PROFESSIONAL RESPONSIBILITY:
BASIC CONCEPTS

MARCIA JOHNSON

AND

LUCKETT ANTHONY JOHNSON

ISBN-13: 978-0-9896936-3-9
ISBN-10: 0989693635

For Adama, Morgan, Luckett, Jules and Vincent

Acknowledgments

We take this opportunity to thank Toni Kogembo, our editor, and Andreience Hines for providing administrative assistance. Thank you

Table of Contents

Introduction

Attorneys and judges in America are guided in their ethical considerations and decisions by the American Bar Association's promulgation of Rules of Professional Conduct and Judicial Code as well as professional ethical standards enacted by state bar associations. Despite these well-defined systems, ethical issues confront legal professionals daily. Some are easily resolved while others prove far more challenging. Disciplinary actions taken against lawyers and judges occur every day, demonstrating the need for state bar associations to uphold ethical standards.

A criminal defense attorney's client may admit to the lawyer that he committed the brutal crimes for which he is charged. What's an ethical lawyer to do?

A civil transactions attorney discovers that documents her client plans to file with the Securities Exchange Commission may be fraudulent. What's an ethical lawyer to do?

A judge presides over a case involving a mortgage company that financed the judge's daughter's home. What's an ethical judge to do?

The first objective of this book is to assist the student in learning the rules of professional ethics and mastering their application via case analysis and real world situations. The second objective is to encourage you, a future attorney, to maintain the highest ethical standards of our profession throughout your career. At times you may encounter many tempting opportunities to forget or ignore your professional obligations. Sometimes you will feel burdened by your various professional duties because the rules of professional responsibility obligate you to a community of players: your client, non-clients, the bar, the judiciary, your colleagues, the public at large and the administration of justice.

The rules of professional conduct are not in themselves standards of morality, but they are based on uniform moral principles that help guide ethical conduct The rules of conduct are not designed to replace your own moral code but to help you identify society's and the profession's expectations of you.

It is incumbent on the professional to know the letter of the law and even more important to understand its meaning and appropriate use on a case by case basis. Some conduct is mandatory while others rely solely on the discretion of the attorney or judge. Violations of mandatory rules may include discipline up to and including disbarment.

You will be exposed to various ethical rules and be presented with cases that illustrate their application. You will also consider hypothetical situations designed to help you more interpret and apply the rules. This book serves as an introduction to professional responsibility, an essential part of law school curriculum and your career.

WHY STUDY PROFESSIONAL RESPONSIBILITY?

For many law students, professional responsibility is merely a curriculum obligation to graduate law school. As such, the course stands as a hurdle to beginning their legal careers. However, the student who gives reasonable attention to the study of professional responsibility during law school will be better prepared to protect their coveted law license later. The study of professional responsibility is the study of ethics and not the study of morals.

Ethics are commonly defined as the rules of moral conduct prescribed by society and its sub-groups, like lawyers.[1] When a lawyer violates mandatory ethical rules of conduct, she may be subject to penalties rangng from private reprimands to being barred from the practice of law altogether.

Morals have more to do with our assessment of what is right or wrong, ethics and morals are not mutually exclusive terms. Rules of ethics are often guided by society's conceptions of what is right and wrong behavior. Society's moral principle against lying is expressed in ethical rules that prohibit a lawyer from lying to a court or tribunal and admonishing the lawyer to be truthful in all her dealings.[2] When the bar association reviews a lawyer's conduct for, say, lying to the court, it considers whether the lawyer's conduct violated a mandatory prohibition enunciated in one or more specific rules of ethical conduct. In other words, the lawyer will not be sanctioned for the moral misconduct of lying per se, but for lying in violation of a specific rule.

Judging Misconduct

The legal profession in America is self-regulating in that the rules of professional conduct to which lawyers and judges must adhere are promulgated by the appropriate state bar association. The state bar associations are typically voluntary organizations whose members are lawyers who are licensed to practice law within that state. These bar associations enact rules or codes of conduct for its members and establish procedures for enforcing those codes.

Usually an ethics committee of the state bar is charged with the responsibility of investigating charges brought against lawyers or judges. In some cases, the bar brings its own charges against the lawyer or judge. The committee, upon due consideration, determines whether a violation of the ethics rules has occurred and prescribes the sanction to be levied against the professional.

In some cases, the professional may choose to defend herself before a civil court rather than to appear before a state bar ethics committee. Either way, the state bar is the petitioner/plaintiff and the professional is the respondent/defendant. So even when seeking relief in civil court, they are appearing before a judge who is by definition a member of the state bar. Thus, the legal profession is also self-enforcing.

---

[1] Merriam-Webster Online, Ethics, available at http://www.merriam-webster.com/dictionary/ethic (last visted July 2, 2014)

[2] ABA Model Rules of Professional Conduct [Rule 3.3]

Ethical codes for lawyers and judges in America

In 1887, the Alabama State Bar Association adopted the first code of lawyer responsibility.[3] Between 1887 and 1905, ten other state bar associations adopted codes of ethics.[4] It was President Theodore Roosevelt's Harvard University commencement address in June 1905 that is credited with giving rise to the first national code of professional ethics.[5] The president expressed a need for leaders, particularly lawyers, to adhere to a high standard of conduct for the betterment of the nation.

Excerpt of President Theodore Roosevelt's 1905 commencement address:

"...This Nation never stood in greater need than now of having among its leaders men of lofty ideals, which they try to live up to and not merely to talk of. We need men with these ideals in public life, and we need them just as much in business and in such a profession as the law. We can by statute establish only those exceedingly rough lines of morality the overpassing of which means that the man is in jeopardy of the constable or the sheriff. But the Nation is badly off if in addition to this there is not a very much higher standard of conduct, a standard impossible effectively to establish by statute, but one upon which the community as a whole, and especially the real leaders of the community, insist. Take such a question as the enforcement of the law. It is, of course, elementary to say that this is the first requisite in any civilization at all. But a great many people in the ranks of life from which most college men are drawn seem to forget that they should condemn with equal severity those men who break the law by committing crimes of mob violence and those who evade the law, or who actually break it, but so cunningly that they can not be discovered, the crimes they commit being not those of physical outrage, but those of greed and craft on the largest scale.

The very rich man who conducts his business as if he believed that he were a law unto himself thereby immensely increases the difficulty of the task of upholding order when the disorder is a menace to men of property; for if the community feels that rich men disregard the law where it affects themselves, then the community is apt to assume the dangerous and unwholesome attitude of condoning crimes of violence committed against the interests which in the popular mind these rich men represent. This last attitude is wholly evil; but so is the attitude which produces it. We have a right to appeal to the alumni of Harvard, and to the alumni of every institution of learning in this land, to do their part in creating a public sentiment which shall demand of all men of means, and especially of the men of vast fortune, that they set an example to their less fortunate brethren, by paying scrupulous heed not only to the letter but to the spirit of the laws, and by acknowledging in the heartiest fashion the moral obligations which can not be expressed in law, but which stand back of and above all laws. It is far more important that they should conduct their business affairs decently than that they should spend the surplus of their fortunes

---

[3] Allison Marston, *Guiding the Professin: The 1887 Code of Ethics of the Alabama State Bar Association*, 49 Ala Law Rev., 470 (1998)

[4] James M. Altman, *Considering the A.B.A.s 1908 Canons of Ethics,* 71 Fordham L. Rev. 2395, 2400 (2003). http://ir.lawnet.fordham.edu/ilr/vol71/iss6/3

[5] Id. and see the full text of the president's address available at http: //www.theodore-roosevelt.com/images/research/txtspeeches/143.txt

in philanthropy. Much has been given to these men and we have the right to demand much of them in return.

Every man of great wealth who runs his business with cynical contempt for those prohibitions of the law which by hired cunning he can escape or evade is a menace to our community; and the community is not to be excused if it does not develop a spirit which actively frowns on and discountenances him. The great profession of the law should be that profession whose members ought to take the lead in the creation of just such a spirit. We all know that, as things actually are, many of the most influential and most highly remunerated members of the bar in every centre of wealth make it their special task to work out bold and ingenious schemes by which their very wealthy clients, individual or corporate, can evade the laws which are made to regulate in the interest of the public the use of great wealth.

Now, the great lawyer who employs his talent and his learning in the highly remunerative task of enabling a very wealthy client to override or circumvent the law is doing all that in him lies to encourage the growth in this country of a spirit of dumb anger against all laws and of disbelief in their efficacy. Such a spirit may breed the demand that laws shall be made even more drastic against the rich, or else it may manifest itself in hostility to all laws. Surely Harvard has the right to expect from her sons a high standard of applied morality, whether their paths lead them into public life, into business, or into the great profession of the law, whose members are so potent in shaping the growth of the national soul.

But in addition to having high ideals it can not too often be said to a body such as is gathered here to-day, that together with devotion to what is right must go practical efficiency in striving for what is right. This is a rough, workaday, practical world, and if in it we are to do the work best worth doing, we must approach that work in a spirit remote from that of the mere visionary, and above all remote from that of the visionary whose aspirations after good find expression only in the shape of scolding and complaining. It shall not help us if we avoid the Scylla of baseness of motive, only to be wrecked on the Charybdis of wrong-headedness, of feebleness and inefficiency. There can be nothing worse for the community than to have the men who profess lofty ideals show themselves so foolish, so narrow, so impracticable, as to cut themselves off from communion with the men who are actually able to do the work of governing, the work of business, the work of the professions.

It is a sad and evil thing if the men with a moral sense group themselves as impractical zealots, while the men of action gradually grow to discard and laugh at all moral sense as an evidence of impractical weakness."[6] ...

The president's address remains pertinent today as a plea to lawyers and judges to attain and uphold the highest standards of ethics in their professions. Following the president's speech, the American Bar Association issued a response by adopting the A.B.A.'s first Canons of Professional Ethics. "The promulgation of Canons was intended to help the legal profession enhance its reputation and, thereby, better perform its important social and political roles as

---

[6] From President Theodore Roosevelt's commencement address, 1905, full text available at http: //www.theodore-roosevelt.com/images/research/txtspeeches/143.txt

5

America's "governing class" by providing ethical standards (1) to judge who should be permitted to become and remain lawyers; (ii) to educate young or inexperienced lawyers; and (iii) to elicit and strengthen lawyers' resolve to conduct themselves in accordance with the highest ethical standards.[7] The ABA code which was adopted by almost all of the states was not self-enforced, but instead was a model for the states to use to adopt their own rules. The current iteration of the rules are incorporated under the ABA *Model Rules of Professional Conduct* and were adopted by the ABA House of Delegates in 1983. They serve as models for the ethics rules of most states.[8]

The A.B.A. Model Rules of Professional Conduct are particularly important to the law student who is required to pass the national bar exam on professional conduct. The exam tests the examinee's knowledge of ethics based on the ABA Model Rules of Professional Conduct and the ABA Judicial Code. The ABA and state codes are based on generally accepted concepts of what the lawyer's responsibilities are.

---

[7] James M. Altman, *Considering the A.B.A.s 1908 Canons of Ethics,* 71 Fordham L. Rev. 2395 (2003). Available at: http://ir.lawnet.fordham.edu/ilr/vol71/iss6/3

[8] See About the Model Rules, ABA Center for Professional Responsibility, available at http://www.americanbar.org/groups/professional_responsibility/publications/model_rules_of_professional_conduct. html and stating in part, "The ABA *Model Rules of Professional Conduct* were adopted by the ABA House of Delegates in 1983. They serve as models for the ethics rules of most states. Before the adoption of the Model Rules, the ABA model was the 1969 *Model Code of Professional Responsibility*. Preceding the Model Code were the 1908 Canons of Professional Ethics (last amended in 1963). To date, California is the only state that does not have professional conduct rules that follow the format of the ABA Model Rules of Professional Conduct. For a listing of the states that have adopted the model rules and amendments to the model rules and links to state ethics rules, visit http://www.americanbar.org/groups/professional_responsibility/publications/model_rules_of_professional_conduct. html

The Lawyer's Responsibilities

Lawyers bear significant burdens to meet the "obligations of their professional calling."[9]   It seems axiomatic that a lawyer is obligated to her client, yet her responsibilities go far beyond the client and include the legal system, the public, and the administration of justice. There are times when these obligations collide and conflicts surface that the lawyer is responsible for resolving. We will explore conflicts more fully later but it is important for the professional to recognize that

---

[9] See ABA Model Rules of Professional Conduct, Preamble [11]

while the lawyer's obligation to their client is normally paramount to other responsibilities there are exceptions that warrant appropriate consideration.[10] The rules also require that the lawyer's obligations extend beyond proper conduct during professional transactions all the way through to his personal and business relationships.[11]

Generally speaking, the lawyer is required to do what is right, fair and just in upholding the lofty tenets of the justice system. The rules help guide the lawyer in understanding what we mean by these terms.

Rules of Reason

The model rules provide that they are rules of reason.[12] In an anti-trust case decided in 1911, the United States Supreme Court introduced the doctrine of the rule of reason when it refused to adopt the government's position that the language of the statute was literal and definitive. The court held that in interpreting the statute, the court would view the rule as *"fixing a standard, that is, by defining the ulterior boundaries which could not be transgressed with impunity, to leave it to be determined by the light of reason, guided by the principles of law and the duty to apply and enforce the public policy embodied in the statute, in every given case whether any particular act or contract was within the contemplation of the statute."*[13] Thus, when interpreting the rules of professional conduct, we are advised to consider the language of the rule in light of the circumstances applicable to the review. In effect, each case will be judged on its own merits and circumstances.

The rules are separate from other remedies under civil or criminal codes; violation of any of the rules will not constitute a basis for a cause of action in a civil or criminal matter outside the realm of enforcement of the rules pursuant to the procedural and substantive rules of the bar.[14]

Lawyer's Responsibility to Client

A lawyer owes fiduciary duties to her client. Those duties include the duty of loyalty and care. The duty of loyalty requires the lawyer to put the client's interest above all else including the lawyer's own interest. The duty of care requires the lawyer to be fully advised in the premises and conduct of the representation. It also requires the lawyer to fully advise the client in all material matters. Before it can be determined whether the lawyer has upheld her duties to her client, it must first be confirmed that the attorney client relationship has been established. Movies may portray a fictional lawyer getting a dollar from the 'client' to show that an attorney-client relationship exists. While payment may provide evidence of the relationship, it is generally irrelevant whether the lawyer was formally retained or paid. The primary question seems to be whether the putative client had the reasonable belief that the relationship had been established.[15]

---

[10] ABA Model Rules of Professional Conduct, Rule 1.6 Comments [6-12]
[11] Id. at preamble [5]
[12] ABA Model Rules of Professional Conduct, Scope [14]
[13] Standard Oil Co. of N.J. v. U.S., 221 U.S.1, 64 (1911)
[14] ABA Model Rules of Professional Conduct, Scope [20]
[15] *Central Die Castig and Mfg. Co., Inc. v. Tokheim Corp.,* 1994 WL 233653, 2 (1994) See also *Westinghouse Electric Corp. v. Kerr-McGee Corp.,* 580 F.2d 1311 (11th Cir.) cert. denied. 439 US 995 (1978)

In Westinghouse Electric Corp. v. Kerr-McGee Corp[16], the United States Supreme Court held that an attorney client relationship exists when the elements of the attorney client privilege are met. The elements are that (1) there is a communication between client and counsel, (2) intended to be and in fact kept confidential, and (3) made for the purpose of obtaining or providing legal advice.[17]

The reliance on the putative client's state of mind could be a problem for the lawyer. Even as a law student you may be approached by family and friends with questions regarding a legal matter because they are aware that you are in law school. Obviously, the law student should not provide legal advice; in some states practicing law without a license is a crime. But similar situations befall lawyers who inadvertently answer questions from persons who believe an attorney client relationship had been created solely by virtue of the communication. Unless the attorney intends to establish the relationship, it is the lawyer's responsibility to clarify that the relationship has not been created. If the lawyer falls victim to the unintended attorney client relationship, she should formally extricate herself immediately in accord with the applicable ethical rules. Otherwise, she could be held to the standards of professional competence, loyalty and care.

Togstad, et al. v. Vesely, Otto, Miller & Keefe and Jerre Miller
291 NW 2d 686 (Minn. 1980)

In August 1971, John Togstad began to experience severe headaches and on August 16, 1971, was admitted to Methodist Hospital where tests disclosed that the headaches were caused by a large aneurism on the left internal carotid artery. The attending physician, Dr. Paul Blake, a neurological surgeon, treated the problem by applying a Selverstone clamp to the left common carotid artery. The clamp was surgically implanted on August 27, 1971, in Togstad's neck to allow the gradual closure of the artery over a period of days.

The treatment was designed to eventually cut off the blood supply through the artery and thus relieve the pressure on the aneurism, allowing the aneurism to heal. It was anticipated that other arteries, as well as the brain's collateral or cross-arterial system would supply the required blood to the portion of the brain which would ordinarily have been provided by the left carotid artery. The greatest risk associated with this procedure is that the patient may become paralyzed if the brain does not receive an adequate flow of blood. In the event the supply of blood becomes so low as to endanger the health of the patient, the adjustable clamp can be opened to establish the proper blood circulation.

In the early morning hours of August 29, 1971, a nurse observed that Togstad was unable to speak or move. At the time, the clamp was one-half (50%) closed. Upon discovering Togstad's condition, the nurse called a resident physician, who did not adjust the clamp. Dr. Blake was also

---

[16] *Westinghouse Electric Corp. v. Kerr-McGee Corp.*, 580 F.2d 1311 (11th Cir.) cert. denied. 439 US 995 (1978).
[17] Id. at 1319

immediately informed of Togstad's condition and arrived about an hour later, at which time he opened the clamp. Togstad is now severely paralyzed in his right arm and leg, and is unable to speak.

Plaintiffs' expert, Dr. Ward Woods, testified that Togstad's paralysis and loss of speech was due to a lack of blood supply to his brain. Dr. Woods stated that the inadequate blood flow resulted from the clamp being 50% closed and that the negligence of Dr. Blake and the hospital precluded the clamp's being opened in time to avoid permanent brain damage. Specifically, Dr. Woods claimed that Dr. Blake and the hospital were negligent for (1) failing to place the patient in the intensive care unit or to have a special nurse conduct certain neurological tests every half-hour; (2) failing to write adequate orders; (3) failing to open the clamp immediately upon discovering that the patient was unable to speak; and (4) the absence of personnel capable of opening the clamp.

Dr. Blake and defendants' expert witness, Dr. Shelly Chou, testified that Togstad's condition was caused by blood clots going up the carotid artery to the brain. They both alleged that the blood clots were not a result of the Selverstone clamp procedure. In addition, they stated that the clamp must be about 90% closed before there will be a slowing of the blood supply through the carotid artery to the brain. Thus, according to Drs. Blake and Chou, when the clamp is 50% closed there is no effect on the blood flow to the brain.

About 14 months after her husband's hospitalization began, plaintiff Joan Togstad met with attorney Jerre Miller regarding her husband's condition. Neither she nor her husband was personally acquainted with Miller or his law firm prior to that time. John Togstad's former work supervisor, Ted Bucholz, made the appointment and accompanied Mrs. Togstad to Miller's office. Bucholz was present when Mrs. Togstad and Miller discussed the case.

Mrs. Togstad had become suspicious of the circumstances surrounding her husband's tragic condition due to the conduct and statements of the hospital nurses shortly after the paralysis occurred. One nurse told Mrs. Togstad that she had checked Mr. Togstad at 2 a. m. and he was fine; that when she returned at 3 a. m., by mistake, to give him someone else's medication, he was unable to move or speak; and that if she hadn't accidentally entered the room no one would have discovered his condition until morning. Mrs. Togstad also noticed that the other nurses were upset and crying, and that Mr. Togstad's condition was a topic of conversation.

Mrs. Togstad testified that she told Miller "everything that happened at the hospital," including the nurses' statements and conduct which had raised a question in her mind. She stated that she "believed" she had told Miller "about the procedure and what was undertaken, what was done, and what happened." She brought no records with her. Miller took notes and asked questions during the meeting, which lasted 45 minutes to an hour. At its conclusion, according to Mrs. Togstad, Miller said that "he did not think we had a legal case, however, he was going to discuss this with his partner." She understood that if Miller changed his mind after talking to his partner, he would call her. Mrs. Togstad "gave it" a few days and, since she did not hear from Miller, decided "that they had come to the conclusion that there wasn't a case." No fee arrangements were discussed, no medical authorizations were requested, nor was Mrs. Togstad billed for the interview.

Mrs. Togstad denied that Miller had told her his firm did not have expertise in the medical malpractice field, urged her to see another attorney, or related to her that the statute of limitations for medical malpractice actions was two years. She did not consult another attorney until one year after she talked to Miller. Mrs. Togstad indicated that she did not confer with another attorney earlier because of her reliance on Miller's "legal advice" that they "did not have a case."

Miller also claimed he related to Mrs. Togstad "that because of the grievous nature of the injuries sustained by her husband, that this was only my opinion and she was encouraged to ask another attorney if she wished for another opinion" and "she ought to do so promptly." He testified that he informed Mrs. Togstad that his firm "was not engaged as experts" in the area of medical malpractice, and that they associated with the Charles Hvass firm in cases of that nature. Miller stated that at the end of the conference he told Mrs. Togstad that he would consult with Charles Hvass and if Hvass's opinion differed from his, Miller would so inform her. Miller recollected that he called Hvass a "couple days" later and discussed the case with him. It was Miller's impression that Hvass thought there was no liability for malpractice in the case. Consequently, Miller did not communicate with Mrs. Togstad further.

Kenneth Green, a Minneapolis attorney, was called as an expert by plaintiffs. He stated that in rendering legal advice regarding a claim of medical malpractice, the "minimum" an attorney should do would be to request medical authorizations from the client, review the hospital records, and consult with an expert in the field. John McNulty, a Minneapolis attorney, and Charles Hvass testified as experts on behalf of the defendants. McNulty stated that when an attorney is consulted as to whether he will take a case, the lawyer's only responsibility in refusing it is to so inform the party. He testified, however, that when a lawyer is asked his legal opinion on the merits of a medical malpractice claim, community standards require that the attorney check hospital records and consult with an expert before rendering his opinion.

Hvass stated that he had no recollection of Miller's calling him in October 1972 relative to the Togstad matter.

This case was submitted to the jury by way of a special verdict form. The jury found that Dr. Blake and the hospital were negligent and that Dr. Blake's negligence (but not the hospital's) was a direct cause of the injuries sustained by John Togstad; that there was an attorney-client contractual relationship between Mrs. Togstad and Miller; that Miller was negligent in rendering advice regarding the possible claims of Mr. and Mrs. Togstad; that, but for Miller's negligence, plaintiffs would have been successful in the prosecution of a legal action against Dr. Blake; and that neither Mr. nor Mrs. Togstad was negligent in pursuing their claims against Dr. Blake. The jury awarded damages to Mr. Togstad of $610,500 and to Mrs. Togstad of $39,000.

On appeal, defendants raise the following issues:

(1) Did the trial court err in denying defendants' motion for judgment notwithstanding the jury verdict?

(2) Does the evidence reasonably support the jury's award of damages to Mrs. Togstad in the amount of $39,000?

(3) Should plaintiffs' damages be reduced by the amount of attorney fees they would have paid had Miller successfully prosecuted the action against Dr. Blake?

(4) Were certain comments of plaintiffs' counsel to the jury improper and, if so, were defendants entitled to a new trial?

In a legal malpractice action of the type involved here, four elements must be shown: (1) that an attorney-client relationship existed; (2) that defendant acted negligently or in breach of contract; (3) that such acts were the proximate cause of the plaintiffs' damages; (4) that but for defendant's conduct the plaintiffs would have been successful in the prosecution of their medical malpractice claim.

This court first dealt with the element of lawyer-client relationship in the decision of Ryan v. Long, 35 Minn. 394, 29 N.W. 51 (1886). The Ryan case involved a claim of legal malpractice and on appeal it was argued that no attorney-client relation existed. This court, without stating whether its conclusion was based on contract principles or a tort theory, disagreed:

> (I)t sufficiently appears that plaintiff, for himself, called upon defendant, as an attorney at law, for "legal advice," and that defendant assumed to give him a professional opinion in reference to the matter as to which plaintiff consulted him. Upon this state of facts the defendant must be taken to have acted as plaintiff's legal adviser, at plaintiff's request, and so as to establish between them the relation of attorney and client.

We believe the evidence shows that a lawyer-client relationship is present here. The thrust of Mrs. Togstad's testimony is that she went to Miller for legal advice, was told there wasn't a case, and relied upon this advice in failing to pursue the claim for medical malpractice. In addition, according to Mrs. Togstad, Miller did not qualify his legal opinion by urging her to seek advice from another attorney, nor did Miller inform her that he lacked expertise in the medical malpractice area. Assuming this testimony is true, as this court must do, we believe a jury could properly find that Mrs. Togstad sought and received legal advice from Miller under circumstances which made it reasonably foreseeable to Miller that Mrs. Togstad would be injured if the advice were negligently given. Thus, there is sufficient evidence in the record to support the existence of an attorney-client relationship.

Defendants argue that even if an attorney-client relationship was established the evidence fails to show that Miller acted negligently in assessing the merits of the Togstads' case. They appear to contend that, at most, Miller was guilty of an error in judgment which does not give rise to legal malpractice. However, this case does not involve a mere error of judgment. The gist of plaintiffs' claim is that Miller failed to perform the minimal research that an ordinarily prudent attorney would do before rendering legal advice in a case of this nature. The record contains sufficient evidence to support plaintiffs' position.

In a related contention, defendants assert that a new trial should be awarded on the ground that the trial court erred by refusing to instruct the jury that Miller's failure to inform Mrs. Togstad of the two-year statute of limitations for medical malpractice could not constitute negligence. The argument continues that since it is unclear from the record on what theory or theories of negligence the jury based its decision, a new trial must be granted.

The defect in defendants' reasoning is that there is adequate evidence supporting the claim that Miller was also negligent in failing to advise Mrs. Togstad of the two-year medical malpractice limitations period and thus the trial court acted properly in refusing to instruct the jury in the manner urged by defendants.

Defendants also indicate that at the time Mrs. Togstad went to another attorney (after Miller) the statute of limitations may not have run and thus Miller's conduct was not a "direct cause" of plaintiffs' damages. As they point out, the limitations period ordinarily begins to run upon termination of the treatment for which the physician was retained. There is other authority, however, which holds that where the injury complained of consists of a "single act," the limitations period commences from the time of that act, even though the doctor-patient relationship may continue thereafter. Consequently, the limitations period began to run on either August 29, 1971, the date of the incident in question, or October 6, 1971, the last time Dr. Blake treated Mr. Togstad. Mrs. Togstad testified that she consulted another attorney "a year after (she) saw Mr. Miller." Thus, since she visited with Miller on October 2, or 3, 1972, if Mr. Togstad's injuries resulted from a "single act" … the limitations period had clearly run by the time Mrs. Togstad consulted another attorney. If, as defendants argue, the statutory period commenced on the date of last treatment, October 6, and Mrs. Togstad's testimony is taken literally, she would have met with a different attorney at a time when perhaps three days of the limitations period remained.

Defendants' contention must be rejected for two reasons. First, at trial defendants apparently assumed that the limitations period commenced on August 29, 1971, and thus did not litigate the instant issue below. Accordingly, they cannot raise the question for the first time on appeal. Further, even assuming the limitations period began on October 6, 1971, it is reasonably inferable from the record that Mrs. Togstad did not see another attorney until after the statute had run. This statement, coupled with the fact that an action was not brought against Dr. Blake or the hospital but instead plaintiffs sued defendants for legal malpractice which allegedly caused Mrs. Togstad to let the limitations period run, allows a jury to draw a reasonable inference that the statutory period had, in fact, expired at the time Mrs. Togstad consulted another lawyer. Although this evidence is weak, it constitutes a prima facie showing, and it was defendants' responsibility to rebut the inference.

There is also sufficient evidence in the record establishing that, but for Miller's negligence, plaintiffs would have been successful in prosecuting their medical malpractice claim. Dr. Woods, in no uncertain terms, concluded that Mr. Togstad's injuries were caused by the medical malpractice of Dr. Blake. Defendants' expert testimony to the contrary was obviously not believed by the jury. Thus, the jury reasonably found that had plaintiff's medical malpractice action been properly brought, plaintiffs would have recovered.

Based on the foregoing, we hold that the jury's findings are adequately supported by the record. Accordingly we uphold the trial court's denial of defendants' motion for judgment notwithstanding the jury verdict.

Defendants next argue that they are entitled to a new trial under Minn.R.Civ.P. 59.01(5) because the $39,000 in damages awarded to Mrs. Togstad for loss of consortium is excessive. In support of this claim defendants refer to the fact that Mr. and Mrs. Togstad were divorced in July 1974 (the dissolution proceeding was commenced in February 1974), and assert that there is "virtually no evidence of the extent of Mrs. Togstad's loss of consortium."

The reasonableness of a jury's damage award is largely left to the discretion of the judge who presided at trial and, accordingly, the district court's ruling on this question will not be disturbed unless a clear abuse of discretion is shown. "Consortium" includes rights inherent in the marital relationship, such as comfort, companionship, and most importantly, sexual relationship. Here, the evidence shows that Mr. Togstad became impotent due to the tragic incident which occurred in August 1971. Consequently, Mrs. Togstad was unable to have sexual intercourse with her husband subsequent to that time. The evidence further indicates that the injuries sustained by Mr. Togstad precipitated a dissolution of the marriage.

We therefore conclude that the jury's damage award to Mrs. Togstad finds sufficient support in the record. Affirmed.

****

Questions:

1. Based on the Togstad facts, would you have found that an attorney-client relationship had been established? Why/Why not?

2. What should Miller have done to avoid liability in this case?

3. Miller nor his associates were well versed in medical malpractice cases. Could (t)he(y) have accepted representation under the model rules?

4. A jury found that Miller had given Mrs. Togstad wrong advice and that but for that advice, she would have won her medical malpractice case. However, the facts state that Togstad waited well past a year to seek a second opinion. Should Miller be liable for her negligence?

5. Distinguish the burden of establishing professional malpractice from establishing violation of rules of professional ethics.

****

WHEN THE CLIENT IS AN ORGANIZATION

The lawyer that represents an organization, may have challenges determining who the client is and to whom the attorney owes a duty. Moreover, the lawyer needs to be able to identify with whom he or she has established the attorney-client relationship. The ABA Model Rules provide that the client is the organization that acts through its human constituents.[18] In effect, when a lawyer represents an organization, it is to that organization that the lawyer has fiduciary duties and while the lawyer must interact with the organization's constituents-- their individual interests are not those that the lawyer must protect. Of course, this relationship may become contentious because the constituents may consider themselves the client because they are the ones who hire and pay the lawyer. However, even though such payment will not be the basis for establishing the relationship, it is commonly the organization's funds that are the source of the payment. Nevertheless, the attorney should ensure that the organization constituents understand the her role and who she represents.

Another challenge for the lawyer in identifying the client is when (s)he works for a government agency. Generally speaking the government lawyer's client is the government agency that employs her/him. To that extent the government lawyer's role differs little from the private lawyer who represents an organization. However, the government lawyer may have a distinct duty to act in the public interest. It is the interest of the public at large that embodies the government agency, begging the question whether the lawyer acts for the public constituent or the agency. At least one author describes it as follows:

> *"In all situations, determination will depend on the context of the representation. The government lawyer can put the representation and client identification in context by examining the structure of authority within the government. The specifics of a state's Constitution, particular statutory provisions of the attorney general's powers and the statutory scheme relating to an individual agency or public officer must be considered. The lawyer may find themselves representing a department or bureau that is part of a branch of government, the branch of government itself, or the government as a whole. In most cases, the government lawyer will represent the governmental entity and the client may be the state agency or officer.[citation omitted] Each situation requires its own analysis.[citation omitted]*
>
> *In short, the task for the government attorney in identifying their client is not an easy one. Regardless, the government attorney must assess the question of client identification on a recurring basis as the answer may change with each new situation or change of circumstance. Failing to do so could result in a breach of ethical duty."[19]*

Competence, Diligence and Communication

A lawyer is required to diligently provide competent legal representation to the client upon and while maintaining reasonable and open communication with the client.[20] Competence is determined by the level of skill and knowledge necessary to represent the client's interests. A

---

[18] ABA Model Rule of Professional Conduct [1.13]

[19] Mark M. Neil, Who is your client? Ethical Considerations for Government Attorneys, National Association of Attorneys General, Program Counsel, NAAGazette, available at http://www.naag.org/who-is-your-client-ethical-considerations-for-government-attorneys.php, last visited June 12, 2014.

[20] ABA Model Rules of Professional Conduct, Rules 1.1, 1.3 and 1.4

lawyer need not possess the necessary skills or knowledge at the time she agrees to represent the client to comply with the rules of conduct. The lawyer need only acquire the necessary skills and knowledge to represent the client. Often, a lawyer will obtain competence through additional study, including continuing legal education programs or by consulting a lawyer competent in the area. If a lawyer does not have the requisite skill and knowledge and the lawyer fails to obtain the skill and knowledge required to represent the client, then the lawyer is not competent to represent the client.

What happens if the circumstances of the representation present an emergency? Will the incompetent lawyer be sanctioned for representing the client? Remember that pursuant to the rule of reason, the circumstances of the representation should be carefully considered. Under the ABA Model Rules of Professional Conduct if the circumstances are such that it would be impractical for the lawyer to obtain the requisite skill and knowledge, then the representation would likely be permitted.[21] However, even in emergency situations, the incompetent lawyer's representation is limited to that appropriate to the emergency.[22]

The model rules also require a lawyer to diligently and promptly provide legal services to the client. Diligence requires the lawyer to exercise the requisite attention and care to the client's case. The lawyer is expected to be fully informed about the matter including all options available to the client and potential consequences of any action taken or omitted. The lawyer is also expected to exercise the degree of caution required by the circumstances of the representation.

Lawyers often have a number of different clients and cases. It is incumbent upon the lawyer not to accept more clients or cases than she can diligently handle. The lawyer should also weigh her professional responsibilities against her personal responsibilities when deciding to accept a case or client.

The diligent lawyer does not neglect his clients or cases nor does he wait until the last minute to perform his work. Procrastination is not a specific rule violation, however, it could constitute evidence of the lawyer's lack of diligence.

Diligence also requires the lawyer to retain competence throughout the representation, to make due inquiry, to investigate the circumstances, and to be prepared by conducting the representation and analyzing the matters thoroughly. In other words, part of the lawyer's diligence is competence.

The lawyer is wise to remember that the case belongs to the client and not to the lawyer. Thus, a lawyer must keep the client fully informed of the progress of the matter as well as the legal strategy that the lawyer will employ. Where the client's consent is required, the lawyer must ensure that the client gives it knowingly and willingly. Such requirement burdens the lawyer with ensuring that all disclosures are made to the client in a way that the client will reasonably understand them. The client's consent is based on the total circumstances reasonably necessary to make an informed decision.

---

[21] ABA Model Rules of Professional Conduct, Rule 1.1
[22] ABA Model Rules of Professional Conduct, Rules 1.1, Comment [3]

Sometimes clients will bombard the lawyer with telephone calls and or impromptu visits that impede the lawyer's ability to handle the case. The lawyer should consult with the client to agree on the method and extent of the consultations in order to avoid communication problems with the client.

The lawyer is bound to follow her client's decisions regarding objectives of the representation even if the lawyer disagrees. In all cases, however, the lawyer is prohibited from engaging or assisting the client to engage in fraudulent or criminal behavior.[23]

Sheridan's Case
148 N.H. 595 (N.H. 2002)

...In August 2001, the Supreme Court Committee on Professional Conduct (Committee) filed a petition with this court against the respondent, William C. Sheridan, requesting that he be suspended for one year from the practice of law. We referred the petition to a Judicial Referee for hearing and recommendation. Thereafter, the Committee served a request for numerous factual admissions upon the respondent. When he failed to respond, the referee issued, upon motion, an order declaring the requests admitted, which we subsequently approved. In sum, the admitted facts constituted violations of Rules 1.1(a), 1.1(b)(5), 1.1(c)(4), 1.3(a), 1.4(a), 1.16(d) and 8.4(a) of the New Hampshire Rules of Professional Conduct (the Rules). After a hearing on sanctions, the referee recommended that the respondent be suspended from the practice of law in New Hampshire for one year. We adopt the referee's recommendation.

The admitted facts are as follows. In the spring of 1999, two individuals sought the respondent's legal services to incorporate their business. The respondent, who was admitted to practice law in New Hampshire and Massachusetts, agreed to incorporate the business in Massachusetts. The respondent generated Articles of Incorporation from his computer, and on May 6, 1999, the incorporators signed the Articles and paid the respondent $1,300.00 for legal services and filing fees. He informed them that he would file the Articles in Massachusetts and obtain a corporate minute book and seal. On May 20, he provided the corporate minute book and seal to the incorporators and told them that they were incorporated. They then began to operate their business. The respondent, however, did not deliver the original signed Articles to the Massachusetts Secretary of State until May 28.

Massachusetts rejected the corporate filing, and returned the Articles as well as the filing fee check to the respondent. The respondent's second attempt to incorporate the business also met with rejection. However, he did not realize that his second attempt had not been successful until ten or eleven months later. He never contacted the incorporators to notify them that the corporation was not properly formed.

The incorporators operated their business for nearly a year before learning that their incorporation papers had been rejected when Massachusetts refused to accept their 1999 corporate tax return. In May 2000, they confronted the respondent with their problem, and it took

---

[23] ABA Model Rules of Professional Conduct [1.2]

him approximately ten days to prepare new incorporation documents. In the meantime, the incorporators retained another lawyer to complete the incorporation process and requested the respondent to provide their case file to new counsel. He failed to do so because he could not find it.

In July 2000, the incorporators filed a professional conduct complaint against the respondent with the Committee. More than eight months later, the respondent supplied the case file to the Committee but still failed to provide the file to his former clients or their new counsel. Further, sometime after the complaint was filed, the respondent discovered $200.00 in his escrow account representing the original filing fee rejected by Massachusetts, which he returned to his former clients. The Committee conducted a hearing in May 2001, but the respondent failed to bring any files or bank records with him. At the hearing, the incorporators identified approximately $5,000 in damages caused by the respondent's failure to properly incorporate their business. Beyond returning the $200.00 filing fee, however, the respondent has not returned any of the sums received for legal services, nor has he made any payments toward the damages caused by his misconduct.

The respondent neither disputes the truth of the facts deemed admitted, nor does he challenge the referee's conclusion that the admitted facts constitute violations of the following Rules:

1.1(a)-failing to represent clients in a competent manner;

1.1(b)(5)-failing to pay attention to schedules and details in incorporating the client's business, so as to assure that the legal matters undertaken would be completed with no avoidable harm to the client's interest;

1.1(c)(4)-failing to undertake actions with regard to the incorporation in a timely and effective manner;

1.3(a)-failing to act with reasonable promptness and diligence;

1.4(a)-failing to keep the clients reasonably informed regarding the status of the matter;

1.16(d)-failing to return the clients' file at the termination of the representation; and

8.4(a)-engaging in conduct in violation of the Rules of Professional Conduct.

The respondent contends that the referee's recommended sanction of a one-year suspension is unduly harsh. He argues that the referee erroneously deprived him of his right to offer evidence to supplement or explain the admitted facts in order to mitigate his misconduct. In addition, based upon the results of an independent psychiatric evaluation which he presented to the referee, the respondent asserts that he has a mental disorder that serves as a mitigating factor and entitles him to reasonable accommodation under the Americans with Disabilities Act (ADA). *See* 42 U.S.C. §§ 12101 *et seq.* (2000). He asserts that the most appropriate sanction would be some form of probation during which he would be required to limit the number of cases he handles in order to provide him "an opportunity to develop his practice, get secretarial help and prove that he [can] perform with attention to detail."

"We retain the ultimate authority to determine the appropriate sanction for a violation of the rules governing attorney conduct." We judge each case on its own facts and circumstances. Our ultimate aim in fashioning a sanction is not to inflict punishment on the offending attorney; rather, we seek "to protect the public, maintain public confidence in the bar, preserve the integrity of the legal profession, and prevent similar conduct in the future." (quotation omitted).

We first address the respondent's contention that the referee erroneously denied him the right to present evidence supplementing and explaining the admitted facts in order to demonstrate relevant mitigating circumstances. Assuming, without deciding, that he had such a right and that he properly preserved it for our review, we conclude that none of the additional evidence described by the respondent mitigates his misconduct.

Specifically, the respondent asserts that the Articles returned to him by Massachusetts bore notations on the first and last pages reflecting initial approval. He contends that "[l]ater, Massachusetts revoked its acceptance of the Articles [by] whit[ing] out [the] acceptance on the last page" but that "acceptance remained noted on the first page." According to the respondent, the Articles were returned to him without a cover page and, because he did not have a secretary, he noticed only the acceptance on the first page and not the rejection on the last page. He claims that in late April or early May 2000, because he had hired a secretary, he discovered that the Articles had actually been rejected. The incorporators soon thereafter confronted him with the defective incorporation, and, he contends, within the next ten days, he spoke with them on several occasions, providing them with new incorporation documents on the tenth day.

The relevance of much of this evidence to the issue of sanctions is questionable. The respondent's initial misperception of the status of the Articles, given the apparent discrepant notations on the first and last pages, bears more on the issue of whether he is culpable in the first instance for failing to pay attention to detail (Rule 1.1(b)(5)). Likewise, his discovery of the defective incorporation shortly before the incorporators confronted him relates to whether he failed to act with reasonable promptness and diligence (Rule 1.3(a)), or failed to keep his clients reasonably informed (Rule 1.4(a)). These issues are probative of whether the respondent violated the Rules of Professional Conduct.

In any event, none of the evidence mitigates the respondent's misconduct. Whether or not the returned incorporation documents lacked clarity in communicating their rejected status, his receipt of the uncashed filing fee check should have been an obvious indicator that his effort to incorporate failed. The respondent, however, did not even notice that the check had been returned because he only first discovered the $200 in his escrow account after the incorporators filed an ethical complaint against him. Further, regarding his late discovery of the failed incorporation, the respondent admitted that he "has no explanation for his failure to notify the incorporators immediately upon his discovery that [the corporation] had not been properly incorporated." Indeed, since it was the incorporators who first confronted him on his failed incorporation effort, we have no way of knowing just how long the respondent would have waited before contacting them or taking steps to remedy his mistake. The delay was unacceptable given the incorporators' continued exposure to personal liability with each passing day.

...The respondent also seeks to explain his admission that he has made no payment to the incorporators, excluding the $200.00 filing fee. He asserts that he has always been willing to reimburse the incorporators and the corporation for damages caused by his conduct but that they have failed to provide him with an itemized list of actual out-of-pocket expenses. The admitted facts belie this claim.

At a May 2001 hearing before the Committee, the incorporators identified approximately $5,000 in damages caused by the respondent's failure to incorporate their business. These damages were attributed to additional accounting and legal expenses relating to incorporation services provided by new counsel and to the state and federal tax returns filed for 1999. The only unknown damages presented at the May 2001 hearing were: (1) any interest and penalties Massachusetts might assess for filing the 1999 corporate tax return before incorporation; and (2) any personal liability for claims that may be incurred by the incorporators which otherwise would have been incurred by the corporation. The estimated $5,000 in damages was sufficiently precise for the respondent to have made some payment. To date, more than one and one-half years later, no payment in any amount has been made.

As a final mitigator, the respondent claims that he has "a mental disorder with a probable biological basis" and that psychiatric medication and use of a secretary would "ameliorate the problem." He claimed to be taking the appropriate medication and blames his lack of a secretary on the Committee for taking past action against him which "wrongfully chilled his ability to advertise [for Bankruptcy clients, his primary area of practice], obtain income and thus obtain a secretary." We conclude that while his apparent mental disorder may offer some explanation for his ethical lapses, it does not justify a lenient sanction.

During the sanctions hearing, the respondent submitted an independent psychiatric evaluation to establish the existence of his apparent mental disorder and explain its effect on his behavior. In November 2001, Dr. Albert Drukteinis conducted the evaluation pursuant to our order in another matter, and opined that the respondent had "a mental disorder with a probable biological basis which [could] benefit from psychiatric treatment." He described the respondent as apparently suffering spells of fatigue and poor mental functioning alternating with periods of high energy and "physical disorder." The doctor did not provide a definitive diagnosis of the respondent's apparent mental disorder, but noted that the respondent's "presentation is characteristic of hypomania seen in Bipolar Disorder (formerly known as Manic Depressive Illness)." He outlined general characteristics of individuals who suffer from Bipolar Disorder to include a tendency to be distracted and disorganized, failing to prioritize or balance their activities appropriately, and intensely pursuing certain objectives at the cost of other obligations. With respect to the respondent in particular, the doctor stated that his "tendency for distractibility and disorganization could easily lead him to miss deadlines as he is hyperfocusing on a project," and that his "mental state deficits are subtle; but, with the high standard of performance that an attorney must maintain, those deficits could be devastating."

The respondent claims that he can overcome his lawyering deficiencies caused by his mental disorder through the structure and organization provided by a secretary. He contends that the Committee engaged in wrongful action against him in the past, which curtailed his primary source of income and forced him to discharge his secretary. Assuming, without deciding, however, that the respondent suffered a mental disorder during the time frame at issue, the mental disorder did not account for much of the misconduct underlying the ethical violations.

The respondent failed to obtain or prepare the proper documents for the Massachusetts incorporation. He told the incorporators that their business had been incorporated a week before he had even filed any documents with the Secretary of State. He never noticed that the uncashed filing fee check was returned to him, or if he did, he failed to understand its significance. Moreover, once he finally discovered the incorporation documents had been rejected, (through, he contends, the aid of a secretary), he failed to appreciate the urgency of the situation and made no attempt to immediately notify the incorporators or remedy his mistake. All of these actions demonstrate grave errors in his professional judgment, which administrative support cannot ameliorate.

The respondent also claims that his apparent mental disorder constitutes a disability under the ADA, and thus requires us to provide him with "reasonable accommodation." He seeks a more lenient sanction of probation to give him an opportunity to financially restore his practice, obtain a secretary and "prove that he could perform with attention to detail." We assume, for the sake of argument, that his ADA claim is properly preserved in the record before us and that we have jurisdiction to adjudicate an ADA claim in the first instance. The evidence presented to the referee, however, is inconclusive as to whether the respondent suffered a "disability" recognized under the ADA.

Dr. Drukteinis made no definitive diagnosis of the respondent's apparent mental disorder. ... Accordingly, we conclude that Dr. Drukteinis' report is insufficient to establish the existence of a disability under the ADA.

The respondent identifies no viable mitigators convincing us to impose a sanction less harsh than suspension. His misconduct demonstrates grave errors in professional judgment in his failure to obtain or prepare updated incorporation documents, misrepresentation of the status of the corporation before he filed incorporation documents, and patent neglect and lack of diligence in apprising his clients of their lack of corporate status, further exposing them to potential liability.

In addition, the respondent has a prior disciplinary record. In the last four years of his fifteen-year law career, we have sanctioned him on three occasions. In 1998, he was publicly censured twice, once for admittedly commingling trust and operating accounts, and again for allowing a civil matter to default. In 2001, he was publicly censured for his lack of diligence and competence in his handling of the probate of a decedent's estate.

We are mindful that suspension is a severe disciplinary measure for any attorney, and do not undertake this sanction lightly. Furthermore, we are sympathetic to the fact that the respondent has suffered various misfortunes in his personal life over the past several years, as revealed in the record. Certainly, these circumstances compounded his apparent mental condition and complicated his ability to remain focused, organized and attentive to detail. Attorneys, however, must maintain a competent level of performance even while suffering trying times in their personal lives. They must be sensitive to the impact external pressures have on their ability to sustain their professional obligations to their clients, and should step aside from their legal representation before their professional obligations are compromised.

After reviewing the admitted facts and considering the respondent's prior discipline, we conclude that suspending the respondent's license to practice law is necessary to protect the public, maintain public confidence in the bar, preserve the integrity of the legal profession, and prevent similar conduct in the future. Accordingly, we order the respondent suspended from the practice of law in New Hampshire for one year, and direct him to reimburse the Committee for all expenses incurred in the investigation and prosecution of this matter. *So ordered.*

****

Questions:

1. ABA Model Rule 1.3 requires a lawyer to "act with reasonable diligence and promptness in representing a client." How did Sheridan's acts specifically fail to meet the requirements of Model Rule 1.3?

2. Attorney provided numerous excuses for his unethical behavior, including mental deficiency. Why were his defenses inadequate to support a more lenient penalty?[24]

3. What is the practical effect on a lawyer's solo practice of being suspended for one year?

4. Consider the fact that Attorney failed to respond to the bar's notices and requests, could this have impacted the court's decision to suspend him?[25] Why? Why not?

****

Joyner v. Commission For Lawyer Discipline
102 S.W. 3d 344 (Tex.App.-Dallas, 2003)

…The Commission for Lawyer Discipline brought this disciplinary action against Roger Joyner, alleging violations of multiple provisions of the Texas Disciplinary Rules of Professional Conduct. Following a nonjury trial, the trial court granted a judgment of partially probated suspension against Joyner. On appeal to this Court, Joyner contends in three issues that the judgment of the trial court was not supported by legally and factually sufficient evidence. We affirm.

---

[24] See Cincinnati Bar Association v Britt, 133 Ohio St.3d 217 (2012)
[25] See Megan Zavieh, Responding to an Ethics Complaint: A How-To Guide, Lawyerist, March 4, 2013 available at http://lawyerist.com/61066/responding-to-an-ethics-complaint-a-how-to-guide/

Factual and Procedural Background

Betty Madge Mills was injured on November 5, 1994. In June 1995, she employed Joyner to pursue a negligence claim arising from the injury. Joyner filed the lawsuit on November 6, 1996. Joyner received interrogatories and requests for production regarding the case in January 1997 but did not answer them. Also in January 1997, counsel for one of the defendants, Farmers Electric Co-op, informed Joyner that suit had been filed two years and one day after the injury occurred and, therefore, he would be filing a motion for summary judgment on limitations grounds. Joyner nonsuited Farmers Electric Co-op. In August or September 1997, Joyner associated Lyle Medlock on the case, and Medlock brought in Craig Bonham shortly thereafter. In November 1997, William E. Reid, counsel for three other defendants, sent Joyner a motion for summary judgment on limitations grounds and notice of the hearing on the motion. No response to the motion was filed, and no one appeared on Mills's behalf at the hearing. The trial court granted summary judgment against Mills on December 19, 1997. No postjudgment motions were filed, and no appeal was filed on Mills's behalf.

The Commission alleged that Mills employed Joyner to represent her in a personal injury matter and that Joyner filed the lawsuit one day after the statute of limitations had run, failed to respond to a motion for summary judgment on limitations grounds, failed to file a motion for new trial or perfect an appeal on Mills's behalf, failed to communicate with Mills about the case, and failed to respond to Mills's requests to return her file. The Commission alleged that Joyner violated several disciplinary rules, including rule 1.01(a) and rule 1.01(b)(1).

The trial court found that Joyner violated rule 1.01 in the matter relating to Mills, and that, as to each violation, Joyner committed professional misconduct as defined in rule 1.06 of the Texas Rules of Disciplinary Procedure. The trial court then imposed sanctions that included a suspension for sixty months, with a two-month active suspension and a five-year probated suspension, subject to various terms and conditions. The court also ordered Joyner to pay $16,316.90 in attorney's fees, expenses, and costs. No findings of fact and conclusions of law were requested or filed. Joyner's motion for new trial was overruled by operation of law. Joyner appealed.

Applicable Law

Rule 1.01 of the Texas Disciplinary Rules of Professional Conduct provides, in part:

(a) A lawyer shall not accept or continue employment in a legal matter which the lawyer knows or should know is beyond the lawyer's competence, unless:

> (1) another lawyer who is competent to handle the matter is, with the prior informed consent of the client, associated in the matter; or

> (2) the advice or assistance of the lawyer is reasonably required in an emergency and the lawyer limits the advice and assistance to that which is reasonably necessary in the circumstances.

(b) In representing a client, a lawyer shall not:

> (1) neglect a legal matter entrusted to the lawyer....

(c) As used in this Rule, "neglect" signifies inattentiveness involving a conscious disregard for the responsibilities owed to a client or clients.

Discussion

Regarding rule 1.01(a), the record shows that Mills employed Joyner to pursue a personal injury case against several defendants. Joyner testified that his primary field of practice was criminal law and that he asked Medlock to help him and Medlock brought in Bonham. Mills testified that she discovered other attorneys were working on her case when Bonham called her and told her he was working on the case; she testified that Joyner never asked for her consent to get another attorney to work on her case. Joyner testified that his contract with Mills did not specifically give him Mills's prior consent to associate Medlock on the case and that he associated Medlock on the case and paid him before telling Mills that Medlock would be working on the case. We conclude that the evidence is undisputed that Joyner did not obtain Mills's consent before associating Medlock or Bonham on the case and that the emergency provision does not apply here. Therefore, this is legally and factually sufficient evidence to show that Joyner violated rule 1.01(a).

Regarding rule 1.01(b), it is undisputed that Joyner entered into a contract with Mills and remained attorney of record in the case. The record shows that Joyner filed Mills's case one day beyond the limitations period. The record also shows that Joyner received interrogatories and requests for production from Reid on January 28, 1997, a response was due thirty-four days later, Joyner did not request an extension of time to respond, and Joyner did not answer the discovery. Bonham testified that a response to the discovery was filed after he began working on the case. Further, it was undisputed that no one responded to the motion for summary judgment, appeared at the hearing, or filed any postjudgment motions or notice of appeal. This is more than a scintilla of evidence that Joyner neglected Mills's legal matter, thus violating rule 1.01(b)(1).

Nevertheless, Joyner argues that the evidence is factually insufficient to support the implied finding that he neglected Mills's legal matter. Joyner argues that he acted in good faith by associating competent counsel after filing the lawsuit and by forwarding documents and papers to them. *See* Tex. Disciplinary R. Prof'l Conduct 1.01 cmt.7 (regarding neglect: "A lawyer who acts in good faith is not subject to discipline, under those provisions [of paragraph (b)] for an isolated inadvertent or unskilled act of omission, tactical error, or error of judgment."). Joyner argues that an assistant in his office, Edward Spears, forwarded the motion to Medlock and Bonham's office for response and handling.

Spears testified that he received the motion for summary judgment in November 1997 and took it to Medlock's office. The motion included notice of the setting of the hearing. Bonham was asked if the motion was delivered to Medlock, who died in 1998. Bonham testified that he did not know if Medlock received the motion but that Bonham thought that if documents had come into Medlock's office, they would have been given to Bonham, since he was the one "doing the primary work on [the case]." Bonham further testified that it was unlikely that the motion was transferred to Medlock's office. Bonham also testified that the motion was not delivered to him or to his secretary. Thus, the evidence was conflicting regarding whether Joyner, or someone in his office, forwarded the motion for summary judgment to Medlock or Bonham.

Joyner also argues that Reid took advantage of Joyner by failing to provide a copy of the motion for summary judgment and the notice of the hearing directly to Medlock and Bonham. Nevertheless, the evidence is undisputed that Joyner remained lead counsel of record for this case, his office received the motion for summary judgment, and Joyner did not share an office with Medlock or Bonham. *See Palmer v. Cantrell,* 747 S.W.2d 39, 41 (Tex.App.-Houston [1st Dist.] 1988, no writ) (holding that "[w]here a single adverse party is represented by two attorneys who are not associated in a firm, we believe that it is sufficient to serve the attorney who is designated as lead counsel because he has 'control in the management of the cause' " and citing rule of civil procedure 8). Joyner cites no authority to support any argument that Reid's failure to send documents and papers to Medlock or Bonham, even if Reid knew they were working on the case, relieves Joyner of his responsibility to Mills under rule 1.01(b)(1).

Considering all the evidence, we cannot say that the evidence supporting the judgment as to rule 1.01(b)(1) is so weak as to be clearly wrong and manifestly unjust. Accordingly, we conclude the evidence is factually sufficient to show that Joyner violated rule 1.01(b)(1).

Conclusion

Because we have concluded that the evidence is sufficient to support the trial court's judgment that Joyner violated rule 1.01, we overrule Joyner's three issues and affirm the trial court's judgment.

****

Questions:

Annie Attorney meets with Cybil Client to discuss representation in a personal injury case. During the conference Annie determines that the statute of limitations runs on the day of the conference. Annie informs Client that Attorney lacks expertise in the area and will have to consult with another lawyer who is an expert in personal injury litigation. Annie also tells Client that the action must be filed that day or the case would be time barred. Client consents to the associated lawyer in writing and Annie files the petition in state court signing the petition as attorney for plaintiff (Client). The next day Annie consults Lonnie Litigator, famed personal injury attorney who agrees to consult on the case. However, no motion to substitute counsel or designation of "new" lead counsel is filed.

1. Is Annie acting in violation of the model rules of professional conduct?

2. When Annie filed the petition, was she in violation of the model rules of professional conduct?

3. If Annie was wrong about the statute of limitations and the actual time did not run until the week following the filing, would Annie be subject to discipline for violating the model rules of professional conduct?

4. If the petition was fatally flawed and Annie had been correct about the statute of limitations (a) would she be subject to discipline for violating the model rules of professional conduct? (b) would she be subject to a professional malpractice claim?

McIntyre v. The Commission For Lawyer Discipline
169 S.W.3d 803 (Tex.App.-Dallas, 2005)

Disciplinary action was brought against attorney. The 192nd Judicial District Court, Dallas County, found misconduct and imposed partially probated eighteen-month suspension. Attorney appealed. The Court of Appeals held that: (1) attorney engaged in specialized bankruptcy proceedings beyond his competency; (2) attorney failed to base his actions upon proper communications with client; (3) false representations were made by attorney in both state court and bankruptcy proceedings; and (4) suspension was warranted. Affirmed.

McIntyre represented Vrasidas Pappas in a state court action against Sally Maglaris in a dispute over the rightful ownership of a restaurant. The result was a judgment in favor of Maglaris. Shortly after the final judgment was entered, McIntyre heard Maglaris was disposing of the restaurant's furniture and fixtures. McIntyre also represented three of Pappas's creditors, who contacted him to obtain advice about the removal of equipment from the restaurant. McIntyre referred the creditors to a bankruptcy lawyer, Joyce Lindauer, suggesting the filing of an involuntary bankruptcy. After the state court trial, but before the involuntary bankruptcy proceeding was initiated, Pappas disappeared. Although he was not able to discuss the matter with Pappas, McIntyre appeared as Pappas's counsel in the bankruptcy proceedings. When the involuntary bankruptcy petition was filed, McIntyre filed a suggestion of bankruptcy in the state trial court where the Maglaris case was pending, requesting immediate injunctive relief against Maglaris. In six paragraphs of his verified motion, McIntyre requested relief for Pappas "on his own behalf and on behalf of the bankruptcy trustee." McIntyre appeared ex parte before the trial judge. The trial judge granted the motion, treating it as a request for temporary restraining order, and set the matter for an injunction hearing.

In bankruptcy court, Maglaris moved to vacate the state trial court's order. United States Bankruptcy Judge Robert C. McGuire did not grant Maglaris's motion, declining to "sit as an appellate court" on the state trial judge's actions. Judge McGuire, however, furnished the state court judge a memorandum opinion, noting the "state court judge may have been misled into signing the order in question." Judge McGuire's opinion noted at the time the suggestion of bankruptcy was filed, no bankruptcy trustee had been appointed, and McIntyre did not represent any bankruptcy trustee for Pappas. Quoting the language in the motion that it was made on behalf of Pappas "and on behalf of the bankruptcy trustee," and the statement that "because all relief requested in this Motion is mandatory under the bankruptcy code and there are no questions of law or fact to be determined by this Court," the motion should be granted, Judge McGuire noted these statements were "legally false."

In an order dated April 27, 2001, state court judge David R. Gibson found "certain representations made to the Court by [McIntyre] … upon which the Court signed its March 30 Order on an *ex parte* basis were inaccurate."

The bankruptcy proceeding in Judge McGuire's court was dismissed… when no one appeared. Pappas's creditors filed a second involuntary proceeding, which was assigned to

United States Bankruptcy Judge Steven A. Felsenthal. In a letter to the United States Trustee dated August 14, 2001, Judge Felsenthal also questioned McIntyre's actions in the bankruptcy proceeding. Judge Felsenthal noted McIntyre had prepared and signed bankruptcy schedules and a statement of financial affairs for Pappas:

McIntyre signed the schedules and statement of financial affairs as attorney for the debtor, even though the signature required a declaration under penalty of perjury that Pappas read the answers and that they are true and correct. Pappas did not read the answers. McIntyre could not attest to the truth and correctness under penalty of perjury for Pappas. McIntyre had no authorization from Pappas to perform these acts.

The judge concluded, "The court is concerned that McIntyre may have submitted false oaths to the court and that he may have engaged in the unethical and improper practice of law that may result in adverse consequences for his purported client."

Appellee filed a disciplinary action against McIntyre, alleging multiple violations of the Texas Disciplinary Rules of Professional Conduct. After a bench trial, the trial judge found McIntyre committed misconduct in violation of rules 1.01(a), 1.03(b), 3.03(a)(3), and 8.04(a)(3). *[citations omitted]* The trial judge filed findings of fact and conclusions of law in support of the judgment. In his conclusions of law, the trial judge found McIntyre represented Pappas in bankruptcy court when he was not competent to do so; represented Pappas in a bankruptcy proceeding without obtaining his client's consent; made false representations to the state court judge; and made false representations in the bankruptcy proceeding. As a sanction, the trial court imposed a partially-probated eighteen-month suspension and ordered as an ancillary sanction $21,347.42 in attorneys' fees. McIntyre appeals.

Discussion

Competent Representation

Appellant's first five issues challenge the trial court's findings and conclusions relating to rule 1.01(a) of the Texas Rules of Disciplinary Conduct. Rule 1.01(a) provides:

A lawyer shall not accept or continue employment in a legal matter which the lawyer knows or should know is beyond the lawyer's competence, unless:

(1) another lawyer who is competent to handle the matter is, with the prior informed consent of the client, associated in the matter; or

(2) the advice or assistance of the lawyer is reasonably required in an emergency and the lawyer limits the advice and assistance to that which is reasonably necessary in the circumstances.

In his first conclusion of law, the trial judge concluded appellant represented Pappas in bankruptcy court when he was not competent to do so, in violation of rule 1.01(a). This conclusion was supported by several findings of fact. Finding of fact sixteen provided:

16. Respondent admitted to the bankruptcy judge in the hearings that he lacked competence to practice bankruptcy law and that he may have done something improper in signing the bankruptcy schedules. His conduct in the bankruptcy hearing led the bankruptcy judge to question his competence to practice before the bankruptcy courts.

In finding of fact fourteen, the trial judge noted appellant was apparently not aware of, and did not seek to learn, the procedures to be followed in order to represent an absent client in bankruptcy court. In finding of fact seven, the trial judge found the bankruptcy trustee had instructed appellant on the steps to be taken to be hired to represent the trustee, but appellant failed to take them.

The comments to rule 1.01(a) provide guidance in determining whether a matter is beyond a lawyer's competence. Comment 2 provides, "relevant factors include the relative complexity and specialized nature of the matter, the lawyer's general experience in the field in question, the preparation and study the lawyer will be able to give the matter, and whether it is feasible either to refer the matter to or associate a lawyer of established competence in the field in question." Tex. Disciplinary R. Professional Conduct 1.01, cmt. 2.

Appellee alleged appellant knew or should have known bankruptcy law was a specialized area of practice and the issues presented were beyond his competence; he failed to associate another attorney competent in the area; he admitted he did not regularly practice bankruptcy law; appellee pleaded appellant admitted "he was not proficient in the practice of Bankruptcy Law"; admitted he had signed bankruptcy schedules under penalty of perjury without authority to do so; and stated he was doing the best he could in "unfamiliar territory."

Appellant next complains about the sufficiency of the evidence. He argues the circumstances surrounding his representation of Pappas in the bankruptcy court constituted an emergency within the meaning of rule 1.01(a). He argues the testimony of numerous witnesses established he handled the matter ethically and competently in the emergency situation. After reviewing all of the evidence, we hold the trial judge's findings are not so contrary to the overwhelming weight of the evidence as to be clearly wrong and manifestly unjust. [The rules do] allow "advice or assistance" by a lawyer in an area beyond his competence "in an emergency," [but] the lawyer must limit the advice and assistance "to that which is reasonably necessary under the circumstances." Appellant continued to represent Pappas in the bankruptcy court after the initial involuntary filing and after the state court judge had addressed Maglaris's removal of property from the restaurant. As noted in his brief, he "prepared and filed Pappas's bankruptcy schedules, attended court hearings, attended the 341 meetings, maintained communications with the bankruptcy trustee and counsel for other parties, informed the trustee of valuable rights that needed to be protected, perfected the state court appeal to preserve the estate's rights, and located alternative counsel for the bankruptcy trustee." These actions went beyond offering advice and assistance to Pappas [under] the circumstances appellant contends constituted the emergency.

Appellant testified he had never represented a client in a bankruptcy case. His experience was limited to representing himself as a creditor in a bankruptcy proceeding on at least two occasions.

Appellant represented to Judge Gibson he sought relief on behalf of the bankruptcy trustee when a bankruptcy trustee had not yet been appointed. He represented to Judge Gibson the relief requested was mandatory under the bankruptcy code. Judge McGuire found both of these representations to be "legally false." Setting aside the question of whether these representations were made intentionally, appellant was at least mistaken as to the applicable procedure and substantive law at the outset of the involuntary bankruptcy.

Later, appellant signed and filed bankruptcy schedules of Pappas's financial affairs under penalty of perjury. Nancy Resnick, an attorney with the United States Trustee's office in charge of monitoring certain cases in the bankruptcy courts, testified "the declaration to be signed under penalty of perjury as to the accuracy of your financial affairs, your assets, and liabilities has to be signed by the debtor." Resnick also testified an attorney can obtain a special power of attorney to represent an absent debtor. Again setting aside any issue of intent, Judge Felsenthal noted appellant was not the debtor and had no authority to sign the schedules under penalty of perjury.

Judge Felsenthal also informed appellant he could not represent the bankruptcy trustee, as he had not obtained an order from the court authorizing him to do so. The bankruptcy trustee, Scott Seidel, testified he assisted appellant with preparing the application for employment because appellant did not know how to prepare one. The application, however, was never filed, so the necessary court order was never obtained. While appellant places the responsibility on Seidel to ensure the application was filed, the end result was that appellant was never properly authorized to represent the trustee. Regardless of appellant's intent, the applicable bankruptcy procedures were not followed.

We hold the evidence was legally and factually sufficient to support the trial court's findings and conclusions that appellant knew or should have known he was not competent to accept and continue employment as Pappas's counsel in bankruptcy. We overrule appellant's first five issues.

Communication

Appellant's next three issues complain of the legal and factual sufficiency of the evidence to support the trial judge's findings and conclusions he violated rule 1.03(b). Rule 1.03(b) provides: "A lawyer shall explain a matter to the extent reasonably necessary to permit the client to make informed decisions regarding the representation."

The trial judge concluded appellant represented Pappas in a bankruptcy proceeding and filed bankruptcy statements and schedules "without first discussing, explaining or the client having consented to such filings" in violation of rule 1.03(b).

Appellant does not contend he consulted Pappas about the bankruptcy proceedings or allege Pappas was aware the bankruptcy cases had been filed. He cites his efforts to reach Pappas through telephone calls to Pappas's sister-in-law. He further contends he could not ethically withdraw from representing Pappas when he had been unable to reach him for only a short time. Appellant contends Pappas's goal, and direction to his lawyer, was to recover his interests in the restaurant. Appellant contends the goal never changed, and he had to act in "exigent circumstances" to protect Pappas's interests.

The trial judge's findings on this issue are based upon appellant's actions in the bankruptcy court, not the state court action. Without his client's knowledge or consent, appellant consented to the involuntary bankruptcy and filed schedules under penalty of perjury on behalf of his client.

[A] California opinion [argued by Appellant] is instructive. There, the client disappeared, and the attorney received two settlement offers. The client had authorized the attorney to accept settlement offers of two-thirds or more of the amount sought in any claim. One settlement offer was for two-thirds of the amount of the claim; the other was for one-half the amount. As to the first offer, the attorney should exercise professional judgment on behalf of the client whether or not to accept the offer. The attorney could not, however, accept any proposed settlement which contained substantive terms at variance with the authority conferred by the client. As to the second offer, the attorney was "not authorized to determine independently what is in Client's best interests from a substantive as opposed to a procedural standpoint." The attorney "cannot know all of the objective and subjective circumstances and considerations that govern Client's substantive decisions, and any decisions outside of client's authorization therefore must be left to client." Therefore, the attorney could not accept the second offer.

Here, while Pappas had instructed appellant to recover his interests in the restaurant, there was no evidence the authority extended to making decisions and representations regarding Pappas's overall financial condition and obligations in bankruptcy court. As the trial judge noted, "Bankruptcy actions taken by the Respondent were such that a reasonable attorney, although a relatively short period of time had lapsed, should have concluded that he was not able to go forward without consultation with his client, especially in light of the fact that the client had no notice of the bankruptcy filing at all." There was sufficient evidence from which the trial judge could conclude appellant failed to "explain a matter to the extent reasonably necessary to permit the client to make informed decisions regarding the representation" in violation of Rule 1.03(b).

Candor Toward the Tribunal

In his ninth, tenth, and eleventh issues, appellant complains of the legal and factual sufficiency of the evidence to support the trial judge's findings and conclusions he violated rule 3.03(a)(3). This rule provides: "A lawyer shall not knowingly: ... (3) in an ex parte proceeding, fail to disclose to the tribunal an unprivileged fact which the lawyer reasonably believes should be known by that entity for it to make an informed decision." Appellant also complains about the sufficiency of the Commission's pleadings to support the judgment.

The trial judge concluded, "Respondent made false representations to the state court judge in violation of Rule 3.03(a)(3), Texas Disciplinary Rules of Professional Conduct."

Appellant urges the evidence is legally and factually insufficient to support the trial judge's findings and conclusions of a violation of rule 3.03(a)(3). Appellant contends there is no evidence of any knowing conduct on his part. He contends his arguments regarding the automatic stay in bankruptcy were "well grounded" in the bankruptcy code, made by "a state court lawyer who did not practice bankruptcy law on a regular basis," who was "focusing solely on protecting the assets" and "not thinking of the legal fine points," and argues he never intended to imply he had been employed as counsel for the bankruptcy trustee. Appellant's motion, however, states unequivocally, six times, that the motion sought relief "on behalf of the bankruptcy trustee," and further states, equally unequivocally, that "all relief requested in this Motion is mandatory under the bankruptcy code and there are no questions of law or fact to be determined by this Court." The evidence showed a bankruptcy trustee had not been appointed at the time of the motion. Appellant verified under oath that all the statements in the motion were based on his personal knowledge and true. Judge Gibson testified he relied on these representations in making his ruling at the ex parte hearing: "My decision was driven by the bankruptcy and representations about the bankruptcy." The trial judge's finding appellant violated rule 3.03(a)(3) is not so contrary to the overwhelming weight of the evidence as to be clearly wrong and manifestly unjust. *See Bellino,* 124 S.W.3d at 385. We overrule appellant's issues nine, ten, and eleven.

Misconduct Involving Dishonesty, Fraud, Deceit or Misrepresentation

In his twelfth and thirteenth issues, appellant challenges the legal and factual sufficiency of the evidence to support the trial judge's findings and conclusions he violated rule 8.04(a)(3). This rule provides: "A lawyer shall not: ... (3) engage in conduct involving dishonesty, fraud, deceit, or misrepresentation."

In his fourth conclusion of law, the trial judge stated: "Respondent made statements in the bankruptcy filings that he could not know were true or accurate and made false representations regarding his status in the bankruptcy proceedings in violation of Rule 8.04(a)(3), Texas Disciplinary Rules of Professional Conduct."

Appellant contends he had the duty and authority to represent Pappas in the bankruptcy, and there was insufficient evidence of any false information in the bankruptcy schedules he filed. Therefore, he argues, there was no or insufficient evidence to support the trial judge's findings and legal conclusion regarding rule 8.04(a)(3). Appellant cites to evidence he had Pappas's authority to recover his interest in the restaurant, and evidence he only signed his own name to the schedules and only listed debts and assets he knew about from representing Pappas for eighteen months. Appellee offered no evidence the debts listed on the schedules were erroneous or false. Professor Moss and Justice Gammage testified there was nothing deceitful in signing the schedules under penalty of perjury where appellant was representing only that he had read the schedules and they were true and correct to the best of his knowledge.

Appellee argues "[i]t was the very filing of the pleadings and documents that constitute the misrepresentation because in doing so McIntyre was representing to the Court and others involved in the proceeding that Pappas knew of the proceedings, that Pappas had consented to the involuntary bankruptcy, and that Pappas approved the financial statement and schedules, when in fact this was not true."

Judge Felsenthal noted, "[t]he problem with this case is that it appears, if you accept the face of the record, that the debtor agreed to the filing. But it hasn't." As noted in the California bar opinion discussed above, an attorney "cannot know all of the objective and subjective circumstances and considerations that govern Client's substantive decisions, and any decisions outside of client's authorization therefore must be left to client." In discussing whether an attorney must or may withdraw from representing an absent client, Professor Moss testified, "[i]t depends on whether you can reasonably and prudently continue to represent him without doing something that you cannot do without his consent." The trial judge found appellant made representations in the bankruptcy court filings "for which he had no knowledge of the truth thereof or the basis for such filings." Appellant himself argues he included on the schedules only information of which he was personally aware. The trial judge concluded appellant signed the declaration pages of the bankruptcy schedules and statements of financial affairs "without Pappas ever having seen the documents, without Pappas' input or completion of the documents, nor any indication that [appellant] knew or could know whether the information was correct, complete and correct." ...The trial judge's finding appellant violated rule 8.04(a)(3) is not so contrary to the overwhelming weight of the evidence as to be clearly wrong and manifestly unjust. *See Bellino*, 124 S.W.3d at 385; *see also Eureste*, 76 S.W.3d at 198 (fraud not the only conduct prohibited by rule 8.04(a)(3); any conduct involving dishonesty, deceit, or misrepresentation also prohibited by rule 8.04(a)(3)). We overrule appellant's twelfth and thirteenth issues.

Sanctions and Attorneys' Fees

In his fourteenth, fifteenth, and sixteenth issues, appellant challenges the legal and factual sufficiency of the evidence to support his suspension from the practice of law and the award of attorneys' fees to appellee. He specifically challenges the trial court's findings he is a continuing threat to his clients and the public; he should be suspended from the practice of law for eighteen months; and he should not practice bankruptcy law without associating a bankruptcy specialist for eighteen months. A trial court has broad discretion to determine the consequences of professional misconduct. *See Eureste*, 76 S.W.3d at 202. An appellate court should only reverse the trial court's decision if the trial court acted in an unreasonable or arbitrary manner, or acted without reference to guiding rules and principles. *Id.* ...

Appellant argues the sanctions are an abuse of discretion because the trial judge did not find any damage to Pappas or to an opposing party and did not find appellant profited by his actions. He also argues the sanction allows appellee to usurp appellant's professional judgment in selecting the means by which to achieve the client's objectives. He also argues the sanction discourages zealous advocacy, requiring an attorney to "sit and do nothing" without specific instructions from the client. The trial judge, however, considered these arguments and noted appellant sometimes went too far in actively urging his and his client's position. He also noted his primary concern in the sanctions was appellant's candor to the court, stating, "you have got to have the respect of the other parties in this process, including the judiciary. That is a very difficult job to do and has to rely upon the attorneys to present matters with them, be candid with them, and present legally and factually correct matters to them." He ordered appellant to attend seminars on the lawyer's creed, in addition to an eighteen month suspension of which ninety days were to be actively served and the remainder to be probated. The record reflects the trial judge acted with reference to the relevant guiding principles and did not act in an unreasonable or arbitrary manner in tailoring the sanctions imposed on appellant.

McIntyre also challenges the award of attorneys' fees to appellee. He concedes appellee may recover reasonable and necessary attorneys' fees under the rules of disciplinary procedure, but argues the fees incurred were neither reasonable nor necessary. He contends the commission was not the prevailing party on the primary issues in the case, and complains the commission failed to segregate its fees between the issues on which it prevailed and the issues on which it did not prevail, and therefore is not entitled to an award of any attorneys' fees. Appellant does not cite authority for this proposition. The trial judge heard evidence from the commission regarding its fees, and appellant vigorously cross-examined the commission's attorney as to the reasonableness and necessity of the fees and costs. The trial judge did not abuse his discretion in the award of attorneys' fees and costs to the commission. We affirm the trial court's judgment.

****

Questions:

1. Attorney seeks your advice about including, in his fee agreement, the following provisions granting him the authority to decide whether to settle a case and sign any necessary settlement documents for a client:

   > *"INABILITY TO CONTACT CLIENT: There have been occasions when clients have failed to communicate with us concerning their whereabouts. This is a rare situation, but when it happens it puts us in an impossible situation. It means that we cannot effectuate a settlement, because in the absence of a valid power of attorney, the client must approve the settlement. This creates a real problem for both attorney and client, because the delay may cause a loss of a very favorable settlement, or the loss of the claim in its entirety if a statue [sic] of limitations is expiring or a lawsuit is to be dismissed for failure to appear or respond.*
   >
   > *LIMITED POWER OF ATTORNEY: To avoid this dilemma, it is our standard practice to obtain a "limited power of attorney" from all of our clients. This limited power of attorney operates as follows: If you do not keep us advised as to where we can contact you, or we are unable to reach or contact you, your signatures(s) on this Agreement authorizes us to act as your attorney-in-fact, and serves as a Special Power of Attorney for the purpose of agreeing to a settlement in our discretion on your behalf, and sign for you any drafts or releases necessary to complete the settlement. We also agree not to settle the case without your authorizing us in advance to do so, unless after diligent efforts we are unable to contact you. In such event we may settle utilizing the Power of Attorney contained in this agreement and will hold your share of recovery in trust for you in accordance with Arizona State Bar requirements. If we settle the case on your behalf, we will hold the funds from settlement in trust until you re-contact us. By signing below you grant us that limited Power of Attorney."*

   May an attorney ask a client for authority to allow the attorney, if the client disappears or otherwise cannot be contacted, to settle the client's case and to sign any drafts or releases necessary to finalize the settlement?

2. Attorney represents the executor of a handsome estate with several beneficiaries and heirs. Executor files the initial papers with the court and, in accordance with the will, is authorized

to serve without bond and minimal court involvement. All creditors are notified and paid and the estate must now be distributed among the heirs and other beneficiaries. However, before the matter can be finalized the executor disappears. After numerous attempts by the attorney to reach him, attorney closes the file but leaves the matter pending with the court. Is attorney subject to discipline?[26]

3. Lawyer represents the wife in a divorce suit, and prior to the final hearing the husband-defendant died. At the time of his death there were two life insurance policies with benefits available to his client amounting to some $12,000. He later received payment of the insurance amounts by mail but was then unable to locate his client and found that she had sold her home, taken her children out of school and remarried. His numerous attempts to locate his client were unsuccessful. Later he received a letter from the client in which she stated that he was welcome to the insurance collections. The postmark on the card showed it was mailed in his city but it had no return address. May the lawyer accept the proceeds of the insurance policies in accordance with the instructions contained in the letter? Discuss fully.[27]

****

ATTORNEY FEES

> A man phones a lawyer and asks, "How much would you charge for just answering three simple questions?"
>
> The lawyer replies, "A thousand dollars."
>
> "A thousand dollars!" exclaims the man. "That's very expensive isn't it?"
>
> "It certainly is," says the lawyer. "Now, what's your third question?"

There is certainly no dearth of jokes about lawyer billing practices. And, of course, humor is the best medicine, isn't it. But is it quite so funny that members of our profession apparently provide so much material for the humorists? Shouldn't we cringe at the thought of our colleagues seriously overcharging clients for work, especially when the work is routine or negligently performed?

Is it right to charge our clients for first class air fare simply because they can afford it? Should we bill separately for our overhead costs or is that included in the hourly rate? Is it acceptable to charge the client a full hour even though we worked for only ¼ or ½ hour?

---

[26] See Tosar v. Sladek, 393 So. 2d 61 (Fla. 3d DCA 1981) In *Tosar v. Sladek*, 393 So. 2d 61 (Fla. 3d DCA 1981).
[27] See Florida Bar ethics opinions, Opinion 61-15

IN THE NEWS:

Based on Various Studies and Client Experiences, the authors created a top ten list about the way lawyers cheat their clients. The intrigue lies not only in the fact that lawyers rip off their clients, but also in the fact that it apparent happens with unacceptable regularity.

The List:

1. **Double billing:** According to a Samford study that the authors cite, "the percentage of attorneys who believed that the practice was unethical fell from 64.7 percent in 1995-96 to only 51.8 percent in 2006-07, even though the practice has been condemned by the American Bar Association and most legal commentators."
2. **Padding hours:** According to that same study, "a distressingly high percentage of attorneys believe that time-based billing results in bill padding and provides incentives for attorneys to perform unnecessary work."
3. **Overhead:** The authors report that Michael Vick's lawyers charged him for their air conditioning as well as for "7,200 billable hours over ten months; equivalent to worign 24 hours a day on the Vick case for 300 straight days."
4. **Trivial tasks:** "Sometimes, law firms use high billing rates to stick clients with unnecessarily expensive bills for research, secretarial work, and other low-level tasks."
5. **Expense accounts:** "Expense reports can be great opportunities to practice greedier billing creativity. You might claim reimbursement for the cost of first-class tickets when actually you flew coach. Or you could claim reimbursement for plane tickets, hotels, and meals when actually you didn't travel at all."
6. **Exorbitant rates:** Some lawyers report to four digit hourly billing rates.
7. **Inefficiency:** You wouldn't think poor work and high rates go together
8. **Negligence:** Clients expect their lawyer to give their best. Is it an ethical violation when the lawyer fails to meet the client's expectations?
9. **Training:** Should lawyers charge clients for on-the-job-training?
10. **Working while sleeping:** While sleeping?

For more read: 10 Ways Lawyers Rip Off Clients http://www.businessinsider.com/10-ways-lawyers-rip-off-clients-2013-7#ixzz32wCe3oxP by Lawrence Delevingne and Gus Lubin.

Attorney Fees: You say tomato

Lawyers are regularly admonished to charge fair and reasonable fees for the services they provide.[28] Determining whether the fee is either fair or reasonable differs based on geography, the lawyer's expertise and reputation, the time that the attorney needs to handle the case, the scope of the representation and the terms of the fee agreement, among other things. These factors could substantially impact the amount of fees that an attorney will charge.

Consider the new attorney who charges $200 an hour to provide legal representation while a more experienced attorney charges $600 an hour to provide the same legal service. To a person who is employed in a position that pays $15.00 an hour neither fee may be fair nor reasonable

---

[28] See for e.g. ABA Model Rules of Professional Conduct [1.5]

but to a person who earns more than $5,000 an hour neither fee seems unreasonable. Nonetheless, to determine whether the attorney's fee meets the fair and reasonable fee standard, we rarely consider the client's ability to pay.[29] Indeed the ABA Model Rules fail to specifically address the client's ability to pay under rule 1.5 or in its comments interpreting the rule. However, the rule and comments make it clear that the factors enumerated in the rule are not exhaustive in determining reasonableness.[30] The rules do provide guidance, however.[31]

Factors commonly used to determine fee reasonableness[32]

1. The time and labor required for the matter, the novelty and difficulty of the questions involved, and the skill necessary to handle the matter properly.
2. The likelihood, if apparent to the client, that taking on this matter will preclude other employment by the lawyer.
3. The fee customarily charged in the locality for similar legal services.
4. The amount involved and the results obtained.
5. Time limitations imposed by the client or by the circumstances of the case.
6. The nature and length of the professional relationship with the client.
7. The lawyer's experience, reputation and ability.
8. Whether the fee is fixed or contingent.

In the Matter of Heather McClure O'Farrell
No. 29S00-0902-DI-76, Indiana Supreme Court (2011)

...Respondent practices law as an attorney of McClure & O'Farrell, PC. ("the Law Office"). The Law Office uses an "Hourly Fee Contract" or a "Flat Fee Contract" in most cases when it represents a party in a family law matter. Both types of contract contain a provision for a nonrefundable "engagement fee." The Commission alleges Respondent improperly charged two clients nonrefundable engagement fees and did not refund unearned fees after the representations ended. The case was submitted to the hearing officer on the parties' stipulation of facts in lieu of an evidentiary hearing.

Count 1. On November 20, 2006, "Client 1" hired the Law Office to prepare and file for dissolution of her marriage, to represent her in the preliminary hearing in that case, and to obtain a protective order against Client l's husband. The Law Office charged Client 1 a $3,000 engagement fee for the cases, plus $131 for filing fees, which Client 1 paid by credit card. Client 1 signed the Law Office's Flat Fee Contract, which contained the following provisions:

> "[The] engagement fee is non-refundable and shall be deemed earned upon commencement of Attorney's work on the case[.]"
> "Attorneys agree to credit any engagement fee received from Client

---

29 *Perdue v. Kenny A. ex rel. Winn*, 130 S.Ct. 1662 (2011)
30 Id. and see comment [1]
31 ABA Model Code of Professional Conduct
32 ABA Model Rules of Professional Conduct [1.5]

toward the flat fee…Said engagement fee shall be due and owing at the time
of execution of this contract. Client agrees to make no demand for a refund or
return of any part of the engagement fee owed or paid."

"In the event that the Client-Attorney relationship terminates prior to the
completion of Attorneys' representation as described ... above, Client and
Attorneys agree Attorneys shall, at the Attorneys' sole discretion, be entitled to
keep the engagement fee paid[.]"

Respondent filed a petition for dissolution of Client 1's marriage ("the Divorce Case") and
a petition for a protective order ("the PO Case") An Ex Parte Order for Protection was entered on
November 22, 2006. On or about November 23, 2006, Client 1 asked her credit card company to
chargeback her payment of $3,131 to the Law Office, which was done. The Law Office
challenged the chargeback, and the credit card company eventually restored the payment of
$3,131 to the Law Office.

On November 28, 2006, Respondent filed motions to withdraw as Client 1's attorney in
the Divorce Case and in the PO Case. Both cases eventually were dismissed. The Law Office
refused to refund any part of the $3,000 Client 1 had paid, saying that the fee was earned upon
receipt pursuant to the Flat Fee Contract.

Count 2 "Client 2" hired the Law Office to represent her regarding her ex-husband's
petition to show cause and petition to modify child support. Client 2 agreed to pay an
"engagement fee" of $1,500 and signed the Law Office's Hourly Fee Contract, which contained
the following provisions:

"[The] engagement fee is non-refundable and shall be deemed earned
upon commencement of Attorney's work on the case[.]"

"Attorneys agree to credit any engagement fee received from Client to
Client's account at Attorneys' prevailing rate as it is established from time to time.
Said engagement fee shall be due and owing at the time of execution of this
contract. Client agrees to make no demand for a refund or return of any part of
the engagement fee owed or paid."

Client 2 paid the $1,500-engagement fee, and later she paid an additional $3,000 under
the terms of the Hourly Fee Contract. The Law Office then offered to complete the
representation for an additional flat fee of $5,000. Client 2 accepted the offer and paid $5,000 to
the Law Office. The Law Office intended the $5,000 flat fee to be non-refundable and deemed
earned upon commencement of the representation. It further intended that the $5,000 flat fee
would pay for the remainder of the representation. The Law Office prepared a written Flat Fee
Contract for Client 2's representation. Although Client 2 never signed it, she confirmed in a
letter to Respondent her understanding that the $9,500 she had paid was payment in full for the
representation. Both parties thus agreed that Client 2's $5,000 payment would constitute payment
in full for the balance of the representation.

37

After paying the Law Firm $5,000, Client 2 told Respondent that her ex-husband had molested their daughter. Respondent advised Client 2 that she could not sign a petition containing such allegations without further investigation and proof. Without further consulting with Respondent, Client 2 reported the molestation allegations to the police, which expanded and complicated the scope of the representation. Due to Client 2's unwillingness to pay any additional fee, Respondent and the Law Office ended their representation of Client 2 and withdrew as her attorney. The Law Office refused to refund any part of the fee paid by Client 2, saying that all fees were earned upon receipt and nonrefundable.

The Commission charged Respondent with violating Indiana Professional Conduct Rule 1-5(a), which prohibits making an agreement for, charging, or collecting an unreasonable fee, and Rule 1.16(d), which prohibits failure to refund an unearned fee promptly.

Discussion

Types of fee arrangements. There are a variety of terms used to describe the types of fee arrangements between attorneys and clients. In this opinion, the following terms will be used for three common types of attorney fees: (1) a "flat fee" is a fixed charge for a particular representation, often paid in full at the beginning of the representation; (2) an "advance fee" is a payment made at the beginning of a representation against which charges for the representation are credited as they accrue, usually on an hourly basis; and (3) a "general retainer" is payment for an attorneys availability, which is earned in full when paid before any work is done.

Regardless of the term used to describe a client's initial payment, its type is determined by its purpose, ie., what it is intended to purchase. When the purpose is to serve as an advance payment to the lawyer of fees the lawyer will earn in the future by doing work for the client, that payment is either a flat fee or advance fee. On the other hand, when the purpose is simply to pay for the lawyer's availability to provide legal services as needed during a period of time, as opposed to payment for work not yet done, the fee is a general retainer. A general retainer acts as an option on the lawyer's future services, often on a priority basis, and precludes the lawyer from undertaking representations that might conflict with representing the client. In some cases, the lawyer may need to turn down unrelated employment to ensure availability if the client calls for immediate assistance. Because this fee is not intended to pay for work, but merely for the lawyer's availability, it is earned on payment and the attorney is entitled to the money even if no services are actually performed for the client, so long as the lawyer provides the bargained-for availability. [citations omitted]

Nonrefundability considerations. In addressing an attorneys use of "special nonrefundable retainer fee agreements" calling for nonrefundable minimum fees, the New York Court of Appeals opined:

> [T] he use of a special nonrefundable retainer fee agreement clashes with public policy because it inappropriately compromises the right to sever the fiduciary services relationship with the lawyer. Special nonrefundable retainer fee agreements diminish the core of the fiduciary relationship by substantially altering and economically chilling the client's unbridled prerogative to walk away from the lawyer. To answer

that the client can technically still terminate misses the reality of the economic coercion that pervades such matters. If special nonrefundable retainers are allowed to flourish, clients would be relegated to hostage status in an unwanted fiduciary relationship—an utter anomaly. Such circumstance would impose a penalty on a client for daring to invoke a hollow right to discharge. [citation omitted]

In a similar vein, we have held: "A corollary of the client's right to discharge a lawyer is that a contract between the client and the lawyer that unduly impairs that right is invalid." [citation omitted] [This court has]... held that an advance fee cannot be nonrefundable and the assertion in a fee agreement that an advance fee is nonrefundable violates the requirement that a lawyer's fee be reasonable. [citation omitted] We continued:

"Where the advance payment is in the nature of a flat fee, however, or for a partial payment of a flat fee, it is not only reasonable but also advisable that the agreement expressly reflect the fact that such flat fee is not refundable *except for failure to perform the agreed legal services. If the legal services covered by a flat fee are not provided as agreed, an attorney must refund any unearned fees."* (emphasis added by court).

In an earlier case... this Court held that the respondent's demand for a nonrefundable $4,500 fee irrespective of any termination of the respondent's employment was an unreasonable fee. We expanded:

"We do not hold that unrefundable retainers are per se unenforceable. There are many circumstances where, for example, preclusion of other representations or guaranteed priority of access to an attorney's advice may justify such an arrangement. But here there is no evidence of, for example, any value received by the client or detriment incurred by the attorney in return for the nonrefundable provision, other than relatively routine legal services. Of course, the client is free to terminate the representation at any time."

... we then advised: "Where a [general] retainer is thus justified, a lawyer would be well advised to explicitly include the basis for such nonrefundability in the attorney-client agreement".

The nature of Respondent's engagement fees. To determine the propriety of the nonrefundable "engagement fees" Respondent charged Clients 1 and 2, we must determine the nature of the fees. The Law Firm's fee agreements state that the engagement fee is "nonrefundable and shall be deemed earned upon commencement of Attorney's work on the case." .... However, "an attorney cannot treat a fee as 'earned' simply by labeling the fee 'earned on receipt' or referring to the fee as an 'engagement retainer.'" Matter of Sather, 3 P.3d 403, 412 (Colo. 2000). "[I]t is the actual nature of the attorney-client relationship, not the label used, that will be determinative." Kendall, 804 N.E.2d at 1160. We therefore turn to the circumstances of Respondent's representations to determine the nature of the fees she charged, which turns on what those fees were intended to purchase.

Respondent contends her engagement fee is paid by a client to induce the Law Firm to take a case and thus is earned on receipt. The Law Firm's fee agreements, however, also provide that the engagement fee would be credited against either Respondent's hourly fee or her flat fee. Thus, if Respondent completed the work called for in the contracts, the entire engagement fee would have been used to purchase the services Respondent rendered. This is evidence that the engagement fees were intended to buy the legal services she agreed to perform rather than simply her availability at the outset.

A contract provision for a nonrefundable general retainer, with or without a recitation of supporting circumstances, cannot be inserted as boilerplate language in all of a firm's fee agreements. Routine inclusion of such a provision in all fee agreements regardless of the circumstances would be misleading; and regardless of what the contract says, the basis for charging a nonrefundable general retainer in a particular case must be supported by the actual circumstances of that case.

In determining the nature of the engagement fees, we finally note that the Law Finn's contract with Client 1 was entitled a Flat Fee Contract and stated explicitly that Client 1 would be billed a "flat fee," which was equal in amount to the engagement fee, for the representation described in the contract. Although Client 2 first signed a contract calling for an hourly fee, the parties later modified it to provide for payment of a fixed additional amount to complete the representation. This, coupled with the absence of evidence justifying general retainers, leads us to conclude that the fees at issue are flat fees for work to be performed.

Respondent's making agreements for and charging nonrefundable flat fees. In addressing flat fees in Kendall, we said it is both reasonable and advisable that a fee agreement expressly reflect that a flat fee is not refundable "except for failure to perform the agreed legal services." However, rather than advise clients of this exception, the Law Firm's Flat Fee Contracts told clients that the fee was nonrefundable "even if the Client-Attorney relationship terminates prior to the completion of Attorneys' representation." The presence of this contract provision, even if unenforceable, could chill the right of a client to terminate Respondent's services, believing the Law Firm would be entitled to keep the entire flat fee regardless of how much or how little work was done and the client would have to pay another attorney to finish the task. We conclude that Respondent violated Rule 1-5(a) by including an improper nonrefundability provision in her flat fee agreements.

The fee agreements not only *stated* that the flat fees were nonrefundable under any circumstances, but Respondent also *treated* them as such. We therefore conclude that Respondent also violated Rule 1-5(a) by charging and collecting flat fees that were nonrefundable regardless of the circumstances, even if Respondent failed to perform the agreed legal services *See* Kendall, 804 NE-2d at 1160. ...

The Court is mindful of the legitimate concern of attorneys that they will go through the initial steps of opening a case and beginning work for a new client, only to have that client discharge them and demand a refund of the entire initial payment as unearned. The solution, however, is not allowing attorneys to charge flat or advance fees upfront that are wholly nonrefundable regardless of the amount of services rendered. As an alternative, a fee agreement could designate a reasonable part of the initial payment that would be deemed earned by the attorney for opening the case and beginning the representation. If a general retainer for availability is justified and additional charges for actual services are contemplated, the contract could include a statement of the amount of the general retainer and the circumstances supporting it along with a provision setting forth how the fees for actual services will be calculated and collected. Even without such contract provisions, "[i]t is well settled that, where the complete performance of an attorney's services has been rendered impossible, or otherwise prevented, by the client, the attorney may, as a rule, recover on a quantum meruit for the services rendered by him [or her]." [citation omitted]

<u>Respondent's failure to refund any part of the flat fees collected from Clients 1 and 2.</u> "if the legal services covered by a flat fee are not provided as agreed, an attorney must refund any unearned fees." Kendall, 804 NE 2d at 1160. Thus, Respondent was obligated under Rule 1.16(d) to refund to Clients 1 and 2 any unearned portion of the flat fees they paid her. The question is how to determine how much of each flat fee was unearned.

The Commission makes no contention that Respondent did not work diligently and professionally in her representation of Client 1 and Client 2. The Commission makes no contention that Respondent's fee, if charged at her hourly rate, would not have exceeded the flat fee each client paid. The Commission argues, however, that if a flat fee representation is not completed, by definition some amount of the flat fee necessarily must be unearned and returned to the client.

With the limited record in this case, we are not prepared to hold that some amount of a flat fee must be returned in all cases in which the attorney-client relationship ends before the work contracted for is completed. Perhaps the entire flat fee could be deemed earned if the client deals unfairly with the attorney or refuses to cooperate with the attorney, and then either fires the attorney or makes continuation of the representation ethically impossible after the attorney expends considerable time and effort on the case. Respondent asserts circumstances like these existed with both Clients 1 and 2. Because this case was submitted to the hearing officer on the parties' limited stipulations, we find the evidence is insufficient to make a definitive determination of how much, if anything, Respondent should have refunded to Clients 1 and 2. The Court therefore concludes *that the Commission* failed to meet its burden of proving by clear and convincing *evidence that* Respondent violated Rule 1.16(d) in the circumstances stipulated for Clients 1 and 2. [Citation omitted]

Conclusion

The Court concludes that in charging nonrefundable flat fees, Respondent violated Indiana Professional Conduct Rule 1.5(a) by making agreements for and charging unreasonable fees. For Respondent's professional misconduct, the Court imposes a public reprimand.

41

****

Questions:

1. Client seeks your professional services which you offer to him for a non-refundable fee of $10,000. After you have fully disclosed to the Client what non-refundable fee means, he signs the contract and initials the bolded print that states "THIS FEE IS NOT REFUNDABLE". The case is messy and Client requires a lot of hand holding, which you personally provide. Moreover, you start work immediately and give the case your all for the thirty days before your Client calls to fire you. He has decided to hire another "more aggressive" lawyer. Client also demands his money back. You refer Client to the contract, remind him of your conversation at the beginning of the representation and let him know in clear terms that you will not refund the money? Are you in violation of the model rules of professional conduct?[33]

2. Attorney Bob Dance agreed to represent Will Flanders's son in a criminal matter for a flat fee of $15,000, with the initial $7,500 paid "up-front" and the remainder paid "after Flanders's son turned himself in to the police." Mance placed about $6,000 of the up-front payment in his client escrow account, with the remaining amount of $1,500 going into his operating account. One week later, Flanders's son turned himself into the police and Dance withdrew the balance of $7,500 from the escrow account and deposited in his operating account. When the attorney-client relationship soured, Flanders demanded his money back, only to learn that Dance had spent all the money. Has Vance violated the model rules of professional conduct?[34] Discuss fully.

****

Hoover Slovacek LLP v. Walton
206 S.W.3d 557 (Tex. 2006)

… In this case, we must determine whether an attorney hired on a contingent-fee basis may include in the fee agreement a provision stating that, in the event the attorney is discharged before completing the representation, the client must immediately pay a fee equal to the present value of the attorney's interest in the client's claim. We conclude that this termination fee provision is contrary to public policy and unenforceable. We affirm the court of appeals' judgment in part, reverse in part, and remand to the court of appeals for further proceedings.

In June 1995, John B. Walton, Jr. hired attorney Steve Parrott of Hoover Slovacek LLP (Hoover) to recover unpaid royalties from several oil and gas companies operating on his 32,500 acre ranch in Winkler County. The engagement letter granted Hoover a 30% contingent fee for all claims on which collection was achieved through one trial. Most significantly, the letter included the following provision:

---

[33] See *Matter of O'Farrell*, No. 29S00-0902-DI-76, 2011 Ind. LEXIS 72 (Ind. Feb. 11, 2011); Also see Ethics Opinion No. 611, The Professional Ethics for the State Bar of Texas
[34] In re Mance, 980 A.2d 1196 (D.C. 2009)

42

You may terminate the Firm's legal representation at any time.... Upon termination by You, You agree to immediately pay the Firm the then present value of the Contingent Fee described [herein], plus all Costs then owed to the Firm, plus subsequent legal fees [incurred to transfer the representation to another firm and withdraw from litigation].

Shortly after signing the contract, Walton and Parrott agreed to hire Kevin Jackson as local counsel and reduced Hoover's contingent fee to 28.66%. Parrott negotiated settlements exceeding $200,000 with Texaco and El Paso Natural Gas, and Walton paid Hoover its contingent fee. Parrott then turned to Walton's claims against Bass Enterprises Production Company (Bass), and hired accountant Everett Holseth to perform an audit and compile evidence establishing the claims' value. *Holseth never completed the audit, but testified that he estimated the value of Walton's claims at $2 million to $4 million.* Meanwhile, Walton authorized Parrott to settle his claims against Bass for $8.5 million.

In January 1997, Parrott made an initial settlement demand of $58.5 million. Bass's attorney testified that Parrott was unable to support this number with any legal theories, expert reports, or calculations, and that the demand was so "enormous" he basically "quit listening." The following month, however, Bass offered $6 million not only to settle Walton's claims, but also to purchase the surface estates of eight sections of the Winkler County ranch, acquire numerous easements, and secure Walton's royalty interests under the leases. Walton refused to sell, but authorized Parrott to accept $6 million to settle only Walton's claims for unpaid royalties. Walton also wrote Parrott and expressed discontent that Parrott did not consult him before making the $58.5 million demand. According to Walton, Parrott responded by pressuring him to sell part of the ranch and his royalties for $6 million. In March 1997, Walton discharged Parrott, complaining that Parrott was doing little to prosecute his claims against Bass and had damaged his credibility by making an unauthorized and "absurd" $58.5 million demand.

Walton then retained Andrews & Kurth LLP, which, in November 1998, settled Walton's claims against Bass for $900,000. By that time, Hoover had sent Walton a bill for $1.7 million (28.66% of $6 million), contending that Bass's $6 million offer, and Walton's subsequent authorization to settle for that amount, established the present value of Walton's claims at the time of discharge. Walton paid Andrews & Kurth approximately $283,000 in hourly fees and costs, but refused to pay Hoover.

When Hoover sought to intervene in the settlement proceedings between Walton and Bass, the trial court severed Hoover's claim, and the parties tried the case before a jury. Richard Bianchi, a former state district judge in Harris County, testified as Hoover's expert witness. Bianchi opined that a 28.66% contingent fee was, "if anything, lower than normal, but certainly reasonable under these circumstances," and that "it would only be unconscionable to ignore the agreement of the parties." He also testified that charging more than Walton ultimately recovered from Bass "doesn't change the deal they made. That's just a bad business deal." In contrast, Walton's local counsel, Kevin Jackson, testified that he had never heard of attorneys charging a percentage based on the present value of a claim at the time of discharge rather than the client's actual recovery, and that the $1.7 million fee was unconscionable.

Discussion

When interpreting and enforcing attorney-client fee agreements, it is "not enough to simply say that a contract is a contract. There are ethical considerations overlaying the contractual relationship." In Texas, we hold attorneys to the highest standards of ethical conduct in their dealings with their clients. The duty is highest when the attorney contracts with his or her client or otherwise takes a position adverse to his or her client's interests. As Justice Cardozo observed, "[a fiduciary] is held to something stricter than the morals of the marketplace. Not honesty alone, but the punctilio of an honor the most sensitive, is then the standard of behavior." Accordingly, a lawyer must conduct his or her business with inveterate honesty and loyalty, always keeping the client's best interest in mind.

Although contingent fee contracts are increasingly used by businesses and other sophisticated parties, their primary purpose is to allow plaintiffs who cannot afford an attorney to obtain legal services by compensating the attorney from the proceeds of any recovery. *Arthur Andersen & Co. v. Perry Equip. Corp.,* 945 S.W.2d 812, 818 (Tex.1997). The contingent fee offers "the potential of a greater fee than might be earned under an hourly billing method" in order to compensate the attorney for the risk that he or she will receive "no fee whatsoever if the case is lost." Id. In exchange, the client is largely protected from incurring a net financial loss in connection with the representation. This risk-sharing feature creates an incentive for lawyers to work diligently and obtain the best results possible. A closely related benefit is the contingent fee's tendency to reduce frivolous litigation by discouraging attorneys from presenting claims that have negative value or otherwise lack merit.

In Texas, if an attorney hired on a contingent-fee basis is discharged without cause before the representation is completed, the attorney may seek compensation in quantum meruit or in a suit to enforce the contract by collecting the fee from any damages the client subsequently recovers. Both remedies are subject to the prohibition against charging or collecting an unconscionable fee. Tex. Disciplinary R. Prof'l Conduct. Whether a particular fee amount or contingency percentage charged by the attorney is unconscionable under all relevant circumstances of the representation is an issue for the factfinder. On the other hand, whether a contract, including a fee agreement between attorney and client, is contrary to public policy and unconscionable at the time it is formed is a question of law.

Although the Disciplinary Rules do not define standards of civil liability for attorneys, they are persuasive authority outside the context of disciplinary proceedings, and we have applied Rule 1.04 as a rule of decision in disputes concerning attorney's fees. Tex. Disciplinary R. Prof'l Conduct preamble ¶ 15. Under the Disciplinary Rules, a fee is unconscionable if a competent lawyer could not form a reasonable belief that the fee is reasonable. Tex. Disciplinary R. Prof'l Conduct. The reasonableness of a fee is determined by considering all relevant circumstances relating to the representation, including:

(1) the time and labor required, the novelty and difficulty of the questions involved, and the skill required to perform the legal services properly;

(2) the likelihood ... that the acceptance of the particular employment will preclude other employment by the lawyer;

(3) the fee customarily charged in the locality for similar legal services;

(4) the amount involved and the results obtained;

(5) the time limitations imposed by the client or by the circumstances;

(6) the nature and length of the professional relationship with the client;

(7) the experience, reputation, and ability of the lawyer or lawyers performing the services; and

(8) whether the fee is fixed or contingent on results obtained or uncertainty of collection before the legal services have been rendered. Tex. Disciplinary R. Prof'l Conduct 1.04(b), *cited in Arthur Andersen,* 945 S.W.2d at 818.

Hoover's termination fee provision purported to contract around the remedies in three ways. First, it made no distinction between discharges occurring with or without cause. Second, it assessed the attorney's fee as a percentage of the present value of the client's claim at the time of discharge, discarding the quantum meruit and contingent fee measurements. Finally, it required Walton to pay Hoover the percentage fee immediately at the time of discharge.

Notwithstanding its immediate-payment requirement, several additional considerations lead us to conclude that Hoover's termination fee provision is unenforceable. In *Levine v. Bayne, Snell & Krause, Ltd.,* we refused to construe a contingent fee contract as entitling the attorney to compensation exceeding the client's actual recovery. 40 S.W.3d 92, 95 (Tex.2001). In that case, the clients purchased a home containing foundation defects, and stopped making mortgage payments when the defects were discovered. *Id.* at 93. They agreed to pay their lawyer one-third of "any amount received by settlement or recovery." *Id.* A jury awarded the clients $243,644 in damages, but offset the award against the balance due on their mortgage, resulting in a net recovery of $81,793. *Id.* The lawyer sued to collect $155,866, a fee equaling one-third of the gross recovery plus pre- and post-judgment interest and expenses. *Id.* In refusing to interpret "any amount received" as permitting collection of a contingent fee exceeding the client's net recovery, we emphasized that the lawyer is entitled to receive the contingent fee " 'only when and *to the extent the client receives payment.'* " *Id.* at 94 (quoting Restatement (Third) Of The Law Governing Lawyers § 35). A reasonable client does not expect that a lawyer engaged on a contingent-fee basis will charge a fee equaling or, as in this case, exceeding 100% of the recovery. In *Levine,* we noted that " '[l]awyers almost always possess the more sophisticated understanding of fee arrangements. It is therefore appropriate to place the balance of the burden of fair dealing and the allotment of risk in the hands of the lawyer in regard to fee arrangements with clients.' " *Id.* at 95 (quoting *In re Myers,* 663 N.E.2d 771, 774–75 (Ind.1996)). We believe Hoover's termination fee provision is unreasonably susceptible to overreaching, exploiting the attorney's superior information, and damaging the trust that is vital to the attorney-client relationship.

Hourly fee agreements and cases in which the prevailing party recovers attorney's fees from an opposing party do not implicate the concerns presented here. Thus, pursuant to statute or a contract between the parties, it is not uncommon for courts to approve fee-shifting awards that exceed the damages recovered by the client. *See, e.g., Hruska v. First State Bank of Deanville,* 747 S.W.2d 783, 785 (Tex.1988) (upholding $12,570 fee where the client recovered $2,920); *Sibley v. RMA Partners, L.P.,* 138 S.W.3d 455, 458–59 (Tex.App.-Beaumont 2004, no pet.) (upholding $82,748 fee where the client stood to recover approximately $43,000).

The Disciplinary Rules provide that a contingent fee is permitted only where, quite sensibly, the fee is "contingent on the outcome of the matter for which the service is rendered." Tex. Disciplinary R. Prof'l Conduct 1.04(d). Hoover's termination fee, if not impliedly prohibited by Rule 1.04(d), is directly forbidden by Rule 1.08(h), which states that "[a] lawyer shall not acquire a proprietary interest in the cause of action or subject matter of litigation the lawyer is conducting for the client, except that the lawyer may ... contract in a civil case with a client for a contingent fee that is permissible under Rule 1.04." *Id.* 1.08(h)(2). Thus, even if Hoover's termination fee provision is viewed as transforming a traditional contingent fee into a fixed fee, it nonetheless impermissibly grants the lawyer a proprietary interest in the client's claim by entitling him to a percentage of the claim's value without regard to the ultimate results obtained.

Hoover's termination fee provision is also antagonistic to many policies supporting the use of contingent fees in civil cases. Most troubling is its creation of an incentive for the lawyer to be discharged soon after he or she can establish the present value of the client's claim with sufficient certainty. Whereas the contingent fee encourages efficiency and diligent efforts to obtain the best results possible, Hoover's termination fee provision encourages the lawyer to escape the contingency as soon as practicable, and take on other cases, thereby avoiding the demands and consequences of trials and appeals. Moreover, the provision encourages litigation of a subset of claims that would not be pursued under traditional contingent fee agreements.

Our conclusion that Hoover's termination fee provision is unconscionable does not render the parties' entire fee agreement unenforceable. "If a contract or term thereof is unconscionable at the time the contract is made a court may refuse to enforce the contract, or may enforce the remainder of the contract without the unconscionable term, or may so limit the application of any unconscionable term as to avoid any unconscionable result."

The court of appeals rendered a take-nothing judgment against Hoover, holding the entire fee agreement unenforceable and denying a recovery in quantum meruit because Hoover failed to present evidence of the reasonable value of its services. 149 S.W.3d at 847. We agree that Hoover no longer has a claim for quantum meruit, but we disagree with the take-nothing judgment. In the trial court, Hoover sought to enforce the contract's termination fee provision. Our holding, however, severs the termination fee provision, leaving a contingent fee contract subject to *Mandell.* The jury (1) found that Walton did not comply with the contract and (2) failed to find that Walton had good cause to discharge Hoover. Under *Mandell,* therefore, Hoover was entitled to its contingent fee: 28.66% of $900,000, or $257,940. In the trial court, and again in his appellate brief, Walton argued that Hoover was entitled to only this amount, and Hoover requested this relief in the alternative in its brief to this Court. In the court of appeals, however, Walton challenged the factual and legal sufficiency of the evidence supporting the jury's finding on the good-cause issue. Because the court of appeals reversed and rendered judgment, it did not reach Walton's sufficiency points. Accordingly, we remand the case to that court for consideration of those issues.

Conclusion

Hoover's termination fee provision penalized Walton for changing counsel, granted Hoover an impermissible proprietary interest in Walton's claims, shifted the risks of the representation almost entirely to Walton's detriment, and subverted several policies underlying the use of contingent fees. We hold that this provision is unconscionable as a matter of law, and therefore, unenforceable. We affirm that part of the court of appeals' judgment reversing the trial court's judgment, but reverse its take-nothing judgment, and remand this case to the court of appeals for further proceedings. Tex.R.App. P. 60.2(a), (d).

****

Questions:

1. Attorney maintains his law office in a small farming community. His clients often pay him in chickens, fruit, bread and Ethiopian linens. The state bar finds out about this and brings charges against the lawyer for violating ethical mandates that a lawyer charge reasonable fees and communicates the bases for his fee to the client. Is Attorney in violation of the ethical mandates regarding attorney fees? Why? Why not?[35]

2. Lawyer and Client agree in writing that lawyer will provide legal services to Client who agrees to pay a per hour rate. However, the contract fails to state what the lawyer's hourly billing rate is. Client receives two bills each invoicing at the rate of $500 an hour. According to client she had failed to look at the entire statement, looking only at the amount that was due. Client paid the first two bills. However, by the time the third bill was received Client's son was visiting from out of town, saw the bill and advised Client that the fee was outrageous for the routine services attorney was providing. Much of what the attorney was doing was general counsel work regarding the sale of various properties client owned. The real estate broker handled most of the details, but Lawyer reviewed all the contracts, participated in various negotiations and conducted independent research about the value of the property that he discovered was located in a flood plain. The work performed by Lawyer could arguably been performed by a paralegal at a rate less than $100 an hour. However, Lawyer was a sole practitioner who had a good professional relationship. He had a single secretary and chose his cases carefully so that he would not have too many cases. If Client protests the billing rate and demands a refund of money she has already paid, what must Lawyer do to comply with the model rules of professional conduct? What <u>should</u> lawyer do?[36]

3. Harry Highstepper is a high profile criminal lawyer. He has defended over ten drug dealers in Federal Court and was able to obtain acquittals for all. He is approached by Melvin Methlab's mother who asks Harry to represent her son who has been charged with multiple crimes including criminal conspiracy, human trafficking and kidnapping. Melvin also faces a charge in an unrelated outstanding warrant for bond forfeiture. Harry admits to Melvin's mother that his fees and expenses exceed that of other attorneys

---

[35] See *In re Grzybek*, 552 N.W.2d 215, 216 (Minn. 1996)

[36] See Daniel L. Abrams, Legal Fees: Ten Things your lawyer may not want you to know, available at http://www.lawyerquality.com/article_fees/

because of his expertise. Harry also tells mother that because the case is high profile and will generate a lot of publicity, he will represent Melvin in all matters under a 25% contingency fee arrangement. Harry reduces the arrangement to writing which provides that Harry will be paid based on 25% of the profits that Melvin makes selling his story. Harry suspects that his own story will sell well also. Melvin's mother and Melvin agree to the fee arrangement and Melvin signs the agreement. Is the fee arrangement permitted under the model rules of professional conduct? Discuss fully.

4. An experienced entertainment law attorney represents Client who is a talented writer and producer of television dramas and mini-series. Client filed a lawsuit to establish and receive royalty payments due to him for one of his highly-rated mini-series. Client did not have the necessary funds to pay the attorney's reasonable hourly rate for undertaking the case so Client proposed instead to pay the attorney 30% of the royalties recovered in the suit. The attorney fee generated under the Client's proposed fee is likely to exceed the amount that the attorney would have received from charging his regular hourly rate. The attorney is ecstatic about the extra fee and intends to put in extra effort to get as high a recovery as possible. Is the attorney subject to discipline for violating the model rules? Discuss fully.

****

Confidentiality

Ethical rules mandate that a lawyer is prohibited from disclosing information that is related to the representation of the client without the client's informed consent. Ethical rules generally permit disclosure where the disclosure is impliedly authorized or when the lawyer reasonably believes the disclosure is necessary to:

a. Prevent reasonably certain death or substantial bodily harm, or

b. Prevent client from committing crime or fraud that will result in substantial financial injury, or

c. Secure legal advice about the lawyer's compliance with the rules of ethics, or

d. Establish a claim or defense on behalf of lawyer in controversy between lawyer and client or other litigation, or

e. Detect and resolve conflicts of interest arising from lawyer's employment status but only if the revealed information would not compromise the attorney-client privilege or otherwise prejudice the client.

The purpose of the rule of confidentiality is to encourage full and open communication between the lawyer and client. The lawyer's duty of confidentiality is discussed in four ABA Model Rules , 1.6 being the foundational rule, 1.8(b), regarding the lawyer's duty to refrain from using confidential information; and rules 1.9 and 1.18 regarding duties to prospective clients.

Confidential information is different from privileged communication subject to attorney-client privilege and shielded by the work product protection. The attorney-client privilege protects the communication between the attorney and client. Work product includes the lawyer's thoughts, notes, observations and research prepared in anticipation of litigation.[37] Both the privilege and the work product protections extend to the communication that will or is sought to be used as evidence in a case.[38] On the other hand, confidential information is secreted for all purposes and extends even after the death of the client.[39] Confidential information is protected regardless of the source, unless the information is publicly available.

It is commonly thought that the reason for the exceptions to the rule of non-disclosure is due principally to public policy considerations. Consider the exceptions enumerated under the ABA Model Rules and you will likely conclude that both the rule and the exceptions are easily employed. However, is not always the case. One stark example of the preeminence of the lawyer's duty of confidentiality (even when faced with public policy considerations against incarcerating innocent people) reveals the complexity of applying the rule.[40]

> In Chicago Illinois, an innocent man, Alton Logan was convicted for murder and sentenced to life in prison. He was 28 years old at the time of his conviction. Twenty-six years later, Logan was exonerated and released from prison at age 54. For the entire time that he was in prison, two lawyers, Dale Coventry and W. Jamie Kunz knew that he was innocent but could not disclose the information because they represented the man who had actually committed the crime. Their client had confessed his role in the crime to the lawyers during their attorney client relationship. The lawyers had obtained their client's consent to disclose the confidential information after the client's death.
>
> Many, including Logan himself, have wondered why the lawyers were unable to disclose the information under the 'certain death or substantial bodily harm' exception. However,

---

[37] Texas Dept. of Mental Health and Mental Retardatioon v. Davis, 775 S.W.2d 467,477 (Tex.App-Austin 1989, no writ)

[38] Martin R. Lueck, Patrick M. Arenz, *Federal Rule of Evidence 502(D) and Compelled Quick Peek Productions*, 10 Sedona Conf. J. 229; 232 (2009)

[39] Deana A. Pollard, *Unconscious Bias and Self-Critical Analysis: The Case for a Qualified Evidentiary Equal Employment Opportunity Privilege*, 74 Wash. L. Rev. 913; 1006 (1999)

[40] See CBS News, *26-Year Secret Kept Innocent Man In Prison*, available at http://www.cbsnews.com/news/26-year-secret-kept-innocent-man-in-prison/. The Logan case involved both the ethical duty of the attorneys to maintain their client's confidence as well as their legal responsibility not to breach the attorney client privilege. Note that in November, 2008 "60 Minutes" covered another possible wrongful conviction involving attorney-client privilege. An attorney for a man who committed suicide in prison has revealed that his client committed a murder for which Lee Wayne Hunt is still incarcerated in North Carolina. The North Carolin Supreme Court refused to hear Hunt's appeal.

the lawyers were advised by the bar and legal experts that the secret could not be disclosed without the client's consent.[41]

> While many lawyers are worried about the erosion of their clients' trust, legal ethicists are worried about the public trust. They suggest that the rules of confidentiality have kept lawyers from doing the right thing for too long.[42]

McClure v. Thompson
323 F.3d 1233 (9th Cir. Or. 2003)

Petitioner, convicted in state court of three counts of aggravated murder, sought federal habeas relief. The United States District Court for the District of Oregon, denied petition. Petitioner appealed. The Court of Appeals, Circuit Judge, held that: (1) district court's finding that petitioner consented to his counsel's disclosure of confidential information concerning locations of bodies of two murder victims was not clearly erroneous; (2) counsel did not advise petitioner of potential harmful consequences of disclosure, invalidating consent; (3) counsel reasonably believed that disclosure was necessary to prevent further criminal acts; and (4) counsel did not act under conflict of interest. Affirmed.

Opinion

Oregon state prisoner Robert A. McClure appeals the district court's denial of his 28 U.S.C. § 2254 habeas corpus petition challenging his jury trial conviction for three aggravated murders. McClure's original defense attorney, Christopher Mecca, placed an anonymous telephone call to law enforcement officials directing them to the locations of what turned out to be the bodies of two children whom McClure was ultimately convicted of killing. The district court rejected McClure's arguments that the disclosure constituted ineffective assistance of counsel, holding there was no breach of the duty of confidentiality and no actual conflict of interest. We affirm.

Background
Offense, Arrest and Conviction

On Tuesday, April 24, 1984, the body of Carol Jones was found in her home in Grants Pass, Oregon. She had been struck numerous times on the head, arms and hands with a blunt object. A gun cabinet in the home had been forced open and a .44 caliber revolver was missing. Two of Jones' children-Michael, age 14, and Tanya, age 10-were also missing. The fingerprints

---

[41]Id. And see Adam Liptak, Lawyer whose Disclosure of Confidence Brought Down a Jusdge is Punished, New York Times, 2003 available at http://www.nytimes.com/2003/04/20/us/lawyer-whose-disclosure-of-confidence-brought-down-a-judge-is-punished.html. Last visited 6.10.14.

[42] Sarah Boxer, Lawyers are Asking, how Secret is a Secret? N Y Times, Aug. 11, 2001

of Robert McClure, a friend of Jones, were found in the blood in the home. On Saturday, April 28, McClure was arrested in connection with the death of Carol Jones and the disappearance of the children.

That same day, McClure's mother contacted attorney Christopher Mecca and asked him to represent her son. As discussed in more detail below, sometime in the next three days, under circumstances described differently by McClure and Mecca, McClure revealed to Mecca the separate remote locations where the children could be found. On Tuesday, May 1, Mecca, armed with a map produced during his conversations with McClure, arranged for his secretary to place an anonymous phone call to a sheriff's department telephone number belonging to a law enforcement officer with whom Mecca had met earlier.

Later that day and the following day, sheriff's deputies located the children's bodies, which were in locations more than 60 miles apart. The children had each died from a single gunshot wound to the head. Mecca then withdrew from representation. On May 3, McClure was indicted for the murders of Carol Jones and her children. At trial, the prosecution produced extensive evidence that stemmed from the discovery of the children's bodies and introduced testimony regarding the anonymous phone call. McClure was found guilty of all three murders and was sentenced to three consecutive life sentences with 30-year minimums. On direct appeal, his conviction was affirmed without opinion.

Disclosure of the Children's Whereabouts

The parties agree that Mecca and McClure met at the jail and spoke on the telephone on a number of occasions between April 28 and May 1. However, the substance of the conversations between McClure and Mecca are the subject of significant dispute.

Mecca recorded his account in notes that he wrote immediately after the children's bodies were discovered. Mecca also gave deposition testimony for McClure's state post conviction proceeding, submitted an affidavit prior to McClure's federal habeas proceeding, and gave testimony at the federal district court evidentiary hearing in the habeas proceeding. In his notes, Mecca wrote that McClure had initially claimed that he was "being framed" for the murder, but that he was nervous about his fingerprints being in the house. He had asked Mecca to help him remove some other potential evidence, which Mecca declined to do. According to the notes, on the Sunday night after McClure's Saturday arrest, Mecca received a "frantic phone call" from McClure's sister, who was convinced that McClure had murdered Jones, but had reason to believe that the children were alive and perhaps "tied up or bound someplace." In response, Mecca set up a meeting with McClure, his sister and his mother at the jail, at which McClure's sister "directly confronted [McClure] and begged him to divulge information about the whereabouts of the kids." McClure and his sister discussed how McClure sometimes did "crazy things" when he was using drugs, but McClure strongly maintained his innocence as to Carol Jones' murder and the children's disappearance.

According to his notes, when Mecca next spoke with McClure on Monday, McClure was less adamant in his denial. Mecca described how, when they met on Monday afternoon, McClure began to tell him of his "sexual hallucinations and fantasies" involving young girls and about "other situations that happened in the past ... involving things he would do while under the influence of drugs." "It was at that time," Mecca wrote, "when I realized in my own mind that he had committed the crime and the problem regarding the children intensified." Mecca wrote that he "was extremely agitated over the fact that these children might still be alive."

After a Monday night visit to the crime scene, Mecca returned to the jail to speak with McClure again, at which time he "peeled off most of the outer layers of McClure and realized that there was no doubt in my mind that he had ... killed Carol Jones." McClure told Mecca he wanted to see a psychiatrist, then launched into "bizarre ramblings." "[E]ach time as I would try to leave," Mecca recalled in his notes, "[McClure] would spew out other information, bits about the children, and he would do it in the form of a fantasy." Mecca wrote that he "wanted to learn from him what happened to those children." He told McClure "that we all have hiding places, that we all know when we go hiking or driving or something, we all remember certain back roads and remote places," and that McClure "related to me ... one place where a body might be" and then "described [where] the other body would be located." Mecca wrote that he "wasn't going to push him for anything more," but "when I tried to leave, he said, and he said it tentatively, 'would you like me to draw you a map and just give you an idea?' and I said 'Yes' and he did[.]" Mecca recorded that "at that time, I felt in my own mind the children were dead, but, of course, I wasn't sure."

Very late on Monday evening, McClure telephoned Mecca at home and said, "I know who did it." Mecca recorded in his notes that the next morning he went to meet with McClure, and asked him about this statement. McClure told Mecca that "Satan killed Carol." When Mecca asked, "What about the kids?" McClure replied, "Jesus saved the kids." Mecca wrote in his notes that this statement "hit me so abruptly, I immediately assumed that if Jesus saved the kids, that the kids are alive[.]" Mecca wrote that he "kind of felt that [McClure] was talking about a sexual thing, but, in any event, I wasn't sure."

Mecca's notes indicate that on Monday, before McClure made the "Jesus saved the kids" comment, and again on Tuesday, immediately after the meeting at which he made that comment, Mecca had conversations with fellow lawyers, seeking advice regarding "the dilemma that [he] faced." After the second of these conversations, which took place Tuesday morning, Mecca arranged for a noon meeting with the undersheriff and the prosecutor. At the meeting, he "mentioned to them that I may have information which would be of interest to the State" and attempted to negotiate a plea. When the prosecutor responded that there would be no deal, Mecca recorded in his notes, "I had made up my mind then that I had to do the correct thing. The only option I had, as far as I was concerned, was to disclose the whereabouts of the body [sic]." (Recall that by the time Mecca wrote these notes, he had learned that the children were dead.) A law enforcement official testified in a federal court deposition that, after both the state bar association and the attorney general "recommended that it would be unwise for Mr. Mecca to provide us information," Mecca "indicated that, even though there might be sanctions, that he still was wanting to provide information that he had regarding the children." Mecca stated that when he spoke with McClure's sister and mother, they were adamant that he do whatever he could to locate the children, and that "[t]hey were still under the impression that one or both of the children were alive, or at least there was a chance they were alive."

Mecca then returned to the jail Tuesday afternoon and, according to his notes, "advised McClure that if there was any possibility that these children were alive, we were obligated to disclose that information in order to prevent, if possible, the occurrence of what could be [the elevation of] an assault to a murder, for instance. I further indicated that if he really requested psychiatric help, to help him deal with his problem, that this perhaps was the first step." "In any event," Mecca recorded in his notes, "he consented." "I arranged to have the information released anonymously to the Sheriff's Department with directions to the bodies." He noted that there was "no provable way to connect" McClure to the information, "but I think it's rather obvious from those in the know, who the information came from."

Mecca testified in his deposition that he thought that if the children were alive, it might relieve McClure of additional murder charges, but that the children were his main concern. When asked if he was "primarily concerned with the children's welfare or ... with Mr. McClure's welfare" at the time he disclosed the location of the bodies, Mecca replied, "At that point I was concerned with the children's welfare." When asked if he explained to McClure that "if they were in fact dead, that revealing the location of the bodies would lead to evidence which could implicate Mr. McClure in their murders," Mecca answered: "No. I don't think I had the presence of mind to sit down and analyze every single detail and go over with him, 'Geez, you know, if they are really dead, why don't you tell me.' " However, he testified, "McClure knew I thought there [was] a chance those kids were alive."

Mecca testified in the deposition that the plan to place the anonymous telephone call was his, but that McClure knew that he planned to do it, and that, in his late-night call, McClure had made clear that he "absolutely" "wanted to disclose where those kids were." When asked, "Did he give you permission to reveal this information?" Mecca responded, "Oh, yes." Mecca also reiterated that he never told McClure of the legal risks involved in disclosing the children's locations.

McClure disagreed with Mecca's account of the events leading up to the anonymous call. In testimony in both the state and federal district court proceedings, he repeatedly insisted that he did not give Mecca permission to disclose any information and that he was reassured that everything he told Mecca would remain confidential. He said Mecca pressured him into disclosing information by setting up the meeting with his sister and mother, and then disseminated that information to his detriment without his knowledge or consent.

McClure testified that Mecca never asked him directly if the children were alive or dead, but that the hypothetical conversations that they had were about where Mecca might find dead "bodies," not live "children." He said his disclosure of those locations was his way of admitting to having killed them. He testified that Mecca never told him that he intended to make an anonymous telephone call.

State Court Decision on Post-Conviction Review

In March 1995, an Oregon circuit court denied McClure's petition for post-conviction review, which had been premised in part on a claim that he had been denied effective assistance of counsel when Mecca revealed confidential communications without his permission and without properly advising him of the consequences of such a disclosure. McClure appealed the denial of post-conviction relief, again raising the ineffective assistance of counsel claim.

District Court Denial of Habeas Relief

The district court denied McClure's federal habeas petition. The court indicated that it found Mecca "highly credible" and that it disbelieved McClure. Noting that "Mecca admits that he did not ... advise petitioner [of the potential adverse consequences of disclosure]," it concluded that under the circumstances, this failure was "not unreasonable." It found that Mecca "informed petitioner that if the children could be alive, they were obligated to disclose the children's location to prevent further harm to them," that McClure was intelligent and engaged in his defense, that "common sense dictates that petitioner understood the consequences of his actions," and that "Mecca's assumption [that McClure was discussing the location of live children] was not unreasonable under the circumstances." It also held that, based on these circumstances, and on the fact that Mecca had attempted to determine whether the children were alive and McClure had led him to believe they were, "Mecca's failure to ask directly whether the children were dead was not unreasonable." McClure timely appealed.

Discussion

McClure's single claim is that habeas relief is appropriate because he received ineffective assistance of counsel under the Sixth Amendment. He asserts three independent grounds on which ineffectiveness could be found. The first two are based on alleged breaches of Mecca's professional duty to maintain client confidentiality. McClure argues that this duty was breached both by a failure to obtain informed consent prior to the disclosure of confidential information and by a failure to inquire thoroughly before concluding that disclosure was necessary to prevent the deaths of the children. The third ground is that the primacy of Mecca's concern for the victims constituted a conflict of interest that rendered Mecca's counsel constitutionally ineffective.

The Duty of Confidentiality

McClure contends that Mecca's disclosure of McClure's confidential statements about the location of the children violated McClure's Sixth Amendment right to effective assistance of counsel. ABA Model Rule of Professional Conduct 1.6 sets forth a widely recognized duty of confidentiality: "A lawyer shall not reveal information relating to representation of a client[.]" Our legal system is premised on the strict adherence to this principle of confidentiality, and "[t]he Supreme Court has long held attorneys to stringent standards of loyalty and fairness with respect to their clients." There are few professional relationships "involving a higher trust and confidence than that of attorney and client," and "few more anxiously guarded by the law, or governed by sterner principles of morality and justice."

As critical as this confidential relationship is to our system of justice, the duty to refrain from disclosing information relating to the representation of a client is not absolute. The ABA Model Rule provides a list of well-established exceptions to the general principle of confidentiality, two of which are pertinent to the present case. First, a lawyer may reveal confidential information if "the client consents after consultation." Second, "[a] lawyer may reveal such information to the extent the lawyer reasonably believes necessary to prevent the client from committing a criminal act that the lawyer believes is likely to result in imminent death or substantial bodily harm[.]" ABA Model Rule of Professional Conduct 1.6(b)(1) (1983).

The duty of an attorney to keep his or her client's confidences in all but a handful of carefully defined circumstances is so deeply ingrained in our legal system and so uniformly acknowledged as a critical component of reasonable representation by counsel that departure from this rule "make[s] out a deprivation of the Sixth Amendment right to counsel." With this uncontested premise as our starting point, we examine whether the circumstances surrounding Mecca's revelation of a confidential client communication excused his disclosure, such that his performance could have been found by the state court and the district court to be constitutionally adequate. Specifically, we look to see if Mecca's client "consent[ed] after consultation" or if Mecca "reasonably believe[d] [the revelation was] necessary to prevent the client from committing a criminal act that [Mecca] believe[d][was] likely to result in imminent death or substantial bodily harm[.]" We conclude that the first of these exceptions does not apply to justify Mecca's behavior, but that the second does.

Consent after Consultation

McClure argues that Mecca rendered constitutionally ineffective assistance because he breached his duty of confidentiality by not obtaining McClure's informed consent before disclosure. The professional standard that allows disclosure of confidential communications when "the client consents after consultation" has two distinct parts: consent by the client, and consultation by the counsel. Our required deference to both the state court's factual findings and the district court's credibility determination leads us to hold that the first of these elements was met. However, despite this deference, we hold that the second element was not met.

Consent

The district court found that McClure "voluntarily drew the map and gave it to Mecca," and that, even in the absence of the words "I consent," Mecca could infer consent from the circumstances and from McClure's conduct. It stated that it found Mecca's testimony "entirely credible and corroborated by his contemporaneous notes which state specifically that petitioner consented to the disclosure."

There is evidence in the record to cast doubt on the consent findings-indeed, enough evidence that if we were sitting as trier of fact, we might find that McClure did not give consent. McClure repeatedly denied that he consented, and certainly would have had good reason not to consent. The state court determination that McClure had consented was made before Mecca clarified that the consent was implied and not express. Moreover, it was based on Mecca's unconditional affirmative response, in his state-court deposition, to the question of whether permission to reveal the information was granted. Only later, in the federal habeas proceeding, did it come to light that Mecca had merely inferred McClure's consent.

Further, Mecca's account of the circumstances from which he inferred McClure's consent changed over the years. His initial account stated that he inferred consent from the fact that

McClure called him at home, drew the map, and gave it to him. It is a significant leap to infer McClure's consent to disclose the map to law enforcement authorities from the fact that McClure gave the map to Mecca. Virtually all clients provide information to their attorneys, but they do so assuming that the attorneys will not breach their duty of confidentiality. Further, Mecca's behavior at the time of the disclosure suggested that he thought he lacked the kind of informed consent that would give him the legal authority to act.

However, the findings reached by the state and district courts are not so "[im]plausible"- particularly in light of the district court's credibility determinations-that they produce a "definite and firm conviction that a mistake has been committed." The district court believed Mecca's account at the evidentiary hearing, disbelieved McClure's, and found the discrepancies in Mecca's testimony to be "minor." Because there are "two permissible views of the evidence, the factfinder's choice between them cannot be clearly erroneous." We therefore hold that McClure gave his consent to the disclosure.

Consultation

However, the mere fact of consent is not sufficient to excuse what would otherwise be a breach of the duty of confidentiality. Consent must also be informed. That is, the client can provide valid consent only if there has been appropriate "consultation" with his or her attorney. Mecca's consultation with McClure regarding his consent to disclosure was addressed in the state court and district court findings. Both courts found that Mecca did not advise McClure about the potential harmful consequences of disclosure. The state court found that "[b]efore petitioner authorized trial counsel to reveal the childrens' [sic] locations to authorities, trial counsel did not advise petitioner that if authorities located the children, he could be further implicated in the criminal activity and the evidence against him would be stronger." The district court found that "Mecca admits that he did not ... advise petitioner [of all potential adverse consequences]."

Emphasizing that McClure was "fully engaged" in his defense and that he was told that the obligation to disclose the children's location arose only if the children were alive, the district court held that "[u]nder the circumstances, Mecca's failure to advise petitioner of all possible adverse consequences was not unreasonable." We believe this holding is inconsistent with the consultation requirement because it does not attach sufficient importance to the role that an attorney's advice plays in the attorney-client relationship.

We disagree with the district court's conclusion that this case was so exceptional that the attorney's basic consultation duties did not apply. It is precisely because the stakes were so high that Mecca had an obligation to consult carefully with his client. In the absence of some other exception to the duty of confidentiality, his failure to obtain informed consent would demonstrate constitutionally deficient performance under the Sixth Amendment.

Prevention of Further Criminal Acts

The State contends that, even if Mecca did not have informed consent, his revelation of client confidences did not amount to ineffective assistance of counsel because he reasonably believed that disclosing the location of the children was necessary in order to prevent further criminal acts. That is, Mecca reasonably believed that revealing the children's locations could

56

have prevented the escalation of kidnapping to murder. This is not a traditional "prevention of further criminal acts" case, because all of the affirmative criminal acts performed by McClure had been completed at the time Mecca made his disclosure. Mecca was thus acting to prevent an earlier criminal act from being transformed by the passage of time into a more serious criminal offense. Nonetheless, we believe that where an attorney's or a client's omission to act could result in "imminent death or substantial bodily harm" constituting a separate and more severe crime from the one already committed, the exception to the duty of confidentiality may be triggered. ABA Model Rule 1.6(b)(1).

This exception, however, requires that an attorney reveal confidences only to the extent that he "reasonably believes necessary to prevent" those criminal acts and imminent harms. *Id.* In assessing the effectiveness of McClure's counsel in light of this standard, the first step is to determine what a constitutionally effective counsel should be required to do before making a disclosure. That is, we must determine what basis the attorney had for believing that the precondition to disclosure was present, and how much investigation he or she must have undertaken before it was "reasonabl[e]" to "believ[e][it] necessary" to make the disclosure to prevent the harm. The second step is to apply that standard to the facts surrounding Mecca's decision to disclose.

McClure is correct that our inquiry must acknowledge the importance of the confidential attorney-client relationship and the gravity of the harm that results from an unwarranted breach of that duty. However, the standard applied in the professional responsibility code asks only if the attorney " *reasonably* believes" disclosure is necessary to prevent the crime. ABA Model Rule 1.6(b)(1) (emphasis added).

Reasonableness of belief may be strongly connected to adequacy of investigation or sufficiency of inquiry in the face of uncertainty. Thus, in determining whether Mecca's disclosure of confidential client information constituted ineffective assistance of counsel, we must examine whether Mecca "reasonably believed" that the precondition for disclosure existed and whether, in coming to that belief, Mecca conducted a reasonable investigation and inquiry.

The ultimate question of the reasonableness of Mecca's belief is a question of law, which we review de novo. In answering that question, however, we look to the facts and circumstances of the case, and as to these facts, we give great deference to the findings of the state court and the district court.

This is a close case, even after we give the required deference to the state and district courts. The choices made by McClure's counsel give us significant pause, and, were we deciding this case as an original matter, we might decide it differently. But we take as true the district court's specific factual findings as to what transpired-including what McClure said and did, and what actions Mecca took and why he took them-and we conclude that Mecca made the disclosure "reasonably believ[ing] [it was] necessary to prevent the client from committing a criminal act that [Mecca] believe[d] [was] likely to result in imminent death or substantial bodily harm[.]" ABA Model Rule 1.6(b)(1). Mecca therefore did not violate the duty of confidentiality in a manner that rendered his assistance constitutionally ineffective.

Conflict of Interest

In addition to his claim that Mecca breached his duty of confidentiality, McClure claims that Mecca was not functioning as the "counsel" guaranteed by the Sixth Amendment because he suffered from a "fatal conflict of interest." McClure argues that Mecca was acting primarily out of concern for the welfare of possible victims rather than in his client's best interests. A conflict of interest constitutes a constructive denial of counsel altogether and is legally presumed to result in prejudice.

It is clear that Mecca's actions were at least partially driven by concern for the lives of the children. He forthrightly indicated as much under oath on more than one occasion. McClure suggests that Mecca's candid statements amount to "a direct admission of an actual conflict." But this is not necessarily so. *At least one case* recognizes both the "wide range of professionally competent assistance" and the need for great leeway for tactical determinations by counsel. Accepting the district court's factual findings as true, Mecca had some basis for believing that the children would be found alive if a prompt search were undertaken, and that this would be beneficial to McClure. Mecca also made an attempt to make a deal with the State in return for the information. His testimony, which the district court regarded as highly credible, repeatedly referred to his concern that McClure's kidnapping charges could become murder charges if the children were allowed to die. The district court specifically found that Mecca "believed the disclosure could have avoided two additional aggravated murder charges and was the best strategic decision for petitioner under the circumstances," and that Mecca "sought to avoid further harm to the children *and* his client's case." (Emphasis added.) Moreover, even if Mecca was acting to preserve the lives of the children rather than to protect the interests of his client, the ethical rule requiring an attorney to act to prevent a crime means that such an action, if based on a reasonable belief, is not inconsistent with the attorney's ethically prescribed duty of loyalty.

To prove an ineffectiveness claim premised on an alleged conflict of interest a petitioner must "establish that an actual conflict of interest adversely affected his lawyer's performance." The client must demonstrate that his attorney made a choice between possible alternative courses of action that impermissibly favored an interest in competition with those of the client. Because McClure cannot identify specific evidence in the record that suggests that his interests were impermissibly impaired or compromised for the benefit of another party, he cannot demonstrate that his counsel "actively represented a conflicting interest." Without this factual showing of inconsistent interests, the conflict is merely possible or speculative. Such a conflict is "insufficient to impugn a criminal conviction."

Conclusion

For the foregoing reasons, we conclude that McClure did not receive constitutionally ineffective assistance of counsel. Accordingly, the district court's denial of McClure's petition for writ of habeas corpus is Affirmed.

****

Questions:

1.   Lillie Lawyer was the subject of a disciplinary investigation regarding charges that she had misappropriated client trust funds. At the hearing Lillie refused to provide any information about the trust funds claiming that disclosure would violate her ethical duty to maintain the client's confidences. Is Lillie prohibited from disclosing this client's confidential information?[43]

2.   Plaintiff was a part-time "of counsel" attorney. She uncovered what she believed to be perjury in an employment case assigned to her by her employer and believed that her employer had fostered the perjury by filing the complaint and defending the client's deposition. Plaintiff informed her employer that she would not work on the case because of the ethical issue. Several weeks later, Plaintiff received notice of termination. Plaintiff did not file a charge against her former employer, opting instead to file a wrongful termination case. Is employer subject to discipline? Will Plaintiff prevail against employer in the wrongful termination case? Discuss fully.[44]

3.   Attorney is faced with the difficult question of whether he can reveal the fact that his client told him that he had committed a crime that someone else had been convicted of. He seeks the advice of his own counsel and when his client discovers that fact, threatens the lawyer with filing a claim against the Attorney with the bar for revealing client confidential information. Is Attorney subject to discipline for the revelation?[45] Discuss fully.

****

In Re: the Disciplinary Proceeding against Douglas Schafer
149 Wn.2d 148; 66 P.3d 1036; 2003 Wash. LEXIS 284 (Wash, En Banc., 2003)

"[We] cannot tolerate for a moment, neither can the profession, neither can the community, any disloyalty on the part of a lawyer to his client.   In all things he must be true to that trust, or, failing it, he must leave the profession."[46]…

On August 12, 1992, William Hamilton contacted his attorney, Douglas Schafer, requesting assistance in forming a corporation to purchase a bowling alley from the estate of Charles Hoffman.   Schafer and Hamilton met on August 17, 1992 to discuss the formation of the corporation.   During either the August 12 or 17 conversation, Hamilton informed Schafer that Grant Anderson was the personal representative and attorney for the Hoffman estate and that Anderson had been " 'milking' " the estate for four years. … Significantly, Hamilton informed Schafer that Anderson was about to become a judge and needed to close the sale of the bowling

---

[43] *In Re: Dyer,* 817 N.W.2d 351 (N.D. 2012)
[44] *Weiss v. Lonnquist,* 2013 Wash. App. Lexis 255 (Wash. App., Feb. 4, 2013)
[45] See *Spratley v. State Farm Mut. Auto Ins. Co.,* 78 P.3d 603 (Utah 2003)
[46] U.S.v. Costen, 38 F. 24 (Circ Ct-Colo, 1889)

59

alley quickly before Anderson assumed the bench. Hamilton said that Anderson was giving Hamilton a good deal on the bowling alley and that Hamilton would repay Anderson " 'down the road.' " Schafer replied that "he did not want to hear about it." In January 1993, Anderson was sworn in as a judge of the Pierce County Superior Court.

In July 1995, nearly three years after Schafer formed the corporation for Hamilton, Schafer represented Donald Barovic in a case before Judge Anderson. Judge Anderson ruled that Schafer's petition was frivolous and without legal merit, and assessed $1,000 in attorney fees against Schafer's client. On the day of Judge Anderson's ruling, Schafer copied the court file for the Hoffman estate and initiated calls to the attorneys involved in that matter. Schafer then met with Hamilton on December 18, 1995, to discuss Hamilton's prior statements about Anderson. Hamilton warned Schafer to "stop 'looking for dirt' " on Judge Anderson.

Over the next month and a half, Schafer researched public records and contacted individuals to discuss Anderson's handling of the Hoffman estate, and also conferred with the attorney who represented Anderson's wife in the Andersons' marriage dissolution. The ex-Mrs. Anderson's divorce attorney recommended that Schafer investigate Anderson's acquisition of a Cadillac. On investigation, Schafer discovered facts leading him to believe that Hamilton had either been paying for Anderson's Cadillac or had given him the funds to purchase it.

Then, on February 1, 1996, Hamilton sent a letter to Schafer terminating their professional relationship, stressing in the letter that Schafer had " 'no authority to disclose any privileged information, relating to your prior representation of me.' " Later that day Schafer met with Hamilton and his new attorney, Philip Sloan. Hamilton and Sloan both emphasized to Schafer that he should not disclose any of the confidences that Hamilton had shared with Schafer and threatened to pursue disciplinary action if Schafer failed to protect Hamilton's confidential information. The next day, Sloan faxed instructions to Schafer " 'not to disclose any communications re Grant Anderson to anyone. If you do-you will be in violation of RPC 1.6.' " Meanwhile, Schafer filed a motion of prejudice and supporting statement in the Barovic case, requesting the case be assigned to a judge other than Anderson. The motion included a reference to his investigation of Anderson's conduct with the Hoffman estate but did not disclose any information from Hamilton at that time.

Over the next several months, Schafer became obsessed with Judge Anderson. He met with a series of legal and government organizations, and eventually the press, revealing his findings about Anderson and Hamilton's dealings. On February 6, 1996, Schafer met with the Pierce County prosecuting attorney to discuss Anderson's alleged improprieties. Two days later he contacted the Federal Bureau of Investigation (FBI). The following day, the prosecutor's office informed Schafer that it was beginning an investigation of Schafer's allegations. On February 13, 1996, Schafer met with an investigator for the Washington Commission on Judicial Conduct (CJC) and provided her with documents related to Anderson's alleged misconduct.

On February 16, 1996, Schafer created a document titled "Declaration Under Penalty of Perjury" (declaration), which revealed contents from his conversations with Hamilton. The relevant section of the declaration states:

On August 12, 1992, I was called by my client, William L. Hamilton, who I previously had advised in several matters including the formation in 1990 of Sound Banking Company (of which he was President/CEO, as he had been at Western Community Bank for about 25 years before its sale), and he requested that I form a new corporation for him immediately. He said that an attorney he knew, Grant Anderson, had been "milking" an estate for four years and was about to become a judge, so he needed to quickly sell the estate's business, Pacific Lanes, in order to close the estate before he took the bench. Hamilton said that he had agreed to buy the business. It was either in that phone conversation or when we met on August 17, 1992, that Hamilton commented that there was no time for an appraisal of the business, that Anderson was giving him a good deal, and that Hamilton would repay him "down the road" by paying him as corporate secretary or something like that. When I heard that comment, I told Hamilton, "I don't even want to hear about it!" I formed his corporation, Pacific Recreation Enterprises, Inc., and had no further involvement with him concerning the purchase of Pacific Lanes. My notes from those conversations and papers Hamilton gave me when we met reflect that the estate was that of Chuck Hoffman. [citation omitted]

Schafer also prepared a memorandum, dated February 29, 1996, addressed to "Appropriate Public Officials," (memorandum) which he provided with his declaration and select files and documents. [citation omitted] Schafer sent his declaration and memorandum to the Washington attorney general's office on March 1, 1996. He then sent the declaration, memorandum and a box of documents to the Washington State Bar Association (WSBA). He sent the declaration and memorandum to the Internal Revenue Service (IRS), Criminal Investigation Division. He also appended the declaration containing Hamilton's confidences, the memorandum and select documents to a motion for discretionary review filed in the Court of Appeals in the Barovic case, but did not seek court assistance to protect the confidentiality of the documents. Upon filing, the content of Hamilton's conversations with Schafer became available to the public at large as a court record. Finally, on April 26, 1996, Schafer provided his declaration and memorandum to The Seattle Times, the Seattle Post-Intelligencer, and The News Tribune.

Outraged at Schafer's disclosures, Hamilton filed a grievance against Schafer with the Washington State Bar Association (WSBA) on July 26, 1996, claiming Schafer violated the Rules of Professional Conduct (RPC) when he disclosed Hamilton's confidential information without authorization. Despite the pending grievance, Schafer went on to author two articles in local newspapers, touting his role in Anderson's disciplinary proceedings and exposing Hamilton's confidences in detail. Hamilton filed a formal complaint on May 26, 1999 (ultimately amended by a hearing officer order), charging Schafer with violation of RPC 1.6, subjecting Schafer to potential sanction under the Rules for Lawyer Discipline (RLD) 1.1(i).

Before the grievance against Schafer was heard, on July 29, 1999, this court issued a decision in In re Disciplinary Proceeding Against Anderson, 138 Wash.2d 830, 981 P.2d 426 (1999), in which we concurred in the findings of the CJC that Judge Anderson had violated Canon 1, Canon 2(A), Canon 5(C)(3), and Canon 6(C). We removed him from his judicial office. Then, by order dated May 4, 2000, we approved a stipulation of discipline, suspending Anderson from the practice of law for two years.

On August 18, 2000, a hearing officer concluded that Schafer had revealed confidences and/or secrets relating to his representation of Hamilton in violation of RPC 1.6(a). After applying the American Bar Association (ABA) standards for lawyer misconduct and considering aggravating and mitigating factors, the hearing officer recommended a six-month suspension from the practice of law and, additionally, that Schafer pay the expenses associated with the proceedings.

Schafer appealed to the WSBA disciplinary board. The 10-member disciplinary board unanimously agreed with the hearing officer's conclusion that Schafer had violated RPC 1.6. But after considering mitigating and aggravating factors, seven of the board members suggested an increased sanction of a one-year suspension from the practice of law.

…The issues before us can be summarized as follows:

(1) Did the hearing officer and the disciplinary board err when they concluded that Schafer violated RPC 1.6?

(2) If not, is there an applicable exception to RPC 1.6 which excused the violation?

(3) If not, what is the appropriate sanction?

We hold that Schafer violated RPC 1.6 when he revealed his client's confidences and secrets and that there is no exception to the rule which excuses the violation in these circumstances. In light of the importance of maintaining a client's confidences and Schafer's willful, unnecessary, and repeated violation of his ethical duty not to betray his client's trust, we hold that a six-month suspension is appropriate.

(1) Did Schafer violate RPC 1.6?

RPC 1.6, as adopted in Washington, states:

(a) A lawyer shall not reveal confidences or secrets relating to representation of a client unless the client consents after consultation, except for disclosures that are impliedly authorized in order to carry out the representation, and except as stated in sections (b) and (c). (Emphasis added.)

RPC 1.6 prohibits an attorney from disclosing client confidences and secrets. A "confidence" is defined by the RPC as "information protected by the attorney-client privilege under applicable law." … A "secret" refers to "other information gained in the professional relationship that the client has requested be held inviolate or the disclosure of which would be embarrassing or would be likely to be detrimental to the client." … We conclude that Hamilton's statements to Schafer qualify as a "confidence" or "secret" under RPC 1.6.

Schafer had represented Hamilton in numerous previous transactions before Hamilton returned to Schafer for his services to create a corporation to purchase a bowling alley. When Hamilton hired Schafer to represent him in that transaction, an attorney-client relationship was established between the two parties again. Hamilton's return to Schafer for his assistance evidences Hamilton's trust in Schafer's professional abilities. Based on this trust, Hamilton freely shared information with Schafer as part of their attorney-client relationship and in the course of forming Pacific Recreation Enterprises, Inc. to purchase the Pacific Lanes bowling alley.

To uphold the valid purposes of RPC 1.6 of encouraging candor and facilitating trust between attorney and client, Hamilton's statements to Schafer warranted protection. Schafer violated this trust by revealing Hamilton's confidences or secrets when he disclosed Hamilton's statements to the Pierce County prosecutor, FBI, CJC, Washington attorney general, WSBA, IRS, three newspapers, his unprotected court filing in the Barovic case, and by including the confidences in articles he had published in two local newspapers. When Hamilton realized that the information that he had shared with Schafer, in full candor under the auspices of the protected relationship, was in jeopardy, he repeatedly demanded that Schafer respect this confidential information. Schafer ignored these demands.

It is a "fundamental principle in the client-lawyer relationship that the lawyer maintain confidentiality of information relating to the representation." ABA, Model Rules of Prof'l Conduct R. 1.6 cmt. 4 (1991). Indeed, "lawyers are regarded as people who know how to keep secrets, as much as they are regarded as litigators or drafters of contracts." ...

But the privilege does not exist merely for the benefit of individuals. The attorney-client privilege has been sustained for centuries because of the fundamental benefits that accrue to society at large. The privilege "promote[s] broader public interests in the observance of law and the administration of justice." Upjohn Co. v. United States, 449 U.S. 383, 389, 101 S.Ct. 677, 66 L.Ed.2d 584 (1981). The attorney-client privilege is pivotal in the orderly administration of the legal system, which is the cornerstone of a just society. The reasoning is tripartite: to maintain the adversarial system, parties must utilize lawyers to resolve disputes; lawyers must know all the relevant facts to advocate effectively; and clients will not confide in lawyers and provide them with the necessary information unless the client knows what he says will remain confidential.[footnote omitted] The confidential relationship that exists between an attorney and client facilitates the full development of facts necessary for proper representation and encourages clients to seek legal assistance early.[footnote omitted]

The privilege also benefits society by helping to prevent crime and other misconduct by encouraging clients to disclose contemplated wrongdoing, giving attorneys a chance to discourage such acts.[footnote omitted] In this regard, it is unfortunate that Schafer did not take the opportunity to counsel Hamilton in 1992 on the possible legal implications of Hamilton's alleged statements.

The attorney-client privilege protects against unjust application of the law on a wide scale. In particular "[t]he attorney-client privilege benefits society by encouraging laymen to seek legal services and thereby learn their legal rights and responsibilities and obtain effective representation in litigation." Developments in the Law-Privileged Communications, 98 Harv. L.Rev.. 1450, 1501 (1985). The privilege has long been considered instrumental in achieving social good because it induces clients to consult freely with lawyers and by doing so acquire expert legal advice and representation that helps them operate within the complex legal system. Id. at 1502. Because the privilege encourages clients to communicate fully with an attorney, lawyers are able to defend clients vigorously against charges and to assure them that the law will be applied justly. Without an effective attorney-client privilege, clients may be inhibited from revealing not only adverse facts but also favorable information that the client might mistakenly believe is damaging. [footnote omitted] …

(2) Is there an applicable exception to RPC 1.6?

A. Exceptions in the RPC:

(b) A lawyer may reveal such confidences or secrets to the extent the lawyer reasonably believes necessary:

> (1) To prevent the client from committing a crime; or
>
> (2) To establish a claim or defense on behalf of the lawyer in a controversy between the lawyer and the client, to establish a defense to a criminal charge or civil claim against the lawyer based upon conduct in which the client was involved, to respond to allegations in any proceeding concerning the lawyer's representation of the client, or pursuant to court order.

(c) A lawyer may reveal to the tribunal confidences or secrets which disclose any breach of fiduciary responsibility by a client who is a guardian, personal representative, receiver, or other court appointed fiduciary. RPC 1.6.

While we laud the principles protecting the sanctity of attorney-client confidences and secrets, we are cognizant that there are occasions when revealing a client's statements may be justified. These occasions are extremely limited, however, consistent with the profession's goals of establishing and maintaining trust in the judicial process.

RPC 1.6(c) indicates that "[a] lawyer may reveal to the tribunal confidences or secrets which disclose any breach of fiduciary responsibility by a client who is a guardian, personal representative, receiver, or other court appointed fiduciary." Schafer contends that he was justified in reporting Hamilton's confidential statements under RPC 1.6(c) because Anderson assumed a fiduciary role as the personal representative of the Hoffman estate. While Schafer may very well have been justified in reporting Anderson's alleged misconduct regarding the estate, he need not have reported his own client's confidences and secrets to accomplish this goal. There is very little doubt that sufficient additional alternative evidence existed in the public records to make revealing Hamilton's confidences unnecessary.

…Furthermore, RPC 1.6(c) permits disclosure "to the tribunal," not to newspapers and a sundry assortment of "appropriate public officials. …

None of Schafer's excuses for his breach of Hamilton's trust are persuasive. He contends that his actions were permissible under RPC 8.3 and RPC 3.3. They were not. RPC 8.3, concerning reporting professional misconduct, states:

(a) A lawyer having knowledge that another lawyer has committed a violation of the Rules of Professional Conduct that raises a substantial question as to that lawyer's honesty, trustworthiness or fitness as a lawyer in other respects, should promptly inform the appropriate professional authority.

(b) A lawyer having knowledge that a judge has committed a violation of applicable rules of judicial conduct that raises a substantial question as to the judge's fitness for office should promptly inform the appropriate authority.

(c) This rule does not require disclosure of information otherwise protected by rule 1.6.

Similarly, the rule pertaining to candor toward the tribunal, RPC 3.3(a)(2), states, "[a] lawyer shall not knowingly [f]ail to disclose a material fact to a tribunal when disclosure is necessary to avoid assisting a criminal or fraudulent act by the client unless such disclosure is prohibited by rule 1.6." Thus, RPC 3.3 also does not mandate disclosure when RPC 1.6 is implicated. The candor required under RPC 3.3 is to the tribunal. Therefore, Schafer could and should have appropriately reported Anderson's alleged indiscretions to the tribunal or the appropriate professional authority, without revealing the confidential information of his own client to the prosecutor's office, the FBI, the IRS and the press. [footnote omitted]...

B. Judicially Created Crime-Fraud Exception

Schafer contends that the judicially created crime-fraud exception also justifies his disclosure of Hamilton's confidences. However, that exception generally does not apply when an attorney seeks to disclose past wrongdoing. This is because the benefit of revealing a past harm that can no longer be prevented does not outweigh the injury to attorney-client relationships that would result by disclosure. See United States v. Zolin, 491 U.S. 554, 562-63, 109 S.Ct. 2619, 105 L.Ed.2d 469 (1989) ...

Washington has never applied the crime-fraud exception to client confidences such as the ones at issue here, yet Schafer invites this court to create such an exception. We decline the invitation.

C. Whistleblower Protection

Schafer further argues that Rule of Lawyer Discipline (RLD) 12.11(b) provides comprehensive protection for anyone who reports lawyer misconduct. He relies on select language from the rule, which states, communications " 'are absolutely privileged, and no lawsuit predicated thereon may be instituted against any grievant, witness or other person providing information.' " Resp't Lawyer's Opening Br. at 55 (quoting RLD 12.11(b)). Schafer fails to cite the beginning of the rule, which limits the protection to "[c]ommunications to the Association, Board of Governors, Disciplinary Board, review committee, hearing officer or panel, disciplinary counsel, special district counsel, Association staff, staff and peer counselors of the Lawyers' Assistance Program, or any other individual acting under authority of these rules." RLD 12.11(b). This list clearly does not include newspapers or other entities independent from the disciplinary process.

D. Washington State and United States Constitutions

Finally, Schafer asserts that his disclosures were protected by the right-to-petition, due process clauses, and the free speech provisions of the federal and state constitutions. His arguments are inconclusive and lack support. As we have recognized, " ' "[N]aked castings into the constitutional sea are not sufficient to command judicial consideration and discussion." ' " State v. Blilie, 132 Wash.2d 484, 493 n. 2, 939 P.2d 691 (1997) (quoting In re Rosier, 105 Wash.2d 606, 616, 717 P.2d 1353 (1986) (quoting United States v. Phillips, 433 F.2d 1364, 1366 (8th Cir.1970))).

3. Sanctions

This court determines disciplinary sanctions by referencing the ABA Standards for Imposing Lawyer Sanctions (1991) (Standards). In re Disciplinary Proceeding Against Johnson, 114 Wash. 2d 737, 745, 790 P.2d 1227 (1990). The Standards consider the following factors when assessing an appropriate sanction: (1) the duty violated; (2) the lawyer's mental state; (3) the potential or actual injury caused by the lawyer's misconduct; and (4) the existence of aggravating or mitigating factors. Standards 3.0.

Under Standard 4.21, suspension is generally appropriate "when a lawyer knowingly reveals information relating to the representation of a client not otherwise lawfully permitted to be disclosed, and this disclosure causes injury or potential injury to a client." …

The hearing officer found only one mitigating factor: Schafer had never been previously sanctioned by the WSBA. We find a second mitigating factor applicable - that because of Schafer's actions, a corrupt judge was exposed and the public was served by the judge's removal from office.

The hearing officer found several aggravating factors. The hearing officer found that Schafer possessed a selfish motive because he was motivated at least in part by a personal vindication, as illustrated by his revelation of Hamilton's confidences and secrets in his motion for discretionary review to the Court of Appeals in the Barovic case (a wholly unrelated matter in which he was the losing attorney) and by faxing his declaration to three newspapers. Additionally, the hearing officer found that Schafer's multiple disclosures evidenced a pattern of misconduct. Schafer could and should have sought to remove the corrupt judge without revealing his client's confidences. Because Schafer would not accept the need for appropriate steps to protect his client's confidences, the hearing officer concluded that Schafer refused to accept the wrongful nature of his conduct. Finally, the hearing officer found that Schafer's substantial experience in the practice of law, 14 years at the time of the disclosures, was an additional aggravating factor. The hearing officer concluded that these factors warranted a six-month suspension.

The disciplinary board concurred with the hearing officer's assessment of the mitigating and aggravating factors, but a majority of the board determined that the factors warranted an increase in the suspension from six months to one year. The board based this increase on Schafer's refusal to acknowledge the wrongful nature of his conduct….

66

We conclude that a one-year suspension is not necessary to protect the public from similar misconduct and that a six-month suspension will suffice. [footnote omitted]   While we applaud the results of Schafer's research into public records revealing Anderson's misconduct, [footnote omitted] we do not condone his unnecessary revelation of client confidences in the process, in particular his sharing of Hamilton's statements with the press, the IRS, the FBI and the prosecutor's office....

Nevertheless, we recognize that an important purpose of attorney discipline is to maintain public confidence in the legal profession.   In re Disciplinary Proceeding Against Halverson, 140 Wash.2d 475, 498, 998 P.2d 833 (2000); In re Disciplinary Proceeding Against McMullen, 127 Wash.2d 150, 163, 896 P.2d 1281 (1995).   Here, Schafer's unethical conduct resulted in the removal of a corrupt judge.   Harsh discipline under these circumstances would likely undermine the public's confidence in the legal profession.

Therefore, we conclude that Schafer should be disciplined for his knowing and willful misconduct, recognizing that two mitigating and several aggravating factors were present. ... This relatively minimal sanction acknowledges the wrongful nature of revealing a client's confidences and serves the purposes of attorney discipline.

We hold that Schafer violated his ethical obligations as an attorney under the RPC when he unnecessarily revealed his client's confidences and secrets beyond the appropriate tribunal designated by the people of the State of Washington for receipt of such complaints.   We conclude that none of Schafer's proposed exceptions to RPC 1.6 excuse him from this violation. To emphasize the importance of maintaining client confidences in an attorney-client relationship, we agree with both the hearing officer and a unanimous disciplinary board that Schafer's knowing disregard for an attorney's code of conduct warrants sanctions.   We conclude that a one-year suspension in these circumstances would be excessive, however, and reduce the sanction to a six-month suspension.

Nix v. Whiteside
475 U.S. 157 (1986)

We granted certiorari to decide whether the Sixth Amendment right of a criminal defendant to assistance of counsel is violated when an attorney refuses to cooperate with the defendant in presenting perjured testimony at his trial.

Whiteside was convicted of second-degree murder by a jury verdict which was affirmed by the Iowa courts. The killing took place on February 8, 1977, in Cedar Rapids, Iowa. Whiteside and two others went to one Calvin Love's apartment late that night, seeking marihuana. Love was in bed when Whiteside and his companions arrived; an argument between Whiteside and Love over the marihuana ensued. At one point, Love directed his girlfriend to get his "piece," and at another point got up, then returned to his bed. According to Whiteside's testimony, Love then started to reach under his pillow and moved toward Whiteside. Whiteside stabbed Love in the chest, inflicting a fatal wound.

Whiteside was charged with murder, and when counsel was appointed, he objected to the lawyer initially appointed, claiming that he felt uncomfortable with a lawyer who had formerly been a prosecutor. Gary L. Robinson was then appointed, and immediately began an investigation. Whiteside gave him a statement that he had stabbed Love as the latter "was pulling a pistol from underneath the pillow on the bed." Upon questioning by Robinson, however, Whiteside indicated that he had not actually seen a gun, but that he was convinced that Love had a gun. No pistol was found on the premises; shortly after the police search following the stabbing, which had revealed no weapon, the victim's family had removed all of the victim's possessions from the apartment. Robinson interviewed Whiteside's companions who were present during the stabbing, and none had seen a gun during the incident. Robinson advised Whiteside that the existence of a gun was not necessary to establish the claim of self-defense, and that only a reasonable belief that the victim had a gun nearby was necessary, even though no gun was actually present.

Until shortly before trial, Whiteside consistently stated to Robinson that he had not actually seen a gun, but that he was convinced that Love had a gun in his hand. About a week before trial, during preparation for direct examination, Whiteside for the first time told Robinson and his associate Donna Paulsen that he had seen something "metallic" in Love's hand. When asked about this, Whiteside responded:

… If I don't say I saw a gun, I'm dead.

Robinson told Whiteside that such testimony would be perjury, and repeated that it was not necessary to prove that a gun was available, but only that Whiteside reasonably believed that he was in danger. On Whiteside's insisting that he would testify that he saw "something metallic," Robinson told him, according to Robinson's testimony:

[W]e could not allow him to [testify falsely], because that would be perjury, and, as officers of the court, we would be suborning perjury if we allowed him to do it; . . . I advised him that, if he did do that, it would be my duty to advise the Court of what he was doing, and that I felt he was committing perjury; also, that I probably would be allowed to attempt to impeach that particular testimony.

…Robinson also indicated he would seek to withdraw from the representation if Whiteside insisted on committing perjury.

Whiteside testified in his own defense at trial, and stated that he "knew" that Love had a gun, and that he believed Love was reaching for a gun, and he had acted swiftly in self-defense. On cross-examination, he admitted that he had not actually seen a gun in Love's hand. Robinson presented evidence that Love had been seen with a sawed-off shotgun on other occasions, that the police search of the apartment may have been careless, and that the victim's family had removed everything from the apartment shortly after the crime. Robinson presented this evidence to show a basis for Whiteside's asserted fear that Love had a gun.

The jury returned a verdict of second-degree murder, and Whiteside moved for a new trial, claiming that he had been deprived of a fair trial by Robinson's admonitions not to state that he saw a gun or "something metallic." The trial court held a hearing, heard testimony by Whiteside and Robinson, and denied the motion. The trial court made specific findings what the facts were as related by Robinson.

The Supreme Court of Iowa affirmed respondent's conviction. *State v. Whiteside*, 272 N.W.2d 468 (1978). That court held that the right to have counsel present all appropriate defenses does not extend to using perjury, and that an attorney's duty to a client does not extend to assisting a client in committing perjury. Relying on DR 7-102(A)(4) of the Iowa Code of Professional Responsibility for Lawyers, which expressly prohibits an attorney from using perjured testimony, and Iowa Code § 721.2 (now Iowa Code § 720.3 (1985)), which criminalizes subornation of perjury, the Iowa court concluded that not only were Robinson's actions permissible, but were required. The court commended "both Mr. Robinson and Ms. Paulsen for the high ethical manner in which this matter was handled."

Whiteside then petitioned for a writ of habeas corpus in the United States District Court for the Southern District of Iowa. In that petition, Whiteside alleged that he had been denied effective assistance of counsel and of his right to present a defense by Robinson's refusal to allow him to testify as he had proposed. The District Court denied the writ. Accepting the state trial court's factual finding that Whiteside's intended testimony would have been perjurious, it concluded that there could be no grounds for habeas relief, since there is no constitutional right to present a perjured defense.

The United States Court of Appeals for the Eighth Circuit reversed and directed that the writ of habeas corpus be granted. *Whiteside v. Scurr*, 744 F.2d 1323 (1984). The Court of Appeals accepted the findings of the trial judge, affirmed by the Iowa Supreme Court, that trial counsel believed with good cause that Whiteside would testify falsely, and acknowledged that, under *Harris v. New York*, 401 U.S. 222 (1971), a criminal defendant's privilege to testify in his own behalf does not include a right to commit perjury. Nevertheless, the court reasoned that an intent to commit perjury, communicated to counsel, does not alter a defendant's right to effective assistance of counsel, and that Robinson's admonition to Whiteside that he would inform the court of Whiteside's perjury constituted a threat to violate the attorney's duty to preserve client confidences. According to the Court of Appeals, this threatened violation of client confidences breached the standards of effective representation set down in *Strickland v. Washington*, 466 U.S. 668 (1984). The court also concluded that *Strickland's* prejudice requirement was satisfied by an implication of prejudice from the conflict between Robinson's duty of loyalty to his client and his ethical duties. A petition for rehearing en banc was denied, with Judges Gibson, Ross, Fagg, and Bowman dissenting. *Whiteside v. Scurr*, 750 F.2d 713 (1984). We granted certiorari, 471 U.S. 1014 (1985), and we reverse.

The right of an accused to testify in his defense is of relatively recent origin. Until the latter part of the preceding century, criminal defendants in this country, as at common law, were considered to be disqualified from giving sworn testimony at their own trial by reason of their interest as a party to the case. [citation omitted]. Iowa was among the states that adhered to this rule of disqualification. *State v. Laffer*, 38 Iowa 422 (1874).

By the end of the 19th century, however, the disqualification was finally abolished by statute in most states and in the federal courts....

In *Strickland v. Washington,* we held that, to obtain relief by way of federal habeas corpus on a claim of a deprivation of effective assistance of counsel under the Sixth Amendment, the movant must establish both serious attorney error and prejudice. To show such error, it must be established that the assistance rendered by counsel was constitutionally deficient in that "counsel made errors so serious that counsel was not functioning as 'counsel' guaranteed the defendant by the Sixth Amendment." *Strickland,* 466 U.S. at 687. To show prejudice, it must be established that the claimed lapses in counsel's performance rendered the trial unfair so as to "undermine confidence in the outcome" of the trial. *Id.* at 694.

In *Strickland,* we acknowledged that the Sixth Amendment does not require any particular response by counsel to a problem that may arise. Rather, the Sixth Amendment inquiry is into whether the attorney's conduct was "reasonably effective." To counteract the natural tendency to fault an unsuccessful defense, a court reviewing a claim of ineffective assistance must "indulge a strong presumption that counsel's conduct falls within the wide range of reasonable professional assistance." *Id.* at 689. ...

Under the *Strickland* standard, breach of an ethical standard does not necessarily make out a denial of the Sixth Amendment guarantee of assistance of counsel. When examining attorney conduct, a court must be careful not to narrow the wide range of conduct acceptable under the Sixth Amendment so restrictively as to constitutionalize particular standards of professional conduct, and thereby intrude into the state's proper authority to define and apply the standards of professional conduct applicable to those it admits to practice in its courts. ...

We turn next to the question presented: the definition of the range of "reasonable professional" responses to a criminal defendant client who informs counsel that he will perjure himself on the stand. We must determine whether, in this setting, Robinson's conduct fell within the wide range of professional responses to threatened client perjury acceptable under the Sixth Amendment.

In *Strickland,* we recognized counsel's duty of loyalty and his "overarching duty to advocate the defendant's cause." Plainly, that duty is limited to legitimate, lawful conduct compatible with the very nature of a trial as a search for truth. Although counsel must take all reasonable lawful means to attain the objectives of the client, counsel is precluded from taking steps or in any way assisting the client in presenting false evidence or otherwise violating the law....

The announced intention of a client to commit a crime is not included within the confidences which [the attorney] is bound to respect.

It is universally agreed that, at a minimum, the attorney's first duty when confronted with a proposal for perjurious testimony is to attempt to dissuade the client from the unlawful course of conduct. [citation omitted]

When false evidence is offered by the client, however, a conflict may arise between the lawyer's duty to keep the client's revelations confidential and the duty of candor to the court. Upon ascertaining that material evidence is false, the lawyer *should seek to persuade the client that the evidence should not be offered* or, if it has been offered, that its false character should immediately be disclosed.

Model Rules of Professional Conduct, Rule 3.3, Comment (1983) (emphasis added). The commentary thus also suggests that an attorney's revelation of his client's perjury to the court is a professionally responsible and acceptable response to the conduct of a client who has actually given perjured testimony. Similarly, the Model Rules and the commentary, as well as the Code of Professional Responsibility adopted in Iowa, expressly permit withdrawal from representation as an appropriate response of an attorney when the client threatens to commit perjury. Model Rules of Professional Conduct, Rule 1.16(a)(1), Rule 1.6, Comment (1983); Code of Professional Responsibility, DR 2-110(B), (C) (1980). Withdrawal of counsel when this situation arises at trial gives rise to many difficult questions including possible mistrial and claims of double jeopardy.

The essence of the brief *amicus* of the American Bar Association reviewing practices long accepted by ethical lawyers is that under no circumstance may a lawyer either advocate or passively tolerate a client's giving false testimony. ...

Considering Robinson's representation of respondent in light of these accepted norms of professional conduct, we discern no failure to adhere to reasonable professional standards that would in any sense make out a deprivation of the Sixth Amendment right to counsel. Whether Robinson's conduct is seen as a successful attempt to dissuade his client from committing the crime of perjury, or whether seen as a "threat" to withdraw from representation and disclose the illegal scheme, Robinson's representation of Whiteside falls well within accepted standards of professional conduct and the range of reasonable professional conduct acceptable under *Strickland.*

The Court of Appeals assumed for the purpose of the decision that Whiteside would have given false testimony had counsel not intervened; its opinion denying a rehearing en banc states:

[W]e presume that appellant would have testified falsely.

. . . Counsel's actions prevented [Whiteside] from testifying falsely. We hold that counsel's action deprived appellant of due process and effective assistance of counsel.

… While purporting to follow Iowa's highest court "on all questions of state law," 744 F.2d at 1330, the Court of Appeals reached its conclusions on the basis of federal constitutional due process and right to counsel.

The Court of Appeals' holding that Robinson's "action deprived [Whiteside] of due process and effective assistance of counsel" is not supported by the record, since Robinson's action, at most, deprived Whiteside of his contemplated perjury. Nothing counsel did in any way undermined Whiteside's claim that he believed the victim was reaching for a gun. Similarly, the record gives no support for holding that Robinson's action also impermissibly compromised [Whiteside's] right to testify in his own defense by conditioning continued representation . . . and confidentiality upon [Whiteside's] restricted testimony….

Whatever the scope of a constitutional right to testify, it is elementary that such a right does not extend to testifying *falsely*. In *Harris v. New York,* we assumed the right of an accused to testify "in his own defense, or to refuse to do so" and went on to hold:

[T]hat privilege cannot be construed to include the right to commit perjury. *See United States v. Knox,* 396 U.S. 77 (1969); *cf. Dennis v. United States,* 384 U.S. 855 (1966). Having voluntarily taken the stand, petitioner was under an obligation to speak truthfully. . . .401 U.S. at 225. ...

On this record, the accused enjoyed continued representation within the bounds of reasonable professional conduct, and did in fact exercise his right to testify; at most, he was denied the right to have the assistance of counsel in the presentation of false testimony. Similarly, we can discern no breach of professional duty in Robinson's admonition to respondent that he would disclose respondent's perjury to the court. The crime of perjury in this setting is indistinguishable in substance from the crime of threatening or tampering with a witness or a juror. ...No system of justice worthy of the name can tolerate a [contrary result].

The rule adopted by the Court of Appeals, which seemingly would require an attorney to remain silent while his client committed perjury, is wholly incompatible with the established standards of ethical conduct and the laws of Iowa, and contrary to professional standards promulgated by that State. The position advocated by petitioner, on the contrary, is wholly consistent with the Iowa standards of professional conduct and law, with the overwhelming majority of courts, and with codes of professional ethics.[47] Since there has been no breach of any recognized professional duty, it follows that there can be no deprivation of the right to assistance of counsel under the *Strickland* standard....

Reversed.

****

Questions:

1. During his murder trial, the defendant insisted, over his Lawyer's vehement advice against it, that he wanted to testify. Defendant testified in a narrative form with no questions from his Lawyer who, after both sides had rested, gave a stirring closing, never mentioning his client's testimony. Defendant was convicted of the murder and sentenced to life without the possibility of parole. After the verdict, defense counsel thanked the jurors for their service and one of the jurors told him that they would probably have voted for acquittal but for the defendant's testimony.

Defendant appealed on the ground of ineffective assistance of counsel, claiming that his testimony was so outrageous and unbelievable that his attorney should never permitted him to testify. Moreover, he claimed that his attorney knew that his testimony was false, because he had told his lawyer a completely different version of the facts at times during

---

[47] See Justice Brennan's concurring opinion where he cautions "Except in the rarest of cases, attorneys who adopt 'the role of the judge or jury to determine the facts,'...pose a danger of depriving their clients of the zealous and loyal advocacy required by the Sixth Amendment." Nix v. Whiteside at 189.

their consultations.[48] As a result, he claimed that lawyer had an ethical obligation to inform the court and or withdraw before the client gave the testimony. Did Lawyer violate the rules of professional conduct? Explain fully.

2. Immediately after stabbing his wife to death, husband telephones his long time neighbor and attorney, told him that he had stabbed the scheming witch to death and asks him what he should do. The attorney advised him not to do anything or talk to anyone until he got there. Once the attorney arrived on the scene, he checked to make sure that the Client's wife was indeed dead, at which time, he instructed Client to telephone the police and 911 for an ambulance. After witnessing Client make the calls, Attorney reminded Client to talk to no one before he left the scene. After attorney heard the emergency sirens, he returned to Client's home giving the impression to the police and emergency care givers that he was just arriving on the scene. He announced that he was Client's lawyer and again admonished Client to say nothing to no one but him.

Client was taken into custody and subsequently released on bail. During the meeting with Lawyer, he tells the circumstances of the murder stating that he had discovered earlier in the day that his wife was planning to leave him and had been systematically withdrawing money out of their bank accounts. That night, when he confronted her about it, she first denied it and then admitted how easy it had been, how he would not be able to prove a thing, that he was stupid and that she only married him for his money. Angered by her confession, he grabbed the poker from the fireplace and stabbed her. Lawyer asked Client whether he was certain that is what happened, and Client, perhaps not as stupid as his wife had thought, replied that everything had been fuzzy about that night and maybe he had blacked out.

Lawyer asked Client, if he was sure that Wife had not come at him with the sewing shears that Lawyer had seen on the floor near wife's body. Client responded that yes she had the shears in her hand that night. Lawyer asked, "So are you saying that you thought she was coming at you to kill you, when you picked up the poker and defended

---

[48] See Commonwealth v Mitchell, 438 Mass. 535 (2003) where the court discusses the various standards for determining whether the Lawyer "knew" under state ethics rules that are based on the ABA Model Rules of Professional Conduct. The court stated: "We first address the defendant's contention that the judge applied the wrong standard to inform the word "knows" in rule 3.3 (e). The question what a criminal defense attorney should do when confronted with client perjury at trial has been a subject of considerable debate. The problem raises both ethical and constitutional concerns. Defense counsel must furnish zealous advocacy and preserve client confidences, but, at the same time, defense counsel has a duty under rule 3.3 (e) to the court. In addition, the problem has constitutional implications by reason of its potential to deprive a defendant of his right to effective assistance of counsel, and his rights to due process and a fair trial, which include his right to testify in his own defense.
Not unexpectedly, courts have adopted differing standards to determine what an attorney must "know" before concluding that his client's testimony will be perjurious. The standards include the following: "good cause to believe the defendant's proposed testimony would be deliberately untruthful," State v. Hischke, 639 N.W.2d 6, 10 (Iowa 2002); "compelling support," Sanborn v. State, 474 So. 2d 309, 313 n.2 (Fla. Dist. Ct. App. 1985); "knowledge beyond a reasonable doubt," Shockley v. State, 565 A.2d 1373, 1379 (Del. 1989); a "firm factual basis," United States ex rel. Wilcox v. Johnson, 555 F.2d 115, 122 (3d Cir. 1977); a "good-faith determination," People v. Bartee, 208 Ill. App. 3d 105, 108, cert. denied, 502 U.S. 1014 (1991); and "actual knowledge," United States v. Del Carpio-Cotrina, 733 F. Supp. 95, 99 (S.D. Fla. 1990) (applying "actual knowledge" standard to require firm factual basis).

yourself?" "Yes, yes...that's it" Client replied. "It was self defense!" Has Lawyer violated the rules of ethics?[49] Explain fully.

3. How would your response to question 2 be different, if Client, in the presence of his Lawyer, gave the statement to the police, whereupon the district attorney's office determined that the evidence supported the self defense claim and consequently decided not to prosecute? Is Lawyer subject to discipline?

4. What if, after the Client's statements, the prosecutor seeks and secures an indictment against Client for involuntary manslaughter, Lawyer negotiates a deal with prosecutor, based on the self defense claim, that Client will plead guilty and get a sentence to be probated for five years. Is Lawyer subject to discipline?

****

Lucas v. State Of South Carolina
352 S.C. 1 (S.C. 2002)

...

Petitioner, Johnny Lee Lucas (Lucas), was convicted of first degree burglary, grand larceny, pointing and presenting a firearm, and possession of a firearm by a convicted felon, in connection with the April 15, 1996, burglary of a North Charleston home. He was sentenced to life without parole for burglary under the recidivist statute, and given five years on each of the remaining charges.

During Lucas' trial, his attorney, William Thrower, moved to be relieved as counsel on the basis that his client intended to call a witness, Rose Marie Brown, who planned to give perjured testimony. The trial judge decided to take Brown's testimony *in camera*. The gist of her testimony was that Lucas had left Brown's house with her husband, Robert Brown, at approximately 9:30a.m. on April 15, 1996, to go see the burglary victim, Mr. Lindenburg; Mrs. Brown believed Lindenburg owed her husband some money. During the *in camera* hearing, it was revealed that Brown's testimony had been written out for her. The statement was in handwritten form, and was not Mrs. Brown's handwriting. She had been given the statement by Lucas' attorney, Mr. Thrower.

Thrower advised the court that he had met with Lucas on Sunday evening and that Lucas had given him the statement to help Brown refresh her memory. However, after talking with Brown in the hallway on the day of trial, it had come to Thrower's attention that her testimony was not going to be truthful. He based this assertion on the fact that when he questioned her as to whether the written statement was the sworn truth, she would only reply that it was what she was going to testify to, and when again asked if everything in the statement were truthful, she would not say so. The trial court denied counsel's motion to be relieved.

---

[49] In the Matter of Steven M. Foley, 439 Mass. 324 (2003)

At the close of evidence, Lucas moved for a mistrial on the ground that, *inter alia,* the lawyer said he didn't want to handle this case, so [he] had ineffective assistance [of counsel]. The trial court denied the motion, ruling that counsel was still there as Lucas' lawyer, notwithstanding Lucas was not obliged to use him if he didn't want. Closing arguments were then made by both Thrower and Lucas. Lucas renewed his motion for a mistrial based upon counsel's backing out on him.

Lucas filed for PCR [post conviction relief] alleging ineffective assistance of counsel in failing to perfect an appeal, and alleging a denial of due process. The PCR court ruled Lucas was entitled to a belated appeal of his direct appeal issues pursuant to *White v. State,* 263 S.C. 110, 208 S.E.2d 35 (1974). Thereafter, this Court affirmed three of Lucas' direct appeal issues pursuant to Rule 220(b), SCACR [South Carolina Appellate Court Rule]. However, we granted certiorari to review the direct appeal issue concerning denial of counsel's motion to be relieved and denial of Lucas' motion for a mistrial.

Issue

Where an attorney forms a good faith basis for suspecting his client is about to present perjured testimony, and thereafter reveals the suspected perjury to the trial court and moves to be relieved as counsel, does the trial court's denial of the motion to be relieved constitute an abuse of discretion, depriving the defendant of a fair trial?

Discussion

Pursuant to Rule 407, SCACR, Rules of Professional Conduct (RPC), Rule 3.3:

(a) A lawyer shall not knowingly ...

> (4) Offer evidence that the lawyer knows to be false. If a lawyer has offered material evidence and comes to know of its falsity, the lawyer shall take reasonable remedial measures.

(b) The duties stated in paragraph (a) continue to the conclusion of the proceeding, and apply even if compliance requires disclosure of information otherwise protected by Rule 1.6.
(c) A lawyer may refuse to offer evidence that the lawyer reasonably believes is false.

Rule 1.6(b) of the RPC permits an attorney to reveal client confidences to the extent the lawyer reasonably believes necessary ... [t]o prevent the client from committing a criminal act.... The notes following Rule 1.6 recognize an exception to the general prohibition against disclosure in that a lawyer may not counsel or assist a client in conduct that is criminal or fraudulent, *see* Rule 1.2(d), and has a duty under Rule 3.3(a)(4) not to use false evidence. If the lawyer's services will be used by the client in materially furthering a course of criminal or fraudulent conduct, the lawyer must withdraw, as stated in Rule 1.16(a)(1)(lawyer must withdraw from representation if representation will result in violation of the Rules of Professional Conduct or other law).

In *Nix v. Whiteside,* 475 U.S. 157, 106 S.Ct. 988, 89 L.Ed.2d 123 (1986), the United States Supreme Court ruled that a criminal defendant's sixth amendment right to effective assistance of counsel was not violated when the attorney refused to cooperate with the defendant in presenting perjured testimony at trial. In *Nix,* the defendant, Whiteside, who was charged with murder, had consistently advised his attorney that although he had not seen a gun in the victim's hand, he was convinced the victim in fact possessed a gun. Shortly before trial, however, Whiteside told counsel he had seen something metallic in the victim's hand. When asked about his change in stories, he told counsel If I don't say I saw a gun, I'm dead. Counsel advised Whiteside that if he insisted upon testifying falsely, counsel would be compelled to advise the court of his belief that Whiteside was committing perjury, and would also move to withdraw as his counsel. Whiteside ultimately testified in accordance with his original version of events, admitting on cross examination that he had not seen a gun in the victim's hand. After he was convicted of murder, Whiteside sought a new trial, claiming he had been deprived of a fair trial by counsel's admonitions not to testify as to seeing something metallic in the victim's hand. The Iowa Supreme Court affirmed the denial of the new trial motion, ruling counsel's actions were not only permissible, but were required under Iowa law.

Thereafter, Whiteside sought federal habeas corpus relief, alleging he had been denied effective assistance of counsel and of his right to present a defense by counsel's refusal to allow him to testify as proposed. The Court of Appeals for the Eighth Circuit agreed, reasoning that an intent to commit perjury, communicated to counsel, does not alter a defendant's right to effective assistance of counsel and that counsel's admonition that he would advise the court of Whiteside's perjury constituted a threat to violate his duty to preserve client confidences. The Eighth Circuit concluded that the prejudice prong of *Strickland v. Washington* was satisfied by an implication of prejudice from the conflict between counsel's duty of loyalty to Whiteside and his ethical duties. The United States Supreme Court reversed in *Nix,* stating, Although counsel must take all reasonable lawful means to attain the objectives of the client, counsel is precluded from taking steps or in any way assisting the client in presenting false evidence or otherwise violating the law. The Court went on to note that under the Iowa Code of Professional Responsibility, the rules do not merely authorize disclosure by counsel of client perjury, they require such disclosure ..., and that the rules expressly permit withdrawal from representation as an appropriate response of an attorney when the client threatens to commit perjury. The Court concluded that counsel's representation fell well within accepted standards of professional conduct, and did not pose the type of conflict which would obviate the need for a showing of prejudice.

The Court stated: Here, there was indeed a conflict, but of quite a different kind; it was one imposed on the attorney by the client's proposal to commit the crime of fabricating testimony ... We find attorney Thrower's actions in the present case consistent with the South Carolina Rules of Professional Conduct. As noted previously, Thrower was prohibited by Rule 3.3. from offering evidence he reasonably believed was false, was authorized by Rule 1.6(b) to reveal confidences necessary to prevent a criminal act, and was permitted to withdraw pursuant to Rule 1.16(a). We find no ethical violation. Moreover, we find no prejudice to Lucas as a result of the trial court's denial of counsel's motion to be relieved.

This court has also addressed the appropriate action of a trial judge when faced with the situation of an attorney attempting to withdraw due to suspected client perjury. While an attorney has an ethical duty not to perpetrate a fraud upon the court by knowingly presenting perjured testimony, the defendant has a constitutional right to representation by counsel. Had the trial judge allowed the withdrawal, any new attorney he appointed would, if faced with the same conflict, have moved to withdraw, potentially resulting in a perpetual cycle of eleventh-hour motions to withdraw. Worse, new counsel might fail to recognize the problem and unwittingly present false evidence.

[M]otions to withdraw must lie within the sound discretion of the trial judge. In making the decision, the trial court must balance the need for the orderly administration of justice with the fact that an irreconcilable conflict exists between counsel and the accused. The court should consider the timing of the motion, the inconvenience to the witnesses, the period of time elapsed between the date of the alleged offense and the trial, and the possibility that any new counsel will be confronted with the same conflict. Here, it is patent that any new attorney would have been confronted with the same dilemma. Moreover, the motion to be relieved came nearly half way through a very serious trial. We find no abuse of discretion in the trial court's denial of the motions to be relieved and for a mistrial.

Finally, we find Lucas has demonstrated no prejudice from denial of counsel's motion to be relieved. Although Lucas himself decided to cross-examine his witnesses, he did so of his own volition, with counsel at his side at all times ready to assist in his defense. Further, counsel made all appropriate motions at the close of both the state's case and the close of evidence, and gave a closing statement to the jury. Accordingly, Lucas has failed to demonstrate in what manner his defense was prejudiced by denial of counsel's motion to be relieved. Lucas' convictions and sentences are AFFIRMED.

IN THE NEWS:

In North Dakota, a lawyer accepted the dual representation of both the alleged "perpetrator" and the alleged victim in a single aggravated assault and terrorizing criminal case. The lawyer also lied to the prosecutor that he had disclosed the dual representation to his partners and that they had approved the representation. The lawyer had the clients execute a waiver of conflict of interest, apparently never considering whether the conflict was non-waiveable.

While the lawyer was charged with violating a number of North Dakota disciplinary rules including conflicts, dishonesty, fraud, deceit and misrepresentation, the ethics panel recommendation may surprise you.

For more, see In the Matter of the Application for Disciplinary Action Against Blake D. Hankey, http://jcorsmeier.wordpress.com/2012/10/23/north-dakota-lawyer-receives-reprimand-for-violating-conflict-of-interest-rules-in-representing-both-the-defendant-and-victim-in-a-single-criminal-case-and-making-false-statements-to-prosecutor/ and see http://www.ndcourts.gov/court/opinions/20120304.htm

---

CONFLICTING INTERESTS

The ethical rules regarding conflicts of interest are designed to ensure that the client is represented by someone who places the client's interest above all others. If a lawyer represents clients with competing interests then it is unlikely that the attorney can fulfill her fiduciary obligation to either client. To fulfill the duty, the lawyer is generally prohibited from having interests that are adverse to an existing client. This conduct is prohibited even if the conflicting interests are unrelated. The lawyer is also prohibited from representing a current client when such representation is adverse to the interests of a former client. In this case the new representation is prohibited only if the case is substantially related to the case the lawyer handled for the former client. If a lawyer is a member of a firm, any conflict the lawyer has that would prohibit him from representing a client is imputed to the law firm. In this case, the other lawyers in the firm would also be prohibited from the representation.

Generally, a lawyer may represent clients with competing interests if both clients give their informed written consent to the representation. In this regard, the lawyer is obligated to ensure that she has fully disclosed the nature of the conflict to all parties. Whether the disclosures are sufficient may be measured by the sophistication of the parties/clients.

The lawyer must also be aware that there may be some conflicts that are non-waiveable.

Various conflicts can occur to the unwary lawyer who has the burden of ensuring that she has no conflicts of interest between clients. It is advisable that a lawyer perform a 'conflicts check' before accepting a new client. This process requires the attorney to inquire of the prospective client a list of all parties, past, present or contemplated that have or could have an interest in the legal matter. Once the attorney has this list of persons that may have interests adverse to the prospective client, the lawyer should examine his and the firm's records to determine whether a potential conflict exists.

Moreover, the lawyer should be careful not to accidentally create an attorney-client relationship. Accidental representation could occur in various circumstances: The attorney who interviews a potential client should not give legal advice or otherwise communicate with the person in a way that the person might reasonably believe that she was communicating with her lawyer. When the lawyer represents a company, she may often communicate with various company employees or representatives. It is important that the lawyer identify who she is representing at the start of any such communication. Of course, it is advisable that the lawyer receive written acknowledgement by all persons involved, that they are aware of whom the lawyer represents, but this may often be impractical.

In some instances, two or more persons may approach the lawyer for representation in the same transaction. The potential clients may believe that they have no conflicts between them and they may be correct. However, there is potential for a conflict in the future and it is up to the lawyer to ensure that she and her clients are protected from such potential conflict. For example, spouses seek the attorney's counsel in securing a divorce. The couple have agreed to the terms of property settlement, there are no children and the marital estate is small. A lawyer should not be tempted by the apparent simplicity of the case. On reviewing the settlement agreement, the lawyer may determine that it is scandalously biased against one of the spouses so that the attorney could not adequately represent both parties. In other words, the lawyer is always required to perform an independent investigation and evaluation of the circumstances to determine whether a conflict or potential conflict exists before accepting the case. There may be times the lawyer is unaware that a potential conflict exists at the time representation is begun. In this case, as soon as the lawyer becomes aware of the conflict she is obligated to diffuse the situation that may require withdrawal from representation.

Stanley v. Board of Professional Responsibility of the Supreme Court of Tennessee
640 S.W.2d 210 (Tenn. 1982)

The hearing committee and the Chancery Court, Anderson County, Wilkes Thrasher, Chancellor, entered judgments in a disciplinary matter. The Supreme Court held that preparation of usurious notes, failure to deal honestly and candidly with clients, and representation of both the victim and defendant in a criminal matter was conduct which seriously reflected upon one's fitness to practice law and warranted permanent disbarment. Affirmed.

The Board of Professional Responsibility charged Harry Parker Stanley with preparation of usurious notes, the lending of money to a client without full disclosure, the failure to deal honestly and candidly with clients, the representation of both the victim and defendant in a criminal matter, incompetency for legal representation, and conflict of interest. The charges were based upon Stanley's conduct in three separate episodes….

Stanley was thirty-three years old at the time of the circuit court hearing. He was admitted to the bar in April 1971, and entered practice with Jimmy D. Turner, in the City of Oak Ridge, Anderson County. Seven months later he opened his own office and has since practiced alone.

John E. Newby

John E. Newby was described by Stanley and Mrs. Shirley Newby as a friend and client of Stanley. Newby was a pharmacist, the owner of Union Prescription Shop in Oak Ridge. One of the witnesses testified that Newby's hobby was spending money. His widow testified that he opened ten drug stores and one camera shop during the last fifteen years of his life and all failed except three; that he was a poor businessman and constantly in financial difficulty.

Stanley testified that beginning about four years before Newby's death in December, 1978, he would lend Newby twenty, fifty or one hundred dollars and would be repaid promptly. Apparently Stanley would be given a note if the amount was as much as one hundred dollars with various items of personal property as collateral. Stanley testified, at one point in the record, that with respect to those loans, either no interest or ten percent interest was charged. Newby died on December 18, 1978. On December 22, 1978, Shirley Newby filed suit against Stanley in the Circuit Court of Anderson County alleging that she and her late husband had borrowed money from Stanley and had given notes that were usurious on their face and that Stanley held jewelry, diamond rings, and other personal property valued in excess of ten thousand dollars, which was described in detail in the petition. She sought and obtained an order restraining Stanley from disposing of the property. The usurious notes were described in this record as follows:

1. A note dated August 22, 1978, in the principal sum of $560.00 bearing interest at twelve percent per annum with an additional ten percent penalty charge for late payment;

2. A note dated August 24, 1978, in the principal sum of $672.00 with interest at twelve percent plus an additional ten percent penalty for late payment.

79

3. A note dated August 30, 1978, in the principal sum of $2,446.50 bearing interest at twelve percent per annum with an additional ten percent penalty for late payment;

4. A note dated September 30, 1978, in the principal sum of $2,563.00 bearing interest at twelve percent per annum with the same penalty for late payment as the preceding notes; and

5. A note dated September 8, 1978, in the principal sum of $7,641.00 bearing interest at the rate of fifteen percent per annum.

The maximum interest rate at the dates of each of said notes was ten percent per annum. Mrs. Newby testified that Stanley supplied the money for the principal amount of each of those notes. Stanley testified that the money loaned belonged to his mother. He admitted that he negotiated all the loans, prepared the notes, transmitted the funds to Newby, and made the collections that were made.

On January 12, 1979, Mrs. Newby's lawsuit against Stanley was settled by entry of an order reciting that Stanley would return all of the property held as collateral to Mrs. Newby and neither party would file or prosecute any suit based upon notes or security instruments executed by Mr. or Mrs. Newby payable to Stanley or his mother. No other terms of the settlement were revealed either in the order or in the testimony of the witnesses in this case.

Stanley's defense was that the interest charge that exceeded ten percent was a service charge. Stanley testified that, at Newby's insistence, Stanley obligated himself to notify Newby a few days in advance of the due dates of payments on the respective notes, and "then appear in person at his place of business in order to collect payment." He further said that Newby "could mail a payment and mail in ten percent at any time." No such terms appeared in the notes and there was no evidence that Newby mailed in payments at only ten percent interest.

… There was absolutely no corroboration, circumstantial or otherwise to support the service charge arrangement….

Stanley also insisted there was no conflict of interest involved in the usurious loan transactions with his client, because there was no lawyer-client relationship, as to those transactions. That conclusion was based on Stanley's testimony that he made the loans to decedent in the role of a friend, not a lawyer; that decedent did not expect or receive any "independent advice" from Stanley in connection with the loan transactions and nothing was misrepresented or withheld from Newby. That was also a patently spurious attempt to avoid the consequences of a lawyer entering into an illegal transaction with a client wherein the lawyer and the client had conflicting interests.

Jane Whittlesay and Ronnie Green

The next episode involved two clients, Janet Whittlesay and her nineteen-year-old friend, Ronnie Green.

According to an Oak Ridge police report that was introduced into evidence, Janet Whittlesay reported the theft of stereo equipment, albums and clothes, valued at approximately seven hundred dollars from the residence where she lived with one Ronald Stevens. After reporting the theft she discovered that her friend Ronnie Green had taken the items and removed them to his home in Cleveland, Tennessee. Whittlesay recovered all of the property and informed the police that she did not want to prosecute, whereupon someone in the police department allegedly threatened her with prosecution for obstructing justice and withholding information.

Ms. Whittlesay sought legal advice from Stanley who testified he did a "limited amount of legal research on the matter of obstruction of justice." In addition, he made two visits to the Oak Ridge Police Department to Sergeant Faust, who apparently made the threat to Ms. Whittlesay. Stanley said that Faust told him, on the first visit, that he was leaving for the day and left him with the impression that he was not interested in the case, but said come back tomorrow. On the next visit Faust was busy and refused to see Stanley. Stanley left a message for Faust that if he was interested in the case he should telephone Stanley. He never heard from Faust thereafter.

For those services to Ms. Whittlesay, Ronnie Green paid Stanley one hundred dollars.

It is not clear from this record who first came up with the idea that Ronnie Green needed the services of a lawyer, but it is clear that Stanley approved of and promoted that idea.

Stanley took Ms. Whittlesay and Green to one Edward M. LaMotte, who was described as a pastoral counsellor. Stanley's version of the visit was that the initial purpose was to help Whittlesay determine whether or not to prosecute Green; that after thirty to forty-five minutes Whittlesay, "resolutely and firmly," came to the conclusion that she would not prosecute Green. But, according to Stanley, it became apparent to LaMotte that Green had "deep seated and serious problems." Then, he continued, "the four of us came to the conclusion ... that he would need ... some type of full-time treatment." Stanley asserted that Green had a drug and alcohol problem.

Stanley testified that Green became his client at LaMotte's place on the Friday evening of the first visit there, in the presence of Whittlesay and LaMotte, prior to Stanley's having met Green's parents. Stanley described the purpose of the employment as follows:

"Q: This was before you had an opportunity to speak with his parents?

A: That is correct. In other words, what he wanted, he wanted my services to reinforce or to act as a paraclete, act as a supporter to advise him of various legal consequences of his acts. He also desired to have Mr. LaMotte stand by to help him. To be the primary counsellor outside of the staff that would be available to him at Freedom House, and also desired to have a counsellor that worked under Mr. LaMotte, and also a counsellor, not an attorney or psychiatrist or doctor, whose role it would be to visit with him and counsel with him at Freedom House in that particular setting, either have that particular agent or Mr. LaMotte himself counsel with him at that particular point.

It was suggested and he desired to have as many people supporting him as he could possibly obtain and that he would need that kind of support."

Stanley was asked if anything remained to be performed as lawyer for Ms. Whittlesay at the time of his employment by Ronnie Green. His response was, "Only ... to make it plain to the police that she had no desire to prosecute Ronnie Green."

On the Saturday following the Friday night meeting with LaMotte, Stanley met with Richard and Bobbie Jean Green, Ronnie Green's parents. Richard Green testified that his son told them Saturday morning that he was in trouble and had an appointment with Stanley at one p.m.; that Stanley had sworn him to secrecy about the nature of the trouble; that when they went to Stanley's office that afternoon Stanley refused to tell them what the trouble was until they paid him a fee; that initially a fee of two thousand dollars was demanded but was later reduced to seven hundred and fifty dollars with a demand for immediate payment; that when informed that they would have to borrow the money from the credit union and that that office was closed until Monday, Stanley insisted that he could procure them an immediate loan which could be repaid from the proceeds of the credit union loan on Monday, that at Stanley's insistence that plan was carried out, to-wit: they gave a note for the loan procured by Stanley for them and brought him the credit union's check for seven hundred fifty dollars on Monday.

The only service rendered by Stanley was to take the Greens and their son back to LaMotte for a counselling session and obtain Ronnie Green's admission to a half-way house where he remained for approximately three weeks. It is crystal clear from the record that the counselling session and admission to a half-way house was accomplished by Stanley keeping alive the threat that Ronnie had committed a serious crime and might yet be sent to the penitentiary. It is not clear at what point in time the Greens realized they had been misled but the following testimony of Mrs. Green under cross examination by counsel for Stanley reflects their ultimate understanding:

"Q: You recognized that as being an act against the law, the act itself?

A: Yes sir. He did break the law, but Mr. Stanley did nothing legally, as far as I know, and I don't know much about lawyers, as far as this goes, but, as far as I know, Mr. Stanley did nothing. Everything was well taken care of before my husband and I were called in on this.

The stereo was taken back. Janet didn't want to prosecute. All of this had been taken care of before my husband and I were brought in."

Stanley deceived an immature youth and his naive parents. He compounded the deception with his lack of understanding of the proper role of a lawyer—which does not include a self-appointed role as a paraclete, comforter, helper, or hand holder, under the guise of legal services and at a lawyer's compensation rate.

Stanley's lack of understanding of conflicts of interest to be avoided by lawyers is exemplified in the following paraphrased questions and answers:

Q: Did you lead Ronnie's parents to believe that unless they employed you he might go to the penitentiary.

A: The plan I had constructed provided the "highest reasonable probability to avoid his having to go into the penitentiary."

Q: Did you consider that if your plan did not work out successfully, that there might be a criminal trial for Ronnie Green and Janet Whittlesay would be the prosecutor?

A: I explained that to them, that that would literally be possible. They knew that was a possibility but Janet said she wouldn't do it.

Q: Despite knowing that and having first represented Miss Whittlesay you accepted employment to represent Ronnie Green in the same matter?
A: With all due respect, I did not see it as the same matter.

Russell Orr

Stanley testified that Russell Orr first retained his services to avoid being prosecuted for passing bad checks. The learned Chancellor's recitation of the relevant facts about this third episode is fully supported by the record, and we adopt the same, together with his conclusions and judgment. That portion of his opinion reads as follows:

"Mrs. Reba June Wallace was a widow with a seventh grade education and at times material to this case she dated Mr. Russell V. Orr when she first came in contact with Mr. H. Parker Stanley. Mr. Orr at that particular time was a bartender at Jerry's Bar on Clinton Highway in late 1977 or early 1978 when some of these transactions materialized. Reba June Wallace subsequently did marry Russell V. Orr and became Mrs. Reba June Wallace Orr.

Mr. Stanley is charged with a conflict of interest in representing Mr. Orr when Mr. Orr had bad checks and sought his help and when loans were made to Mr. Orr, and then it is charged that Mr. Stanley also represented his mother in the case of Stanley versus Orr with respect to back rent due to his mother from Mr. Orr, and generally the charges of the Disciplinary Board also state that Mr. Stanley's conduct in this regard also reflected upon his fitness to practice law. Without burdening this opinion unnecessarily with a maze of facts and details, it does appear that a sum total of thirteen thousand dollars worth of mortgages were placed against the little home of Mrs. Reba June Wallace Orr.

Mrs. Orr very positively stated that she did not know the nature of these obligations and that she felt she had been misinformed and that she did not understand the legal import or significance of some of these documents. In any event in due time appropriate legal action was filed on behalf of Mrs. Reba June Orr and these thirteen thousand dollars in obligations were disposed of for approximately one thousand dollars. …

It is also apparent from the Exhibits to Mrs. Reba June Wallace Orr's testimony and from the transcript that the notes payable to Mr. Stanley's mother were usurious as evidenced by the transcript at page 184, line 14, and transcript 190, line 24.

Mr. Stanley himself said, 'I told him [Orr] that *we* would renew the note and that at that particular time the note would bear a higher rate of interest than ten percent as ten percent was not sufficient to renew the note. He knew *us* well enough to know that if *we* told him we would, we would renew it. I told him that he could trust us and that we would run it for two years that he could then renew the note. He asked what rate of interest the rate would be at the end of that. I indicated that I thought the maximum rate would then be raised to fourteen and a half to fifteen ....' (Emphasis supplied)

The Court concludes that the we and the us refers to Mr. Stanley and his mother—this conclusion is inescapable. Mrs. Stanley said that her son did not tell her to insert the interest rate of fourteen and a half percent, but Mr. Orr told her, 'Parker said put fourteen and a half percent as the interest rate.' There's no attached document of explanation with regard to the Orr matter and as in the Newby case the alleged document of explanation has been conveniently discarded or thrown away.

Mr. Stanley simply cannot divorce himself from involvement in this Orr transaction. After all from the lips of his own mother the Court heard her answer and her deposition at page 28, lines 21 and 22, when she was asked this question, 'Is it true that your son routinely makes the business decisions for you.' Answer unqualifiedly and without any suffix or prefix, she answered yes.

From all of which and from the clear and convincing evidence the Court concludes that Mr. Stanley is guilty of the specifically enumerated improprieties with regard to the Orr-Wallace transactions.

Aside from the specifically designated charges the Court feels that it is appropriate to comment upon the quality of Mr. Stanley's professional services. Again after attentively listening to Mr. Stanley's testimony and after carefully observing his manner and demeanor on the witness stand the Court concludes that Mr. Stanley's incompetence is exceeded only by his lack of remorse and his inability to recognize his wrong doing.

Nevertheless the Court now returns to the central theme or the major thrust of these proceedings. The Court has re-read the transcript, re-examined the Exhibits, analyzed the testimony by the oral witnesses and by the deposition, and the Court has given due consideration to the arguments of counsel, and the Court concludes that Mr. H. Parker Stanley is guilty as charged by the Disciplinary Board of the Supreme Court. In particular Mr. Stanley is guilty of participation in usurious transactions, of conflict of interest, and is most assuredly guilty of conduct which seriously reflects upon his fitness to practice law." Affirmed.

****

Questions:

1. Lawyer represents company that is charged with vicarious liability for the acts of one of its supervisors. Both company and supervisor are named as defendants in the lawsuit. Plaintiff, a former company employee charges that the supervisor wrongfully terminated his employment. Would it be a violation of the model rules of professional conduct for Lawyer to represent both the company and the supervisor?[50]

2. Lawyer has been appointed by the court to represent Client in a criminal prosecution. Client has plead "not guilty" claiming an alibi for the time of the offense. The chief witness against Client is one of Lawyer's former clients. Lawyer will be required to cross-examine the former client about, among other things, the prior conviction in which lawyer represented former Client. As soon as Lawyer sees former client's name on the state's witness list, he moves the court to withdraw from the current representation. The judge denies the motion and orders Lawyer to continue with the representation. Will lawyer be in violation of the model rules of professional conduct if he pursues the representation? What should Lawyer do to ensure compliance with the rules of ethics?[51]

****

In Re Guaranty Insurance Services, Inc., Relator
343 S.W. 3d 130 (Tex. 2011)

What happens when a law firm's efforts to screen a conflict fail, permitting a non-lawyer who worked on one side of a case at one firm to work on the other side of the same case at the opposing firm? Here, the trial court disqualified the second firm, reasoning there was a conclusive presumption that the non-lawyer had shared confidential information, despite evidence he had not. A divided court of appeals denied mandamus relief. 310 S.W.3d 630, 634. Given our prior decisions on the subject—particularly our recent decision in *In re Columbia Valley Healthcare System, L.P.,* 320 S.W.3d 819 (Tex. 2010) (orig. proceeding), issued four months after the court of appeals' decision below—we conclude disqualification was not warranted. Further, because the improper disqualification was a clear abuse of discretion for which there is no adequate remedy by appeal, mandamus relief is warranted. *See In re Prudential*

---

[50] See generally, Janet A. Savage, Conflicts of Interest issues in simultaneous representation of employers and employees in employment law, American Bar Assoc 2002, available at
http://www.bnabooks.com/ababna/ethics/2002/savage.doc

[51] See e.g. Ohio Sup. Ct., Bd of Comm'rs on Grievances & Discipline, Opinion 2013-4 [Advisory Opinions of the Board of Commissioners on Grievances and Discipline are informal, nonbinding opinions in response to prospective or hypothetical questions regarding the application of the Supreme Court Rules for the Government of the Bar of Ohio, the Supreme Court Rules for the Government of the Judiciary, the Ohio Rules of Professional Conduct, the Ohio Code of Judicial Conduct, and the Attorney's Oath of Office.] and see North Carolina Ethics Opinion 14 (2003)

85

Ins. Co., 148 S.W.3d 124, 13 *5-36* (Tex. 2004) (orig. proceeding) (describing when mandamus relief may issue); *NCNB Tex. Nat'l Bank v. Coker, 765 SW 2d 398, 400 (Tex.1989)(orig. proceeding)(granting mandamus in context of* improper disqualification). We conditionally grant mandamus relief and direct the trial court to vacate its disqualification order.

The non-lawyer in this story is paralegal Clyde Williams; the two firms are Godwin Pappas Langley Ronquillo, LLP (Godwin Pappas) and Strasburger & Price, LLP (Strasburger). Like many corporate battles, the litigation underlying this mandamus proceeding was a multi-suit affair. The lawsuit from which Strasburger was ultimately disqualified is suit number two in the litigation between Trans-Global Solutions, Inc. (Trans-Global) and Guaranty Insurance Services, Inc. (Guaranty). Trans-Global first sued Guaranty, an insurance agent, for allegedly failing to obtain appropriate insurance. Guaranty prevailed and brought suit number two (the underlying suit), seeking indemnity for the defense costs it incurred in the first suit. Strasburger represents Guaranty in the underlying suit. Trans-Global was first represented by Godwin Pappas in the underlying suit and is now represented by Kane Russell Coleman & Logan, PC (Kane Russell).

In July 2005, Williams began work as a paralegal at Godwin Pappas. While there, he billed a total of 6.8 hours in the underlying suit, reviewing the file to identify persons with knowledge of relevant facts, preparing an initial draft of a response to Guaranty's request for disclosures, assisting in document production, and communicating with opposing counsel. Williams left Godwin Pappas in November 2006. The attorneys handling the case left the firm in August 2008 for Kane Russell, taking the case with them.

In October 2008, Williams applied for a paralegal position at Strasburger. In his Employee Application, he identified Godwin Pappas as one of his previous employers, and Strasburger ran an initial conflicts check, which came back clear. At the firm's request, Williams also identified two potential conflicts due to his previous work on matters in which Strasburger represented another party. Strasburger ran a separate conflicts check on those and restricted his access to documents related to them. Williams attested that he failed to identify the underlying suit as a potential conflict because he did not remember having billed any hours for it.

In addition to the conflicts check, the firm instructed Williams several times prior to his work on this case not to disclose confidential information he gained during his previous employment—specifically during his orientation, and through the Strasburger Employee Information Handbook and a confidentiality agreement. Williams signed the handbook and the agreement. Both required him to notify his supervising attorney immediately if he became aware of a matter on which he previously worked.

Williams started work at Strasburger in January 2009. At that point, the underlying suit was already underway. The trial court granted partial summary judgment in Guaranty's favor that March, determining Trans-Global was contractually obligated to indemnify Guaranty for the defense costs incurred during the first suit. In July 2009, Williams's supervising attorney at Strasburger asked him to organize the pleadings and discovery in this case. Williams again failed to recognize the conflict and to notify the supervising attorney of its existence. In September 2009, Williams affixed bates labels to documents produced to Trans-Global and attached redacting tape to passages highlighted by an attorney. In total, Williams billed about 27 hours on the case at Strasburger.

Emails between Strasburger and Kane Russell regarding routine discovery matters made reference to Williams as a Strasburger legal assistant. A Kane Russell attorney recognized Williams as a former Godwin Pappas employee and notified Strasburger of the conflict. Strasburger immediately instructed Williams to discontinue working on the matter, not to view or access any documents related to the case, and not to disclose any information he had obtained during his employment with Godwin Pappas. Trans-Global moved to disqualify Stra.sburger. Though Trans-Global disputes this fact before our Court, the record is clear that Trans-Global conceded during the disqualification hearing that no confidences were actually shared. After conducting that hearing, the trial court granted Trans-Global's motion and entered findings of fact and conclusions of law. In brief, it reasoned the journey was irrelevant when the final destination included a non-lawyer on both sides of the same case. It held that evidence Strasburger instituted a screening procedure for non-lawyers was immaterial under Texas law because the screening procedure did not prevent Williams from actually working on the opposite side of the case. Williams's actual work on opposite sides created a genuine threat of disclosure, which meant he was conclusively presumed to have shared confidential information, despite evidence he had not.

Guaranty unsuccessfully sought mandamus relief in the court of appeals, which essentially agreed with the trial court's analysis. While conceding Strasburger's screening procedures were "exemplary," it explained that those procedures, "however thorough, must actually be effective in order to rebut the presumption." 310 S.W.3d at 632 *(citing Phoenix Founders, Inc. v. Marshall, 887 S.W.2d 831, 833 (Tex. 1994) (orig. proceeding))*. It reasoned that "where a paralegal has actually been allowed to work on both sides of the same litigation, even the most exhaustive attempts at screening cannot be deemed effective" and concluded the trial court did not abuse its discretion. *Id.* at 633-34. A dissenting justice took the position that a non-lawyer's actual work on both sides of the case by itself did not mandate disqualification of the second firm. *Id.* at 634 (Waldrop, J., dissenting).

Our conflict-of-interest jurisprudence recognizes distinctions between lawyers and non-lawyers, their duties, and their likelihood of contact with confidential information. We have held that a lawyer who has previously represented a client may not represent another person on a matter adverse to the client if the matters are the same or substantially related. *In re Columbia*, 320 S.W.3d at 824. If the *lawyer* works on a matter, there is an *irrebuttable* presumption that the lawyer *obtained* confidential information during the representation. *Phoenix Founders*, 887 S.W.2d at 833. When the lawyer moves to another firm and the second firm represents an opposing party to the lawyer's former client, a second *irrebuttable* presumption arises—that the lawyer has *shared* the client's confidences with members of the second firm. *Id.* at 834. The effect of this second presumption is the mandatory disqualification of the second firm. *See id.* at 833-34.

But the rule is different for non-lawyers. A *non-lawyer* who worked on a matter at a prior firm is also subject to a *conclusive* presumption that confidences were *obtained*. *In re Am. Home Prods. Corp.*, 985 S.W.2d 68, 74 (Tex. 1998) (orig. proceeding); *Phoenix Founders*, 887 S.W.2d at 834. This rule serves "to prevent the moving party from being forced to reveal the very confidences sought to be protected." *In re Am. Home*, 985 S.W.2d at 74 *(quoting Phoenix Founders*, 887 S.W.2d at 834) (quotation marks omitted). However, the second presumption—that confidences were *shared* with members of the second firm—may be rebutted where non-lawyers are concerned. *Phoenix Founders*, 887 S.W.2d at 835. As applies here, then, there is a conclusive presumption that Williams obtained confidential information, but Strasburger may be free to rebut the presumption that Williams shared those confidences with it. The issue is whether Strasburger can do so in this situation and, if so, whether it has.

> The only way to rebut the rebuttable presumption is:
> (1) to instruct the legal assistant "not to work on any matter on which the paralegal worked during the prior employment, or regarding which the paralegal has information relating to the former employer's representation," and (2) to "take other reasonable steps to ensure that the paralegal does not work in connection with matters on which the paralegal worked during the prior employment, absent client consent."

In re Am. Home, 985 S.W.2d at 75 (quoting *Phoenix Founders*, 887 S.W.2d at *835).* A simple, informal admonition to a non-lawyer employee not to work on a matter on which he worked before is not enough. *In re Columbia*, 320 S.W.3d at 826. And the "other reasonable measures must include, at a minimum, formal, institutionalized screening measures that render the possibility of the non-lawyer having contact with the file less likely." *Id.* Thus, effective screening methods may be used to shield the employee from the matter in order to avoid disqualification. *Id.* at 824 (citations omitted).

But we have never said that ineffective screening measures merited automatic disqualification for non-lawyers. On the contrary, we have explained that in most cases, disqualification is not required provided "the practical effect of formal screening has been achieved." *Phoenix Founders*, 887 S.W.2d at 835 (citation omitted). In *re Columbia*, we equated this to "effective screening," and cited to the six *Phoenix Founders* factors that guide such an inquiry:

> (1) the substantiality of the relationship between the former and current matters; (2) the time elapsing between the matters; (3) the size of the firm; (4) the number of individuals presumed to have confidential information; (5) the nature of their involvement in the former matter; and (6) the timing and features of any measures taken to reduce the danger of disclosure. 20 S.W.3d at 824-25 *(citing Phoenix Founders*, 887 S.W.2d at 836).

Whether screening actually works is not determinative. Instead, the "ultimate question in weighing these factors" is whether the second firm "has taken measures sufficient to *reduce* the potential for misuse of confidences to an *acceptable* level." *Phoenix Founders*, 887 S.W.2d at 836 (emphasis added).

We have also explained that knowledge of a conflict can be central to this analysis:

> The non-lawyer should be cautioned. . . that the employee should not work on any

matter on which the employee worked for the former employer. . . . *When the new firm becomes aware of such matters,* the employing firm must also take reasonable steps to ensure that the employee takes no action and does no work in relation to matters on which the employer worked in the prior employment, absent client consent after consultation. *Grant v. Thirteenth Court of Appeals,* 888 S.W.2d 466, 467-68 (Tex. 1994) (per curiam) (orig. proceeding) (emphasis added) (quoting ABA Comm. on Ethics and Prof l Responsibility, Informal Op. 1526 (1988)).

We reiterated the flexibility of this approach as well as the significance of knowledge in *In re Columbia,* which expounded upon the thrust of our prior holdings:

> Despite the screening measures used, the presumption of shared confidences becomes conclusive if: (1) information related to the representation of an adverse client has in fact been disclosed, (2) screening would be ineffective or the non-lawyer necessarily would be required to work on the other side of a matter that is the same as or substantially related to a matter on which the paralegal has previously worked; or (3) the non-lawyer has actually performed work, including clerical work, on the matter at the lawyer's directive if the lawyer reasonably should know about the conflict of interest. 320 S.W.3d at 828.

Because Williams actually worked on both sides of this case, the third scenario discussed in *In re Columbia is* implicated. Today we clarify, under that scenario: The presumption of shared confidences is *rebuttable* if the non-lawyer has actually performed work on the matter at a lawyer's directive and the lawyer reasonably should *not know about the conflict of interest.* Put differently, if the non-lawyer has actually worked on the matter, the presumption of shared confidences is *not rebuttable unless* the assigning lawyer should *not* have known of the conflict. The question, then, is whether Williams's supervising attorney reasonably should have known that Williams worked on the same case at Godwin Pappas before coming to Strasburger. First, on this record, the supervising attorney reasonably should not have had such knowledge, rendering the presumption rebuttable. Second, Strasburger succeeds in rebutting this presumption. We discuss each in turn.

Prior to Williams's discovery by a Kane Russell attorney, there is no evidence Strasburger was ever notified of the conflict. Williams never informed Strasburger that he had worked on the suit. And the fact that he worked less than seven hours on the case certainly supports Williams's claim that he simply forgot he had engaged with the litigation; the fact that he willingly disclosed two other potential conflicts suggests he was not averse to disclosing potential conflicts.

Further, the conflicts check came back clear. Trans-Global argues Strasburger would have discovered the conflict but for its ineffective screening system in screening conflicts. ... Aside from its computerized conflicts check, Strasburger had specifically asked Williams to identify any conflicts of which he was aware. In addition, Trans-Global conceded that Strasburger's system was adequate during the oral hearing on the motion to disqualify, at one point stating, "we have no complaints about their screening procedure," and remaining mum when the trial court stated that Trans-Global had conceded that Strasburger's screening methods were sufficient to *meet the Phoenix Founders* and *In re American Home* standards. The failure of a screening method to actually screen a tainted party will not translate into disqualification where "the practical effect of formal screening has been achieved." *Phoenix Founders, 887* S.W.2d at *835* (citation omitted). That effect was achieved here because there is no evidence the supervising attorney reasonably should have known about the conflict.

The screening was also effective under the fact-intensive, multi-factor inquiry of *Phoenix Founders.* There was undoubtedly a substantial relationship between the former and current matters—they stemmed, after all, from the same litigation. However, it is worth noting that by the time Williams first worked on the case as a Strasburger employee in July 2009, summary judgment had limited the scope of the matter, leaving only the determination of the amount of attorney fees from the first suit and whether fees could be recovered in the second indemnity suit. The other factors further indicate effective screening. Almost two years passed between Williams's exit from Godwin Pappas and his application to Strasburger; another three months after that passed before he gained employment there; and another six months after that went by before he actually worked on the case. Only one person—Williams--is presumed to have confidential information, and Williams's minimal work on the case (less than 34 hours across both firms) also suggests effective screening. Finally, the evidence indicates that Strasburger took numerous measures, … to prevent and later to address the danger of disclosure.

Strasburger clears the hurdles to presumption-rebuttal erected by *In re American Home* and *Phoenix Founders.* At the outset, via his orientation, the Strasburger Employee Information Handbook, and the confidentiality agreement, Strasburger instructed Williams not to engage with matters on which he had worked previously. Those documents also directed Williams to notify his supervising attorney immediately if he realized a conflict. Strasburger also took other reasonable steps to ensure Williams did not work on matters from his prior employment. Specifically, it had in place formal, institutionalized screening procedures, which even the court of appeals noted were "nothing if not thorough." 310 S.W.3d at 633. The trial court similarly noted Strasburger had "presented evidence that it had instituted a screening procedure for non-lawyers," and even Trans-Global itself stated "we have no complaints about their screening procedure." Strasburger also presented evidence that it strictly adhered to its formal screening process when it hired Williams. When Williams identified two closed matters on which he had worked and in which Strasburger had also been involved, Strasburger removed his access to those files. Strasburger also ran a conflicts check based on Williams's previous employers, and it revealed no additional conflicts. Williams signed a confidentiality agreement, certifying that he disclosed the existence of any conflict of interest of which he was aware at the time. He also acknowledged receiving, reading, and signing the Employee Information Book, which informed him of his duty to keep confidential information obtained during his previous employment.

Further, Williams attested that upon discovering the conflict, Strasburger instructed him not to work further on this case, not to access related documents, and not to disclose any information. While such a restriction is not a stand-alone requirement for rebutting the presumption, these additional steps further distinguish this case from others where we have disqualified firms for a non-lawyer's actual work on both sides of a case. For example, in *In re*

Columbia, the paralegal had similarly performed limited work on both sides of the same case. 320 S.W.3d at 823. But the second law firm did not have any formal screening measures in place and, upon realizing a conflict existed, did not immediately remove the non-lawyer's access to the case. *Id.* In fact, the supervising attorney asked the non-lawyer to work on the case even after the conflict came to light. *Id.* Strasburger's efforts after discovering the conflict parallel and reinforce its thorough attempts to preempt the conflict in the first place.

For these reasons, and without hearing oral argument, *see* Tx. R. App. P. 52.8(c), we conditionally grant mandamus relief and direct the trial court to vacate its order granting the motion to disqualify. We are confident the trial court will comply, and the writ will issue only if it does not.

****

Note:

Generally speaking, courts have taken the position that Model Rule 5.3 requires the lawyer to "make reasonable efforts to ensure that the firm has in effect measures giving reasonable assurance that the person's conduct is compatible with the professional obligations of the lawyer". The Guaranty court appears to expand the law firm's duty to ensure that the screening methods extend beyond what the screening the lawyer would be subject to under rule 1.9(b). That rule prohibits the lawyer from *knowingly* representing "a person in the same or substantially related matter in which a firm with which the lawyer formerly was associated had previously represented a client (1) whose interests are materially adverse to that person *and* (2) about whom the lawyer had acquired information protected by Rules 1.6 and 1.9(c) that is *material to the matter;…*" The Guaranty court emphasizes the quality of the screening without first determining that no screening was required as the two prerequisites had not been met since the information that the paralegal may have had access to at the old firm was immaterial to the matter at bar. A different analysis might be required for those jurisdictions that have adopted the Restatement of Law Governing Lawyers which provides at §124 a screen/screening process even if the lawyer's information is not significant.[52]

Texaco, Inc. v. The Honorable Ricardo H. Garcia, Judge
891 S.W.2d 255 (1995)

In this original proceeding, Relators Texaco, Inc. and Texaco Refining and Marketing Inc. ("Texaco") seek a writ of mandamus directing the trial judge (1) to vacate his June 7, 1994 order denying Texaco's motion to disqualify and (2) to grant Texaco's motion to disqualify. Pursuant to Rule 122 of the Texas Rules of Appellate Procedure, without hearing oral argument, a majority of the court conditionally grants the writ of mandamus.

Plaintiffs James G. Holten and Quail Valley, Ltd. d/b/a Valley View Shopping Center sued Texaco and others alleging that a shopping center has been contaminated by the migration of

---

[52] See ABA Model Rules of Professional Responsibility, Rule 1.9; Restatement of the Law Governing Lawyers §124 and Freivogel on Conflicts, Changing Firms-Screening- Part I available at *www.freivogelonconflicts.com/changingfirmsscreeningparti.html*

petroleum products from a Texaco-brand service station and by the disposal practices followed by Texaco, the service station operator and the previous owner of Plaintiffs' property and the adjoining property on which the Texaco station was built. Plaintiffs are seeking to recover economic and environmental damages and allege causes of action for negligence, gross negligence, trespass, nuisance, strict liability, negligence per se, misrepresentation, fraud and fraudulent concealment. Texaco filed a motion to disqualify Plaintiffs' attorney, Ronald Secrest and the firm of Beck, Redden & Secrest, alleging that Mr. Secrest and the name partners of the firm formerly practiced with the firm of Fulbright & Jaworski which was the long-time counsel to Texaco and its related, affiliated and subsidiary companies. Between 1985 and 1992, during the tenure of Mr. Secrest and the other named partners of Beck, Redden & Secrest at Fulbright & Jaworski, Fulbright & Jaworski represented Texaco in no fewer than 106 litigation matters and of those 106 matters, 9 cases specifically dealt with environmental contamination and property damages. As counsel for Texaco and many of its affiliated companies, Fulbright & Jaworski's partners and associates would have participated in multiple negotiations and legal consultations requiring access to privileged and confidential information.

While he was a Fulbright & Jaworski partner, Mr. Secrest participated in defending Texaco in another environmental contamination lawsuit—David M. Cummings, et al. v. Texaco Chemical Co., et al. in the Federal District Court of the Eastern District of Texas. In Cummings, the plaintiffs alleged that Texaco and others polluted the plaintiffs' land with leaking and/or improper disposal of petroleum by-products, chemicals and hazardous wastes. In this case, the Plaintiffs allege that Texaco and others polluted their land by improperly disposing and handling of certain battery cases which contained lead, and petroleum products which leaked from underground storage tanks. Plaintiffs allege that the materials migrated into and contaminated their land from the adjoining property. The causes of action alleged in Cummings, as in this one, included trespass, negligence, nuisance, strict liability and negligence per se. [footnote omitted] The trial judge denied the motion to disqualify.

Texaco argues that the trial judge abused his discretion when he denied the motion to disqualify. We agree.

Rule 1.09(a) states in pertinent part that "[w]ithout prior consent, a lawyer who personally has formerly represented a client in a matter shall not thereafter represent another person in a matter adverse to the former client ... if it is the same or a substantially related matter." Rule 1.09(b) states that "[e]xcept to the extent authorized by Rule 1.10 [concerning successive government and private employment], when lawyers are or have become members of or associated with a firm, none of them shall knowingly represent a client if any one of them practicing alone would be prohibited from doing so by paragraph (a) [of Rule 1.09]."

Relators are required to "prove the existence of a prior attorney-client relationship in which the factual matters involved were so related to the facts in the pending litigation that it creates a genuine threat that confidences revealed to his former counsel will be divulged to his present adversary." *NCNB Texas National Bank v. Coker,* 765 S.W.2d 398, 400 (Tex.1989). The Plaintiffs' allegations in this case involve similar liability issues, similar scientific issues, and similar defenses and strategies as were present in Cummings. The factual matters involved in Cummings appear to be so related to the facts in this case "that it creates a genuine threat that confidences revealed to his former counsel will be divulged to his present adversary." Although we do not presume that Mr. Secrest has revealed confidential information of Texaco to his present client, he should be disqualified from further representation in the pending litigation. *See NCNB Texas National Bank v. Coker,* 765 S.W.2d at 400. Consequently, the trial judge abused his discretion when he denied Texaco's motion to disqualify concerning Mr. Secrest. In addition, since Mr. Secrest is disqualified, the entire firm of Beck, Redden & Secrest is also disqualified. *See* Rule 1.09(b) ("when lawyers are or have become members of or associated with a firm, none of them shall knowingly represent a client if any one of them practicing alone would be prohibited from doing so...."). Consequently, the trial judge abused his discretion when he denied Texaco's motion to disqualify.

Pursuant to Rule 122 of the Texas Rules of Appellate Procedure, without hearing oral argument, a majority of the court conditionally grants the writ of mandamus. The writ will issue only if the trial judge refuses to act in accordance with this opinion.

United States of America v. Daniels
163 F. Supp. 2d 1288 (D.Kan., 2001)

… On February 14, 2001, a grand jury returned a first superseding indictment which charges defendant with 36 counts of health care fraud in violation of 18 U.S.C. § 1346, seven counts of mail fraud in violation of 18 U.S.C. § 1341 and four counts of perjury in violation of 18 U.S.C. § 1623(a). …

Several of the victims identified in the indictment have filed medical malpractice suits against defendant. The law firm of Logan & Logan represents defendant in a number of these suits. On August 28, 2001, the Logan & Logan law firm entered its appearance in this action. Mr. Bath and Mr. Morris remain as counsel for defendant. The government argues that the Logan & Logan law firm may have a conflict of interest because defendant's malpractice insurance carrier is paying its legal fees.

Analysis

Rule 1.7(b) of the Kansas Rules of Professional Conduct provides that "[a] lawyer shall not represent a client if the representation of that client may be materially limited by the lawyer's responsibilities to another client or to a third person, or by the lawyer's own interests, unless: (1) the lawyer reasonably believes the representation will not be adversely affected; and (2) the client consents after consultation." An actual conflict of interest results if counsel is "forced to make choices advancing other interests to the detriment of his client."

Here, the dangers ordinarily present with a third-party fee arrangement are significantly mitigated by two factors. First, in addition to Logan & Logan, defendant is represented by two capable and experienced criminal defense attorneys who are not hindered by any actual or potential conflict. During the case, defendant may consult these independent attorneys regarding any concern he may have about the advice of Logan & Logan or whether a potential criminal defense strategy is consistent with coverage for any adverse judgments in the civil actions. The government has not shown that the same scrutiny of third-party fee arrangements applies where a defendant is represented by two additional law firms which defendant has personally retained and for whose services he is personally responsible. Second, the third party in this case is an insurance company, not a co-defendant or an anonymous leader of a criminal enterprise.

Pursuant to established insurance law principles, insurance companies often hire independent counsel to represent an insured while reserving the right to later contest coverage. In such circumstances, retained counsel owe their duty of loyalty to the insured, not the insurance carrier. Likewise, the conflicts rules in the Model Rules of Professional Conduct are based on the principle that loyalty is an essential element in the lawyer's relationship to a client. See Comment to Rule 1.7 of the Model Rules. In contrast to a co-defendant or an uncharged leader of a criminal enterprise who may not understand the ethical obligations of retained counsel, an insurance carrier necessarily understands that retained counsel owes its duty of loyalty to the defendant, not the insurance carrier who pays them. Likewise, the Logan & Logan law firm has evinced a clear understanding of its ethical obligation to defendant and has articulated in no uncertain terms its willingness and ability to discharge that obligation. Based on the Court's *in camera* review, the Court finds that the third-party fee arrangement in this case does not create a conflict, or a likelihood of a potential conflict, for the Logan & Logan firm.

This case presents a slightly different wrinkle because the insurance carrier is not obligated to provide Dr. Daniels counsel in this matter. Because counsel's duty of loyalty is to Dr. Daniels, not the insurance carrier, the Court finds that the voluntary nature of the payments is not material to the conflicts determination. In the civil context, insurance companies often provide a defense (at least initially) while contesting an obligation to defend or indemnify an insured. Even in such "voluntary" payment situations, counsel retained by the insurance carrier owes their duty of loyalty to the insured.

The government suggests that Logan & Logan may be in a "conflicts dilemma" because through the civil suits, it has access to information which it would not have in the criminal case absent a Court order under Rule 17(c), Fed.R.Crim.P., and which it could use in the criminal case only by violating the limited authorizations and releases provided by the civil plaintiffs. Attorneys are often faced with similar decisions. For example, the Court may rule that certain topics (though favorable to the attorney's client) are inadmissible. The attorney, armed with knowledge of the inadmissible information, must conduct his examination so that he avoids the excluded topics. The government does not explain how such "dilemmas" present ethical conflicts. If Logan & Logan is prohibited from presenting certain information because of the limited releases in the civil cases or because such information is irrelevant (issues which the Court need not decide at this stage), its attorneys will have to abide by that ruling just as any other attorney. The fact that Logan & Logan represents defendant in the civil actions does not change the analysis. The issue is an evidentiary one, not an ethical one.

In sum, the Court finds that Logan & Logan's representation of Dr. Daniels does not constitute an actual conflict of interest. Logan & Logan and defendant do not have inconsistent interests.

Even if a conflict of interest existed by virtue of the insurance carrier's payment of fees for Logan & Logan, the firm may still represent defendant because (1) counsel reasonably believes (as does the Court) that the representation will not be adversely affected by any potential conflict and (2) defendant has knowingly and voluntarily consented after consultation with independent counsel. See Rule 1.7(b) of the Model Rules of Professional Conduct.

… Based on the Court's *in camera* review of the documents submitted by defendant and his counsel, the Court finds that no actual or potential conflict arises from Logan & Logan's representation of defendant in this matter. To the extent any such conflict might arguably exist, defendant has knowingly and voluntarily consented to Logan & Logan's representation after consultation with independent counsel.

In the Matter of James V. Tsoutsouris
748 N.E.2d 856 (Ind. 2001)

In disciplinary hearing, the Supreme Court held that: (1) sexual relationship with client was misconduct, and (2) such misconduct warranted 30 day suspension.

The respondent, James V. Tsoutsouris, engaged in a sexual relationship with his client while he was representing her in a dissolution matter. He claims such a relationship was not improper. Alternatively, he argues that even if it were, it merits only a private reprimand. We disagree and suspend him from the practice of law in Indiana for 30 days.

Within that review framework, we now find that a client hired the respondent in 1994 to represent her in a child support modification action filed by her first husband. The client paid the respondent a total fee of $350. While that child support matter was pending, the client also hired the respondent to represent her in a dissolution action against her second husband.

While the respondent was representing the client in the fall of 1994, the respondent and the client began dating and engaged in consensual sexual relations several times. The respondent did not inform the client how a sexual relationship between them might impact his professional duties to her or otherwise affect their attorney/client relationship.

The respondent ended the sexual relationship a few weeks after it began in 1994. The client hired the respondent for a third legal matter in 1996. In 1997, the client sought psychological treatment. One of the subjects discussed during that treatment was her personal relationship with the respondent three years earlier.

The respondent contends his consensual sexual relationship with his client during his representation of her does not violate the *Rules of Professional Conduct*. He bases that argument on the lack of evidence establishing that his sexual relationship with the client impaired his ability to represent the client effectively. The respondent contends that a sexual relationship between attorney and client in Indiana is professional misconduct only when it affects the quality of the attorney's representation of the client. The respondent also suggests that Indiana law in 1994 was ambiguous with respect to the impropriety of sexual relations between attorney and client. Therefore, he argues a finding of misconduct would be inappropriate because he was unaware of his obligations to avoid sexual contact with his client at the time of such contact.

Rule 1.7(b) prohibits representation of a client if the representation "may be materially limited ... by the lawyer's own interests." Although the rule contains general exceptions in instances where the lawyer reasonably believes that the representation will not be adversely affected and the client consents after consultation [*see* Prof. Cond. R. 1.7(b)(1) and (2)], these exceptions will not generally avail when the "lawyer's own interests" at issue are those related to a lawyer/client sexual relationship. In effect, the respondent argues that sexual relationships between lawyers and clients ought to be authorized unless there is evidence of impaired representation. We decline to adopt that position.

Twenty-five years ago this Court suspended a lawyer for sexual misconduct with clients and warned of the professional conflicts such intimate associations create. In a subsequent case involving the same attorney accused of similar misconduct, this Court ruled that the intermeshing of a lawyer's professional duties with the lawyer's personal sexual interests creates a situation where "the exercise of professional judgment on behalf of a client would be affected by personal interests" in violation of Rule 5–101(A).

We believe the better practice is to avoid all sexual contact with clients during the representation. In their professional capacity, lawyers are expected to provide emotionally detached, objective analysis of legal problems and issues for clients who may be embroiled in sensitive or difficult matters. Clients, especially those who are troubled or emotionally fragile, often place a great deal of trust in the lawyer and rely heavily on his or her agreement to provide professional assistance. Unfortunately, the lawyer's position of trust may provide opportunity to manipulate the client for the lawyer's sexual benefit. Where a lawyer permits or encourages a sexual relationship to form with a client, that trust is betrayed and the stage is set for continued unfair exploitation of the lawyer's fiduciary position. Additionally, the lawyer's ability to represent effectively the client may be impaired. Objective detachment, essential for clear and reasoned analysis of issues and independent professional judgment, may be lost.

We hold that the respondent violated Prof.Cond.R. 1.7(b) and prejudiced the administration of justice in violation of Prof.Cond.R. 8.4(d).

Given our finding of misconduct, we must determine an appropriate sanction. In doing so, we consider the misconduct, the respondent's state of mind underlying the misconduct, the duty of this court to preserve the integrity of the profession, the risk to the public in allowing the respondent to continue in practice, and any mitigating or aggravating factors. As a mitigating factor only, we find no evidence that the respondent's sexual relationship with his client actually impaired his representation of her. In fact, the client hired the respondent to handle another legal matter for her after the sexual relationship ended but before disciplinary charges were filed against the respondent. Moreover, the respondent has not been disciplined previously during his 33 years of practicing law. Given these mitigating factors, we conclude a 30–day suspension from the practice of law is warranted. ...

****

Note: While the ethics rules appear intrusive into the actions of consenting adults, bar associations and courts have routinely recognized that certain sexual relationships between the lawyer and client are particularly troublesome and should be subject to discipline.   The rule especially protects the vulnerable client.   In one case, *Oklahoma Bar Association v. Anderson* (OK, 2005) 109 P.3d 326, 331) the court found that the sexual relationship was prejudicial to the administration of justice. [53]

ABA Formal Ethics Opinion No. 92-364 gives other examples of clients that have retained a lawyer in a time of crisis, including a criminal client, probate client or immigration client.

Attorney Grievance Commission Of Maryland v. Stein
373 Md. 531, 819 A 2d 372 (2003)

Charles F. Stein, III, respondent, drafted a will for his client providing a substantial gift to himself where the client did not have the benefit of independent counsel in relation to the gift. Respondent engaged in an impermissible conflict of interest and violated Rule 1.8(c). The only real issue before this Court is the appropriate sanction to be imposed.

The Attorney Grievance Commission, acting through Bar Counsel, filed a petition with this Court for disciplinary action against respondent alleging a violation of the Maryland Rules of Professional Conduct. The Commission charged respondent with violating Rule 1.8(c). We referred the matter to Judge Susan Souder of the Circuit Court for Baltimore County to make findings of fact and proposed conclusions of law.

Judge Souder held a hearing in the Circuit Court for Baltimore County. The parties entered into a stipulation of facts and based upon those stipulated facts, the hearing court entered its ruling. …

Judge Souder concluded that respondent violated Rule 1.8(c). The hearing court noted that respondent prepared a will for his client, Mrs. Lindinger, to whom he was not related. The will provided a substantial gift from the client to respondent, and the client was not represented by independent counsel in connection with the gift. Judge Souder also found that there was no indication that any improper influence or duress was brought to bear upon the client by respondent or anyone else and that respondent had suggested to his client many other alternative legatees for the gift.

No exceptions were taken by either party to the hearing court's ruling. The dispute between Bar Counsel and respondent centers upon the sanction to be imposed in this case. Respondent concedes the violation of Rule 1.8(c) but argues that the appropriate sanction is a reprimand. On the other hand, Bar Counsel recommends an indefinite suspension, with

---

[53] See Wendy Patrick Mazzarella, How Close Can You Get to Your Client?, 2009, published on line at California Bar Journal, July 2014 available at http://apps.calbar.ca.gov/mcleselfstudy/mcle_home.aspx?testID=12

respondent's right to seek reinstatement conditioned upon his renunciation of any interest in the residuary bequest left to him in the will he prepared for his client.

The primary purpose in imposing discipline on an attorney for violation of the Rules of Professional Conduct is not to punish the lawyer but rather to protect the public and the public's confidence in the legal profession. *Attorney Grievance Comm'n v. Powell,* 369 Md. 462, 474, 800 A.2d 782, 789 (2002). Disciplinary proceedings also are aimed at deterring other lawyers from engaging in similar conduct. *Id.* at 474-75, 800 A.2d at 789. The purpose, however, "is not to punish the lawyer or to provide a basis upon which to impose civil liability." *Attorney Grievance Comm'n v. Monfried,* 368 Md. 373, 394, 794 A.2d 92, 104 (2002). When this Court imposes a sanction, it protects the public interest "because it demonstrates to members of the legal profession the type of conduct which will not be tolerated." *Attorney Grievance Comm'n v. Mooney,* 359 Md. 56, 96, 753 A.2d 17, 38 (2000). Finally, the public is protected when sanctions are imposed that are commensurate with the nature and gravity of the violations and the intent with which they were committed. *Attorney Grievance Comm'n v. Awuah,* 346 Md. 420, 435, 697 A.2d 446, 454 (1997).

We have no doubt that respondent violated Rule 1.8(c), which provides that a lawyer shall not prepare an instrument, including a testamentary gift, giving the lawyer any substantial gift from a client except where the lawyer is related to the client or where the client is represented by independent counsel. The Rule is mandatory and contains no provision for waiver of the requirement to consult with independent counsel. The independent counsel required by the Rule must be truly independent-the requirement of the Rule may not be satisfied by consultation with an attorney who is a partner of, shares space with, or is a close associate of the attorney-drafter.

Discipline for violation of Rule 1.8(c) is a question of first impression for this Court. We view the violation as a most serious one. There are many potential dangers inherent in an attorney drafting a will in which he or she is the beneficiary. Conflict of interest, the attorney's incompetency to testify because of a transaction with the deceased, the attorney's ability to influence the testator, the possible jeopardy to probate of the entire will if its admission is contested, the possible harm to other beneficiaries and the undermining of the public trust and confidence in the legal profession are some of the dangers. The Supreme Court of Ohio in *Disciplinary Counsel v. Galinas,* 76 Ohio St.3d 87, 666 N.E.2d 1083 (1996) stated:

> "A client's dependence upon, and trust in, his attorney's skill, disinterested advice, and ethical conduct exceeds the trust and confidence found in most fiduciary relationships. Seldom is the client's dependence upon, and trust in, his attorney greater than when, contemplating his own mortality, he seeks the attorney's advice, guidance, and drafting skill in the preparation of a will to dispose of his estate after death. These consultations are often among the most private to take place between an attorney and his client. The client is dealing with his innermost thoughts and feelings, which he may not wish to share with his spouse, children and other next of kin.

"[E]ven with the best intentions, an attorney risks the possibility of exploiting his client when their interests become so intertwined. We therefore reconsidered the ethical propriety of the situation and resolved that these risks are untenable."

Respondent suggests that the appropriate sanction is a reprimand. In mitigation, he argues that he was not aware of the specific rule in question; that he is sixty-nine years of age and was admitted to the Bar in 1961; that he is presently semi-retired; and that he has had no prior disciplinary sanction imposed against him. Further, he concludes that there was no undue influence imposed upon the client and that the will reflects her true intent.

Respondent's defense of ignorance of the rule is no defense at all. Lawyers admitted to practice in this State are deemed to know the Rules of Professional Conduct and have the obligation to act in conformity with those standards as a requirement to practice law.

Respondent acknowledges that the idea to grant him a portion of the residuary was his suggestion. Respondent stood to gain $116,988.79 from the estate, a not insubstantial amount. Respondent knew, or should have known, that drafting a will in which he was named a beneficiary created an obvious and facial conflict of interest. He appeared to recognize the conflict of interest in recommending that Mrs. Lindinger consult with other counsel, albeit not independent counsel outside respondent's firm. When she did not, he proceeded to draft the will. Respondent acted with conscious awareness of the nature of his conduct.

We find an indefinite suspension is warranted in this case. While respondent's lack of prior ethical violations is a mitigating factor, it does not justify a reprimand. As stated above, we consider a violation of Rule 1.8(c) to be most serious. Respondent's conduct undermines the public confidence in the legal profession in a particularly egregious manner.

In addition to an indefinite suspension, Bar Counsel urges us to require as a condition of reinstatement that respondent disclaim his interest in Mrs. Lindinger's estate. Bar Counsel has not directed us to any case in the country that has required an attorney as a condition of reinstatement or as a condition to continue in practice to return money received from an estate or to renounce or disclaim a bequest. Under the circumstances presented in this case, we decline to do so.

Indefinite suspension is the appropriate sanction. ...

****

Questions:

1. Lawyer represents a business entity that is comprised of two persons, one of whom is the Lawyer's uncle. The relationship and the business go well for more than ten years before the two parties decide to go their separate ways, each believing the other has caused them and the business harm. Lawyer decides that he will represent his Uncle because he knows that the acts and decisions of the business partner were principally responsible for

the harm. If lawyer represents Uncle, will he be subject to discipline under the model rules?

2. Potential Client approaches you about representing her in a lawsuit against Orange Computers. You are able to determine that the likelihood of recovery is good. Based on the estimated recovery, your contingent attorney fee will be at least $400,000. During your conflicts check, you discover that your family limited partnership (FLP) owns less than 500 of the outstanding shares of Orange Corporation, which represents less than ½ of 1 percent. You are a limited partner in the FLP. May you represent Potential Client without violating the ABA model rules of professional conduct?

3. Attorney and Client have become friends over the course of their ten-year professional relationship. Client approaches Attorney about the two of them investing in a commercial real estate multi use development. Preliminary numbers show a respectable return on investment and Attorney is very interested in participating as an investor. May the Attorney engage in the business relationship with Client?

4. An attorney is general counsel for a publicly traded corporation. Plaintiffs sued the corporation alleging they had been harmed by the corporation's negligence in disposing of toxic waste materials. The plaintiffs alleged that the corporation was guilty of various criminal and civil acts in violation of its state charter. The chairman of the board of the corporation believes that the lawsuit is ill-advised and that the plaintiffs lack standing to charge the corporation with ultra vires acts. However, the defendant's motion to dismiss was denied. Subsequent motions for summary judgment and judgment as a matter of law were also denied. Thereafter, Attorney strongly urged the corporation to settle the case to avoid final judgment that could order damages in the millions of dollars against the corporation. Corporation refused to settle under any conditions because it believes the trial judge is wrong and, if necessary, it will take its case to the appellate courts. Attorney steadfastly believes that the case should be settled and that the corporation's strategy is detrimental to the corporation. Will Attorney be required to withdraw under the model rules of professional conduct?

****

The Impaired Client

Rules of conduct often address the lawyer's ethical role when representing an impaired client. A client is considered impaired if they have not reached the age of majority and have not been emancipated, or they suffer a mental or physical incapacity that renders them unable to understand or make decisions affecting their representation. Such impairment could include drug or alcohol addiction, mental disease or psychiatric disorder, or age including geriatrics related impairment.

In any circumstance the rules provide that the lawyer is required to represent the interests of the client.[54] Specifically, the model rules provide that the lawyer's duty is to maintain a normal

---

[54] See Timothy David Edwards, The Lawyer as Counselor Representing Impaired Client, American Bar Association, GPSolo, October/November 2004 available at http://www.americanbar.org/newsletter/publications/gp_solo_magazine_home/gp_solo_magazine_index/lawyercou

relationship with the client.[55] This requires the lawyer to permit the client to make decisions and manage his affairs as any other client would.[56] What is normal may be subject to various interpretations, but, in any event, when the client's dimished capacity makes it impossible to maintain an ordinary or normal relationship, the attorney continues to have a duty to the client. In order to meet her obligations the lawyer, when the lawyer reasonably believes the client is at risk of substantial physical, financial or other harm due to the client's incapacity, is expected to take reasonable measures to protect the client's interests.[57]

Safekeeping Client's Property

The lawyer has an ethical responsibility to maintain certain client property during the course of and even after representation. The model rules provide that the lawyer's responsibility is to segregate the client's property from her own.[58] A client's property may consist of tangible and intangible goods. Much of the focus of model rule 1.15 is on client funds and what an attorney must do to comply with her obligations under the rule. But client property may also consist of files, papers, documents and other things that the client has given to the lawyer for safe keeping.

Client Funds

Bar associations and their members will generally not tolerate an attorney misusing, misapplying or otherwise mishandling client funds. Money that the client gives the lawyer as advances on attorney fees or for payment of expenses belong to the client. When the attorney receives client funds, (s)he has an obligation to deposit those funds in a client trust account. The client trust account must be segregated from the attorney's operations, professional and personal accounts. The lawyer must refrain from using funds in the client trust account for any reason other than the specific purpose of the funds.

A lawyer may not borrow money from the client trust fund for any reason. However, an attorney who has been paid a retainer and deposited those funds in the client trust is eligible to pay those funds out to himself once the work for which the payment is made is completed. Such disbursements may be made in accordance with the retainer agreement. In no event, may an attorney take funds from the client trust account to pay business or personal expenses on the theory that the fees will be earned in the future. An attorney who uses the client's funds inappropriately may be guilty of theft.

On the other hand, once the characterization of the funds changes from client property to attorney property, as is the case when the fee is earned, the attorney fee must be removed from the client trust. Otherwise, the retention of the funds in the client trust account constitutes commingling and violates the rules of ethics.

---

nselor.html discussing the expanded role of the lawyer who represents the impaired client. Last visited June 11, 2014.
[55] ABA Model Rules of Professional Conduct [1.14a]
[56] ABA Model Rules of Professional Conduct [1.14a] comment [1]
[57] ABA Model Rules of Professional Conduct [1.14b] permitting the attorney to consult with appropriate persons other than the client in order to protect the client as well as seeking the appointment of a guardian, conservator or guardian ad litem.
[58] ABA Model Rules of Professional Conduct [1.15]

Proof of safekeeping

Attorneys are required to maintain records of account for the client for a period of time after the representation is terminated.[59] The attorney is expected to maintain detailed records of account that comply with generally accepted accounting practices. While many law firms may hire financial personnel, including bookkeepers, it is better practice for the lawyer not to permit non-lawyers signing authority on any client account.

Non-monetary property

One of the most contentious points for lawyers and their clients is who owns the file. The general rule is that the lawyer is the representative of the client and therefore work produced, including client files, belong to the client.[60] This means that documents, information as well as tangible property that the client gives to the lawyer belong to the client. However, whether the lawyer's work product belongs to the client depends on the jurisdiction involved. The Restatement of the Law Governing Lawyers states that the client is entitled to the entire file, including "such original and copies of other documents possessed by the lawyer relating to the representation as the *client or former client reasonably needs.*"[61]*emphasis added.*

The Restatement also provides that the primary exception that allows a lawyer to refuse disclosure of documents is those created and retained only for internal review. Moreover, the attorney is not permitted to provide files to a client that would compromise important interests of other clients.[62]

Non-monetary property consists of more than files and work product. For example, material that the lawyer retrieves from third parties during the representation as well as property the client delivers to the lawyer to keep from third parties is generally treated as property belonging to the client.

The People of the State of Colorado v. Clyne
945 P. 2d 1386, 97 CJ C.A.R. 2405 (1997)
Supreme Court of Colorado, En Banc.

Attorney discipline proceeding was brought. The Supreme Court held that pursuant to attorney's conditional admission and consent, disbarment was warranted for misconduct which included misappropriation of client funds. So ordered.

---

[59] The ABA Model Rules require that the records be maintained for five years after the representation terminates. This period may differ between states.
[60] See *Resolution Trust Corp v. H----------, P.C.*, 128 F.R.D. 647 (N.D. Tex. 1989)
[61] Restatement (Third) of the Law Governing Lawyers §46(3)
[62] ABA Model Rules of Professional Conduct, Rule 1.7 Comments [6]

The parties in this lawyer discipline case entered into a stipulation, agreement, and conditional admission of misconduct pursuant to C.R.C.P. 241.18. In the conditional admission, the respondent consented to disbarment. An inquiry panel of the supreme court grievance committee approved the conditional admission and recommended that the respondent be disbarred. We accept the conditional admission and the inquiry panel's recommendation.

The respondent was licensed to practice law in this state in 1980. The conditional admission details the respondent's actions in numerous matters. We here only summarize the contents of the conditional admission for the purpose of this opinion and order.

A. The Brenner Matter

The respondent represented Charles Brenner in a personal injury case in which Brenner was injured in an automobile accident. After recovering settlements from the insurer of the other automobile, and from underinsured motor vehicle coverage, and deducting the applicable contingent fees and paying the client the balance, the respondent settled the PIP benefits claim for $25,000. Brenner was supposed to receive $16,666.67 from this settlement, but in December of 1993 the respondent misappropriated the funds for his personal and business use. The respondent's trust account records disclose that the respondent dissipated the entire $16,666.67.

During the same time period, he also represented Brenner in matters involving a recreational vehicle (RV) park and a social security case. On or about August 13, 1993, Brenner paid the respondent $1,500 to represent him in the RV case. The respondent improperly deposited this advance fee into his operating account rather than his trust account. In the social security case, the respondent failed to timely file an appeal, did not notify Brenner of his failure to do so, and did not withdraw.

B. The Shippy and Boren Matters

In April 1995, Charlotte Shippy and Gloria Boren hired the respondent to assist an individual in his efforts to reduce his prison sentence. The respondent agreed to file a motion for reconsideration of the sentence and told them that if that did not succeed he would appeal the matter to the state supreme court if necessary. On May 30, 1995, Boren paid the respondent $2,500 as an advance fee, and Shippy signed an hourly fee agreement.

In August or September 1995, Shippy and Boren discovered that the respondent had closed his law office in Durango. After they filed a request for investigation with the Office of Disciplinary Counsel in November, the respondent sent them a letter in December 1995 indicating that personal problems had caused him to close his office. The respondent also returned Boren's $2,500 advance fee and the documents provided to him.

C. Insufficient Funds Checks

On June 6, 1995, the local district attorney asked the respondent to pay his outstanding balance of $101.25 for copies of discovery documents. On August 1, 1995, the district attorney's office received the respondent's check in the proper amount. The check was returned on two occasions for insufficient funds. An investigation of the respondent's operating account by the Office of Disciplinary Counsel revealed that between November 1994 and September 1995, the respondent had 105 checks returned for insufficient funds, most of which the bank eventually honored.

D. The Caudill Matter

On July 13, 1995, the respondent agreed to represent Marshall A. Caudill on a misdemeanor charge for a flat fee of $400. Unable to reach the respondent after that date, Caudill was forced to appear in court by himself. The respondent never entered an appearance on behalf of Caudill, although he cashed Caudill's $400 check on July 13, knowing that he intended to close his law office the next day.

E. Danny L. Nielson, D.C.

Dr. Nielson, an Arizona chiropractor, provided treatment to four injured members of the Sirimarco family following an automobile accident. In July and August 1993, the Sirimarcos signed agreements with Dr. Nielson and the respondent authorizing the respondent to pay Dr. Nielson's bills directly and to withhold such sums from any settlement or judgment obtained on their behalf.

Dr. Nielson, whose outstanding medical bills for the Sirimarcos totaled $8,344, was unable to contact either the respondent or the Sirimarcos. He discovered in August 1995 that the insurer had settled the Sirimarcos' claims the preceding February for an amount exceeding $20,000.

F. The State Grievance Board

A client retained the respondent in February 1994 to file a complaint with the state grievance board concerning one or more members of the local mental health community. After months of trying unsuccessfully to reach the respondent, the client discharged the respondent by letter dated November 23, 1994, and asked for the return of his file. On December 2, 1994, however, the two met and the respondent indicated that he would file the complaint without charge to the client. On July 17, 1995, the client learned from the state grievance board that the respondent had never filed the complaint. The client then sent the respondent a second termination letter on July 20, 1995, and requested return of all of his documents. The respondent had not returned the documents as of the date of the conditional admission in this case.

G. Disciplinary Counsel

During the course of the investigation of the respondent's trust account, the investigative counsel for the Office of Disciplinary Counsel discovered that on numerous occasions between 1992 and 1995 the respondent issued checks drawn on his trust account for personal expenses and law office operating expenses; and that he commingled earned and unearned fees received from clients as well.

H. The Vigil Matter

In December 1994, Elroy A. Vigil hired the respondent to represent him on criminal charges in La Plata County. Vigil paid the respondent a $1,000 flat fee. After the respondent made one or two court appearances, Vigil learned in March or April 1996, that the respondent's telephone had been disconnected and his law office closed.

The respondent has agreed to disbarment. The inquiry panel recommended disbarment. We have previously found disbarment appropriate in similar cases when a lawyer accepts fees from clients, fails to perform legal services, and then effectively abandons the clients, thereby misappropriating the unearned fees.

It is hereby ordered that Mark Raymond Clyne be disbarred and that his name be stricken from the list of attorneys authorized to practice before this court, effective thirty days after the announcement of this opinion. Prior to and as a condition of any petition for readmission, the respondent must demonstrate that he has made full restitution to all parties.

****

Question:

In determining the appropriate sanction for violating a rule of professional conduct, a court will look at extenuating circumstances including Respondent's remorse and commitment to righting the wrongs. Should service in the military constitute a mitigating factor? See Cincinnati Bar Association v Britt.[63]

****

Resolution Trust Corp. v. H----, P.C.
128 F.R.D. 647 (U. S. D. C., N.D. Texas-Dallas Division, 1989)

... This case began when Plaintiff requested a temporary restraining order against Defendant, asserting that H—— might be altering documents in its files. Upon the transfer of the files to Defendant's counsel's offices, that request was dropped. However, the parties could not agree on access to or the ultimate ownership of the files, so Plaintiff again requested the Court to require the Defendant to turn over the files. A hearing was held on September 27, 1989. The Court then entered an interim Order which:

1. required Defendant to turn over to Plaintiff all original and duplicate original documents;
2. prohibited anyone from removing or altering any documents in the files;
3. permitted Defendant to withhold from Plaintiff attorneys' notes and legal memoranda contained in the files, and
4. required the parties to submit briefs on the issue of the ownership of the files.

After reviewing the briefs and the relevant case law, the Court has determined, for the reasons set forth below, that the entire contents of the files belong to Plaintiff.

---

[63] 133 Ohio St.3d 217 (2012)

The starting point for the analysis is, of course, Texas law. The Texas State Bar rules provide that a lawyer must "promptly pay or deliver to the client as requested by a client, the funds, securities, or other properties in the possession of the lawyer which the client is entitled to receive." DR 9–102(B)(4). Both the Texas Bar and the Houston Court of Civil Appeals have held that this rule applies to documents in an attorney's files. [citation omitted]

... Defendant has a number of objections. First, Defendant argues that this rule applies only to materials that the client had previously given to the attorney. Documents created by the attorney are not the client's property, according to Defendant, and thus do not fall within the rule.

Second, Defendant distinguishes the instant suit, asserting that it already turned over virtually the entire contents of the files to Caprock during the ordinary course of its representation of Caprock. For example, H—— gave Caprock copies of all transaction-oriented documents and records created by the firm, such as loan papers. Defendant insists that Plaintiff's request is duplicative, since Plaintiff ought to have nearly all of the material requested in its own files. Further, Defendant argues that the few materials which it acknowledges Plaintiff does not possess—attorneys' notes and legal memoranda—are "the personal property of the individual attorneys who drafted and prepared documents." Defendant argued at the hearing that such material may be protected by the work product doctrine and/or the attorney-client privilege.

Plaintiff admits none of these defenses and asserts title to the entire contents of the files. Both parties cite *Nolan v. Foreman,* 665 F.2d 738, *reh'g denied,* 671 F.2d 1380 (5th Cir.1982), in support of their respective positions. In that case the Fifth Circuit stated that "a client has the right to return of his papers on request." *Id.* at 742, *citing Hebisen v. State, supra,* at 868. While the support this case provides for Plaintiff's argument is obvious, Defendant finely parses the statement to find support for its position. Defendant argues that the use of the word "return," as opposed to "turn over," implies that the Fifth Circuit was only referring to those papers given by the client to the attorney for use during his representation. Thus, the client was only entitled to the "return" of his previously-owned documents.

This is a creative reading of the case, but it is unpersuasive, for the same reason that the Texas Bar Rule does not decide the issue. Neither the Fifth Circuit nor the Texas Bar has defined precisely *which* materials in the file belong to the client. If, as is quite possible, the Fifth Circuit believed that the entire file belonged to the client, then the use of the word "return" only reflects the Circuit's underlying assumption that every document in the entire file became the client's property as soon as each document was created. The parties admitted at the hearing the virtually universal practice of former attorneys transferring the entire client file to new counsel. In such cases, former attorneys do not withhold anything from the file, and any materials which they wish to keep are copied at their own expense.

Defendant concedes this practice, but asserts that this rule only applies when the file is to be turned over to another attorney and not to the client. Alternatively, Defendant argues that since this representation terminated amidst charges of misconduct by the Plaintiff against Defendant, Defendant has a right to withhold the documents in anticipation of litigation over its conduct.

The first argument, that the practice only applies when a file is turned over to another attorney, is contrary to the fiduciary and agency nature of the relationship between a client and an attorney. The relationship between a client and an attorney has been held by Texas courts to be one of "[t]he most abundant good faith; absolute and perfect candor or *openness* and honesty; the *absence of any concealment* or deception, however slight." ...

The second objection, that this case involves allegations of misconduct by the former client against the former firm, and thus the firm has the right to retain the files in anticipation of litigation, fails for precisely the same reason. So long as an attorney represents his client, he owes that client a fiduciary duty to disclose all information to the client. *See Willis v. Maverick,* 760 S.W.2d 642, 645 (Tex.1988). If conflict develops, either side may terminate the relationship, and upon termination, the client is entitled to the fruits of the attorney's labor until that point. If charges are filed against the firm, the firm may retrieve those documents it feels are relevant to its defense through discovery. But so long as the files were created in the course of the representation of the client, they belong to the client.

Finally, the Court considers the attorney-client privilege and work-product doctrine as reasons or excluding attorneys' notes and legal memoranda. The attorney-client privilege clearly is inapplicable in this situation, since it belongs to the client. *Bearden v. Boone,* 693 S.W.2d 25, 27 (Tex.App.—Austin 1985, no writ). Thus, an attorney may not raise it against his own client.

The work-product doctrine is equally inapplicable. The doctrine protects materials that are not covered by the attorney-client privilege but are prepared in anticipation of litigation and contain material revealing attorney's thoughts or strategies. *Texas Dept. of Mental Health and Mental Retardation v. Davis,* 775 S.W.2d 467, 471 (Tex.App.—Austin 1989, no writ). None of the materials at issue here were prepared in anticipation of litigation, unless H—— claims that it created materials in anticipation of litigation with its own client. Such a statement would be an admission of a breach of the fiduciary duty owed by H—— to Caprock, and it could hardly serve as a basis for this Court to allow H—— to prohibit Plaintiff from obtaining those documents.

More importantly, the protection afforded by the doctrine is for the benefit of the client, and thus cannot be used by his own attorney against him. "[T]he work product doctrine does not apply to the situation in which a client seeks access to documents or other tangible things created or amassed by his attorney during the course of the representation." *Spivey v. Zant,* 683 F.2d 881, 885 (5th Cir.1982).

The one remaining contention is that Defendant already delivered to Caprock, during the course of its representation, virtually all of the documents contained in the current files. Defendant asserts that photocopying the entire file would cost between $70,000 and $80,000, an unfair burden when Plaintiff is simply trying to fill in the gaps in Caprock's own carelessly-kept files.
This argument is a red herring. First, Defendant is not obligated to copy the files, only to turn them over. Second, most, if not all, of the documents in Defendant's files were copied at *Caprock's* expense from the originals given to Caprock. Since the files were paid for by Caprock, they belong to Plaintiff. Any documents Defendant wishes to keep may be copied at its own expense. And while Defendant may anticipate that much of the file will be needed if litigation

over its representation ensues, Defendant is entitled to receive copies of the relevant documents through discovery.

Conclusion

An attorney is hired to represent the interests of his client, and every service provided by the attorney, including the creation of legal memoranda and attorney's notes and the copying of documents, is paid for by the client. To allow the attorney to decide which materials may or may not be revealed to the client from its files would deny the client the full benefit of the services for which he paid, often dearly. Even more important, giving such a power to an attorney would fundamentally undermine the fiduciary nature of the relationship between an attorney and a client. Such an alteration is unwarranted and untenable. "It is a sound public policy which exacts utmost fidelity of attorneys, and that policy should not be weakened by the whittling down process or the adding of numerous exceptions to the rules calling for its application." *Henderson Jp. Shell Oil Co.,* 208 S.W.2d 863, 866 (Tex.), *cert. denied,* 335 U.S. 884, 69 S.Ct. 233, 93 L.Ed. 423 (1948).   Accordingly, Defendant is Ordered to turn over to Plaintiff the entire contents, including previously withheld attorneys' notes and legal memoranda, of all files maintained for Caprock Savings and Loan Association by H—— which are currently in the possession or control of H——, or an agent of the law firm, within 15 days of the date of this Order.

Judy v. Preferred Communication Systems, Inc.
29 A.3d 248 *(Court of Chancery-Delaware, 2011)*

Plaintiff Michael D. Judy moved to enforce a subpoena and compel the production of documents from his former counsel, Potter Anderson & Corroon LLP ("Potter Anderson"). Approximately four months ago, Potter Anderson withdrew from representing Judy for reasons including unpaid bills. Potter Anderson and Judy could not resolve their fee dispute, and Potter Anderson asserted a retaining lien over its files. Judy contends that he needs the documents held by Potter Anderson in order to prepare for trial. I have concluded that under the facts presented, Judy is entitled to the documents he seeks, but only if he first posts security in the amount Potter Anderson has requested, *viz.,* cash in escrow or a secured bond equal to 70% of the firm's outstanding receivable.

I. Factual Background

Judy owns shares of Preferred Communication Systems, Inc. ("Preferred" or the "Company"). Between 1998 and 2000, Preferred obtained licenses to provide wireless telecommunications services in Puerto Rico, the U.S. Virgin Islands, and certain portions of the United States. Over a decade later, Preferred has yet to capitalize on its licenses, and the record reveals significant disputes over whether Charles M. Austin, the Chairman, President and sole director of the Company, breached his fiduciary duties by failing to properly maintain the licenses. At present, the Company is little more than a shell with neither operations nor cash.

A. Potter Anderson Commences Litigation.

In February 2009, Judy formed Preferred Spectrum Investments, LLC ("PSI") as a vehicle for investors in Preferred to seek change at the Company. Judy serves as President of PSI. In May

2009, Judy and PSI retained Potter Anderson to pursue claims against the Company and Austin. Later that month, Potter Anderson served a demand for books and records on the Company pursuant to Section 220 of the General Corporation Law, 8 *Del. C.* § 220. After the Company rejected the demand, Potter Anderson filed suit. In July, Potter Anderson filed a second action seeking to compel a meeting of stockholders pursuant to Section 211 of the General Corporation Law, 8 *Del. C.* § 211. Potter Anderson also filed a plenary action seeking declaratory and injunctive relief against Austin. The three actions were consolidated, and Potter Anderson moved for summary judgment on its claims for relief under Sections 220 and 211. During a hearing on September 29, 2009, Chancellor Chandler granted summary judgment on the Section 220 and Section 211 issues. He ordered production of the books and records and directed that a meeting of stockholders be held on December 9, 2009.

B. The Court Appoints a Receiver.

The December 2009 meeting was not to be. In preparation for the Court-ordered meeting, Preferred produced a list of stockholders to which Judy objected. Potter Anderson then sought the appointment of a receiver to determine which stockholders could vote at the meeting. During a hearing on December 4, 2009, Chancellor Chandler deferred the annual meeting and appointed Richard L. Renck, Esq., as receiver. ...

C. The March 2010 Engagement Letter

By March 2010, Judy and PSI had fallen behind in their payment obligations to Potter Anderson. Facing the prospect of a significant litigation commitment going forward, Potter Anderson asked Judy and PSI to execute an updated and confirmatory engagement letter (the "March 2010 Engagement Letter"). They did. In addition, over the next several months, other members of PSI retained Potter Anderson with respect to their rights vis-à-vis Preferred, and each signed an addendum agreeing to be bound by the March 2010 Engagement Letter.

Between March and April 2010, Judy and other investors in Preferred filed an assortment of objections to the receiver's report. Chancellor Chandler scheduled a three-day trial to resolve the objections for July 6–8, 2010. The parties embarked in earnest on discovery and other pre-trial preparations.

D. Potter Anderson Secures The Disputed Documents.

In April 2010, Potter Anderson served discovery requests on the Company and Austin. Among other things, the requests sought copies of the Company's corporate records. The Company and Austin refused to produce any documents, contending that the receiver had possession of all documents that the Company and Austin intended to produce. In an effort to secure documents from other sources, Potter Anderson moved for commissions to obtain corporate documents from Hallett & Perrin, P.C., the Company's former corporate and securities counsel, and Robert Forrester, its counsel before Hallett & Perrin. The Company and Austin objected to the commissions. The parties crossed swords via motions to compel and for protective order. By letter decision dated June 11, 2010, Chancellor Chandler ordered the Company and Austin to produce the documents and overruled the objections to commissions.

On June 22, 2010, counsel to the Company and Austin advised Potter Anderson that there were original documents responsive to the discovery requests at a storage facility in Texas. Defense counsel suggested that Potter Anderson could look at the materials while in Texas for a previously scheduled deposition or have the documents brought to the deposition site. On June 23, defense counsel made available to Potter Anderson at the deposition location over 35 boxes of original Company documents. Potter Anderson took custody of the documents and shipped them to its Delaware office. None of the documents had been Bates stamped, and Potter Anderson undertook the tasks of processing and reviewing the documents.

In September, the Chancellor advised the parties that he would not proceed with trial until the receiver was paid.

E. Potter Anderson's Payment Problems

By the end of 2010, Judy and PSI had fallen behind by over two months in their payments to Potter Anderson, and the firm anticipated ongoing litigation in 2011. Potter Anderson advised Judy and PSI in writing that it could not continue to provide legal services unless (i) the firm received a substantial payment on the past due amounts, (ii) the clients committed to a payment plan, and (iii) the clients undertook to pay future invoices in a timely manner. After negotiations, Potter Anderson, Judy, and PSI entered into an agreement dated January 7, 2011, pursuant to which Potter Anderson agreed to forego a portion of its outstanding fees, and Judy and PSI agreed to pay off the balance on a specified schedule and satisfy all future invoices within thirty days of receipt (the "January 2011 Agreement").

Based on the January 2011 Agreement, Potter Anderson continued its representation. Unfortunately, although Judy and PSI initially made certain payments, Potter Anderson did not receive any payments after January 2011. In March 2011, in part due to unpaid bills, Potter Anderson moved to withdraw. Chancellor Chandler granted the motion on March 16.

Potter Anderson and its former clients have been unable to resolve their fee dispute. On July 15, 2011, Potter Anderson initiated arbitration proceedings and asserted an attorneys' retaining lien over its files, including the 35 boxes of documents secured through its litigation efforts. On July 22, 2011, Judy served a subpoena on Potter Anderson seeking the original documents that Potter Anderson obtained from the defendants and third parties. Potter Anderson objected to the subpoena, citing its retaining lien. Judy moved to enforce the subpoena and compel the production of documents.

II. Legal Analysis

"An attorney's retaining lien is the right of an attorney to detain possession of his client's property acquired in the course of rendering professional services." *Eagle Poultry Co. v. Camden Fire Ins. Ass'n,* 1963 WL 64648, at *1 (Del.Ch. July 18, 1963). The lien extends to "documents, money or other property in [the attorney's] possession belonging to his client which [the attorney] acquired in the course of his professional relationship." *Royal Ins. Co. v. Simon,* 174 A. 444, 446 (Del.Ch.1934). It is "a common-law lien, which has its origin in the inherent power of courts over the relations between attorneys and their clients." *Everett, Clarke & Benedict v. Alpha Portland Cement Co.*, 225 F. 931, 935 (2d Cir.1915). ...

"Retaining liens are widely accepted in the United States, and have been compared to mechanic's or artisan's liens. Lawyers are merely afforded the same advantage enjoyed by workmen who labor on behalf of others." *Bennett v. NSR, Inc.*, 553 N.E.2d 881, 882 (Ind.Ct.App.1990) (footnote omitted). The Restatement (Second) of Agency treats the attorney's lien as a specific application of the general principle that an agent has a right to retain money, goods, or documents of the principal to secure payment of the agent's compensation....

"The value of the attorney's retaining lien is principally in the leverage which it gives the attorney over a client who fails or refuses to pay for services rendered, through the embarrassment and inconvenience caused the client by withholding papers, documents, and other valuables...." [citation omitted] "While such a lien has no intrinsic value, it is an extremely valuable tool, because of the inconvenience caused to the client by withholding his property. If the client does not need the files' contents, the attorney will probably not be paid through assertion of the lien." [citation omitted). ...

The right of an attorney to assert a retaining lien and inconvenience his former client by keeping his file contrasts sharply with the ethical obligations of an attorney to provide the former client with his file and act reasonably to protect the interests of the former client. Rule 1.16(d) of the Delaware Lawyers' Rules of Professional Conduct provides that [u]pon termination of representation, a lawyer shall take steps to the extent reasonably practicable to protect a client's interests, such as giving reasonable notice to the client, allowing time for employment of other counsel, surrendering papers and property to which the client is entitled and refunding any advance payment of fee or expense that has not been earned or incurred. ... As the United States District Court for the Northern District of Illinois observed when considering a challenge to a retaining lien,

> *We are therefore faced with a direct conflict between two well-established principles: An attorney may hold a client's property under an attorney's retaining lien, but a client should have his property returned to him when his attorney withdraws. Although both principles are well established, neither is absolute. Both are judicial devices, the former for the protection of the attorney, the latter for the protection of the client.* (citation omitted).
>
> *The retaining lien also potentially conflicts with "an equally important third interest—effective judicial administration."*

Both the court and the former client have an obligation to make sure the lawsuit proceeds in a fair and reasonable manner. A disgruntled attorney does not have the right to disrupt a court's calendar and frustrate their former client's chances of success, nor is a disgruntled client justified in not paying an attorney a reasonable fee for services rendered. *Carrizales v. Bd. of Educ.*, 2004 WL 2385028, at *2 (N.D.Ill. Oct. 22, 2004). "The conflict between the withdrawn attorney and the former client should not be allowed to delay the underlying action." *Lucky–Goldstar*, 636 F.Supp. at 1063. At the same time, "[i]n attempting to move the underlying action forward and accommodate these competing interests, the court should not interfere unnecessarily in the dispute between the lawyer and client." *Id.* That dispute should be resolved in the proper forum, which often will not be the court addressing the lien. *See id.* Here, the parties' fee dispute will be resolved in the arbitration that Potter Anderson initiated in July 2011.

Confronted with these competing interests, the vast majority of courts have upheld attorney retaining liens, but crafted a host of bright-line and near bright-line exceptions to their enforcement. The resulting thicket of decisions conflicts on numerous points. A minority of jurisdictions have rejected or dramatically limited the circumstances under which an attorneys' retaining lien can be asserted. Other (and in my view better reasoned) decisions openly recognize the need for balancing. Most prominently, in *Lucky–Goldstar,* the United States District Court for the Northern District of Illinois applied a balancing test using factors identified by the American Bar Association's 256 Standing Committee on Ethics and Professional Responsibility (the "ABA Committee"). *See* 636 F.Supp. at 1063–64. After noting that the ethical rules exhort lawyers to forego their legal right to sue a client for a fee "unless necessary to prevent fraud or gross imposition by the client," the ABA Committee concluded that "the same standard should be applied in determining whether or not to exercise an attorney's lien." *Id.* at 376 (internal quotation marks omitted). The ABA Committee then identified seven factors for a lawyer to consider when analyzing the "fraud or gross imposition" standard:

> *the financial situation of the client, the sophistication of the client in dealing with lawyers, whether the fee is reasonable, whether the client clearly understood and agreed to pay the amount now owing, whether imposition of the retaining lien would prejudice important rights or interests of the client or of other parties, whether failure to impose the lien would result in fraud or gross imposition by the client, and whether there are less stringent means by which the matter can be resolved or by which the amount owing can be secured. Id.*

Having identified these factors, the ABA Committee offered concise suggestions as to how they might balance out:

If, for example, exercise of the retaining lien would prejudice the client's ability to defend against a criminal charge, or to assert or defend a similarly important personal liberty, the lawyer should ordinarily forego the lien. Similarly, if the court, or other parties, or the public interest would be adversely and seriously affected by the lien, the lawyer should be hesitant to invoke it. Financial inability of the client to pay the amount owing should also cause the lawyer to forego the lien because the failure to pay the fee is not deliberate and thus does not constitute fraud or gross imposition by the client. The lawyer should forego the lien if he knew of the client's financial inability at the beginning or if he failed to assure agreement as to the amount or method of calculating the fee. Assertion of the lien would be ethically justified when the client is financially able but deliberately refuses to pay a fee that was clearly agreed upon and is due, since this conduct would constitute gross imposition by the client. *Id.* …

Delaware courts have yet to consider the myriad issues raised by attorney retaining liens. Only three Delaware cases mention the lien… Each opinion merely describes it in passing. …None delves into the parameters of the lien or considers the conflicting interests involved in its application to particular facts.

Delaware's only other nod to retaining liens appears in Rule 1.16(d) of the Delaware Rules of Professional Conduct, which replicates Model Rule of Professional Conduct 1.16(d) *in haec verba*. Like the Delaware cases, Rule 1.16(d) makes only passing reference to a retaining lien and avoids using the term. It states: "Upon termination of representation, a lawyer shall take steps to the extent reasonably practicable to protect a client's interests, such as ... surrendering papers and property to which the client is entitled.... *The lawyer may retain papers relating to the client to the extent permitted by other law.*" Del. Lawyers' Rules of Prof'l Conduct R. 1.16(d) (emphasis added). Comment 9 to the Delaware Rule, which is identical to Comment 9 to the Model Rule, cautions: "Even if the lawyer has been unfairly discharged by the client, a lawyer must take all reasonable steps to mitigate the consequences to the client. *The lawyer may retain papers as security for a fee only to the extent permitted by law.*" *Id.* at cmt. 9 (emphasis added). Rule 1.16(d) thus acknowledges the possibility of a lien but does not provide any guidance about when, how, and to what degree a lawyer might assert it.

From these limited authorities, I can glean that Delaware recognizes attorney retaining liens, but not much else. In my view, a multi-factor balancing approach like that followed in *Lucky–Goldstar* best allows a court to gauge when and to what degree an attorney's retaining lien should be respected. After engaging in a fact-specific balancing of interests, a court can take into account the competing interests of the attorney, the client, and the judicial system, determine whether the lien should be enforced in whole or part, and evaluate whether the partial or complete release of the lien should be conditioned on the client providing alternative security. On the facts of this case, balancing the interests calls for granting the motion to compel and requiring Potter Anderson to release its lien conditioned on Judy posting adequate security. I start with the relative interests of Potter Anderson and Judy in the disputed documents. Judy argues that Potter Anderson has no legitimate interest in the original documents it holds because those documents comprise Preferred's corporate records and therefore are not property of Potter Anderson's client. Descriptions of the attorney retaining lien, whether the brief references in the Delaware cases or lengthier descriptions from other jurisdictions or treatises, universally refer in various forms to an attorney's right to retain documents and other property "belonging to" the former client. Judy asserts that a bright-line rule bars an attorney from asserting a retaining lien unless the client holds title to the disputed property.

Judy forgets that our legal system long ago moved beyond conceiving ownership as unitary and indivisible. Multiple parties may hold differing interests in an asset with relative priorities and rights. ... Judy and Potter Anderson became entitled to possess Preferred's original corporate records when Preferred produced them in response to Chancellor Chandler's order. As between Preferred on the one hand and Judy on the other, Preferred holds the superior interest. ...

I now turn to the *Lucky–Goldstar* factors, which start with the financial situation of the client. Because attorneys are not immune to financial difficulties, and because a client could take advantage of a law firm's distress or over-investment in a matter, I broaden this factor to consider the financial situations of both client and counsel.

In this case, neither side has identified any particular financial difficulties. Judy and PSI have not suggested that they cannot pay or are *in extremis*. To the contrary, they have engaged multiple other law firms both within and outside of Delaware. In addition to their own fees, Judy and PSI are also paying the legal fees of *all other objectors* in this litigation, with the exception of Preferred Investors Association. For its part, while Potter Anderson does not appear to be in financial distress, the firm understandably would like to collect a receivable in the vicinity of half a million dollars. That is already a discounted amount, because Potter Anderson wrote off a portion of its fees as part of the January 2011 Agreement. Because it appears that Judy could pay and has simply chosen not to, the first factor favors upholding Potter Anderson's lien. ...

The second *Lucky–Goldstar* factor calls for evaluating the sophistication of the client in dealing with lawyers. Judy is clearly sophisticated and knowledgeable in this regard. During all stages of Potter Anderson's representation, Judy simultaneously consulted with other lawyers, and Potter Anderson has interacted with at least four law firms located in Washington, D.C., all retained by Judy and PSI. ... Judy's familiarity with lawyers and the legal process favors maintaining the Potter Anderson lien.

The third and fourth *Lucky–Goldstar* factors examine whether the disputed fee is reasonable and whether the client clearly understood and agreed to pay the amount owed. ...In the January 2011 Agreement, Judy and PSI extracted a write-off from Potter Anderson, agreed to pay the discounted amount according to a payment schedule, and undertook to pay future invoices within thirty days. Judy drafted the January 2011 Agreement and negotiated its terms directly with Potter Anderson. There can be no question that Judy and PSI clearly understood and agreed to pay the outstanding amounts. The arms' length bargaining over the compromise memorialized by the January 2011 Agreement provides strong evidence that the resulting terms are reasonable. The third and fourth factors favor Potter Anderson.

The fifth *Lucky–Goldstar* factor asks whether imposition of the retaining lien would prejudice important rights or interests of the client or other parties. There is inherently some prejudice to Judy and other litigants from enforcing the retaining lien. As noted, a retaining lien functions by imposing some degree of inconvenience on the former client. This is not a case, however, where the resulting inconvenience is disproportionate or unfairly prejudicial, such as where upholding the lien would interfere with the client's ability to defend against a criminal charge or protect a similarly important liberty interest. *See Lucky–Goldstar,* 636 F.Supp. at 1062–64. As Judy describes it, the merits claims in this action seek "a determination of the identity of the Company's stockholders, warrant holders and note holders; the validity and entire fairness of Mr. Austin's issuance of 800,000 shares of common stock to himself; and the validity of the 2007 Reorganization of the Company." Mot. to Compel ¶ 12. In other words, this is a civil dispute over economic interests in a privately held entity. Although the Court regards every matter on its docket as significant, and the case has obvious importance to the parties, the litigation has now been pending for over two years. No external deadline or upcoming event has been identified that would require an expedited decision or otherwise prevent the Court from modifying the case schedule (if warranted) to protect all parties' rights. There accordingly is no risk of disproportionate inconvenience or unfair prejudice that would merit overriding Potter Anderson's lien.

I now jump to the seventh *Lucky–Goldstar* factor, which asks "whether there are less stringent means by which the matter can be resolved or by which the amount owing can be secured"? The attorney's interest protected by the retaining lien is a pecuniary interest in payment. Courts now commonly resolve the competing interests of attorney, client, and judicial system by requiring the production of the case file conditioned on the client posting alternative security to protect the lawyer's pecuniary interest. To my mind, this *Lucky–Goldstar* factor predominantly turns on whether the posting of security can protect adequately the attorney's pecuniary interest and, if so, what form and amount of security is warranted.

Different factual scenarios will affect whether the posting of security provides a solution. The financial pressures facing the attorney and client necessarily re-enter the analysis. If the client is impecunious, then the retaining lien may have little practical value, and it could be appropriate to require only a fraction of the amount as security. *See New World Mktg. Corp. v. Garcia,* 76 B.R. 68, 69 (E.D.Pa.1987) ("Given a client in bankruptcy, with no likelihood of distribution to unsecured creditors, the lien asserted by [the law firm] does not represent a significant property interest."). If the attorney and former client can obtain a prompt decision on the merits of their dispute, then the attorney may have less need for the lien's protection and potentially could make due without it or with security for only a portion of the disputed amount. The justification for a retaining lien might also be undermined or non-existent if the attorney pursued the case on contingency or with the expectation of being compensated through fee-shifting at the end of the case. *See, e.g. Misek–Falkoff v. Int'l Bus. Machs. Corp.,* 829 F.Supp. 660, 664 (S.D.N.Y.1993) (overruling retaining lien in part because litigation was brought with expectation that counsel would obtain compensation under fee-shifting provisions of federal law).

After considering this *Lucky–Goldstar* factor, I conclude that requiring Judy and PSI to post security will protect adequately Potter Anderson's pecuniary interest. ... The[se] facts support requiring security equal to the full amount of the agreed-upon but unpaid fee. At the same time, Potter Anderson recently initiated an arbitration to resolve the fee dispute and presumably will obtain a relatively prompt result, a fact that reduces to some degree Potter Anderson's need for full security. Under the circumstances, I likely would require Judy to post security equal to 100% of the outstanding fees or at most apply a small discount. Potter Anderson has responsibly requested only 70%, less than what I would impose, and I therefore adopt Potter Anderson's figure.

Finally, I decline to consider the sixth *Lucky–Goldstar* factor, which asks whether failing to impose the lien "would result in fraud or gross imposition by the client." ...Our Supreme Court has held that the Delaware Lawyers' Rules of Professional Conduct may not be applied in extra-disciplinary proceedings solely to vindicate the legal profession's concerns in such affairs. Unless the challenged conduct prejudices the fairness of the proceedings, such that it adversely affects the fair and efficient administration of justice, only [the Delaware Supreme Court] has the power and responsibility to govern the Bar, and in pursuance of that authority to enforce the Rules for disciplinary purposes. *In re Infotechnology,* 582 A.2d 215, 216–17 (Del.1990). In reaching this holding, the Supreme Court relied on the Scope of the Rules, which states:

Violation of a Rule should not give rise to a cause of action nor should it create any presumption that a legal duty has been breached. The Rules are designed to provide guidance to lawyers...

III. Conclusion

For the foregoing reasons, the motion to compel is granted, conditioned on Judy posting adequate security. An order has been entered consistent with this opinion.

****

Note: For additional information on attorney retaining liens see John Leubsdorf, Against Lawyer Retaining Liens, 72 Fordham L. Rev. 849 (2004) providing an overview of the lien and its effects and see Kathleen D. Britton, Attorneys' Retaining Liens, 6 J of the Legal Prof 263 (1981) providing a historical perspective of the lien.

****

Declining or Terminating Representation

There are times when an attorney may need to decline to represent a prospective client or to withdraw from representation of a client. For example, the lawyer normally must not accept a case that would result in a conflict of interest. When the lawyer is not competent to handle the case, she must decline representation.

In some instances a lawyer will consider withdrawal because the relationship between the lawyer and client is irreconcilable. Ethical rules generally classify the attorney's ability to withdraw in two categories, mandatory withdrawal and permissive withdrawal. The model rules require withdrawal when the (1) representation results in a violation of the Rules of Professional Conduct or other law; (2) when the lawyer's mental or physical condition materially impairs the lawyer's ability to represent the client or (3) when the lawyer is discharged.[64]

When withdrawal is mandatory in a matter that is pending before a court, the lawyer must adhere to the rules regarding notice or permission from the court to withdraw.[65]

Under certain circumstances, a lawyer will be permitted to withdraw from representation as long as the withdrawal poses no materially adverse affect on the client. However, best practices dictate that the lawyer not withdraw for mere convenience in light of the lawyer's fiduciary obligations to the client. If the lawyer does seek to withdraw (s)he must comply with notice requirements of the applicable rules. The lawyer must also act in every reasonable way to ensure the client is not adversely affected by the withdrawal including providing the client with the client files and other property.[66]

---

[64] ABA Model Rules of Professional Conduct [1.16a]
[65] ABA Model Rules of Professional Conduct [1.16c]
[66] ABA Model Rules of Professional Conduct [1.16d]

Even under circumstances that require mandatory withdrawal, a lawyer may be ethically required to retain a matter when a court or tribunal orders the lawyer to do so. It will be the lawyer's burden to seek remedy through, for example, application for mandamus. [67]

Hawkins v. The Commission For Lawyer Discipline
988 SW 2d 927, (Tex.App. El Paso, 1999)

In attorney disciplinary proceedings,the Court of Appeals held that: (1) attorney could not decide that he was not competent to handle appointed matter and refuse to comply with court order to continue his appointed representation of criminal defendant; (2) Rules of Professional Conduct were not void for vagueness; (3) evidence was sufficient to find violations of rules barring neglect of legal matter, requiring compliance with order for continued representation, and requiring reasonable steps to protect client's interests upon termination of representation; and (4) trial court did not abuse its discretion in balancing evidence and applying it in terms of statutory factors to impose one-year suspension from practice of law followed by three-year probated suspension. Affirmed as modified....

Facts

On August 8, 1994, Midland County Court at Law Judge James Fitz-Gerald issued an order appointing Hawkins to represent Daniel Wayne Sundy in a criminal matter. Sundy was charged with possession of marijuana, two ounces or less, a Class B misdemeanor. Sundy, who was infected with the HIV virus, claimed that his illness required him to use marijuana in order to digest food. Sundy had never previously been arrested. On August 29, 1994, Hawkins filed a "Motion for Appointment of an Effective and Competent Attorney." In the motion, Hawkins contended that he was not competent to practice criminal law and therefore could not represent Sundy without violating Rules 1.01 and 6.01 of the Texas Disciplinary Rules of Professional Conduct. Despite his contentions of incompetence, Hawkins filed motions for speedy trial, jury trial, andq to suppress evidence. Hawkins also filed a request for a court reporter and statement of facts, a motion for production of evidence for examination, and a motion for appointment of experts. On September 7, 1994, Hawkins attended a docket call on behalf of Sundy, and on September 12, he appeared for a scheduled trial date, which was continued.

Although he had claimed to be incompetent in his motion for appointment of competent counsel, Hawkins filed a "Motion for Payment of Fees to Charity in Lieu of Payment to Allan Hawkins" on September 12, 1994. In this motion, Hawkins noted that he had been required "to be in contact with Mr. Sundy and risk exposure to the HIV virus and death" and to "expend a great deal of time and effort to provide emergency representation" to Sundy, which, Hawkins maintained, caused "great inconvenience to Allan Hawkins and his other clients...." Hawkins requested that $2,000 be paid to the Permian Basin Aids Coalition in honor of Sundy as payment for Hawkins' "emergency" representation of Sundy which was, in Hawkins' own words, "above and beyond the call of duty for an attorney and member of the bar of the State of Texas."

---

[67] ABA Model Rules of Professional Conduct [1.16c]

On September 20, 1994, the County Attorney offered Sundy a plea agreement, which included payment of a fine. Hawkins sent a copy of the written offer to Sundy, but refused to discuss the merits of the offer with him or advise him whether to accept the agreement. Meanwhile, Hawkins told the prosecutor that Sundy did not have money and therefore could not accept the agreement. In response to the plea offer, Hawkins filed a second motion for appointment of effective counsel along with a brief outlining his incompetence to assist Sundy with the plea negotiations. Judge Fitz–Gerald held a hearing on the second motion. Evidence at the hearing established that Hawkins had served as an Assistant State's Attorney in North Dakota where he had also handled some criminal defense matters such as guilty pleas, traffic tickets, and game violations. He had handled appointed criminal matters in the Midland district courts along with co-counsel. Judge Fitz–Gerald found Hawkins competent to represent Sundy and issued an order requiring him to continue representing Sundy as appointed counsel.

Upon receiving Judge Fitz–Gerald's order, Hawkins sent a letter to Sundy, the text of which was:

> I am enclosing a copy of an order which I received today. Judge Fitz–Gerald has decided that you are not entitled to a lawyer.
> Judge Fitz–Gerald swore an oath to God and to man that he would uphold the *Constitution* and laws of the United States and Texas. He has decided that you are not entitled to a lawyer.
>
> Apparently you are only entitled to a lawyer if a cash pay-off is made. I will not make a cash pay-off to obtain judicial favoritism. I believe it is a crime. Apparently that means that you don't get a lawyer. That is peculiar.
>
> I must know even less about the *Constitution* than I thought. I thought the United States *Constitution* applies to you. I thought you are entitled to a lawyer under the *Constitution*.
>
> Although I am not permitted to represent you on the substance of this matter. I have done what I can do. I wish you well. (Emphasis in original).

Sundy, understandably confused, contacted Hawkins for an explanation. Hawkins was "very reluctant" to talk to Sundy, but told Sundy that he (Hawkins) was no longer his attorney and that Sundy should look for another lawyer. Sundy continued to call Hawkins a few times a month in an attempt to see what was happening in his case.

On January 6, 1995, Sundy's case was set for docket call. Although Hawkins admittedly received notice of the docket call, he did not attend nor did he notify Sundy of the setting. At the docket call, Sundy's case was set for a January 23, 1995 trial. Hawkins did not appear for trial, nor did he inform Sundy of the trial date. Sundy's failure to appear resulted in a proceeding to forfeit his bond. In response to a call from the district clerk's office concerning the possible revocation of Sundy's bond, Hawkins wrote to the court as follows:

> Today my office received a call for Mr. Daniel Sundy. I do not represent Daniel Sundy. This is not news. The court knows it. The file in your office demonstrates

that. I am not his courier. I do not work for him. He does not work for me. He is not at this office. He is not at this telephone number.

If you wish to contact Mr. Sundy, do not call me or write me.

If you wish to contact Mr. Sundy, contact Mr. Sundy. Mr. Sundy is easy to contact. He responds to contacts. Mr. Sundy moved to Midland County so that he would be available when the court needed him. I will not act as an intermediary between the court and Mr. Sundy. I will not pass messages back and forth. If you have any message for him it is up to you to contact him.

On February 1, 1995, Sundy received notice that the court intended to revoke his bond. Sundy panicked and called the clerk's office. The clerk told Sundy that a warrant for his arrest had been issued and he should come to the courthouse to straighten the matter out. The clerk tried to reach Hawkins, but could not get him. Judge Alvin Walvoord later found Sundy in the courthouse foyer crying in "a very highly excitable state ... very disturbed and agitated." Judge Walvoord learned that there was a problem with Sundy's bond, but because the judge was on recess from a trial, he could not assist Sundy. He found another judge who was available to hold a hearing for Sundy, and contacted the County Attorney. After a hearing at which Sundy apparently represented himself, Sundy's bond was reinstated. The day after the bond hearing, Hawkins wrote to the court as follows:

I was out of office yesterday. Last evening I reviewed telephone messages and found a message from Fonda Love related to a hearing yesterday. As the Court knows, I do not represent Mr. Sundy.

After the February bond hearing, the trial court appointed new counsel for Sundy, and the matter was resolved quickly for a fine plus court costs, and Sundy's plea of guilty to possession of paraphernalia.

The Commission for Lawyer Discipline initiated a disciplinary proceeding against Hawkins which was eventually tried in district court before Judge George M. Thurmond. The trial court found that Hawkins violated Texas Rules of Professional Conduct 1.01(b)(1), 1.15(c), and 1.15(d). Judge Thurmond assessed a one-year suspension from the practice of law followed by a three-year period of probated suspension against Hawkins. Hawkins appeals with forty-two points of error.

Interpretation of The Rules

The majority of the relevant facts in this case are not disputed. What is hotly contested is the appropriate interpretation of the Rules of Professional Conduct in terms of Hawkins' behavior. In Points of Error One, Four, Five, Six, Fourteen, Fifteen, Eighteen, Nineteen, Twenty, Twenty-five, Twenty-six, and Thirty-seven, Hawkins contends that the trial court erred in finding that his conduct violated the Rules of Professional Conduct, and in finding that Rules 1.01(b)(1), 1.15(c), and 1.15(d) applied to him at all. Each of these points is dependent upon Hawkins' interpretation of the Rules and his translation of the conduct the Rules required of him. The Commission, on the other hand, contends that the trial court correctly interpreted the Rules to find Hawkins' conduct in violation.

When considering the Rules, as when considering statutes, the appellate court should look to the entire Rule rather than to one phrase, clause, or sentence. One provision or part should not be given meaning or construction out of harmony or inconsistent with the other provisions. Accordingly, we will review the trial court's interpretation of the Rules as we would review the trial court's interpretation of statutes. Questions of statutory interpretation are questions of law that are not entitled to a presumption of validity. We therefore review the trial court's interpretation of the Rules de novo.

According to Hawkins' interpretation of the Rules, Rule 1.01(a) required him to decline to represent Sundy. Rule 1.01(a) mandates

(a) A lawyer shall not accept or continue employment in a legal matter which the lawyer knows or should know is beyond the lawyer's competence, unless:

(1) another lawyer who is competent to handle the matter is, with the prior informed consent of the client, associated in the matter; or

(2) the advice or assistance of the lawyer is reasonably required in an emergency and the lawyer limits the advice and assistance to that which is reasonably necessary in the circumstances.

Hawkins maintains that Rule 1.01(a) required him to decline to represent Sundy despite his appointment and despite Judge Fitz–Gerald's order to continue the representation because the Rule places the determination of competence solely on the attorney. Accordingly, Hawkins argues, he had to defy the appointment and Judge Fitz–Gerald's order or be in violation of the Rules. Hawkins argues that Rule 3.04(d) further supports his actions. Rule 3.04(d) states that an attorney may not [k]nowingly disobey, or advise the client to disobey, an obligation under the standing rules of or a ruling by a tribunal except for an open refusal based either on an assertion that no valid obligation exists or on the client's willingness to accept any sanctions arising from such disobedience. *Tex. Disciplinary R. Prof'l Conduct 3.04(d).*

Since Hawkins professes to have held a good faith belief that he could not represent Sundy pursuant to Rule 1.01(a), he urges that no valid obligation for him to do so existed and he was forced to openly refuse to follow Judge Fitz–Gerald's order. Thus, Hawkins contends that his open refusal to acknowledge representation of Sundy even after Judge Fitz–Gerald's order insulates him from discipline under the Rules.

Hawkins fails, however, to consider other provisions of the Rules which belie his construction. It is important to recognize that different parts of the Rules apply to different situations in which an attorney may find him or her self. Rule 1.01(a), the Rule Hawkins relies upon, is stated in general terms of "employment in a legal matter." Another section of the Rules, however, is directed specifically at court appointments. Rule 6.01, entitled "Accepting Appointments by a Tribunal" and placed under the heading "Public Service," states, in pertinent part, that:

A lawyer shall not seek to avoid appointment by a tribunal to represent a person except for good cause, such as:

(a) representing the client is likely to result in violation of law or rules of professional conduct. *Tex. Disciplinary R. Prof'l Conduct 6.01(a)*.

A specific statutory provision ordinarily controls over a general one. Accordingly, when an attorney obtains a representation by appointment, the attorney may not merely decline the representation as provided under the more general Rule 1.01(a), but must "seek to avoid" the appointment only for good cause pursuant to Rule 6.01. We find the phrase "seek to avoid appointment by a tribunal" implies a showing to the tribunal of good cause. In other words, the attorney may not simply decide that he or she is not competent to handle the appointed matter and decline or refuse the representation without the court's permission. We find Professors Sutton and Schwerk's comments on the operation of Rule 6.01 in appointment situations worth repeating here:

Though generally a lawyer may freely reject any person's offer of professional employment, a different standard applies when that offer emanates from a court. ...

[A] lawyer may decline a representation that could not possibly be handled by the lawyer in a competent manner due to the matter's complexity, a representation wherein the lawyer is unfamiliar with the subject matter of the case, and where the lawyer has insufficient time to acquire the requisite degree of competence. Nevertheless, lawyers can abuse this exception by utilizing it when they presently lack the legal background and training necessary to competently handle a matter but they know they could remedy those defects through reasonable efforts. The ability to attain a law degree and a law license betokens a considerable ability to grasp legal issues. Thus, courts may expect that lawyers will make a good faith effort to utilize those abilities to acquire the requisite degree of competence before they invoke this exception, just as they would if they were approached about taking on an unfamiliar type of matter that they nonetheless believed would be rewarding. *Robert P. Schwerk & John F. Sutton, Jr., A Guide to the Texas Disciplinary Rules of Professional Conduct, 27A HOUS. L. REV. 398–400 (1990).*

To an extent, Hawkins followed the mandate of <u>Rule 6.01</u> by filing his motions for appointment of competent counsel and appearing before Judge Fitz–Gerald to argue that his continued defense of Sundy would violate a Rule of Professional Conduct (Rule 1.01(a)) because the matter was beyond his competence.

But importantly, once Judge Fitz–Gerald ordered Hawkins to continue the representation, another Rule came into play. Rule 1.15(c) directs that "[w]hen ordered to do so by a tribunal, a lawyer shall continue representation notwithstanding good cause for terminating the representation." Hawkins' refusal to represent Sundy after he was ordered to do so by Judge Fitz–Gerald runs afoul of Rule 1.15(c). Further, Hawkins' use of Rule 3.04 to justify his refusal to act for Sundy even after Judge Fitz–Gerald's order is, like his reliance on Rule 1.01(a) rather than on Rule 6.01, a misapplication of a Rule germane to a set of circumstances different from his own. When read in isolation, Rule 3.04(d) seems to allow an attorney to defy any court order so long as it is done openly and is based on an assertion that no valid obligation exists. This appears to be precisely what Hawkins did. *Tex. Disciplinary R. Prof'l Conduct 1.15(c).*

Placed in context of the Rule as a whole, however, application of Rule 3.04(d) to Hawkins' situation becomes less than clear. Rule 3.04 is entitled "Fairness in Adjudicatory

Proceedings." The Rule speaks in terms of refraining from "obstruct[ing] another party's access to evidence," "falsify[ing] evidence," violating "established rule[s] of procedure or of evidence," asking questions "intended to degrade a witness" or engaging in "conduct intended to disrupt the proceedings." Thus, the Rule is aimed at fairness between the parties to a suit and fairness of the adversarial process. It is rulings within that process that fall under Rule 3.04(d). The appointment of counsel for an indigent criminal defendant is not a ruling that occurs within the adjudicatory proceeding itself.

Moreover, we find another application of the "specific versus general" rule in the interplay between Rules 3.04(d) and 1.15(c). Whereas Rule 3.04(d) refers generally to any ruling of a court, Rule 1.15(c) is specifically directed to an order by the court to continue representation. Rule 1.15(c) forbids an attorney from discontinuing a representation in violation of a court order even if good cause for terminating the representation exists. Accordingly, we find that Rule 3.04(d) is inapplicable when the ruling in question is an order to continue representation. Instead, the more specific Rule 1.15(c) applies to such an order.

Additionally, Rule 1.15(c) serves to shield an attorney who holds an honest belief that he or she is incompetent to represent an appointed client from ethical repercussions resulting from the continued court ordered representation. By explicitly requiring the lawyer to accede to the tribunal's ruling to continue representation despite the lawyer's misgivings, Rule 1.15(c) protects the lawyer against a charge of wrongdoing. Accordingly, Hawkins could have followed Rule 1.15(c), continued to represent Sundy, and been protected from any perceived ethical violations based on his alleged lack of criminal law skills without needing to rely on a refusal to represent Sundy under Rule 3.04(d).

Vagueness

In his second and third points, Hawkins contends that the trial court erred in failing to strictly construe the Rules in his favor, and erred in applying the Rules to him on the ground that the Rules are vague and ambiguous. At the outset, we note that disciplinary proceedings are civil in nature. With the nature of the proceedings in mind, we turn to Hawkins' complaints of vagueness and failure to construe the Rules strictly.

…We find that the Rules of Professional Conduct gave Hawkins fair and adequate notice of the conduct expected of him. Contrary to Hawkins' assertions, the Rules provide a clear distinction between the actions necessary to decline or withdraw from voluntary employment on the one hand and those necessary to decline or withdraw from appointed representations or court ordered representations on the other. …We find that the ordinary person, or in this case, the ordinary attorney, exercising ordinary common sense could sufficiently understand and comply with the Rules. We therefore overrule Hawkins' second and third points.

Application of the Law to the Facts

We find ample evidence in the record to support the trial court's finding of violations of these Rules. With regard to Rule 1.01(b), the record reflects that Hawkins neglected Sundy's defense by failing to advise Sundy when Sundy specifically requested advice, failing to appear for a docket call despite admittedly receiving notice of the setting, failing to appear for a potential trial date which would have been known to Hawkins had Hawkins appeared for the docket call, and failing to appear to defend Sundy on the revocation of his bond despite the trial court's telephone request to do so.

The record also displays more than sufficient evidence that Hawkins failed to continue representation of Sundy after Judge Fitz–Gerald's order in violation of Rule 1.15(c). It is undisputed that after a hearing on Hawkins' competence, Judge Fitz–Gerald ordered Hawkins to continue to represent Sundy. Instead, Hawkins wrote to Sundy and told Sundy that the judge had determined Sundy was not entitled to a lawyer to defend him. Hawkins refused to act on Sundy's behalf when appropriately noticed by the court and instead wrote letters to the court claiming that he did not represent Sundy and would not act as Sundy's "courier." Even after being ordered to continue as Sundy's counsel, Hawkins ignored docket call and thereby missed a potential trial date resulting in the threatened revocation of Sundy's bond.

Even under Hawkins' interpretation of the Rules, he failed to comply with Rule 1.15(d) after he allegedly "declined" to represent Sundy. Before new counsel was appointed for Sundy, Hawkins refused to advise Sundy when he requested advice, ignored the docket call and did not inform Sundy of it, missed a potential trial setting, and refused to defend Sundy against the revocation of his bond. These omissions amply illustrate Hawkins' failure to take "steps to the extent reasonably practicable to protect a client's interests" as Rule 1.15(d) requires.

…   The trial court's Finding of Fact Six impliedly finds neglect of Sundy's case in that it states Hawkins "failed to notify his client of scheduled court proceedings...." The same finding also satisfies, at the very least, the element of Rule 1.15(d) requiring that an attorney take reasonable steps to protect a client's interests even after termination of a representation. Finding Five satisfies, at the very least, an element of Rule 1.15(c) in that it states Hawkins "refused to continue with his representation of the Defendant despite the Court's ordering him to do so." As we have already discussed pursuant to Hawkins' twelfth, seventeenth, twenty-second, and twenty-seventh points, the evidence is sufficient to support any elements left unstated in the trial court's Findings of Fact. Accordingly, we overrule Hawkins' eleventh, thirteenth, and sixteenth points of error.

Defects in the Underlying Appointment

In his thirty-fourth point, Hawkins maintains that his appointment to represent Sundy was fundamentally flawed. In this single point of error, Hawkins makes three different contentions. First, he alleges that the Midland Bar Plan under which he was initially appointed to represent Sundy created an unconstitutional "taking" of his services. Second, he contends that some lawyers are treated differently than others under the Plan thus violating principles of equal protection. Finally, Hawkins argues that under the Plan, he was appointed at random and not on the basis of merit as required by the Texas Code of Judicial Conduct. We note that neither of the first two contentions were raised to the trial court. Accordingly, they are waived. The constitutionality of a statute or rule will be considered only when the question is properly raised and a decision becomes necessary and appropriate to the disposal of the case. Predicates for complaints on appeal must be preserved at the trial court level by motion, exception, objection, or some other vehicle.

Sanctions Outside the Court's Authority

Hawkins alleges in his thirty-fifth point that the trial court had no authority to impose any sanction on him other than those delineated in Texas Rule of Disciplinary Procedure 1.06(T). The trial court's judgment suspended Hawkins from the practice of law for one year, and imposed a three-year probated suspension to be served after the year's suspension. The trial court further required Hawkins to comply with the following conditions during the term of probated suspension:

1. Respondent shall not violate any of the provisions of the Texas Disciplinary Rules of Professional Conduct nor any provisions of the State Bar Rules;

2. Respondent shall not violate the laws of the United States of any other state other than minor traffic violations;

3. Respondent shall maintain a current status regarding membership fees in accordance with Article III of the State Bar Rules;

4. Respondent shall comply with Minimum Continuing Legal Education (MCLE) requirements in accordance with Article III of the State Bar Rules;

5. Respondent shall comply with Interest on Lawyers Trust Account requirements in accordance with Article XI of the State Bar Rules;

6. Respondent shall comply with all requests for information forwarded to him by any grievance committee of the State Bar of Texas;

7. Respondent shall cooperate fully with the General Counsel's office in their efforts to monitor compliance with this order; and

8. Respondent shall provide fifteen (15) hours per month of pro bono services to indigent persons, as referred to him by the Midland County Bar Association, in need of wills, powers of attorney, and similar services and instruments within his field of expertise. Respondent shall begin this service on September 1, 1998 and continue until August 31, 2000. Respondent shall send a report to the State Bar of Texas, 201 Main Street, Suite 1150, Fort Worth, Texas 76102, stating that he has complied with this condition of probation. The report is due to the State Bar of Texas Fort Worth office by the 15th of each month following the previous month.

Hawkins contends that the portion of the trial court's judgment requiring him to comply with the list of eight conditions is outside the bounds specified in Rule 1.06. We disagree. Our reading of the judgment reveals that the eight conditions are imposed as conditions of Hawkins' probated suspension. Rule 1.06(T)(5) allows the trial court to probate a suspension "upon such reasonable terms as are appropriate under the circumstances." Thus, the imposition of the conditions is authorized by the Rule. We find that the conditions are appropriate and therefore overrule Hawkins' thirty-fifth point.

Error in Sanction

In his thirty-sixth, thirty-eighth, and fortieth points, Hawkins contends that the trial court failed to consider the factors set out in Disciplinary Procedure Rule 3.10 when it considered and imposed sanctions on Hawkins. Rule 3.10 requires the trial court to consider the following twelve factors: nature and degree of the misconduct; seriousness of and circumstances surrounding the misconduct; loss or damage to clients; damage to the profession; assurance that those who seek legal services in the future will be insulated from the type of misconduct found; profit to the attorney; avoidance of repetition; deterrent effect; maintenance of respect for the legal profession; conduct of Respondent during the course of the Committee action; trial of the case; other relevant evidence concerning the Respondent's personal and professional background. We find that the trial court appropriately considered each of these factors in fashioning Hawkins' sanction in this case. The evidence showed that Hawkins intentionally disobeyed a court order to represent the indigent Sundy in spite of Rule 1.15(c) which clearly required him to do so. Worse, Hawkins wrote to Sundy after Judge Fitz–Gerald's order and told Sundy that Judge Fitz–Gerald had found Sundy was not entitled to an attorney. Although he clearly understood that he was under court order to represent Sundy, Hawkins ignored a docket call which led to further failures to appear and the eventual bond revocation hearing, which Hawkins also failed to attend despite telephone notice from the court. Hawkins wrote snide letters to the trial court in response to notice of hearings, while failing to even communicate the content of these notices to Sundy. The degree and seriousness of Hawkins' misconduct in a case where a gravely ill man's liberty was at stake profoundly and negatively impacted the profession and respect for the profession in the eyes of the public. The trial court correctly concluded that a serious sanction was needed to deter others from similar conduct.

Additionally, the Commission presented evidence that a serious sanction was needed to deter Hawkins from repeating his conduct. Hawkins admitted that he had previously filed ten to twenty similar objections to appointments in criminal cases, and had filed recusal motions against almost every judge who had appointed him. … Hawkins alleged in the motion that the judiciary of Midland County was extorting bribes, yet he admitted that he had no evidence that any judge actually requested or took a bribe.

Attorney's Fees Award

In his forty-second point, Hawkins contends that the evidence is insufficient to support the trial court's award of $15,000 in attorney's fees to the Commission. We find, however, that the parties stipulated $15,000 was a reasonable and necessary fee for the litigation. Accordingly, we find the evidence sufficient to support the trial court's award and we overrule Hawkins' forty-second point.

Conclusion

Having considered and overruled each of Hawkins' points of error with the exception of Point of Error Forty-one, we reform the trial court's judgment to delete any reference to an agreement or an agreed judgment … and we affirm the judgment as modified.

In re Gonzalez
773 A.2d 1026 (CCA-DC, 2001)

In 1997, Gonzalez, who is also a member of the Virginia bar, was retained by A.A. and A.A.'s company, D.B.I., to defend a suit which had been brought against them in the Circuit Court for Fairfax County, Virginia. Problems arose in the lawyer-client relationship when A.A. and D.B.I.

failed to make payments to Gonzalez in accordance with their retainer agreement. During the early months of 1998, Gonzalez wrote a number of letters to A.A. in which he complained that he had not been paid. Gonzalez also accused A.A. in these letters of failing to cooperate with him in preparing a defense and of making untrue representations to him. Gonzalez warned that, unless these problems could be promptly and amicably resolved, he would move to withdraw as counsel.

The relationship between lawyer and clients did not improve, and on May 8, 1998, in accordance with his warning, Gonzalez faxed and mailed to A.A. a "Notice of Intent to File Motion for Leave to Withdraw," as well as a "Motion for Order Permitting Withdrawal from Representation." A copy of the motion was mailed to the attorney for the adverse party in the Circuit Court action against A.A. and D.B.I. In his motion, Gonzalez represented that his clients were not paying their bills in a timely manner and that they had failed to cooperate with him in preparing for trial. Gonzalez further alleged that [A.A.] has missed appointments on a number of occasions, failed to timely provide information necessary to the case, *and made misrepresentations to her attorneys.* (Emphasis added.)

Attached to Gonzalez' initial motion were copies of seven of the letters in which he had berated A.A. for her alleged non-cooperation and, in two of the letters, for misrepresenting certain facts to him. In these letters, Gonzalez revealed, *inter alia,* the amounts allegedly owed to him by A.A. and D.B.I. In one of the letters filed with his motion, Gonzalez advised A.A.:
Your exposure is in the tens of thousands. The complainant asks for approximately $1 million. [Plaintiff's] attorney talks of a realistic figure around $90,000. At a minimum there is about $40,000 at stake from his payments to you.

Shortly after Gonzalez first moved to withdraw, and before he had re-filed his motion so as to comply with the Circuit Court's requirements, … a new attorney entered an appearance for A.A. and D.B.I., and a stipulation was filed substituting the new attorney for Gonzalez. Dissatisfied with Gonzalez' representation, however, A.A. made a complaint against him to District of Columbia Bar Counsel. In correspondence with Bar Counsel, A.A. expressed her concern regarding Gonzalez' "failure to perform legal services for me properly," and she claimed that Gonzalez had "breache[d] his obligation of confidentiality to me by revealing privileged matters detrimental to my ongoing lawsuit."

On or about August 27, 1999, in response to A.A.'s complaint, former Bar Counsel issued a "Specification of Charges" against Gonzalez in which he summarized the foregoing facts. Bar Counsel alleged, *inter alia,* that Gonzalez had knowingly revealed a confidence or secret of his client, in violation of Rule 1.6(a)(1) of the District's Rules of Professional Conduct and Disciplinary Rule DR 4-101(B)(1) of the Virginia Code of Professional Responsibility. The case was referred to an "ad hoc" Hearing Committee, and a hearing was held on October 6, 1999. On January 12, 2000, the Committee issued proposed findings of fact and conclusions of law in which it set forth the events described above. The Committee concluded that Gonzalez had not revealed a "secret" of his clients because, in the Committee's view, the principal facts disclosed by Gonzalez "should not be deemed information gained in the professional relationship between Gonzalez and his clients." The Hearing Committee further reasoned that to the extent any information revealed by Gonzalez was gained in his professional relationship, the disclosure was not detrimental or embarrassing to A.A.

Bar Counsel excepted to the Hearing Committee's findings, and the matter was heard by the Board on Professional Responsibility. The Board disagreed with the Hearing Committee's analysis and concluded that "the information [Gonzalez] included in the motion to withdraw and its attachments at least constituted 'secrets' within the meaning of Virginia DR 4-101(B)." Noting Gonzalez' argument that the Circuit Court would not have been prepared to grant Gonzalez' motion to withdraw if Gonzalez had failed to submit a reasonably detailed justification for the relief sought, the Board stated:

We do not think the need for support for his motion can justify Respondent's decision to make public his client's secrets. Even in situations recognized in the rules as exceptions to the ban on revealing client secrets, the attorney is obligated to reveal only the minimum information necessary under the circumstances and to take steps to minimize any harm to the client's interest. * * * In addition, there is no reason those documents could not have been provided to the [Circuit] Court *in camera,* so that the [Circuit] Court could be satisfied that the motion had a factual foundation, without harm to the client's interests.

Observing that Gonzalez had "made a mistake he is not likely to make again," the Board concluded that "an informal admonition is the appropriate sanction," and directed Bar Counsel to issue the admonition. Gonzalez now asks us to hold that no discipline is warranted.

Legal Discussion

... Disclosure of clients' secrets.

At the times relevant to this proceeding, Virginia's DR 4-101(B)(1) provided, with exceptions not here applicable, that a lawyer shall not "knowingly ... [r]eveal a confidence or secret of his client." ... We take no position on the question whether there has been disclosure in this case of A.A.'s "confidence[s]," *id.,* for we agree with the Board that Gonzalez revealed secrets gained in his professional relationship with A.A. and D.B.I. This conclusion would be inescapable even if we were to confine ourselves to the text of Gonzalez' motion to withdraw, and it is reinforced by the contents of the letters attached thereto. In the body of the motion, which Gonzalez submitted to the court for filing and mailed to opposing counsel in the underlying litigation, Gonzalez alleged that A.A. not only missed appointments and failed to provide necessary information, but also "made misrepresentations to her attorneys." We think it obvious that a public allegation by a client's own lawyer that the client deliberately lied to him would be "embarrassing" to the client and "would be likely to be detrimental" to her, within the meaning of DR 4-101(A). Indeed, it is difficult to understand how a reasonable person could conclude otherwise.

The Hearing Committee was of the opinion that "[t]he conduct of [A.A.] that is depicted in Gonzalez' [motion and] letters did not come to Gonzalez as a part of his fact-gathering for the case he was handling," and that therefore it "should not be deemed 'information gained in the professional relationship' between Gonzalez and his clients." We are unable to agree with this analysis. ... Chief Judge Howard T. Markey, sitting by designation, has eloquently captured the essence of the professional obligation at issue in this case:

The broad commitment of the lawyer to respect confidences reposed in him is his talisman. Touching the very soul of lawyering, it rests upon a "privilege" which is that of the client, not that of the lawyer. Inaccurately described as the "lawyer's privilege against testifying," the privilege of clients to bind their lawyers to secrecy is universally honored and enforced as productive of social values more important than the search for truth. ...[citations omitted]

... Gonzalez argues that he was obliged to disclose the information at issue because, under local court practice, his motion to withdraw would otherwise have been denied. This contention is somewhat undermined by Gonzalez' inability, at oral argument, to cite any authority for, or to identify a single concrete example of, the purported local practice to which he alluded. In any event, we agree with the Board that Gonzalez could have submitted his documentation *in camera,* and that he could also have made appropriate redactions of the material most potentially damaging to his clients (*e.g.,* his allegations that A.A. had misrepresented facts to him and his suggestion, in one of the letters, that a demand of $90,000 by the plaintiffs in the underlying litigation might be reasonable).

As noted in Virginia's Ethical Consideration 2-41, [a] lawyer should not withdraw without considering carefully and endeavoring to minimize the possible adverse effect on the rights of his client and the possibility of prejudice to his client as a result of his withdrawal. Even when he justifiably withdraws, a lawyer should protect the welfare of his client by giving due notice of his withdrawal, suggesting employment of other counsel, delivering to the client all papers and property to which the client is entitled, cooperating with counsel subsequently employed, *and otherwise endeavoring to minimize the possibility of harm.* Va. S.Ct. Prof. Resp. Canons, EC 2-41 (Michie 1998) (emphasis added).

Contrary to this admonition, Gonzalez revealed secret information about his clients in his motion to withdraw and in the attachments thereto, and he failed to take steps to minimize the possibility of harm. ...

We recognize, as did the Board, that if his substantive complaints against A.A. and her company were warranted, then Gonzalez faced a difficult situation. But Bar Counsel and the Board have both recommended an informal admonition, the least severe of the available sanctions. No party has sought, and we are not disposed to impose, any sterner discipline. We have no doubt that Gonzalez revealed his client's secrets, and an appropriate (if relatively modest) sanction is called for. Accordingly, Bar Counsel is hereby directed to issue an informal admonition to Gonzalez. *So ordered.*

Lawyer Disciplinary Board v. Farber
200 W.Va. 185 (1997)

This case is before this Court upon a review of the October 17, 1996, findings and recommendation of the Hearing Panel Subcommittee of the Lawyer Disciplinary Board of the West Virginia State Bar concerning the respondent, Michael C. Farber, an attorney practicing in Sutton, West Virginia. The respondent was charged, *inter alia,* with revealing confidential information concerning a client and with threatening that client, in violation of the *West Virginia Rules of Professional Conduct.* According to the Hearing Panel Subcommittee and the Office of

Disciplinary Counsel, the charges were substantiated, and sanctions are warranted. The respondent, however, contends that no ethics violations occurred.

This Court has before it the findings and recommendation, all matters of record and the briefs and argument of counsel. For the reasons expressed below, this Court is of the opinion that the above charges were established by clear and convincing evidence. Moreover, although the Hearing Panel Subcommittee recommends that the respondent's license to practice law in West Virginia be suspended for one year, this Court concludes that, under the circumstances of this case, a four-month suspension, supervised practice and the payment of costs are more appropriate.

Regrettably, the respondent has had previous problems concerning professional ethics. In *Committee on Legal Ethics v. Farber*, 185 W.Va. 522, 408 S.E.2d 274 (1991), *cert. denied*, 502 U.S. 1073, 112 S.Ct. 970, 117 L.Ed.2d 135 (1992), this Court upheld the findings of the Disciplinary Committee that the respondent had (1) misrepresented facts in order to lend support to accusations of wrongdoing, (2) falsely accused a circuit judge of criminal conduct and (3) engaged in a pattern and practice of contemptuous and disruptive behavior revealing a "tendency to lash out with irrational and reckless accusations [.]" 185 W. Va. at 534, 408 S.E.2d at 286. In that case, this Court ordered that the respondent's license be suspended for three months and that, upon return, his practice be supervised by another attorney. We further ordered, in *Farber*, that the respondent pay the costs of the proceeding. Thereafter, in *Committee on Legal Ethics v. Farber*, 191 W.Va. 667, 447 S.E.2d 602 (1994), this Court, noting that the respondent had not properly complied with the supervised practice requirement and had not paid the costs previously awarded, continued the suspension of the respondent's license, until such time as supervision and reimbursement agreements were reached with the State Bar. Soon after, the respondent's license to practice law was reinstated with the understanding that his practice would be supervised until March 1, 1996, by George M. Cooper, also of Sutton, West Virginia.

The facts giving rise to this case occurred during the respondent's period of supervision. On September 26, 1995, G. Ernest Skaggs, an attorney, appeared in the Circuit Court of Greenbrier County, West Virginia, and entered a plea of nolo contendere to the charge of obstructing an officer. The charge arose from an incident in January, 1994 between Skaggs and two law enforcement officers. Pursuant to *W.Va.Code*, 61-5-17 [1931], the offense of obstructing an officer, a misdemeanor, carried with it a fine of not less than $50 nor more than $500 and possible imprisonment not exceeding one year. During the plea hearing, Skaggs was represented by the respondent, and, as the transcript of that hearing indicates, the circuit court determined that the plea was voluntary and without any promise concerning punishment. *Call v. McKenzie*, 159 W.Va. 191, 220 S.E.2d 665 (1975). Skaggs' sentencing was scheduled for November 3, 1995.

Shortly thereafter, Skaggs wrote a letter to the respondent dated October 8, 1995, in which he suggested that the respondent had misled him with regard to the sentence to be imposed. According to the letter, the respondent told Skaggs, before the nolo contendere plea was taken, that the circuit judge had agreed to impose no punishment for the offense beyond a $50 fine, but that, following the plea, the respondent suggested to Skaggs that he could not promise what the punishment would be. Skaggs indicated in the letter that he intended to file a motion to set the plea aside.

Upon receipt of the October 8, 1995, letter, the respondent immediately telephoned Skaggs concerning the problem. Although the record does not reveal the substance of the conversation between the two, Skaggs hung up the telephone twice on the respondent. On October 13, 1995, Skaggs filed a *pro se* motion to set the plea aside.

On October 17, 1995, the respondent filed a motion to withdraw as Skaggs' counsel. As indicated to the Hearing Panel Subcommittee and to this Court, the respondent based the motion to withdraw upon the contention that Skaggs had either testified falsely at the plea hearing (during which Skaggs had indicated that no promises had been made to him as to the punishment for the offense) or intended to testify falsely upon the motion to set the plea aside (in contradiction to the plea hearing). Upon the latter point, the respondent has asserted that it would be "a fraudulent act by Mr. Skaggs to attempt to set aside his plea."

Nevertheless, the respondent's motion to withdraw went beyond setting forth allegations supportive of the above contention and denying that the respondent had indicated that the circuit judge had agreed to a $50 fine. An affidavit attached to the motion indicated that Skaggs had engaged in "a flat-out-lie" and that "Skaggs had expressed the view that he thought he would have been convicted of battery had the issue been presented to the jury." It appears certain that Skaggs' statement concerning battery, as described by the respondent, was made to the respondent during the course of the attorney-client relationship. Moreover, the motion to withdraw containing Skaggs' statement was filed by the respondent prior to the final disposition of Skaggs' case.

Shortly after the filing of the motion to withdraw as counsel, the respondent sent a letter to Skaggs dated October 25, 1995. As that letter stated in part: "What you are doing here is so disgusting to me personally and professionally, I'm going to do everything in my power to even the score with you."

In November, 1995, the circuit court conducted a hearing in Skaggs' case concerning the charge of obstructing an officer. Although the record herein does not reveal the sentence ultimately imposed, the circuit court, during the hearing, denied Skaggs' motion to set the plea of nolo contendere aside. The circuit court, however, granted the respondent's motion to withdraw as counsel. The granting of the motion to withdraw was reflected in an order entered by the circuit court on November 27, 1995.

On March 8, 1996, the Investigative Panel of the Lawyer Disciplinary Board filed a statement of formal charges alleging, *inter alia,* that the respondent had violated the *West Virginia Rules of Professional Conduct,* (1) by revealing confidential information concerning Mr. Skaggs in the motion to withdraw and (2) by threatening Mr. Skaggs in the letter of October 25, 1995. In particular, the statement of formal charges alleged that the respondent's conduct violated Rule 1.6(a), which states that a lawyer shall not "reveal information relating to representation of a client unless the client consents after consultation," Rule 1.8(b), which states that a lawyer shall not "use information relating to representation of a client to the disadvantage of the client unless the client consents after consultation," Rule 1.9(b), which states that a lawyer "who has formerly represented a client in a matter shall not thereafter ... use information relating to the representation to the disadvantage of the former client," and Rule 8.4(d), which states that it is professional misconduct for a lawyer to " engage in conduct that is prejudicial to the administration of justice." ...

[T]he Hearing Panel Subcommittee found that the respondent violated the *West Virginia Rules of Professional Conduct* (1) by revealing confidential information concerning Mr. Skaggs in the motion to withdraw as counsel and (2) by threatening Mr. Skaggs in the letter of October 25, 1995. In response, the respondent contends that both the motion and the letter should be viewed in the context of what the respondent has characterized as Skaggs' fraudulent attempt to withdraw his plea to the offense of obstructing an officer. According to the respondent, he was merely reacting to a belief that Skaggs had either testified falsely during the plea hearing of September 26, 1995, or intended to testify falsely upon the motion to set the plea aside. Thus, the respondent places great emphasis upon Rule 1.16 of the *West Virginia Rules of Professional Conduct,* concerning a lawyer's duty to withdraw from representation where a client engages in improper conduct, and Rule 3.3 of those Rules, concerning a lawyer's duty to avoid the making of false statements to a legal tribunal. As Rule 1.16(b) states in part:

[A] lawyer may withdraw from representing a client if withdrawal can be accomplished without material adverse effect on the interests of the client, or if:
(1) the client persists in a course of action involving the lawyer's services that the lawyer reasonably believes is criminal or fraudulent;
(2) the client has used the lawyer's services to perpetrate a crime or fraud;
(3) the client insists upon pursuing an objective that the lawyer considers repugnant or imprudent[.]

The assertions of the respondent notwithstanding, the issue before the Hearing Panel Subcommittee, and now before this Court, is not whether the respondent had good reason under Rule 1.16 or Rule 3.3, or other authority, to withdraw as Skaggs' attorney. Inasmuch as the attorney-client relationship between the respondent and Skaggs clearly deteriorated in October, 1995, the respondent may, very well, have had legitimate grounds for the motion to withdraw. Nor does the issue involve the assertion of Skaggs that the respondent misled him with regard to the sentence to be imposed for obstructing an officer. Rather, the concern is with the respondent's method of withdrawing and whether his conduct, in so doing, violated the *West Virginia Rules of Professional Conduct.*

In this case, the respondent's motion to withdraw and subsequent letter went beyond the type of communication appropriate to the termination of an attorney-client relationship. In the experience of this Court gained in reviewing the many records in cases before us, we may safely say that motions to withdraw as counsel are ordinarily rather attenuated. Here, attached to the motion to withdraw was an affidavit in which Skaggs was accused of telling a lie and said to have stated that "he thought he would have been convicted of battery had the issue been presented to the jury." Manifestly, those statements were significant in view of the fact that Skaggs, at that time, was continuing to litigate his guilt or innocence upon the charge of obstructing an officer. Moreover, the respondent's conduct culminated with the letter of October

25, 1995, in which the respondent stated to Skaggs that "I'm going to do everything in my power to even the score with you."

As Disciplinary Counsel's brief before this Court properly observes: "[A] difficult client does not give an attorney license to turn on the client and engage in a vindictive campaign[.]" Here, the respondent acted out of anger, rather than professionally, toward Skaggs. Nor did the respondent seek the approval of his supervising attorney concerning his actions. As Disciplinary Counsel stated before the Hearing Panel Subcommittee:

The motion to withdraw and the affidavit are really the substance of attorney-client conversations. They are couched in terms such as could cause harm to Mr. Skaggs' position in the pending case and they make negative comments about Mr. Skaggs. Some examples of these comments are Mr. Skaggs has expressed the view that he thought he would have been convicted of battery had the issue been presented to the jury. ....

We think that his letter of October 25, 1995, threatens that ... 'I'm going to do everything in my power to even the score with you,' is most telling of his motivation for his conduct.

Clearly, the statements of the respondent, at issue, in the motion to withdraw and in the letter of October 25, 1995, were inappropriate and unnecessary. The statements revealed confidential information, were potentially to the disadvantage of Skaggs and were threatening. ...Thus, this Court confirms the findings of the Hearing Panel Subcommittee that the respondent's conduct violated Rule 1.6(a), Rule 1.8(b) and Rule 1.9(b), which Rules prohibit revealing confidential information concerning a client or using information relating to the representation of a client "to the disadvantage" of the client, and Rule 8.4(d), which states that it is professional misconduct for a lawyer to "engage in conduct that is prejudicial to the administration of justice." *[citations omitted]*

With regard to the sanction to be imposed,...although the respondent's discipline by this Court in previous cases is a factor to be considered in the severity of the current sanction to be imposed, this Court is not unmindful of the fact that a series of heated exchanges occurred between the respondent and Skaggs, who is also an attorney, and that the respondent attempted to follow what he perceived to be a viable method of extricating himself from the attorney-client relationship. Therefore, while not condoning the respondent's actions in any way, this Court is of the opinion that a four-month suspension, rather than a one-year suspension, is warranted. Moreover, as in the past, we direct the West Virginia State Bar and the respondent to develop and execute a written agreement pursuant to which the respondent will practice law under supervision upon the termination of his suspension. The period of supervision shall be for a period of two years. In that regard, we respectfully note the death of George M. Cooper, the respondent's previous supervising attorney. Finally, this Court directs the respondent to pay the costs of these proceedings.

Upon all of the above, this Court declines to adopt the recommended one-year suspension. Instead, this Court directs that the respondent shall be suspended for four months and, thereafter, shall practice under supervision for a period of two years. In addition, the respondent shall pay the costs of these proceedings.

Duties Owed Clients upon Sale of Law Practice

There are various reasons that a lawyer might want to sell her law practice, change of careers, disbarment and retirement are all reasons for selling the practice. For such sellers, the ethical questions can be numerous, not the least of which is just what the lawyer is selling.

Selling Clients

A lawyer's sale of her law practice does not necessarily include the transfer of clients, their files or their business. The client always retains the right to decide whether he will become the client of the buyer or will seek alternate representation. The duty to inform the client is that of the seller. The rules of ethics generally require that all clients be informed of certain matters. ABA Model Rule 1.17(c) requires the seller to inform the client of the proposed sale, the client's right to retain other counsel and the fact that the client's consent to the transfer of the client's files will be presumed unless the client acts timely.

Often, the seller and buyer will take additional action to assure that the seller's clients will likely follow the buyer. The seller is interested in maximizing the value of the business and therefore the purchase price and the buyer's interest is in securing a thriving business. Therefore it is often in both the seller's and buyer's best interest if the clients are also informed of the seller's confidence that the buyer will perform well for them and also to present the buyer's resume in order to encourage the client to stay with the new buyer.

Typically, an agreement that limits the right of an attorney to practice law is unenforceable. However, when a non-compete agreement is part of the sale of practice, it will commonly be enforced because it is exempt from the prohibition in ABA Model Rule 5.6.[68]

Ethics Advisory Opinion

UPON THE REQUEST OF A MEMBER OF THE SOUTH CAROLINA BAR, THE ETHICS ADVISORY COMMITTEE HAS RENDERED THIS OPINION ON THE ETHICAL PROPRIETY OF THE INQUIRER'S CONTEMPLATED CONDUCT. THIS COMMITTEE HAS NO DISCIPLINARY AUTHORITY. LAWYER DISCIPLINE IS ADMINISTERED SOLELY BY THE SOUTH CAROLINA SUPREME COURT THROUGH ITS COMMISSION ON LAWYER CONDUCT.

Ethics Advisory Opinion 02-14: Law Firm has been in existence since 1989 and has maintained most client files at the conclusion of the legal matters. Lawyer A has been with the firm since its inception but is now ready to wind down his career. Lawyer B, who was hired in 1998, will remain with the firm. Lawyer B has had no contact with the vast majority of clients of the firm prior to 1998.

---

[68] ABA Model Rules of Professional Responsibility, Rule 5.6 comment [3]

Questions:

1. What ethical obligations does Lawyer B owe to the former clients of Lawyer A?

2. What obligations does Lawyer A have in maintaining the files of former clients?

3. How long must a file be maintained? Under what circumstances may a file be destroyed?

4. Should a file be returned to the client at the close of the practice?

Summary:

1. If Lawyer B is purchasing Lawyer A's existing practice, then Rule 1.17 applies and Lawyer A should retain the files of inactive clients and Lawyer B would have no more of an ethical obligation to Lawyer A's inactive clients than he had prior to the purchase. Unless Lawyer B was involved with the inactive client prior to the purchase, Lawyer B would have no ethical obligations to Lawyer A's clients. If Lawyer B is continuing the existing firm, then the inactive clients are still clients of the firm and Lawyer B would have a continuing duty to those clients, including the general duties of competence, confidentiality, communication, and conflicts of interest.

2. If Lawyer B purchases Lawyer A's practice pursuant to Rule 1.17, then Lawyer B should not take possession of the files of Lawyer A's former clients and is not obligated to them. If Lawyer B merely continues the existing firm's practice, then the files remain files of the firm and Lawyer B would be required to maintain those files as he would maintain any other file of the firm.

3. Because a client file is the property of the client, under Rule 1.15 it is appropriate for the lawyer to retain records of the property for a minimum of six years after the end of the representation. File contents should not be disposed of until such time as it is reasonable to believe that their disposal will not prejudice or potentially prejudice the rights of the client.

4. Rule 1.16(d) requires that upon termination of representation, the lawyer shall return papers and property to which the client is entitled.

Opinion:

It would appear from the facts given, that Lawyer A and Lawyer B are the only lawyers in the firm. Lawyer B's ethical obligations relating to the former clients of Lawyer A depend on whether Lawyer B is purchasing Lawyer A's law practice or continuing the representations undertaken by Lawyer A. If a purchase, both Lawyer A and Lawyer B have an obligation to ensure that the requirements of Rule 1.17 are followed. Rule 1.17(a)(4)(iv) presumes that the selling lawyer will retain files of inactive clients unless specific actions are undertaken. It stands to reason, then, that if Lawyer B will not take possession of Lawyer A's inactive files, that he would also owe no ethical duties to the inactive clients to which those files pertain. The Comment to Rule 1.17 makes note of the continuing duties to an inactive client that remain vested in the selling lawyer. In the event of the sale of a law practice, the purchasing attorney owes no ethical obligations to the inactive clients of the selling attorney whose files remain in the possession of the selling attorney.

Conversely, if Lawyer B is not purchasing Lawyer A's practice, but is continuing the existing firm, then the clients are clients of the firm and the firm has an ongoing obligation to them. Inactive clients refer to clients whose files have been closed due to completion or termination of the representation. As a practical matter, Lawyer B's continuing ethical obligations to those inactive clients may be limited. However, Lawyer B's agreement to take over the firm is tantamount to accepting representation of all the clients of the firm, the inactive clients of A become the inactive clients of Lawyer B, and the general duties any law firm owes its inactive clients remain.

If Lawyer B does not wish to take on the responsibilities inherent in an ongoing practice, including the obligations to the inactive clients as well as the responsibility for their files, Lawyer B should purchase Lawyer A's law practice pursuant to Rule 1.17, and insist that Lawyer A retain possession of all his inactive client files.

Separate from the issues regarding Lawyer B's responsibilities to inactive clients and their files is the issue of how long any client file must be kept and under what circumstances may a client file be destroyed. Rule 1.15 deals with the safekeeping of a client's property. In SC Bar Ethics Adv. Op. #98-33, we indicated, in the absence of an agreement with the client, the attorney should retain files for at least six years and may place the files on computer disks or other electronic media. Depending on the nature of the material, retention beyond six years may be necessary if destruction might prejudice the client. See SC Bar Ethics Adv. Op. #95-18. The safest course is to enter into a reasonable agreement with the client regarding file retention. SC Bar Ethics Adv. Op. #92-19.

With regard to returning a file at the close of a law practice, Rule 1.16 (d) of the SCACR provides, "upon termination of representation, a lawyer shall take steps to the extent reasonable and practical to protect a client's interests...surrendering paper and property to which the client is entitled... the lawyer may retain papers relating to the client to the extent permitted by other law." Rule 1.15(b) states, "except as stated in this rule or otherwise permitted by law or by agreement with the client, a lawyer shall promptly deliver to the client or third person any funds or other property that the client or third person is entitled to receive..."1 If a client file contains property belonging to the client and (1) it has not already been returned to the client, (2) no written agreement governing the file's retention has been entered into between the client and the lawyer, and (3) the client has not abandoned its property after reasonable notice, then the client file should be returned to the client at the close of the practice. If a client file does not contain any property belonging to the client, then there is no duty to return the file to the client at the close of the practice unless the failure to return the file to the client will prejudice the client in any way.

REVIEW QUESTIONS

1. A lawyer is prohibited from conflicts of interest unless the client gives "informed consent". What does "Informed consent" require?

2. Not all states require lawyers to participate in continuing legal education courses annually. State X does not. What, if anything would Attorneys in State X be required to do under the model rules of professional conduct?

3. Attorney represented Client in a federal RICO action. The government's case was not good and they did not want the Client to be found not guilty. The government believed that Client was a low level participant in the conspiracy and needed leverage to get the folk at the top who they believed Attorney also represented. In an effort to build their case against their targets, the government seized all of Attorney's assets, claiming that Attorney was a participant in the criminal enterprise because he knew or reasonably should have known that his clients were running a criminal business and that the Attorney was paid from the proceeds of the criminal enterprise. The government believed that Attorney would willingly identify his clients in order to regain access to his assets. Following the seizure, the government subpoenaed the Attorney to release the source(s) of all income he earned or received during the prior five years. The subpoena demanded that Attorney reveal the name of each client and each case that was the basis for the income. Attorney fully disclosed the government's request to his clients, most of whom told the Attorney not to reveal the information. Consequently, Attorney refused to provide the information to the government. Is Attorney subject to discipline for refusing to furnish the information to the government?

4. Attorney was retained by Client to represent him. Client paid Attorney $5,000 but due to the complexity of the case, a reasonable attorney fee would be close to $25,000. Client's partner believed the suit was unfounded and motivated by malice. Partner sent Attorney a check for $25,000 for payment of Client's fee. Partner told Attorney not to tell Client of the payment. Is it proper for Attorney to accept Partner's check?

5. Your client has confessed to a murder of a security guard and shows you irrefutable proof of his claim. The police have arrested, the prosecutor has charged and the grand jury has issued an indictment against another man for the crime. Charged with one count of capital murder, one count of assault with a deadly weapon, multiple counts of felony burglary, robbery and a host of other associated crimes, the defendant faced the death penalty if convicted. After a two-week trial, Defendant was sentenced to life imprisonment without the possibility of parole. Defendant was represented by competent counsel and the record is vacant of reversible error. Throughout the trial defendant declared that he was innocent of the crime. Are you able to reveal the fact that it is your client who is guilty without violating the model rules of professional conduct?

6. Attorney represented Client First last year in a case where First was a plaintiff against a large corporation. The cause of action sounded in breach of contract. Attorney vigorously represented First who won resoundingly. This year, Client Second, a different corporation

seeks to retain Attorney to hire it in representing it against a plaintiff who has brought a similar cause of action as First had. If Attorney were to represent Different, she would have to argue the opposite position she took when representing First. Will Attorney be permitted to represent Different without violating the model rules of professional conduct?

7. Attorney represents a man suspected of murdering his wife and four children. Man is not charged with the offense but during the course of representation admits to Attorney that he committed the offenses. One year after his confession, Client commits suicide leaving a suicide note that said "everything you might want to know about my family, I told Attorney". Police investigating the suicide, contact Attorney and ask that he reveal everything that Client told him. Attorney claims attorney client privilege and refuses to reveal the confession. Prosecutors argue that there is no privilege that protects the communication because the Client is deceased. May Attorney reveal the confession under these circumstances?

8. Similar facts as in question 7, except here, Client is not a suspect. Instead police arrest a neighbor who was seen near the victims' home on the night of the crime. Neighbor vehemently denies committing the crime, but is nonetheless tried and convicted. Neighbor is sentenced to life in prison without the possibility of parole. Will Attorney be permitted to reveal his Client's confession?

9. Attorney represents Client in a criminal case where Client was accused of violating State Blue Sky laws. Client was acquitted but only after a witness perjured testimony. After the acquittal, the perjury became clear and Attorney is charged with suborning perjury. In her defense, Attorney reveals that Client had not told her about the perjury until after the case was over. She also reveals that Client had told Attorney after the trial that he and witness had intentionally orchestrated the perjured testimony. Finally, Attorney reveals that Client told her that she was not to reveal his confidences. Is Attorney subject to discipline for revealing her Client's confidence?

10. Prospective Client (PC) meets with Attorney to discuss the possibility of representation. After the meeting, PC decides not to hire Attorney. During the meeting, however, PC had disclosed highly incriminating information to Attorney. Because PC never hired Attorney, prosecutors call Attorney to testify about what PC had said during their meeting. Attorney refuses to disclose the information, notwithstanding the fact that he was never PC's attorney. Is Attorney permitted to make the disclosure?

11. Attorney represents Client in a civil action. Client and the opposing party are neighbors who have been embroiled in a bitter feud for more than a decade. One day, Client tells Attorney that the opponent makes him so mad that he has been thinking about "going to his house and killing him with his bare hands". Attorney has heard similar from Client before and does not believe Client is likely to do any such thing. A week later, Opponent is found dead after having been suffocated in his home. The neighbor's wife finds out about Client's warning to Attorney so she sues Attorney for wrongful death in civil district court. She also seeks to have Attorney disbarred. Is Attorney subject to civil liability for failure to report Client's threat? Has Lawyer violated the model rules? What should Lawyer do to comply with the rules?

ATTORNEYS, ADVISORS AND COUNSELORS AT LAW

> ## *IN THE NEWS:*
>
> Brian Keith Banks was a high school football star who had been highly sought after by various universities. He had orally agreed to attend and play for University of Southern California (USC) but was accused of rape by a high school classmate. The prosecutors offered a deal, plead guilty and face up to 18 months in prison or proceed to trial where he risked conviction and a prison sentence for up to 41 years. Banks's lawyer told him he had ten minutes to decide after advising him to take the deal. Banks plead no contest and was sentenced to six years in prison, five years probation and required to register as a sex offender for the rest of his life.
>
> After spending five years in prison, his accuser admitted to lying. He has been exonerated and has attempted to go back to playing football.
>
> Most criminal cases are settled through plea bargaining. But it has to be a gut wrenching decision for the attorney who must counsel a client she believes is innocent to take the plea because the only alternative appears to be conviction at trial and a harsher sentence. Is it ethical for an attorney to give that advice?
>
> Not only is defense counsel challenged in the plea bargaining scenario, but what of the prosecutor who believes the defendant may not be guilty. Is it ethical for the prosecutor to pursue the case?
>
> For more, see: Brian Banks' Lawyer's Dilemma: The Ethics of Counselling An Innocent Client To Plead Guilty, http://ethicsalarms.com/2012/05/31/brian-banks-lawyers-dilemma-the-ethics-of-counselling-an-innocent-client-to-plead-guilty/

A Lot at Stake

Law students spend almost three years in school learning to think like a lawyer. Thinking like a lawyer commonly implies that in a given situation, you can identify the problems or issues and logically and methodically identify the potential strengths and weaknesses of the possible solutions. Clients entrust their problems to lawyers because of their ability to think like a lawyer (think analyticaslly).

Once the lawyer has thought the case through, (s)he must be able to communicate what she has learned to the client. Commonly, the lawyer must relay to the client all the options and potential solutions discovered, and also counsel the client regarding which approach is best. In this regard, the lawyer helps counsel the client from the logical perspective of a neutral observer. Relying on the lawyer's skill, professionalism and fiduciary duties to the client, the lawyer must advise the client.

In advising the client, the lawyer counsels the client on strategy and procedures to effect the client's preferred results. Ethically, the lawyer is required to advise the client candidly and without interference from pressures other than the lawyer's independent judgment. However, the lawyer is not limited to legal judgment, and may consider social, economic, moral and other factors, in rendering advice.[69]

Advice to third parties

Generally, the attorney advises his client. Lawyers should refrain from giving advice to non-clients, because, among other reasons, such advisement could lead to the unintentional consequence of creating an attorney client relationship.[70] On the other hand, there are times when the lawyer's obligation to the client requires the lawyer to render an opinion or evaluation that she reasonably believes third parties will rely. In this situation, the lawyer must believe that the opinion or evaluation is in the client's interests.

These situations may occur in more instances than expected. For example, business lawyers are often requested by client's auditors to provide legal impressions about legal matters that a client has pending. Part of such audit may be a legal opinion about the likely outcome of the legal matter reported. It is incumbent upon the lawyer to refrain from disclosing client confidential matters as well as information that would not be in the client's interest. This responsibility could easily conflict with the lawyer's obligation to be truthful in his representations to third parties.[71]

Lawyers as third-party neutrals

During the history of US courts, as court dockets filled with legal disputes, alternative resolution methods were sought. These methods, including mediation and arbitration have grown over the past decades. Lawyers increasingly became certified arbiters or mediators. In such capacity, the lawyer does not represent either of the parties to the dispute but instead serves as an independent third party that considers all sides and attempts to reach a fair resolution to the problem. Ethically, lawyers who serve in these positions, in addition to putting all parties on notice regarding his or her role as mediator/arbiter should conduct a conflicts check to ensure that no conflict of interest will bar his or her service.

In the Matter of F. Mikell Harper
351 S.C. 575 (S.C. 2002)

Disciplinary Counsel brought discipline action against attorney. After parties entered into consent agreement, the Supreme Court held that attorney's conduct in advising client to invest in company in which he had substantial interest warranted definite suspension for nine months. Ordered accordingly.

In this attorney disciplinary matter, respondent and Disciplinary Counsel have entered into an Agreement for Discipline by Consent pursuant to Rule 21, RLDE, Rule 413, SCACR. In

---

[69] ABA Model Rules of Professional Conduct [2.1]
[70] *Central Die Casting and Mfg. Co., Inc. v. Tokheim Corp.,* 1994 WL 233653, 2 (1994) See also *Westinghouse Electric Corp. v. Kerr-McGee Corp.,* 580 F.2d 1311 (11th Cir.) cert. denied. 439 US 995 (1978)
[71] ABA Model Rules of Professional Conduct [4.1]

the agreement, respondent conditionally admits misconduct and consents to a definite suspension from the practice of law for a period of up to nine months. We accept the agreement and suspend respondent for nine months. The facts as admitted in the agreement are as follows. In 1997, this Court suspended respondent for 60 days for engaging in business dealings with a client. In the Matter of Harper, 326 S.C. 186, 485 S.E.2d 376 (1997).

Facts

Respondent was retained by Client, a personal acquaintance, to represent Client in various matters from January 1993 through September 1994. Client had previously recovered a sum of money in a divorce proceeding and, after consulting respondent, invested the funds in Waterhouse II, L.P (Waterhouse), a company in which respondent owned a substantial interest. Waterhouse owned property in Beaufort County, South Carolina and planned to construct and operate an assisted living complex for elderly people.

Client invested $69,500 in Waterhouse through loans evidenced by four promissory notes. The first note was in the amount of $49,500 and executed by Atlantis Title Agency (Atlantis Title), which was the general partner of Waterhouse and solely owned by respondent. The note was secured by 11% of the shares of stock in Waterhouse. A second note in the amount of $25,000 was also executed by Atlantis Title and secured by 7% of the shares of stock in Waterhouse.

A third note in the amount of $15,000 and secured by 2 1/2 % of the shares of stock in Waterhouse was executed by another acquaintance of respondent (Acquaintance) and prepared by respondent. The fourth note, also prepared by respondent, was in the amount of $5000 and unsecured. None of these notes were paid on maturity or thereafter by respondent or Acquaintance. Throughout all periods relevant to this agreement, respondent, Atlantis Title, and Acquaintance owned interests in Waterhouse, and respondent was the sole owner of Atlantis Title.

After respondent began representing Client, respondent became aware that Acquaintance was having significant financial difficulties, was involved in a divorce, and had filed for bankruptcy protection. However, respondent failed to advise Client of Acquaintance's financial difficulties. Respondent was also aware that Atlantis Title would be unable to honor Client's notes upon maturity, but failed to notify Client. Respondent did not advise Client how to seek legal recourse against Acquaintance and Atlantis Title, and did not inform Client that Client might have had certain remedies of recision[sic] relating to the issuance of stock in Waterhouse. Respondent also failed to advise Client that she might have been able to seek additional security for payment of the notes. Further, respondent failed to advise Client of possible conflicts of interest and that she should seek independent legal advice concerning her investments in Waterhouse.

As a result of the default on the notes, Client initiated legal proceedings. Respondent consented to an order of judgment against him to expedite recovery by the Client from respondent's insurance carrier. As a result, Client has partially recovered her claimed losses under a confidential settlement agreement with the insurance carrier.

Law

Respondent admits that his conduct violated the following Rules of Professional Conduct, Rule 407, SCACR: Rule 1.1 (failing to provide competent representation); Rule 1.2 (failing to abide by a client's decisions concerning the objectives of representation, and failing to consult with the client as to the means by which they are to be pursued); Rule 1.3 (failing to act with reasonable diligence and promptness while representing a client); Rule 1.4 (failure to keep a client reasonably informed about the status of a matter and failing to promptly comply with requests for information); Rule 1.7 (a lawyer shall not represent a client if the representation of that client may be materially limited by the lawyer's responsibilities to another client or to a third person, or by the lawyer's own interests); Rule 1.8 (a lawyer shall not enter into a business transaction with a client or knowingly acquire an ownership, possessory, security or other pecuniary interest adverse to a client unless the terms of the transaction are in writing and fair and reasonable to the client and the client is given an opportunity to seek advice from independent counsel); Rule 2.1 (failing to exercise independent professional judgment and render candid advice to client); Rule 8.4(a) (violating the Rules of Professional Conduct); and Rule 8.4(e) (engaging in conduct prejudicial to the administration of justice).

Conclusion

We find that respondent's misconduct warrants a definite suspension. Accordingly, we accept the Agreement for Discipline by Consent and suspend respondent from the practice of law for nine months. Within fifteen days of the date of this opinion, respondent shall file an affidavit with the Clerk of Court showing that he has complied with Rule 30 of Rule 413, SCACR.

****

REVIEW QUESTIONS

1. Client asks Lawyer's advice regarding a law that recently took effect. The law required companies that "employed" undocumented workers to report such workers to the federal authorities within thirty days or be subject to arrest, fines up to $5,000 per worker not reported per day and up to 5 years in prison. Client believes in open borders and that the law violates his right to freely associate. Attorney advises him that the law is enforceable unless successfully challenged and that during the interim, he would be subject to arrest and other penalties for employing undocumented workers. Attorney also advises Client that the law may have a loophole in that it does not appear to cover independent contractors. Attorney explains what an independent contractor is and what was required to meet the independent contractor status. Attorney also tells Client that because the law was untested, she did not know how effective claiming independent contractors would be. Client then fired all his employees, including the documented workers and contracted with them in accordance with the information that he received from his Attorney. Is Attorney subject to discipline?

2. Corporation has recently been served with a shareholder demand. In response corporation seeks counsel. The law firm agrees to conduct an investigation of the claims and to reach a decision regarding the corporation's responsibility under the circumstances. There is no prior relationship between the law firm and any of the parties involved. Law firm charges the corporation a hefty legal fee for their investigation which concludes that the corporation should reject the shareholder demand. In a thorough written report, the law firm points out the various reasons that the corporation had not acted wrongfully, that the directors and officers were protected by the business judgment rule and that the shareholder should take nothing. Law firm was aware that the report would likely be relied upon by a court and claimant. Does the law firm have any duty to the non-clients who may rely on their report?

3. Mediator, a licensed attorney attempts to settle a dispute between the parties before her. Each of the parties is represented by counsel. The dispute arises from the sale of real property that Seller sold to Purchaser who then sold it to Third party. Seller had failed to reveal that there was a five year option on the property. The original sale occurred within the second year of the option agreement. The second sale occurred during the third year and in the fourth year, Optioner attempted to exercise the option only then to discover the property had been sold. Optioner demands specific performance. Who does mediator represent?

4. Same facts as in question three above. Attorney for Seller was formerly an associate in the law firm where mediator was a partner and had on various occasions worked under Mediator's supervision. Mediator thought highly of Attorney. Mediator also knew the Lawyer for the Optioner and believed him to be a bit of a cad who took short cuts in handling his cases and clients. Mediator did not know either of the other attorneys. Will Mediator violate the model rules of professional conduct if she fails to recuse herself?

5. Lawyer sits as the arbitrator in a dispute between two parties. Later, one of the parties asks the Lawyer to represent her in an action against the other party, based substantially on the facts discussed during the earlier arbitration. Will Lawyer violate the model rules of professional conduct if she represents the party?

* * * * * * * * * * * * * * * *

IN THE NEWS:

Strategy vs Frivolity

Lawyers are trained beginning first year in law school that it is wrong to file a frivolous or defense. However, how they are trained after leaving law school is another story altogether. Consider, for example, the lesson provided at one seminar for trucking industry insurance defense lawyers where a speaker explained his defense strategy:

Even in a case of clear liability against a truck driver or a trucking company, the defendant truck driver and trucking company should deny fault and place all of the blame on the plaintiff, because utilizing such a strategy will allow "defense-leaning jurors" to ultimately side with the plaintiff-leaning jurors on fault. Then, because the defense-leaning jurors have caved in on liability, they will now be "owed a favor" by the plaintiff-leaning jurors. The favor comes in the form of "keeping the verdict down."

For more, see: Frivolous Defense: A Case From Trucking, http://www.romanolawgroup.com/blog/frivolous-defense-a-case-from-trucking/

Lawyers have ethical responsibilities to ensure that the claims and defenses they file are meritorious, that litigation is conducted expeditiously, that representations made to the court are honest, that the matter is performed with civility to the opposing party and counsel and that the administration of justice is protected and preserved. In addition, the prosecutor in a criminal case has especial ethical obligations.

During your first year in civil procedure class, you learned about the lawyer's duty to ensure the claim or defense was meritorious.[72] You undoubtedly also learned about the lawyer's role in ensuring that cases are handled expeditiously.[73] A basic tenet of professional ethics is that the lawyer will conduct herself honestly in her professional and personal life. The challenge for the lawyer is to identify the conduct demanded of her when following the letter of the rule works to the disadvantage of her client. For example, your client wishes to pursue a matter that you believe is being pursued to harass the opponent. However, the claim meets the 'meritorious' threshold because there is a legal basis for it. Does the ethical lawyer pursue the matter on behalf of the client? When is it ethically permissible for the attorney to employ legal methods for the purpose of delaying rather than expediting litigation? What does the lawyer do when her client in a criminal defense case insists on perjuring himself during his trial testimony?

What is required from the attorney in these situations may vary between jurisdictions. For example, in some jurisdictions, the attorney who believes her client will offer perjurious testimony, may permit the client to testify using a narrative approach.[74] A comment to the ABA

---

[72] Consider Rule 11, Federal Rules of Civil Procedure
[73] ABA Model Rules of Professional Conduct, Rule 3.2 Comment [1]
[74] See ABA Model Rules of Professional Conduct [Rule 3.3 comment 7]

model rules provide that the lawyer cannot refuse to allow the client to offer the testimony unless the lawyer knows that the client is lying.[75]

In effect, the lawyer is often placed in a position somewhere between permissible advocacy and conduct that is outside the boundaries imposed by ethical obligations.[76]

Prosecutors and advocacy

Because they represent the government, prosecutors exercise a power and authority that few others hold in our society.[77] The quagmire presented by the advocate's varying roles may be more daunting for the criminal prosecutor. In our adversarial system of justice, it is often viewed as the role of the prosecutor to pursue convictions. Often considered a lofty goal to get criminals off the streets, in fact the prosecutors' role is supposed to be about ensuring just results.

In Berger v. United States, the United States Supreme Court recognized the prosecutor's role as more lofty than winner or loser of an adversarial battle.[78] While stating that the prosecutor has a duty to prosecute with earnestness and vigor, the court also said that it was as much his duty to refrain from improper methods calculated to produce a wrongful conviction as it is to use every legitimate means to bring about a just one. The court stated that in a criminal prosecution the prosecutor's goal is not that it shall win a case, but that justice shall be done.[79] A prosecutor's overzealous acts could cause justice to be substantially delayed or to be denied altogether.[80]

Zealous Advocacy

[A]n advocate, in the discharge of his duty, knows but one person in all the world, and that person is his client. To save that client by all means and expedients, and at all hazards and costs to other persons, and, amongst them, to himself, is his first and only duty; and in performing this duty he must not regard the alarm, the torments, the destruction which he may bring upon others. Separating the duty of a patriot from that of an advocate, he must go on reckless of the consequences, though it should be his unhappy fate to involve his country in confusion.

statement by
Henry Lord Brougham in 1820 in *Queen Caroline's Case*[81]:

Among the lawyer's responsibilities is that of zealous advocacy of her client's position. Even as some states have dropped "zealous" from describing the attorney's duty of advocacy,[82] the

---

[75] See ABA Model Rules of Professional Conduct [Rule 3.3 comment 9]

[76] For e.g. Qualcomm Inc v Broadcom Corp., 548 F.3d 1004 (U.S.Ct.App.-Fed., 2008) where the plaintiff's lawyers concealed a pertinent fact in the case

[77] Brian A. Sun, The Overzealous Prosecutor, 18 Litigation 38 (1991-1992)

[78] 295 U.S. 78, 55 S Ct. 629 (1935)

[79] Id. at 633

[80] See Robert P. Mosteller, *The Special Threat of Informants to the Innocent Who are not Innocents: Producing "First Drafts." Recording Incentives, and Taking a Fresh Look at the Evidence*, 6 Ohio St J of Crim L 519 ( ) citing Robert P. Mosteller, *The Duke Lacrosse Case, Innocence, and False Identifications: A Fundamental Failure to "Do Justice,"* 76 FORDHAM L. REV. 1337, 1337 (2007).

[81] Monroe H. Freedman, *Henry Lord Brougham and Zeal*, 34 Hofstra L. Rev. 1319 (2006)

[82] See Lawrence J. Vilardo and Vincent E. Doyle III, Where Did the Zeal Go?, American bar Association, Journal of the Section of Litigation, Fall 2011 where authors state "New York adopted the ABA Model Rules of Professional Responsibility in 2009, but omitted "zeal" altogether –even from the preamble". *See* Paul C. Saunders, *Whatever*

requirement has remained part of the ABA's rules of ethics since the beginning.[83] In some instances, the lawyer's duty to provide zealous advocacy supercedes the lawyer's duty to the "truth". For example, criminal defense attorneys are entitled to force the prosecutor to prove their case beyond a reasonable doubt, notwithstanding the lawyer's belief that the client is guilty of the crime charged. The reconciliation between what appears to be two opposing duties is that the defense lawyer's duty to the client is in keeping with his duty to the administration of criminal justice system of advocacy.

Lawyers in civil cases may file motions for the purpose of excluding evidence--arguably the truth, because it is not in the client's interests. In some instances, truth may lie in the way of the administration of justice. In other words, when the lawyer acts within his role as advocate, zealous representation of the client's interest is not only acceptable and proper but right. The challenge for some lawyers may be the determination when zealousness stops and overzealousness begins.

Overzealousness begins at that point when the lawyer steps outside the legal and ethical bounds of advocacy.[84] Just where the point lies often depends on the circumstances.

Olmstead v. U.S.
277 U.S. 438, 48 S.Ct. 564, 66 A.L.R. 376 72 L.Ed. 944 (1928)

...

The petitioners were convicted in the District Court for the Western District of Washington of a conspiracy to violate the National Prohibition Act (27 USCA) by unlawfully possessing, transporting and importing intoxicating liquors and maintaining nuisances, and by selling intoxicating liquors. Seventy-two others, in addition to the petitioners, were indicted. Some were not apprehended, some were acquitted, and others pleaded guilty.

The evidence in the records discloses a conspiracy of amazing magnitude to import, possess, and sell liquor unlawfully. It involved the employment of not less than 50 persons, of two sea-going vessels for the transportation of liquor to British Columbia, of smaller vessels for coastwise transportation to the state of Washington, the purchase and use of a branch beyond the suburban limits of Seattle, with a large underground cache for storage and a number of smaller caches in that city, the maintenance of a central office manned with operators, and the employment of executives, salesmen, deliverymen dispatchers, scouts, bookkeepers, collectors, and an attorney. In a bad month sales amounted to $176,000; the aggregate for a year must have exceeded $2,000,000.[85]

Happened To 'Zealous Advocacy'?, 47 New York L. J. 245 (2011) available at http://www.cravath.com/files/Uploads/Documents/Publications/3272850_1.pdf
[83] ABA Model Rules of Professional Conduct, Preamble & Scope
[84] See generally Monroe H. Freedman, In Praise of Overzealous Representation-Lying to Judges, Deceiving Third Parties, and Other Ethical Conduct, 772 Hofstra L.Rev. 771 (2006)
[85] [In 2014 funds that would be $2,378,834 and $27,032,208 respectively; see www.calculator.net/inflation-calculator.html?cstartingamount1].

Olmstead was the leading conspirator and the general manager of the business. He made a contribution of $10,000 to the capital; 11 others contributed $1,000 each. The profits were divided, one-half to Olmstead and the remainder to the other 11. Of the several offices in Seattle, the chief one was in a large office building. In this there were three telephones on three different lines. There were telephones in an office of the manager in his own home, at the homes of his associates, and at other places in the city. Communication was had frequently with Vancouver, British Columbia. Times were fixed for the deliveries of the 'stuff' to places along Puget Sound near Seattle, and from there the liquor was removed and deposited in the caches already referred to. One of the chief men was always on duty at the main office to receive orders by the telephones and to direct their filling by a corps of men stationed in another room-the 'bull pen.' The call numbers of the telephones were given to those known to be likely customers. At times the sales amounted to 200 cases of liquor per day.

The information which led to the discovery of the conspiracy and its nature and extent was largely obtained by intercepting messages on the telephones of the conspirators by four federal prohibition officers. Small wires were inserted along the ordinary telephone wires from the residences of four of the petitioners and those leading from the chief office. The insertions were made without trespass upon any property of the defendants. They were made in the basement of the large office building. The taps from house lines were made in the streets near the houses.

The gathering of evidence continued for many months. Conversations of the conspirators, of which refreshing stenographic notes were currently made, were testified to by the government witnesses. They revealed the large business transactions of the partners and their subordinates. Men at the wires heard the orders given for liquor by customers and the acceptances; they became auditors of the conversations between the partners. All this disclosed the conspiracy charged in the indictment. Many of the intercepted conversations were not merely reports, but parts of the criminal acts. The evidence also disclosed the difficulties to which the conspirators were subjected, the reported news of the capture of vessels, the arrest of their men, and the seizure of cases of liquor in garages and other places. It showed the dealing by Olmstead, the chief conspirator, with members of the Seattle police, the messages to them which secured the release of arrested members of the conspiracy, and also direct promises to officers of payments as soon as opportunity offered.

The Fourth Amendment provides:

'The right of the people to be secure in their persons, houses, papers, and effects, against unreasonable searches and seizures, shall not be violated, and no warrants shall issue, but upon probable cause, supported by oath or affirmation, and particularly describing the place to be searched, and the persons or things to be seized.'

And the Fifth:

'No person * * * shall be compelled in any criminal case to be a witness against himself.'

It will be helpful to consider the chief cases in this court which bear upon the construction of these amendments.

146

Boyd v. United States, 116 U. S. 616, 6 S. Ct. 524, 29 L. Ed. 746, was an information filed by the District Attorney in the federal court in a cause of seizure and forfeiture against 35 cases of plate glass, which charged that the owner and importer, with intent to defraud the revenue, made an entry of the imported merchandise by means of a fraudulent or false invoice. It became important to show the quantity and value of glass contained in 29 cases previously imported. The fifth section of the Act of June 22, 1874 (19 USCA § 535), provided that, in cases not criminal under the revenue laws, *the United States attorney, whenever he thought an invoice, belonging to the defendant, would tend to prove any allegation made by the United States, might by a written motion, describing the invoice and setting forth the allegation which he expected to prove, secure a notice from the court to the defendant to produce the invoice, and, if the defendant refused to produce it, the allegations stated in the motion should be taken as confessed, but if produced the United States attorney should be permitted, under the direction of the court, to make an examination of the invoice, and might offer the same in evidence.* [emphasis added] ...

The court held the act of 1874 repugnant to the Fourth and Fifth Amendments. ...Concurring, Mr. Justice Miller and Chief Justice Waite said that they did not think the machinery used to get this evidence amounted to a search and seizure, but they agreed that the Fifth Amendment had been violated....

The next case, and perhaps the most important, is Weeks v. United States, 232 U. S. 383, 34 S. Ct. 341, 58 L. Ed. 652, L. R. A. 1915B, 834, Ann. Cas. 1815C, 1177, a conviction for using the mails to transmit coupons or tickets in a lottery enterpise. The defendant was arrested by a police officer without a warrant. After his arrest, other police officers and the United States marshal went to his house, got the key from a neighbor, entered the defendant's room, and searched it, and took possession of various papers and articles. Neither the marshal nor the police officers had a search warrant. The defendant filed a petition in court asking the return of all his property. The court ordered the return of everything not pertinent to the charge, but denied return of relevant evidence. After the jury was sworn, the defendant again made objection, and on introduction of the papers contended that the search without warrant was a violation of the Fourth and Fifth Amendments, and they were therefore inadmissible. This court held that such taking of papers by an official of the United States, acting under color of his office, was in violation of the constitutional rights of the defendant, and upon making seasonable application he was entitled to have them restored, and that by permitting their use upon the trial the trial court erred....

The United States takes no such care of telegraph or telephone messages as of mailed sealed letters. The amendment does not forbid what was done here. There was no searching. There was no seizure. The evidence was secured by the use of the sense of hearing and that only. There was no entry of the houses or offices of the defendants....

Neither the cases we have cited nor any of the many federal decisions brought to our attention hold the Fourth Amendment to have been violated as against a defendant, unless there has been an official search and seizure of his person or such a seizure of his papers or his tangible material effects or an actual physical invasion of his house 'or curtilage' for the purpose of making a seizure.

We think, therefore, that the wire tapping here disclosed did not amount to a search or seizure within the meaning of the Fourth Amendment. ...

Mr. Justice Brandeis (dissenting).

The defendants were convicted of conspiring to violate the National Prohibition Act (27 USCA). Before any of the persons now charged had been arrested or indicted, the telephones by means of which they habitually communicated with one another and with others had been tapped by federal officers. To this end, a lineman of long experience in wire tapping was employed, on behalf of the government and at its expense. He tapped eight telephones, some in the homes of the persons charged, some in their offices. Acting on behalf of the government and in their official capacity, at least six other prohibition agents listened over the tapped wires and reported the messages taken. Their operations extended over a period of nearly five months. The typewritten record of the notes of conversations overheard occupies 775 typewritten pages. By objections seasonably made and persistently renewed, the defendants objected to the admission of the evidence obtained by wire tapping, on the ground that the government's wire tapping constituted an unreasonable search and seizure, in violation of the Fourth Amendment, and that the use as evidence of the conversations overheard compelled the defendants to be witnesses against themselves, in violation of the Fifth Amendment.

The government makes no attempt to defend the methods employed by its officers. Indeed, it concedes that, if wire tapping can be deemed a search and seizure within the Fourth Amendment, such wire tapping as was practiced in the case at bar was an unreasonable search and seizure, and that the evidence thus obtained was inadmissible. But it relies on the language of the amendment, and it claims that the protection given thereby cannot properly be held to include a telephone conversation.

'We must never forget,' said Mr. Chief Justice Marshall in McCulloch v. Maryland, 4 Wheat. 316, 407 4 L. Ed. 579, 'that it is a Constitution we are expounding.' Since then this court has repeatedly sustained the exercise of power by Congress, under various clauses of that instrument, over objects of which the fathers could not have dreamed. [citations omitted] We have likewise held that general limitations on the powers of government, like those embodied in the due process clauses of the Fifth and Fourteenth Amendments, do not forbid the United States or the states from meeting modern conditions by regulations which 'a century ago, or even half a century ago, probably would have been rejected as arbitrary and oppressive.' [citation omitted]. Clauses guaranteeing to the individual protection against specific abuses of power, must have a similar capacity of adaptation to a changing world. ...Time works changes, brings into existence new conditions and purposes. ...

When the Fourth and Fifth Amendments were adopted, 'the form that evil had theretofore taken' had been necessarily simple. Force and violence were then the only means known to man by which a government could directly effect self-incrimination. It could compel the individual to testify-a compulsion effected, if need be, by torture. It could secure possession of his papers and other articles incident to his private life-a seizure effected, if need be, by breaking and entry. Protection against such invasion of 'the sanctities of a man's home and the privacies of life' was provided in the Fourth and Fifth Amendments by specific language. Boyd v. United States, 116

U. S. 616, 630, 6 S. Ct. 524, 29 L. Ed. 746. But 'time works changes, brings into existence new conditions and purposes.' Subtler and more far-reaching means of invading privacy have become available to the government. Discovery and invention have made it possible for the government, by means far more effective than stretching upon the rack, to obtain disclosure in court of what is whispered in the closet.

Moreover, 'in the application of a Constitution, our contemplation cannot be only of what has been, but of what may be.' The progress of science in furnishing the government with means of espionage is not likely to stop with wire tapping. Ways may some day be developed by which the government, without removing papers from secret drawers, can reproduce them in court, and by which it will be enabled to expose to a jury the most intimate occurrences of the home. Advances in the psychic and related sciences may bring means of exploring unexpressed beliefs, thoughts and emotions. ...

The evil incident to invasion of the privacy of the telephone is far greater than that involved in tampering with the mails. Whenever a telephone line is tapped, the privacy of the persons at both ends of the line is invaded, and all conversations between them upon any subject, and although proper, confidential, and privileged, may be overheard. Moreover, the tapping of one man's telephone line involves the tapping of the telephone of every other person whom he may call, or who may call him. As a means of espionage, writs of assistance and general warrants are but puny instruments of tyranny and oppression when compared with wire tapping.

... The makers of our Constitution undertook to secure conditions favorable to the pursuit of happiness. They recognized the significance of man's spiritual nature, of his feelings and of his intellect. ... Applying to the Fourth and Fifth Amendments the established rule of construction, the defendants' objections to the evidence obtained by wire tapping must, in my opinion, be sustained. It is, of course, immaterial where the physical connection with the telephone wires leading into the defendants' premises was made. And it is also immaterial that the intrusion was in aid of law enforcement. Experience should teach us to be most on our guard to protect liberty when the government's purposes are beneficent. *Men born to freedom are naturally alert to repel invasion of their liberty by evil-minded rulers. The greatest dangers to liberty lurk in insidious encroachment by men of zeal, well-meaning but without understanding. Independently of the constitutional question, I am of opinion that the judgment should be reversed. [emphasis added]*

Blackburn v. Goettel-Blanton
898 F.2d 95 (C.A. 9th, 1990)

This is a case of litigation run amok. A minor dispute that long ago should have been resolved by the parties without the help of lawyers has been transformed into an attorney-fee-generating machine. While yielding only $6,654 in damages, it has resulted in more than $133,000 in billings for plaintiffs alone. We consider, *inter alia,* whether Hawaii law permits an attorney's fees award to exceed the underlying judgment.

Facts
There's no doubt about it: Sheryl Goettl–Blanton breached a contract. Four years ago, she agreed to buy a condominium for $245,000, signed the appropriate forms and made a small

down payment. She even moved in. A month later, she changed her mind and refused to go through with the deal. The would-be sellers, Joseph and Mary Louise Blackburn, sued Blanton under the contract, as was their right. After much procedural wrangling, the case came to trial and the district court awarded the Blackburns damages of $6,654, prejudgment interest of $14,707.14, costs of $14,262.56 and attorney's fees of $61,250.

On appeal, Blanton challenges the award of attorney's fees. She contends that the amount awarded was excessive, and that the district court erred in denying her motions for a more detailed evidentiary hearing and for sanctions. While most of her contentions lack merit, we agree with defendant that the fees award exceeded Hawaii's statutory ceiling.

Discussion

Hawaii law prohibits awards of attorney's fees except where authorized by statute, stipulation or agreement. *Food Pantry, Ltd. v. Waikiki Bus. Plaza, Inc.*, 58 Haw. 606, 575 P.2d 869, 878 (1978). Here, the Deposit Receipt, Offer and Acceptance (DROA) signed by the parties stated that "the prevailing party shall be entitled to recover all costs incurred *including reasonable attorney fees* " (emphasis added). That agreement is tempered, however, by Hawaii Revised Statutes § 607–17 (1985), which provides, in relevant part, that where a contract "provides for a reasonable attorney's fee, not more than twenty-five per cent shall be allowed." Thus, we can affirm the attorney's fees award of $61,250 only if three requirements are met: (1) the Blackburns were the prevailing party; (2) the amount awarded was reasonable; and (3) the amount does not exceed the statutory twenty-five percent ceiling.

I

Blanton does not dispute that plaintiffs satisfy the first requirement; she focuses her attack on the second—the reasonableness of the award. We review the reasonableness of the district court's award of fees for abuse of discretion. *See Sharp v. Hui Wahine, Inc.*, 49 Haw. 241, 413 P.2d 242, 245 (1966). The thrust of Blanton's argument is that this case was so simple—her breach of contract so self-evident—that plaintiffs could not legitimately have amassed attorney's fees in excess of $133,000. Although we are strongly tempted by the logic of this argument, we must reject it.

This case presents clearly the dilemma faced by individuals who must seek redress through our legal system for concrete, yet modest, legal claims. Under a breach of contract theory, the plaintiffs were entitled only to the benefit of their bargain. This did not amount to much: When defendant breached the agreement, the condominium was still worth more or less what she had agreed to pay for it; all plaintiffs were entitled to recover, therefore, was the roughly $6000 it cost them to undo some minor physical alterations to the property and to find a new buyer. Yet, as anyone who has dealt with the law knows only too well, a $6000 claim is hardly worth litigating; it often costs more than that to hire a lawyer just to file a complaint. As here, the solution often adopted is to pile on a lot of big-ticket claims.

Thus, plaintiffs sued not only for breach of contract but also for intentional misrepresentation, negligent misrepresentation, willful and reckless breach, harassment and abuse of process. By the time they were finished, they were asking for more than $1 million, an amount more nearly worth fighting about. Defendant, for her part, further raised the stakes by removing the case to federal court, filing a counterclaim and heaping on every conceivable procedural and substantive defense. What had started out as a small contract squabble had suddenly become a major case.

Litigation has its own perverse logic and, the ante once having been raised more or less by mutual assent, the parties were locked into a wide-ranging and costly battle. The Blackburns sought extensive (and expensive) discovery as to *why* defendant had breached the contract. While irrelevant to their underlying contract claim, this discovery was relevant to their tacked-on claim for punitive damages. When defendant resisted, plaintiffs filed repeated motions to compel discovery and for sanctions.

Eventually, plaintiffs prevailed only on their contract claim, recovering approximately $6000 in damages, plus interest. They spent considerably more than that in litigating the case, however, and, given the scope of the claims and counterclaims, the district court concluded that a $61,250 award was reasonable. On this record, we are unable to conclude that the district court abused its discretion in awarding this amount of attorney's fees.

Moreover, even if the district court had determined that the tort claims did arise out of the contract, defendant could have argued that plaintiffs did not prevail on these claims. Both the DROA and section 607–17 have a prevailing party limitation. *See* pp. 96-97 & n. 3 *supra*. While the Hawaii Supreme Court has declared that fees can be recovered "where a party prevails on the disputed main issue, even though not to the extent of his original contention," *see Food Pantry,* 575 P.2d at 879, a strong argument might have been made that the inflated tort claims, not the relatively minor contract claim, were the focus of plaintiffs' lawsuit. As defendant did not raise any of these arguments, we do not consider them.

II

Plaintiffs, however, face an even more serious obstacle in recovering attorney's fees in this litigation, namely the twenty-five percent ceiling of section 607–17. Section 607–17 is a curious statute: it sets out a pithy, seemingly bright-line rule, yet its meaning is unclear. The section establishes a twenty-five percent ceiling on attorney's fees awards, but fails to identify the figure to which the percentage applies—presumably, either the judgment, the amount sought in the complaint or the value of the contract. The district court used the last of these figures; it awarded the Blackburns fees of $61,250, *i.e.,* twenty-five percent of the $245,000 contract price of the condominium.

We are unable to agree with the district court's construction of the statute. Our review of Hawaii caselaw leads us to the conclusion that section 607–17 limits an award of fees to twenty-five percent of the judgment. … In other words, if plaintiffs prevail, as here, the court may award them fees of up to twenty-five percent of the judgment. However, if a defendant wins—in which case there is no money judgment—the court can award her up to twenty-five percent of the amount prayed for in the complaint. … Here, plaintiffs prevailed; consequently, they were entitled to reasonable fees not to exceed twenty-five percent of the judgment. The judgment consisted of $6,654 in damages, plus $14,707.14 in prejudgment interest. *[citation omitted]* Accordingly, the total judgment was $21,361.14 and the fees award may not exceed $5,340.29. On remand, the district court may award any reasonable amount up to this ceiling.…

Conclusion

Lawsuits have become particularly inappropriate devices for resolving minor disputes. They are clumsy, noisy, unwieldy and notoriously inefficient. Fueled by bad feelings, they generate much heat and friction, yet produce little that is of any use. Worst of all, once set in motion, they are well-nigh impossible to bring to a halt.

This case is not atypical: A relatively minor dispute mushroomed into a full-blown war of attrition in which both sides suffered substantial casualties. The district judge called it "a cold turkey case" and he was right. Yet the parties trudged through four years of expensive and frustrating litigation all the same. As is quite often the case when litigation ends, neither side will be satisfied with the result we reach today.

We vacate the award of attorney's fees and remand to the district court. On remand, the court is instructed to award the Blackburns reasonable attorney's fees not to exceed $5,340.29 on their breach of contract claim, and reasonable fees for defending against defendant's counterclaim.

United States of America v. Sattar, a/k/a "Abu Omar," a/k/a "Dr. Ahmed," Stewart and Yousry
395 F.Supp.2d 79 (U S District Court, S.D. New York, 2005)

On February 10, 2005, after a lengthy trial, a jury found each of the defendants—Ahmed Abdel Sattar ("Sattar"), Lynne Stewart ("Stewart"), and Mohammed Yousry ("Yousry")—guilty on each of the counts in which they were charged in the seven-count superseding indictment ("S1 Indictment").

Count One of the S1 Indictment charged Sattar, Stewart, and Yousry with conspiring to defraud the United States in violation of 18 U.S.C. § 371. Count Two charged Sattar with conspiring to murder and kidnap persons in a foreign country in violation of 18 U.S.C. § 956. Count Three charged Sattar with soliciting persons to engage in crimes of violence in violation of 18 U.S.C. § 373. Count Four charged Stewart and Yousry with conspiring, in violation of 18 U.S.C. § 371, to provide and conceal material support to be used in preparation for, and in carrying out, the conspiracy alleged in Count Two. Count Five charged Stewart and Yousry with a substantive count of providing and concealing material support to the Count Two conspiracy, in violation of 18 U.S.C. §§ 2339A and 2. Counts Six and Seven charged Stewart with making false statements in violation 18 U.S.C. § 1001. See *United States v. Sattar*, 272 F.Supp.2d 348 (S.D.N.Y.2003) ("*Sattar I*"); *United States v. Sattar*, 314 F.Supp.2d 279 (S.D.N.Y.2004) ("*Sattar II*"). The jury found that the conspiracy charged in Count Two was solely a conspiracy to murder—and not to kidnap persons—in a foreign country, and that the crimes solicited as charged in Count Three were murder and conspiracy to murder.

At the conclusion of the Government's case, all defendants moved for a judgment of acquittal pursuant to Rule 29 of the Federal Rules of Criminal Procedure on the grounds that the evidence was insufficient to sustain a conviction. ... At the conclusion of all of the evidence and after the jury verdict, the defendants again moved for judgment of acquittal, and the Court reserved judgment.

... Each of the defendants has moved for a judgment of acquittal on each of the counts in which they are charged, but the only substantive arguments with respect to the insufficiency of the evidence have been raised by Stewart with respect to the Counts in which she is charged— namely Counts One, Four, Five, Six, and Seven.

Count One of the S1 Indictment alleges that, from about June 1997 through about April 2002, defendants Sattar, Stewart, and Yousry, as well as Sheikh Omar Abdel Rahman ("Abdel Rahman) and Rifaoi Ahmad Taha Musa, a/k/a "Abu Yasir" ("Taha"), together with others known and unknown, conspired to defraud the United States, in violation of 18 U.S.C. § 371, by obstructing the Department of Justice and the Bureau of Prisons in the administration and enforcement of the Special Administrative Measures ("SAM's") applicable to the imprisoned Sheikh Abdel Rahman. Stewart argues that there was insufficient evidence both of the existence of the Count One conspiracy and of her specific intent to join the conspiracy. In particular, Stewart argues that her actions were not calculated to deceive the Government, but rather to defy it openly. None of these arguments have merit.

The Court instructed the jury that, "in this case, the term 'conspiracy to defraud the United States' refers to charges that the defendants agreed to [employ] deceitful or dishonest means toward the Department of Justice and its agency, the Bureau of Prisons, in order to obstruct, interfere with, impair, impede, or defeat the administration and enforcement of Special Administrative Measures upon inmate Sheikh Omar Abdel Rahman." See *United States v. Ballistrea*, 101 F.3d 827, 831 (2d Cir.1996).

The evidence at trial was more than sufficient to show that Stewart conspired with Yousry, Sattar, Abdel Rahman, and others to defraud the United States Department of Justice and the Bureau of Prisons. Stewart's knowledge of the existence of the conspiracy to defraud and her intent to participate in it were inferable from her conduct and her statements.

The evidence showed that the Special Administrative Measures imposed upon Sheikh Abdel Rahman prohibited him from, among other things, passing or receiving communications from third persons with few exceptions. Abdel Rahman was permitted to communicate with his attorneys, but only with respect to legal matters. He could receive visits only from his attorneys and certain family members, and could communicate by telephone only with his legal spouse and his attorneys. Any correspondence to or from Abdel Rahman was required to be screened by the FBI to determine whether it contained either overt or covert requests for illegal activities, or actual or attempted circumvention of the SAMs. The SAMs also strictly prohibited Abdel Rahman from communicating with the news media in any manner, including through his attorneys. The SAMs required the attorneys of record for Abdel Rahman to sign an affirmation that counsel and anyone acting at counsel's behalf would abide by the SAMs.

The evidence further proved that in signing the attorney affirmations, Stewart affirmed, among other things, that she and her staff would abide by the SAMs; that she would not use her meetings with Abdel Rahman to pass messages between him and third parties; that she would not pass his messages to the media; and that she would be accompanied by a translator during prison visits only for the purpose of communicating with Abdel Rahman concerning legal matters. The affirmations specifically provided that the attorney understood that the Bureau of Prisons was relying on the sworn representation in affording Abdel Rahman the opportunity to meet or speak with the attorney.

A rational jury could find that Stewart and her co-defendants knew of the existence of the SAMs and the limitations the SAMs placed on Abdel Rahman's ability to communicate with others. A rational jury could find that, despite this knowledge, the defendants acted together to employ deceitful or dishonest means towards the Department of Justice and the Bureau of Prisons in order to obstruct the administration and enforcement of SAMs upon Abdel Rahman. The defendants did this primarily by smuggling messages to and from Abdel Rahman and by disseminating his statements to the media in the form of two press releases in June 2000, announcing his withdrawal of support for a cease-fire.

In March 1999, Stewart and Yousry visited Abdel Rahman at the Federal Medical Center in Rochester, Minnesota ("FMC Rochester").

The Islamic Group ("IG") is an organization that had been designated a "foreign terrorist organization" by the [United States] Secretary of State. Under the cease-fire, the IG had suspended terrorist operations in Egypt in an effort to persuade the Egyptian government to release IG leaders, members, and associates who were in prison in Egypt. Prior to the March 1999 visit to Abdel Rahman, Sattar had received a letter from two individuals named Gamal Sultan and Kamal Habib, who requested an opinion from Abdel Rahman as to whether the Islamic Group should form a political party in Egypt. A rational jury could find that, during the course of the March 1999 visit, Stewart and Yousry relayed to Abdel Rahman the requests from Taha and from Sultan and Habib, and received Abdel Rahman's response.

In response to Sultan's and Habib's letter, Abdel Rahman rejected the proposal that the Islamic Group form a political party. Abdel Rahman stated that the "cessation of violence" was a "matter of tactics and not of principle." In response to Taha's request for Abdel Rahman's support in ending the cease-fire, Abdel Rahman stated that he had "no objection," even though others were calling for the halt of violence. Significantly, Abdel Rahman instructed that "[n]o new charter, and nothing should happen or be done without consulting me, or informing me."

Following the visit, Sattar relayed Abdel Rahman's messages to both Taha and Mustafa Hamza ("Hamza"). Taha told Sattar that he wanted the letter for him "a little stronger."

Stewart and Yousry next visited Abdel Rahman at FMC Rochester on May 19 and 20, 2000. Three days before that visit, on May 16, 2000, Stewart signed an attorney affirmation again making the representations explained above. Stewart submitted the attorney affirmation to the United States Attorney's Office on May 26, 2000, ten days after she signed it, and six days after the May 2000 prison visit. A rational jury could find that during the visit, Stewart violated her affirmation.

The May 2000 visit was, unbeknownst to Stewart and Yousry, recorded on videotape. During that visit, Stewart and Yousry secretly brought into the prison a number of letters for Abdel Rahman. Among the correspondence was a letter from Sattar containing a message from Taha seeking Abdel Rahman's support in ending the cease-fire. In the letter, Sattar and Taha asked

154

Abdel Rahman to take a "more forceful position," and to "dictate some points" that could be announced by Stewart to the media.

On May 19, 2000, the first day of the visit, Stewart had Yousry read to Abdel Rahman the letter from Sattar with Taha's message. Stewart testified that Yousry translated Sattar's letter with Taha's message to her before their visit with Abdel Rahman on May 19, 2000. Stewart, who had brought Sattar's letter into the prison concealed in a legal pad, handed the letter to Yousry shortly before Yousry read it to Abdel Rahman. When Stewart passed the letter to Yousry, she mentioned to him that Abdel Rahman would need to think about his response to the letter, and Yousry so informed Abdel Rahman. Just before Yousry was about to read Taha's message to Abdel Rahman, Yousry saw the prison guards outside the window of their meeting room and alerted Stewart to that fact. Yousry instructed Stewart to talk to Abdel Rahman, as if they were engaged in a conversation. Stewart and Yousry then laughed while acknowledging that if the prison guards discovered that they were reading the letter to Abdel Rahman, they would be "in trouble." While Yousry read Sattar's and Taha's message to Abdel Rahman, Stewart and Yousry actively concealed that fact from the prison guards. Stewart pretended to be participating in the conversation with Abdel Rahman by making extraneous comments about food and eating.

On May 20, 2000, during the second day of the visit, Abdel Rahman dictated letters to Yousry in response to Taha's and Sattar's message. In his letter, Abdel Rahman stated, among other things, "what use is the initiative ... where we declared the halt of violence ... and the government continues to arrest the Islamic Group members, puts them to military trials, continues to execute and re-arrest them?" He urged that the opposition voice be heard and that Taha should be given "his natural right ... as head of the Group ... [if not] the least is to have the person in charge consult with him...."

During Abdel Rahman's dictation, Stewart actively concealed the conversation between Abdel Rahman and Yousry from the prison guards by again engaging in covering noises. Among other things, Stewart again periodically interrupted the dictation with extraneous comments and told Yousry to talk to her from time to time "for the sake of talking about something." After the visit, Stewart and Yousry brought out of the prison Abdel Rahman's dictated letters in response to Taha's and Sattar's message. Once back in New York, the letters were provided to Sattar, who relayed Abdel Rahman's message to Hamza and Taha. Stewart testified that, after the visit, Yousry translated for her Abdel Rahman's response to Sattar's and Taha's letter. Sattar told Taha that while the details of Abdel Rahman's message were relayed to Taha and Hamza, and the lawyer would meet with the press, the details of the message would not be conveyed publicly.

Following the May 2000 visit, Sattar spoke with Yousry, Taha, and Yassir Al-Sirri ("Al-Sirri") about the release of Abdel Rahman's statement. During a June 4, 2000 telephone conversation with Taha, Sattar told Taha that the release of Abdel Rahman's statement would not impact Sattar but "it will have an impact on the person would issued the statement." On the next day, June 5, 2000, Sattar spoke with Yousry about issuing a press release with Abdel Rahman's message. During their conversation, Sattar stated that he had spoken with Stewart about the content of the press release and he told Yousry also to speak with Stewart about it. Yousry suggested that the three of them meet to discuss the press release. On June 11, 2000, Sattar spoke with Al-Sirri about Abdel Rahman's withdrawal of support for the cease-fire, and about how to time the press release in order to maximize the value of the news coverage.

On June 13, 2000, Stewart and Sattar relayed Abdel Rahman's withdrawal of support for the cease-fire to Reuters reporter Esmat Salaheddin, who was based in Cairo, Egypt. Salaheddin testified at trial as to his conference call with Stewart and the accuracy of his article. In disseminating Abdel Rahman's statement, Stewart told Salaheddin that "Abdel Rahman is withdrawing his support for the cease-fire that currently exists." Stewart also told Salaheddin that "[prison authorities] may bar me from visiting him because of this announcement." The following day, Reuters and various Middle Eastern newspapers published articles about Abdel Rahman's withdrawal of support for the Islamic Group's cease-fire in Egypt.

As part of her case, Stewart entered into evidence a transcript that showed that while discussing with Yousry the fact that there were IG members blaming Sattar in the Arabic media for disseminating Abdel Rahman's statement and calling it a fabrication, Stewart states that she was "risking my whole career" in disseminating Abdel Rahman's statement, and that she was not doing it "lightly."

Stewart's dissemination of Abdel Rahman's withdrawal of support for the cease-fire and its publication in the media produced conflict within the Islamic Group between pro-cease-fire and pro-violence factions, with pro-cease-fire advocates denying that Abdel Rahman had issued the withdrawal. Stewart and Sattar responded by issuing Abdel Rahman's reaffirmation of his withdrawal of support for the cease-fire on June 21, 2000, by relaying it to Salaheddin. The statement reaffirmed that everything that was said in the previous statement was correct and that Abdel Rahman said those things. The statement also stated, "… I did not cancel the cease-fire. I do withdraw my support to the initiative. I expressed my opinion and left the matters to my brothers to examine it and study it because they are the ones who live there and they know the circumstances where they live better than I. I also ask them not to repress any other opinion within the Gama'a, even if that is a minority opinion." The jury could reasonably find that the "other opinion" was a reference to Taha.

On July 13 and 14, 2001, Stewart and Yousry visited Abdel Rahman at FMC Rochester. …This visit was also recorded on videotape without the knowledge of Stewart and Yousry. During this visit, at Sattar's request, Stewart and Yousry brought a message to Abdel Rahman from his son, Mohammed Abdel Rahman, which urged Abdel Rahman to continue to support an end to the cease-fire. They also secretly brought to Abdel Rahman messages and correspondence from other persons.

During this visit, Stewart and Yousry also told Abdel Rahman that Sattar had been informed that the U.S.S. Cole had been bombed on Abdel Rahman's behalf, and that Sattar was asked to convey to the United States Government that other things would follow if it did not free Abdel Rahman. Abdel Rahman said that negotiations should go through a lawyer. While Yousry was informing Abdel Rahman about these things, Stewart actively concealed the conversations between Yousry and Abdel Rahman from the prison guards by, among other things, tapping a water bottle on the table while stating that she was "just doing covering noises."

All of the evidence presented was more than sufficient to establish, beyond a reasonable doubt, that Stewart, Yousry, and Sattar participated in a conspiracy to defraud the United States. From the evidence of the concerted actions of Stewart, Yousry, and Sattar to relay Sattar's, Taha's, and Mohammed Abdel Rahman's messages to and from Abdel Rahman during prison visits, in violation of the SAMs, a rational jury could find the existence of the Count One conspiracy to defraud the United States regarding the SAMs. A rational jury could further infer the existence of the conspiracy from Stewart's and Yousry's concerted efforts to conceal from the prison guards and officials their conversations regarding Taha's and Sattar's messages to Abdel Rahman and Abdel Rahman's responses to them. A rational juror could also infer from the actions and words of each of the defendants that they knowingly participated in the conspiracy.

Stewart argues that there was insufficient evidence to prove the existence of a conspiracy to defraud the Government because Stewart's violations of the SAMs were entirely open and notorious and that this shows that Stewart's actions were designed to "defy, and not to defraud." (Stewart Reply Mem. at 6.) Stewart points in particular to her public dissemination of the press release following the May 2000 prison visit. This argument has no merit. A reasonable jury could certainly find that Stewart gained access to Abdel Rahman by deceit and dishonest means. ...This was not a case of defiance of the SAMs as opposed to the dishonest effort to violate them. As the Court noted in two prior opinions, Stewart had ample opportunities to challenge the SAMs and the attorney affirmations within the legal system, but chose not to do so.

Stewart also argues that there was no conspiracy to defraud because the Government actually recorded the May 2000 and July 2001 prison visits. This argument is also unavailing. ...

The Court of Appeals for the Second Circuit has frequently noted that the "essence of conspiracy is the agreement and not the commission of the substantive offense." *United States v. McDermott*, 245 F.3d 133, 137 (2d Cir.2001) (citation omitted). For a jury to find a defendant guilty of a conspiracy charge, the Government need not prove that the underlying substantive offense was actually committed. See *United States v. Rosengarten*, 857 F.2d 76, 78 (2d Cir.1988) (Section 371 conspiracy to defraud "need not involve the violation of a separate statute"). For the reasons explained above, a rational jury could find that the defendants, including Stewart, conspired to use deceitful and dishonest means to obstruct the administration and enforcement of the SAMs. The fact that the conspiracy did not in fact deceive the Government does not undermine the existence of the conspiracy. Further, the fact that prison visits were recorded by the Government does not undermine the evidence that the defendants were in fact conspiring to use deceitful and dishonest means. There is no evidence that Stewart and Yousry were aware that their visits were being recorded. Their actions were calculated to prevent the prison authorities from discovering what Stewart and Yousry were doing during their visits.

In addition, Stewart argues that the Government did not offer evidence sufficient to dispute Stewart's testimony that the purpose of her actions was to provide zealous representation to Abdel Rahman. (Stewart Mem. at 51.) This argument also fails. The jury was entitled to disbelieve the defendant's testimony and use its disbelief to supplement the other evidence against the defendant. See *Morrison*, 153 F.3d at 50; *Stanley*, 928 F.2d at 577. The jury could disbelieve that zealous representation included filing false affirmations, hiding from prison guards the delivery of messages to Abdel Rahman, and the dissemination of responses by him that were obtained through dishonesty. Moreover, the Court specifically charged the jury on good faith with respect to Count One, and a rational jury could find, consistent with that charge and all of the evidence, that the Government had proved bad faith. The defendants' motions for judgment of acquittal pursuant to Rule 29 on Count One are therefore denied.

…The Court has considered all of the arguments. To the extent not specifically addressed herein, the arguments are either moot or without merit. For the reasons stated above, all of the pending motions are denied.

****

Side Bar: Lynne Stewart was convicted and sentenced in 2005 to serve 28 months in prison. In 2010, she was resentenced to 10 years in prison for perjury at her trial. Immeidately upon conviction in 2005, Stewart was disbarred. On December 31, 2013, she was given a compassionate release order because she has been diagnosed with terminal breast cancer.[86]

****

The People of the State of Colorado v. Ain
35 P.3d 734 (Colo. 2001)

Attorney discipline proceeding was brought. The Office of the Presiding Disciplinary Judge held that attorney's knowing conversion by retaining unearned client funds for an extended period of time, in conjunction with her abandonment of clients, misrepresentations to other clients and to the court, and her disregard of court orders, warranted disbarment and order of restitution. Disbarment ordered. The Complaint in this action was filed February 12, 2001. Ain did not file an Answer to the Complaint. On April 13, 2001 the People filed a Motion for Default. Ain did not respond. On June 6, 2001 the PDJ issued an Order granting default, stating that all factual allegations set forth in the Complaint were deemed admitted pursuant to C.R.C.P. 251.15(b). The default Order also granted default on certain violations of The Rules of Professional Conduct ("Colo.RPC") alleged in the Complaint which were deemed admitted, default on certain other violations, which were subsequently dismissed by Order dated July 5, 2001.

Ain has taken and subscribed to the oath of admission, was admitted to the bar of the Supreme Court on October 27, 1987 and is registered upon the official records of this court, registration number 17112. Ain is subject to the jurisdiction of this court pursuant to C.R.C.P. 251.1(b).

The Brown Matter

Sue Brown ("Brown") hired Ain to represent her in a potential discrimination/wrongful termination action against Brown's employer. After initially filing a claim on Brown's behalf, Ain failed to specify Brown's claims for relief for several months despite opposing counsel's

---

[86] See Lorenzo Ferrigno and Ray Sanchez, *Dying defense lawyer Lynne Stewart released from jail*, *CNN Justice Report, January 1, 2014, available at* www.cnn.com/2013/12/31/justice/**lynne-stewart**-compassionate-release, *last visited June 29, 2014.*

requests that she do so; she failed to respond to opposing counsel's correspondence; she failed to timely and adequately provide discovery; she missed scheduled meetings with the client, and she failed to comply with the court's order requiring her to formally set forth Brown's claims. Consequently, Ain failed to act with reasonable diligence and promptness and neglected Brown's matter in violation of Colo. RPC 1.3 (an attorney shall not neglect a legal matter entrusted to that attorney).

Ain violated Colo. RPC 3.4(c)(an attorney shall not knowingly disobey an obligation under the rules of a tribunal) by failing to comply with the court's order directing her to file a complaint that formally stated her client's claims against the various defendants. Ain failed to keep Brown informed about the status of the matter in violation of Colo. RPC 1.4(a)(an attorney shall keep a client reasonably informed about the status of a matter and promptly comply with reasonable requests for information). Ain failed to make reasonable efforts to expedite the client's matter in violation of Colo. RPC 3.2(an attorney shall make reasonable efforts to expedite litigation consistent with the interests of a client). Ain knowingly misrepresented to her client that she was proceeding adequately in the case when in fact she was not. Such conduct is a violation of Colo. RPC 8.4(c)(engaging in conduct involving dishonesty, fraud, deceit, or misrepresentation). After withdrawing as Brown's attorney, Ain failed to return Brown's papers upon request in violation of Colo. RPC 1.16(d)(upon termination of representation, taking steps to the extent reasonably practicable to protect a client's interests, and refunding any advance payment of any fee not earned).

The Baker Matter

Dr. and Mrs. Baker (the "Bakers") retained Ain in August 1996, to represent them in a dispute over an automobile service contract with an automobile manufacturer. They paid Ain a $500 cost retainer and later paid her an additional $600. Ain provided incompetent advice to the Bakers with regard to the statute of limitations applicable to their claim in violation of Colo. RPC 1.1(an attorney shall provide competent representation to a client). Ain engaged in numerous acts of neglect in violation of Colo. RPC 1.3(neglect of a legal matter): she filed a complaint on behalf of the Bakers after the statute of limitations had expired; she tendered a check for filing costs drawn on her operating account with insufficient funds on deposit to cover the check; she failed to respond to opposing counsel's correspondence when advised of the legal deficiencies in the case; she delayed the case by failing to produce the clients' vehicle for inspection despite being requested to do so numerous times by defense counsel; she failed to respond to discovery requests; she neglected to interview certain essential witnesses for over sixteen months; she failed to draft a trial management order; she failed to obtain an expert opinion, and she failed to prepare the matter for trial.

Ain violated Colo. RPC 1.4(a) (an attorney shall keep a client reasonably informed about the status of a matter and promptly comply with reasonable requests for information) by repeatedly failing to respond to the Bakers' requests for information. Ain failed to communicate the client's rejection of the settlement offer to the defendant manufacturer; she failed to advise the clients of opposing counsel's correspondence regarding deficiencies in the lawsuit and affirmative defenses; she failed to advise the Bakers of the defendants' dispositive motions and Ain's failure to timely respond to the motions; she failed to inform the Bakers of the court's ruling on the motions and that the court dismissed their case, and she failed to inform them of the judgment against herself and her clients jointly and severally in the amount of $11,438.60 for attorney fees and $215.27 in costs.

Ain violated Colo. RPC 1.15(a) (an attorney shall hold clients' property separate from the attorney's own property) by placing the Bakers' $500 cost retainer in her operating account and commingling their funds with her own funds. Ain violated Colo. RPC 8.4(c)(engaging in conduct involving dishonesty, fraud, deceit, or misrepresentation) by misrepresenting to the court that she could not file a timely response to a summary judgment motion due to the client's failure to provide her with an affidavit when in fact she had never requested that the Bakers prepare an affidavit. Ain's repeated misrepresentations to the Bakers regarding the status of the case constitutes additional violations of Colo. RPC 8.4(c).

Ain violated Colo. RPC 3.2 (an attorney shall make reasonable efforts to expedite litigation consistent with the interests of a client) by failing to produce the Bakers' vehicle for inspection which precipitated delay in the case, and failing to make reasonable efforts to expedite litigation. Ain knowingly disobeyed a court order in violation of Colo. RPC 3.4(c)(an attorney shall not knowingly disobey an obligation under the rules of a tribunal) by failing to appear for her rule 69 deposition when ordered to do so by the court. Ain violated Colo. RPC 1.16(d)(an attorney shall, upon termination of representation, take steps to the extent reasonably practicable to protect a client's interests) by failing to return the Bakers' file when requested.

The Page/Densmore Matter

Nancy Page and her son, Case Densmore, hired Ain in late 1998 to represent Densmore regarding a dissolution of his marriage. Densmore paid Ain a $500 retainer. Ain was aware that Densmore was psychologically vulnerable. Densmore had recently attempted suicide as a result of the failed marriage. Ain incorrectly informed Densmore that the dissolution proceeding would take only forty-five days due to the short duration of the marriage. Such advice was incompetent and a violation of Colo. RPC 1.1 (an attorney shall provide competent representation to a client). Ain violated Colo. RPC 1.4(a) (an attorney shall keep a client reasonably informed about the status of a matter and promptly comply with reasonable requests for information) by repeatedly failing to return Densmore's phone calls and failing to communicate with Densmore from late 1998 to late summer 1999. Indeed, after her initial meeting with Densmore, in which she stated that the matter would be resolved within forty-five days, Ain failed to take any further legal action on the case. Such Failure to act with reasonable diligence and promptness in the representation is a violation of Colo. RPC 1.3(neglect of a legal matter). Notwithstanding her complete failure to take any steps to advance her client's dissolution of marriage, in late summer 1999, Ain told Page that she would check on the status of the case and thereby engaged in knowing deceit. Ain knew there was no case to check on and, by misleading Page, violated Colo. RPC 8.4(c).

Ain failed to make reasonable efforts to expedite litigation consistent with the client's interests in violation of Colo. RPC 3.2 (failure to expedite litigation). Ain violated Colo. RPC 1.15(b) (upon receiving funds or other property in which a client has an interest, an attorney shall promptly deliver to the client any funds or other property that the client is entitled to receive and render a full accounting) by failing to provide an accounting when Densmore requested she provide him with one.

To find abandonment rather than merely neglect, there must be proof that the attorney—during a given time period—was required to accomplish specific professional tasks for the client, failed to accomplish those tasks, and failed to communicate with the client. The proof must objectively indicate that the attorney has deserted, rejected and/or relinquished the professional responsibilities owed to the client.

In the present case, a finding of abandonment is warranted. The totality of facts which reveal the level of Ain's misconduct establish that she deserted, rejected and/or relinquished the professional responsibilities owed to her client and thereby abandoned him.

In addition, Ain accepted $500 from Densmore in return for her professional services. Despite her repeated assurances to her client suggesting the case was progressing, Ain performed no professional services for her client. Even after her client had demanded an accounting and filed a Request for Investigation, Ain did not refund the unearned $500. Ain's failure to refund the unearned $500 to her client for more than a year knowing that she had not performed the services for which the funds were paid is sufficient evidence to conclude that Ain knowingly converted her clients funds in violation of Colo. RPC 8.4(c)(engaging in conduct involving dishonesty, fraud, deceit, or misrepresentation).

In November 1999, Ain contacted Kenny Crumpton, an inmate at the Department of Corrections in Canon City, Colorado, with regard to a post-conviction challenge. Ain had no family or prior professional relationship with Crumpton and was soliciting him primarily for monetary gain. Ain's solicitation of Crumpton as a client violated Colo. RPC 7.3(a) (a lawyer shall not solicit professional employment from a prospective client with whom the lawyer has no family or prior professional relationship where a significant motive for the lawyer's doing so is the lawyer's pecuniary gain).

In December 1999, Crumpton executed the fee agreement, paid Ain a retainer in the amount of $600 and provided her with several hundred pages of court transcripts. An attorney/client relationship was established. Ain spoke with Crumpton two weeks later after the initial meeting in November 1999. Ain did no further work on Crumpton's legal matter. Thereafter, Crumpton attempted to contact the respondent on at least eleven occasions without success. Eventually, Crumpton received a recording stating that the respondent's telephone had been disconnected. Crumpton wrote to the respondent by certified letter asking that she get in touch with him. Crumpton has not heard from Ain since December 1999. Such conduct by an attorney constitutes a violation of Colo. RPC 1.4(a) (failure to communicate) and Colo. RPC 1.3 (neglect of a legal matter). The totality of facts establish by clear and convincing evidence that Ain deserted and/or rejected her professional responsibilities regarding her client, and thereby abandoned her client

Moreover, Ain's retention of Crumpton's retainer for over a year after she abandoned his case constitutes conversion in violation of Colo. RPC 8.4(c). From the evidence presented it is reasonable to infer that her retention of the unearned funds was knowing.

161

In both the Page/Densmore and the Crumpton matters, Ain's retention of the unearned clients' funds for an extended period of time constituted knowing conversion. Colorado law provides that in the absence of substantial mitigating factors, disbarment is the presumed sanction when an attorney knowingly misappropriates clients' funds.

In both the Page/Densmore and Crumpton matters, the extent of Ain's neglect rose to the level of abandonment. The presumed sanction for knowing conversion coupled with abandonment of an attorney's clients also results in disbarment.

In addition to Ain's knowing conversion and abandonment of her clients, her misrepresentations to the clients in the Baker and Brown matters, her misrepresentation to the court in the Baker matter, and her disregard of court orders in the Brown and Baker matters support the PDJ and Hearing Board's conclusion that the presumed sanction is disbarment.

Determination of the appropriate sanction requires the PDJ and Hearing Board to consider aggravating and mitigating factors pursuant to ABA *Standards* 9.22 and 9.32 respectively. No mitigating factors were presented. However, several aggravating factors are evident. Densmore was a particularly vulnerable client and Ain was aware of his vulnerability.

It is therefore Ordered:

Phyllis M. Ain, attorney registration number 17122 is disbarred from the practice of law effective thirty-one days from the date of this Order.

Prior to readmission to the practice of law, Ain must establish that she has refunded and paid restitution within twelve (12) months from the date of this Order to:

A. Dr. Robert Baker in the sum of $6,926.96 plus interest at the statutory rate from February 8, 2000;

B. Nancy Page in the amount of $500 plus statutory interest from January 1, 1999,

C. Kenny Crumpton in the amount of $600 plus statutory interest from December 1, 1999.

Prior to readmission to the practice of law, Ain must establish that she has complied with all prior orders of court in the Baker lawsuit referenced in the Complaint.

Ain is Ordered to return the files to Sue Brown and Dr. Robert Baker within ninety (90) days of the date of this Order.

Ain is Ordered to pay the costs of these proceedings; the People shall submit a Statement of Costs within ten (10) days of the date of this Order. Respondent shall have five (5) days thereafter to submit a response thereto.

In the Matter of Steven C. Litz

721 N.E.2d 258 (Ind. 1999)

Attorney discipline proceeding was brought. The Supreme Court held that attorney's publication in three local newspapers of letter in which he stated that client whom he represented in prosecution for neglect of a dependent had committed no crime, criticized the prosecutor's decision to retry his client following the reversal of her conviction on appeal, and mentioned that client had passed lie detector test constituted misconduct warranting public reprimand. Public reprimand ordered.

The respondent, Steven C. Litz, defended a woman accused of neglect of a dependent. While a retrial of that case proceeded, the respondent caused to be published in several newspapers a letter which stated his client had committed no crime, criticized the prosecutor's decision to retry the case, and mentioned that his client had passed a lie detector test. For that, we find today that the respondent violated Ind. Professional Conduct Rule 3.6(a), which forbids attorneys from making extrajudicial statements which they know or reasonably should know have a substantial likelihood of materially prejudicing an adjudicative proceeding.

The parties agree that the respondent represented a client in criminal proceeding in Morgan County in which a jury found the client guilty of neglect of a dependent resulting in serious bodily injury. The respondent represented the client in the appeal of her conviction and succeeded in obtaining a reversal of the conviction from the Indiana Court of Appeals. The Court of Appeals remanded the case to the trial court, finding that the lower court erred in determining that evidence of "battered women's syndrome" was irrelevant and inadmissible in the first trial.

After remand on June 2, 1997, the trial court set the matter for a new jury trial on November 3, 1997. On June 25, 1997, a "Letter to the Editor" written and submitted by the respondent appeared in the Bloomington, Indiana *Herald–Times* and the Mooresville, Indiana *Times*. An identical letter from the respondent appeared in the June 26, 1997, edition of the *Indianapolis Star*. The respondent's letter stated that his client had spent the "last 18 months in jail for a crime she did not commit" and revealed that she had passed a lie detector test. The letter also decried the decision to retry his client, characterizing it as "abominable." The letter stated:

> *In a time when the public is fascinated with criminal trials and often perceives grave injustice being done to victims of crimes, I thought your readers would be interested to know that here in Morgan County, the prosecutor has elected to retry my client ... [h]er boyfriend ... murdered [her] daughter ... in October 1995. [The client] was subsequently charged with neglect of a dependent because she allegedly knew that leaving [her daughter] with [the boyfriend] would endanger her life.*
>
> *She was convicted in January 1996 and sentenced to 20 years in prison, the maximum possible for the crime. Her conviction was recently reversed by the Indiana Court of Appeals because it said [the client] did not receive a fair trial due to the judge's refusal to allow her to present evidence that she suffered from battered woman's syndrome.*

163

In the weeks preceding her daughter's murder, [the boyfriend] had beaten [the daughter] and allegedly raped [the client] at knifepoint. She reported the beating and rape to the Connersville police who, because they were friendly with [the boyfriend], released him at the scene of the alleged rape.

Ironically, [the client] was given a lie detector test (which she passed) to make sure that she had not hurt her daughter and that she had been raped. Fearful of her life, she moved away from [the boyfriend], only to return to him a week later.

Tragically but not surprisingly, she believed his promises to her that he would get help, that he would never harm [the daughter] again and that he would provide a life for her. Two weeks later, [the daughter] was brutally murdered.

[The client] has spent the last 18 months in jail for a crime she did not commit. Anyone who has the slightest familiarity with battered woman's syndrome knows that the batterer frequently promises to change, and all too often his victims accept those words—even when they come after one's child has been injured.

While the ability to say she could have left comes easily, the fact is that the single greatest difficulty for battered women is leaving their attackers. [The client] has come to learn this at the horrible expense of her daughter's life. Perhaps others in situations such as hers can learn from [her] that the time to leave is now, not after a life-altering event occurs.

The decision to re-prosecute [the client] is abominable. Our system of justice was never intended to repeatedly exact punishment from someone.

She has lost the dearest thing to her, and our citizens should voice their concern that she continues to be penalized for being the victim of a brutal, terrifying man who convinced her that her and her daughter's safety would be protected.

On September 29, 1997, the respondent, on behalf of the client, filed a *Motion for Change of Venue* from Morgan County, citing "prejudicial pre-trial publicity." The court granted the motion.

Indiana Professional Conduct Rule 3.6(a) provides:

A lawyer shall not make an extrajudicial statement that a reasonable person would expect to be disseminated by means of public communication if the lawyer knows or reasonably should know that it will have a substantial likelihood of materially prejudicing an adjudicative proceeding.

Indiana Professional Conduct Rule 3.6(b) provides that certain types of extrajudicial statements referred to in subsection (a) are "rebuttably presumed" to have a substantial likelihood of materially prejudicing an adjudicative proceeding, including the results of any examination or test, any opinion as to the guilt or innocence of a defendant in a criminal case that could result in incarceration, or information that the lawyer knows or reasonably should know is likely to be inadmissible as evidence in a trial. Prof.Cond.R. 3.6(b)(3), (4), (5).

Preserving the right to a fair trial necessarily entails some curtailment of the information that may be disseminated about a party prior to trial, particularly where trial by jury is involved. *Comment* to Prof.Cond.R. 3.6. The respondent's letters to area newspapers created a substantial likelihood of material prejudice to the pending jury retrial of the respondent's own client. Some of the statements contained therein presumptively presented that risk: his description of evidence that could have been inadmissible at trial (i.e., the fact and result of the lie detector test), and his opinion that his client did not commit the crime for which she was charged. Further, the respondent's identification of the prosecution's decision to retry the case as "abominable," despite the fact that retrial of the case was well within the prosecutor's discretion, tended to contribute to a pre-trial atmosphere prejudicial to the prosecution's case. In sum, the respondent's letters created an environment where a fair trial was much less likely to occur. Additionally, the respondent effectively set the stage for his own subsequent motion for change of venue based on prejudicial pre-trial publicity. Accordingly, we find that the respondent's published commentary created a substantial likelihood of materially prejudicing retrial of his client's criminal case, and thus violated Prof.Cond.R. 3.6(a).

The parties agree that the appropriate sanction for the misconduct is a public reprimand. Among the factors we consider in assessing the adequacy of that proposed sanction are aggravating and mitigating circumstances. In mitigation, the parties agree that the respondent has not previously been the subject of a disciplinary proceeding, that he cooperated with the Commission, and that he continued to represent the client through the resolution of her case. No factors in aggravation were cited.

We view the respondent's actions as a purposeful attempt to gain an unfair advantage in retrial of his client's case. Although the respondent had no real selfish motive (and instead apparently sought only to advocate zealously his client's cause), he nonetheless was bound to do so only within the bounds of our ethical rules. His public comments were inappropriate because they threatened or in fact impinged the prospect of a fair trial for his client. Whether extrajudicial statements of this sort warrant reprimand or suspension is fact sensitive. Here, we take into account the fact that the respondent's primary motivation appears to have been the welfare of his client. We are also cognizant while assessing the proposed sanction of our policy of encouraging agreed resolution of disciplinary cases. We find that, in this case, the agreed sanction of a public reprimand is appropriate.

* * * * * * * * * * * * * *

Questions

        1.   In 2012, HLN reporter Nancy Grace interviewed Drew Peterson's defense lawyer during his murder trial for the murder of his fourth wife.[87] Lawyer, Joel Brodsky, said that three pathologists will testify that all the dead woman's bruises were consistent with skin problems and rough sex 'with her boyfriend' who slept in her house the night before her death. Grace also asked Brodsky why Peterson was laughing in the courtroom during the trial. Brodsky explained that Peterson did not laugh when the jury was in the courtroom and that the only reason that he laughed at all was because he had been isolated from the public for three years. Were any of these lawyer's statements on the Nancy Grace show in violation of the model rules of professional conduct? Discuss fully.

        2.   Would your response to question one above be the same if the trial was over at the time of the television interview?

        3.   The court in Lix stated "We view the respondent's actions as a purposeful attempt to gain an unfair advantage in retrial of his client's case." Discuss what the court meant by "unfair advantage" and distinguish that from a "fair" advantage.

                      ****

Falk, etc., et al. v. Gallo, etc., et al.
901 N.Y.S. 2d (2010)

Plaintiffs brought action against defendants, alleging breach of contract. The Supreme Court, Nassau County, granted defendants' motion to disqualify plaintiffs' attorney. Plaintiffs appealed. The Supreme Court, Appellate Division, held that attorney was a necessary trial witness. Affirmed.

The plaintiffs commenced this action, inter alia, to recover damages for breach of contract. The defendants moved to disqualify the plaintiffs' attorney on the ground that he was a necessary trial witness for the defendants because he was present during conversations between the parties regarding the terms of the oral agreement at issue. The Supreme Court granted the defendants' motion, and we affirm.

The disqualification of an attorney is a matter that rests within the sound discretion of the Supreme Court. A party's entitlement to be represented by counsel of his or her choice is a valued right which should not be abridged absent a clear showing that disqualification is warranted.

The advocate-witness rules contained in the Code of Professional Responsibility provide guidance, but are not binding authority, for the courts in determining whether a party's attorney should be disqualified during litigation. Rule 3.7 of the Rules of Professional Conduct provides

---

[87] Nancy Grace grills Drew Peterson's attorney, http://www.hlntv.com/video/2012/08/06/nancy-grace-grills-drew-petersons-attorney, last visited 7.3.14

that unless certain exceptions apply, "[a] lawyer shall not act as an advocate before a tribunal in a matter in which the lawyer is likely to be a witness on a significant issue of fact". Here, since the plaintiffs' attorney was the only person, other than the parties, who had knowledge of any discussions regarding the terms of the oral agreement underlying this litigation, he is "likely to be a witness on a significant issue of fact" (Rules of Professional Conduct. Accordingly, the Supreme Court properly granted the defendants' motion to disqualify the plaintiffs' attorney.

****

Questions:

1.   In a paternity action, admitted father (Tyler) is represented by Lawyer who is his father (Richard).[88] Tyler has given Richard informed written consent to represent him but baby's mother (Kayla) seeks to have lawyer disqualified. Lawyer had formerly represented the Kayla's father in his divorce action but had never represented Kayla. If Richard continued to represent Tyler, would he be in violation of model rule 3.7? Why or why not?

2.   Has Tyler been denied his right to counsel of his choice if the court were to grant Kayla's moion to disqualify Richard? Why or why not?

3.   In Falk, the court reasoned that the defendant's attorney should be disqualified because he was the only person who could testify on a significant issue of fact. What result if there were witnesses in addition to the attorney who during cross examination asks the testifying witness. "Isn't it true that you stated, in my presence, that you had every intention of avoiding the contract at the time the document was executed?" Has attorney violated model rules of professional conduct? If so, how ; if not why not?

****

REVIEW QUESTIONS

1. Attorney represents Client in a case based on statutory construction. Numerous cases have already held the statute constitutional and enforceable. However, Attorney believes that she can secure a settlement for the benefit of her Client if she were to pursue her claim against the defendant. Attorney knows that her claim must not be frivolous but she remembers her law professor telling her that it "did not take much imagination to make a claim creative and meritorious". Attorney then manufactures a creative basis for pursuing the claim despite precedence. Is Attorney subject to discipline?

2. Lawyer files a lawsuit that he knows is barred by applicable statute of limitations. Is Lawyer subject to discipline?

3. Lawyer accepts payment of attorney fees from Client to prosecute a personal injury claim. Lawyer deposits the fee in his operations account but six months later has yet to do anything to pursue the Client's claim. Is Lawyer subject to discipline?

---

[88] See Kennedy v. Eldridge, 201 Cal.App.4th 1197 (2011)

4. Lawyer files a motion that she knows will likely fail. Is Lawyer subject to discipline?

5. Attorney represented Hospital that sought a judicial ruling that a patient in question be removed from life support. Patient's family argued that such removal would constitute murder and that court should rule against the hospital. Hospital needed a ruling in its favor to establish a precedent for the hospital. The case was before a judge the hospital felt would rule in its favor because the judge had shown concern about the quality of life for a person who languished on life support. Before making her decision, the judge asked the Lawyer for the hospital about the patient's condition. The Attorney responded "grave", knowing that the patient had died less than thirty minutes before. The judge rendered her ruling in favor of the hospital. Is Attorney subject to discipline?

6. Attorney represented a Client who discovered that she had offered false testimony on a critical issue. Client informed Attorney who asked to recall Client. As Attorney suspected, opposing counsel objected on the ground that Client's testimony would be cumulative and duplicative. In response, Attorney quickly withdrew his request, having made effort to correct any incorrect testimony. Has Attorney violated the model rules of professional conduct?

7. Lawyer files a trial brief with the court that failed to address a case that was directly adverse to Lawyer's position. The case was not cited by opposing counsel either but was legal authority in the controlling jurisdiction. Before making his decision, judge finds the case, admonishes the attorneys and reports both of them to the state bar for disciplinary action. Lawyer defends stating he had conducted extensive research but had not located the case prior to the judge's discovery. Is Lawyer subject to discipline when it is clear that he had not intentionally mislead the tribunal? Is opposing counsel subject to discipline?

8. Criminal defendant insists on testifying in his case over his lawyer's objection. Defendant faces life in prison without the possibility of parole on each of three counts of murder. Defendant believes he has nothing to lose by giving perjured testimony and he informs Lawyer that is his intent. In response, Lawyer moves to withdraw, which motion is denied. Lawyer then calls defendant to the stand and permits defendant to testify in a narrative form without asking a single question. Defendants' testimony is perjured. Is Lawyer subject to discipline under the model rules of professional conduct? [See how Texas treats the dilemma in Texas Disciplinary Rules of Professional Conduct, Rule 3.03 comments 9-12.]

9. Distinguish the Lawyer's duty of candor to the Court from the Lawyer's duty of fairness to opposing counsel.

10. Defense counsel represents criminal defendant who confesses to Lawyer that he committed the crime. Defense counsel does nothing. One week after the confession, Defendant gives Lawyer a key to a storage facility, tells the lawyer where the facility is located and reaffirms that Lawyer is not to mention any of this information to the prosecutor. When Lawyer asks what's in the storage facility, Client smirks and responds, "wouldn't they all like to know". Under these circumstances is Lawyer required to disclose the Client's confession? Is Lawyer required to turn over the key to avoid facing discipline?

****

IN THE NEWS:

Online Research Of Jurors: Ethics in the 21rst Century

In April 2014, "the American Bar Association's Committee on Ethics and Professional Responsibility ("ABA") gave lawyers the go-ahead to scour jurors' or potential jurors' publicly available social-media accounts, blogs, and websites such as Facebook, LinkedIn LNKD +0.41% and Twitter. Although lawyers might be expected to breathe a sigh of relief that they can now engage in conduct considered acceptable and expected for most other professions without the threat of professional discipline, the opinion actually adds to the confusion about how existing ethical rules are applied in the ever evolving world of social media. Indeed, just two and three years ago respectively, two different New York bar associations concluded that the conduct the ABA just approved could be considered a violation of New York's Rules of Professional Conduct. Thus, whether and how an attorney can research his or her jury pool may depend entirely on where that jury is sitting."

The ABA opinion leaves a lot to the lawyer's imagination, which is not good for the lawyer who is trying to determine whether his/her actions rise to the level of an ethical violation, here not contacting jurors.

Read more at Conducting Online Research of Jurors Just Got Less Perilous -- Or Did It? Catherine Foti, *Contributor*, 4/30/2014, http://www.forbes.com/sites/insider/2014/04/30/conducting-online-research-of-jurors-just-got-less-perilous-or-did-it/ Also see ABA Formal Opinion 466, entitled "Lawyer Reviewing Jurors' Internet Presence".

Self-Representation

Some people represent themselves in transactions and in litigation. There is some evidence that self-representation is on the rise.[89] Americans have the right to self-representation.[90] When the lawyer is on the other side of a self-represented person (pro se), there are certain ethical standards to which the lawyer must adhere. Of course, the lawyer must be honest in all matters. The lawyer is also required to act in such a way to ensure the unrepresented person does not misunderstand the lawyer's role, especially in transactional matters not requiring litigation.

When the opponent is represented by counsel, the lawyer must not contact the represented party if he knows the party has counsel. In that case, the lawyer must direct all communication to the person's lawyer unless the person's lawyer consents to the direct communication or unless the communication is authorized by law.

---

[89] Drew A. Swank, The Pro Se Phenomenon, 19 BYU J of Pub L 373 (2005)
[90] Id. Citing Tiffany Buxton, Foreign Solutions to the U.S. Pro Se Phenomenon, 34 Case W Res. J. Int'l L 103, 109 (2002).

State Bar of Arizona Ethics Opinion

95-07: Communication with Represented Party; Communication with Corporate Employees

The ethical propriety of communicating with current or former employees of opposing party will depend upon (1) whether the acts, omissions or statements of the employee may be imputed to the employer; and (2) whether the employee is represented by counsel. [ER 4.2]

Facts

An attorney desires to interview witnesses who are (1) current and (2) former employees of an opposing party in litigation under the following circumstances:

(a) where the testimony may be detrimental to the employer;

(b) where the employee may have witnessed an unlawful act of the employer or its agent; and

(c) where the employee's situation is similar to that described by the plaintiff.

ER 4.2 Communication with Person Represented by Counsel

> In representing a client, a lawyer shall not communicate about the subject of the representation with a party the lawyer knows to be represented by another lawyer in the matter, unless the lawyer has the consent of the other lawyer or is authorized by law to do so. …

Opinion

This opinion will address in turn communications with a witness who is first a current employee, and then a witness who is a former employee, of an adverse party represented by counsel, with respect to each of the three enumerated circumstances, in the absence of consent by the adverse party employer's counsel.

ER 4.2 permits communications with consent or when "authorized by law to do so". A properly issued subpoena and notice of deposition presumably constitutes authorization by law. This opinion assumes that the "interviews" sought to be conducted will not be pursuant to any lawfully issued subpoenas. This opinion is limited to the question of communications with non-governmental employees and former employees, and with respect to matters that are the subject of potential or pending civil litigation. Communications with respect to pending or potential criminal or civil enforcement by a government authority are beyond the scope of this opinion.

The American Bar Association Committee on Ethics and Professional Responsibility issued Formal Opinion 95-396, Communications With Represented Persons, on July 28, 1995. Although Opinion 95-396 does not bear directly on the questions presented to this Committee and addressed in this

Opinion, it is consistent with this Opinion (except to the extent that the Arizona Court of Appeals limited communications with former employees in Lang v. Superior Court, 170 Ariz. 602, 826 P.2d 1228 (App. 1992), see infra. at p. 4) and the ABA Opinion provides an otherwise comprehensive analysis of the rule; the reader therefore is referred to it for general guidance.

I. Current Employee

A. Witness's testimony may be detrimental to the employer

That the testimony of the employee may be detrimental to her employer is not determinative. The Comment to ER 4.2 states as follows:

> In the case of an organization, this rule prohibits communications by a lawyer for one party concerning the matter in representation with **persons having a managerial responsibility** on behalf of the organization, and with any other person whose act or omission in connection with that matter may be imputed to the organization for purposes of civil or criminal liability or whose statement may constitute an admission on the part of the organization.

If the employee does have managerial responsibility with the employer, ER 4.2 prohibits communication by a lawyer for the party adverse to the employer with such employee without the employer's lawyer's consent. On the other hand, such communication with a non-managerial employee is not so proscribed, unless an act or omission of the non-managerial employee may be imputed to the employer for purposes of civil or criminal liability, or the statement of such non-managerial employee may constitute an admission on the part of the employer.

The Comment to ER 4.2 goes on to state:

> If an agent or employee of the organization is represented in the matter by his or her own counsel, the consent by that counsel to a communication will be sufficient for purposes of this rule.

Thus, counsel for a party wishing to communicate with a non-managerial employee of an adverse party should ascertain from the employee (or beforehand if possible) whether or not she is represented in connection with the matter that is the subject of the proposed communication, and if so, obtain the consent of the employee's counsel. Often, the employer has offered to provide the employee with her own counsel, who may have been engaged at the time of the communication by counsel for the party adverse to the employer, or the employer's own counsel also represents the employee.

B. Employee may have witnessed an unlawful act by the employer

That the employee may have witnessed an unlawful act of his employer or representative is not relevant to whether communication by counsel for a party adverse to the employer is permitted under ER 4.2. Whether or not such communication is permissible under ER 4.2 is governed by the commentary to the rule as set out in section I.A. above.

C. Employee's situation is similar to that described by the plaintiff

That employee may be in a situation similar to that described by the plaintiff in the lawsuit also is not relevant to whether or not communication by counsel for a party adverse to the employer is permitted under ER 4.2. Whether or not such communication is permissible under ER 4.2 is governed by the commentary to the rule as set out in section I.A. above.

II. Former Employee

A. Witness's testimony may be detrimental to the employer

That the testimony of the former employee may be detrimental to her former employer is not determinative. The Arizona Court of Appeals held in Lang v. Superior Court, 170 Ariz. 602, 826 P.2d 1228 (App. 1992) that communication with a former employee by counsel for a party adverse to the former employer is permissible in the absence of consent by counsel for the employer, unless the acts or omissions of the former employee gave rise to the underlying litigation. In the language of the Comment to ER 4.2, communication is prohibited if "an act or omission [of the former employee] . . . may be imputed to the organization for purposes of civil or criminal liability . . . ." The court also held in Lang that communication was prohibited without the consent of the former employer's counsel if the former employee has some ongoing relationship with the employer in connection with the litigation.

B. Employee may have witnessed an unlawful act of his former employer

That the former employee may have witnessed an unlawful act by his former employer or representative is not relevant to whether communication by counsel for a party adverse to the former employer is permitted under ER 4.2. Whether or not communication with a former employee is permitted under such circumstances is governed by the same analysis set out in section II.A. above.

C. Employee's situation is similar to that described by the plaintiff

That the former employee's situation may be similar to that described by the plaintiff is not relevant to whether or not communication by counsel for a party adverse to the former employer is permitted under ER 4.2. Whether or not communication with a former employee is permitted under such circumstances is governed by the same analysis set out in section II.A. above.

****

Questions:

1. Former employee is contacted by plaintiff's attorney in a case against former employer. Former employee is represented by counsel in an unrelated matter. Nevertheless plaintiff's attorney contacts lawyer seeking permission to discuss his case with the former employee. Both the former employee and her attorney consent to the discussion. When former employer, who is also represented by an attorney, discovers the communication, she vehemently objects to the conversation and files a complaint against plaintiff's

attorney with the state's bar. Has plaintiff's lawyer violated the model rules of professional conduct? Explain the bases your answer.

2. An employee of your corporate client is being deposed by opposing counsel. In the middle of the questioning, he begins to ask questions based on confidential information that, to your knowledge, your client has only shared with you. You object on privilege grounds and call for a break — at which time you discover your opponent is in possession of a cache of private correspondence between you and your client. The other lawyer explains that the information was provided directly to him by the Client's staff. He claims that because he inadvertently received it through no fault of his own, he used it to prepare his case. Under relevant case law and ethics rules, what remedies are open to you?[91]

3. Lawyer represents client who is suing the corporation that you represent. One evening, Lawyer approaches company's janitor while he was dumping the trash, and asks if he may have the trash bags from the CEO's office. Janitor asks why Lawyer needs it and Lawyer tells him that he is suing the company and believes the CEO's trash contains information that would be helpful to his case. Janitor then hands him the trash from the CEO's office. Is Lawyer's communication with company janitor prohibited by the model rules of professional conduct?[92]

4. Employee is represented by counsel who is not contacted by opposing counsel about matters related to a lawsuit by a third party against the employer. Without contacting the represented employee, Employer's lawyer contacts the employee who gives statements, none of which are adverse to the employer's interests. Has Lawyer violated the model rules of professional conduct?

****

Abeles v. The State Bar of California
9 Cal.3d 603, 510 P.2d 719, 108 Cal.Rptr. 359 (1973)

This is a proceeding to review a recommendation of the Disciplinary Board that petitioner be suspended from the practice of law for 60 days. Petitioner, who was admitted to practice in 1955, has no prior disciplinary record. In the instant proceeding he was charged with, inter alia, wilfully violating rule 12 of the Rules of Professional Conduct, which provides that "A member of the State Bar shall not communicate with a party represented by counsel upon a subject of controversy, in the absence and without the consent of such counsel. ..." (See Bus. & Prof. Code, § 6077.) Petitioner denied the charges.

---

[91] See Wendy L. Patrick, You Saw What? Inadvertent disclosure and the attorney-client privilege, California Bar Journal, July 2014 available at http://apps.calbar.ca.gov/mcleselfstudy/mcle_home.aspx?testID=52, last visited 7.4.14
[92] See Suzanne Lever, You Can't Touch This—A Look at the Anti-Contact Rule, North Carolina State Bar, available at http://www.ncbar.com/ethics/eth_articles_16,3.asp, last visited 7.4.14.

About 1965 a joint venture for the production of a film was entered into between William Bates, L. Jensen, and Neil Stein, doing business as Golden Land Properties, and Apostolof Film Productions, Inc. (hereafter called Apostolof, Inc.), a corporation formed by Stephen Apostolof. A disagreement arose between Golden Land Properties and Apostolof, Inc., and as a result thereof a lawsuit was filed in April 1967. The action was captioned Bates, Jensen and Stein, doing business as Golden Land Properties, v. Apostolof, Inc., et al. Slavitt, Edelman and Weiser appeared on the pleadings as counsel of record for the plaintiffs, and petitioner represented the defendants.

Various documents were filed in the action, and in December 1967 Apostolof's deposition was taken. After that date there was no further activity in the litigation until 1969, at which time new counsel was substituted for Jerry Edelman of the above named firm.

Before June 11, 1968, Stein and Apostolof met accidentally at a restaurant. According to Apostolof, at that time Stein denied having filed the lawsuit and at a later meeting repudiated the accusations in the complaint. Apostolof testified that he repeated Stein's remarks to petitioner and asked petitioner to prepare for Stein's signature an affidavit containing the remarks.

On June 11, 1968, Stein and Apostolof met petitioner at his office. Petitioner testified that Stein told him that Stein "was not represented by ... Edelman" and had "never authorized ... Edelman to file any action," and petitioner's testimony was corroborated by Apostolof and Joseph Copelan, an attorney who had an office in the same suite as that of petitioner.

In the absence and without the consent of Slavitt, Edelman and Weiser, petitioner then submitted to Stein for his signature an affidavit that denied having authorized the filing of the action and repudiated various allegations in the complaint, and Stein signed the affidavit. Before doing so Stein asked whether he should not consult with his attorney Barton Schuman, who had an office in the same building as that of petitioner, and petitioner replied that he did not think it was necessary to do so. The affidavit has never been used.

Additional evidence was presented relating to whether the firm of Slavitt, Edelman, and Weiser was authorized to act for Stein in the action against Apostolof, Inc. Edelman testified: Before the action was filed he discussed the complaint with Stein and the other plaintiffs. He also discussed with them and attorney Schuman the terms of Edelman's representation of Golden Land Properties, and it was agreed by Stein and the others that Edelman would be paid a specified hourly fee. Edelman did not have a written retainer agreement.

Stein testified: He never met with Edelman regarding the action against Apostolof, Inc., and never discussed with Edelman what Edelman's compensation would be for representing the plaintiffs in that action. However, Stein authorized Bates to file that action and to retain Edelman for that purpose and Stein considered that Slavitt, Edelman and Weiser represented him in the Apostolof case. In a deposition Stein stated that he did not consider that the foregoing firm represented him "personally."

Petitioner testified: He was aware that Slavitt, Edelman and Weiser appeared as the attorneys of record for the plaintiffs in the action against Apostolof, Inc. However, when Stein signed the affidavit petitioner did not believe that the foregoing firm represented Stein. Petitioner believed Stein's statements that Stein "was not represented by ... Edelman" and "never authorized ... Edelman to file any action." Also petitioner "thought Stein was [his] client, and thought they had filed an action for [his] client without [the client's] consent." He assumed that Stein was his client because petitioner prepared the joint venture agreement between Golden Land Properties and Apostolof, Inc., and represented "the individuals there" and when Stein said he never authorized the action petitioner felt that Stein should have been named a party defendant. It was petitioner's understanding that if a partner refuses to join in a lawsuit he must be made a party defendant. Petitioner had no recollection of trying to contact Slavitt, Edelman and Weiser on June 11, 1968, and when asked "Did you ever question Mr. Edelman about his representation of Mr. Stein?," petitioner replied, "I never had any reason to until June 11, 1968. I assumed he wasn't on June 11th."

The Findings and Recommendations

The local committee found, inter alia, that "Bates obtained consent from Stein to file an action through ... Slavitt, Edelman and Weiser against Apostolof, Inc. with ... Bates, ... Jensen, and ... Stein named as plaintiffs" and that the "nature and extent of the attorney-client relationship between [that firm] and Stein is not clear." The local committee concluded that there was insufficient proof that petitioner wilfully violated rule 12 and recommended that the proceeding be dismissed.

The board, without receiving additional evidence, unanimously adopted new findings. It found, inter alia, that "... At all pertinent times herein [petitioner] knew that ... Slavitt, Edelman et al., represented the plaintiffs [in the action in question] and [petitioner] ... failed to obtain the consent of [that] law firm ... to [the communication between petitioner and Stein on June 11, 1968]."

The board also found, as did the local committee, that Stein told Apostolof that Stein had not authorized the filing of any action against Apostolof, Inc., that Apostolof told petitioner what Stein said, and that Stein thereafter similarly stated to petitioner that Slavitt, Edelman and Weiser had no authority to file the litigation on Stein's behalf.

Petitioner's Contentions

...Petitioner ... claims (1) that the evidence does not support a finding that (a) Stein was "a party represented by counsel" or (b) petitioner knew that Stein was so represented; (2) that at the time of the events in question there was no "subject of controversy"; and (3) that the record does not support a determination that any breach of rule 12 was wilful. He asserts that rule 12, in referring to "a party represented by counsel" contemplates "not merely that the attorney act as ostensible representative of a party, but that he actually be such." We do not agree with petitioner's construction of rule 12 or with his foregoing claims.

Rule 12 prohibits communication "upon a subject of controversy" with "a party represented by counsel" in the absence and without the consent of such counsel. (See *Turner v. State Bar*, 36

Cal.2d 155, 158 [222 P.2d 857].) This rule "is necessary to the preservation of the attorney-client relationship and the proper functioning of the administration of justice. ... It shields the opposing party not only from an attorney's approaches which are intentionally improper, but, in addition, from approaches which are well intended but misguided.

"The rule was designed to permit an attorney to function adequately in his proper role and to prevent the opposing attorney from impeding his performance in such role. ..." (*Mitton v. State Bar*, 71 Cal.2d 525, 534 [78 Cal.Rptr. 649, 455 P.2d 753].)

In view of the purposes of the rule we believe that "a party represented by counsel" includes a party who has counsel of record whether or not that counsel was in fact authorized to act for the party. If the quoted words were interpreted to include counsel of record only if such counsel was in fact authorized to act for the party, harm could result to attorney-client relationships and to the administration of justice. Under the latter interpretation an opposing attorney could deal directly with a party, who was known to the attorney to have counsel of record, upon a subject of controversy with impunity in some cases, even though the counsel of record had actual authority to act for the party, since it might be impossible to show that the opposing attorney had knowledge of that authority and wilfully violated rule 12.

Here it was stipulated that "During all times herein relevant Slavitt, Edelman & Weiser appeared on the pleadings as being counsel of record for the plaintiffs in [the action against Apostolof, Inc.]" and that Stein was named as one of the plaintiffs in that action. Petitioner admittedly knew that the foregoing firm appeared as counsel of record for the plaintiffs and that Stein was named as a plaintiff. Thus the record supports findings that Stein was a party represented by counsel within the meaning of rule 12 and that petitioner knew that Stein had counsel of record in the action.

Petitioner contends that at the time of the events in question there was no "subject of controversy" because the action against Apostolof, Inc., was inactive and apparently had been abandoned. However, it was stipulated that the affidavit petitioner submitted to Stein for his signature contradicted allegations in the complaint in that action and it appears without dispute that the action was still pending. Accordingly, the communication was "upon a subject of controversy" even though the action may then have been inactive. It could not be assumed that the action had been abandoned.

It is for a "wilful breach" of the Rules of Professional Conduct that Business and Professions Code section 6077 authorizes discipline. ..."To establish a wilful breach, it must be demonstrated that the person charged acted or omitted to act purposely, that is, that he knew what he was doing or not doing and that he intended either to commit the act or to abstain from committing it. [Citations omitted] The wilfulness or intent may be proved by direct or by circumstantial evidence. [Citations omitted]" (*Millsberg v. State Bar*, 6 Cal.3d 65, 74 [98 Cal.Rptr. 223, 490 P.2d 543], quoting from *Zitny v. State Bar*, 64 Cal.2d 787, 792 [51 Cal.Rptr. 825, 415 P.2d 521].) "'It is ... immaterial that petitioner may have been ignorant of the provision ... that he violated.'"(*Millsberg v. State Bar, supra*, at p. 75, quoting from *Zitny v. State Bar, supra*, at p. 793.) "A mistake of law made in good faith may be a defense to an alleged violation of Business and Professions Code section 6067 (oath upon admission) [citation] but "In contrast section 6077 proscribes any wilful violation of the Rules of Professional Conduct and does not make knowledge of the rules an element of the offense." (*Zitny v. State Bar* at 793)(*Millsberg v. State Bar, supra*, at 75)

Here, as we have seen, admittedly petitioner knew that Slavitt, Edelman and Weiser appeared as counsel of record for the plaintiffs in the action against Apostolof, Inc. Petitioner also must have known that he was communicating with one of the plaintiffs (Stein) in the absence and without the consent of that firm and must have been aware of the contents of the affidavit that he submitted to Stein for his signature.

We conclude that petitioner knew what he was doing and intended to commit the act. Thus his breach of rule 12 was wilful. It is immaterial that petitioner may have been mistaken as to the scope of rule 12, since knowledge of the rules is not an element of the offense.

Petitioner contends that in any event 60 days' suspension, as recommended by the board, is excessive. As we have seen, six board members thought such discipline excessive. The fact that petitioner has no prior disciplinary record is a matter in his favor (see *Mrakich v. State Bar of California, supra*, 8 Cal.3d 896, 907), and his instant misconduct may have reflected only an error in judgment based on his misinterpretation of rule 12 and Stein's statement to him that Stein was not represented by Edelman. Under the circumstances we are satisfied that a public reprimand will constitute sufficient discipline. This opinion shall serve as such reprimand.

****

Question:

The court found that the petitioner intentionally violated rule 12 an further that his action may have been caused by his misunderstanding of the rule's prohibitions. Howver, the court also found that the mistake of the law was insufficient to shield him from discipline. Conform those findings to the court's conclusion that the "error in judgment based on his misinterpretation of rule 12" supported minimal sanction.

****

State of Oklahoma, ex rel., Oklahoma Bar Association v. Butner
1998 OK 133 (Okla. 1998)

Disciplinary proceeding was brought against attorney for allegedly communicating with adverse party represented by counsel, and the trial panel recommended dismissal of the complaint. The Supreme Court, Simms, J., held that attorney did not have reason to know that woman, who was referred to attorney after her former attorney had failed to file divorce action for her 16 years earlier, was currently represented by new attorney. Attorney exonerated.

Complainant, Oklahoma Bar Association, brought disciplinary proceedings against Respondent, George William Butner, Claiming Butner violated Rules 1.1, 1.3, 4.2, 8.4(c), and 8.4(d) of the Oklahoma Rules of Professional Conduct. After a hearing before a Trial Panel of the Professional Responsibility Tribunal, the Trial Panel concluded that Butner had not violated the Oklahoma Rules of Professional Conduct and recommended that the complaint against him be dismissed.

Events precipitating this complaint began in 1980 when Lee Stillwell, a member of the Oklahoma Bar Association, failed to file a divorce action after being employed to do so. Butner entered the situation in 1996 when Stillwell asked Butner to speak to the ex-wife of his former client in an effort to facilitate the divorce which should have occurred over 16 years before.

The bar complaint alleged Butner violated the following Rules Governing Disciplinary Procedure: 1.1 (competence), 1.3 (diligence), 4.2 (communication with person represented by counsel), 8.4(c) (conduct involving fraud, dishonesty or deceit), and 8.4(d) (conduct prejudicial to the administration of justice). At the hearing, the Bar Association dismissed its claims for violations of Rules 1.1, 1.3 and 8.4(c), leaving the only issues remaining the alleged violations of Rules 4.2 and 8.4(d). After de novo review, we agree with the Trial Panel and find the Bar Association was unable to meet its burden in establishing that George Butner violated Rules 4.2 and 8.4(d).

Facts

In 1980, Mr. & Mrs. Clayton were getting a divorce. Mr. Clayton hired Lee Stillwell, who is now an associate district judge, to represent him in the divorce. Mrs. Clayton had accompanied Mr. Clayton to his appointment with Stillwell to sign the waiver of divorce. She had paid $230.00 to Stillwell, on Mr. Clayton's behalf because he was unable to pay the fee and neither Mr. nor Mrs. Clayton wanted the matter delayed due to non-payment. Lee Stillwell did not represent Mrs. Clayton.

In 1996, Mrs. Clayton, now Smith, needed documentation of her divorce for routine paperwork in conjunction with a missionary trip she was planning with her now husband, who is a minister. She discovered there was no record of her divorce in Hughes County, where she understood her divorce to have been granted, or in neighboring Seminole County. Very concerned and upset, she contacted Stillwell in an effort to discover what the problem was. Neither the petition for divorce nor the waiver had been filed because Stillwell's file was then packed away when Stillwell left private practice to join the district attorney's office.

After being contacted by Mrs. Smith, Stillwell asked George Butner if he would be willing to speak with Smith and try to help her with the divorce problem. After coming to Seminole County to speak with Stillwell, Smith then went across the street to see Butner, Stillwell having suggested Butner might be able to help her.

The thrust of the bar's allegations concerning Rule 4.2 center around the theory that Butner represented the interests of Stillwell, as opposed to the interests of Mrs. Smith. In Butner's unopposed testimony, he stated that he did not discuss with Stillwell his advice to Mrs. Smith, venue options for Mrs. Smith, or use of the original 1980 petition to facilitate a quicker divorce for Smith.

There is no evidence of improper communications between Stillwell and Butner; nothing to indicate the advice he gave Smith was influenced by Stillwell or some concern for Stillwell; and no substantive evidence that Butner was attempting to hide matters to save Stillwell embarrassment. There is nothing in the record to indicate Butner was representing the interests of Stillwell, especially as against the interests of Mrs. Smith.

Smith did not retain Butner as her attorney and at the conclusion of their only meeting, she mentioned that she was going to retain a Stillwater attorney instead, William Boyce. Boyce had previously helped Smith confirm the unfiled divorce by checking Hughes and Seminole County records.

Butner accepted no money from Smith, but did act as courier for the reimbursement of $230, the 1980 fee, between Stillwell and Smith. He did so at Boyce's request. Butner also conveyed Stillwell's apologies when he gave Boyce the reimbursement. Butner spoke to Boyce on the phone about possible options of waiving venue and using the 1980 petition to possibly avoid the notice requirements and get the divorce done faster, essentially repeating the discussions he had with Smith. It was during the course of this conversation that Butner made a comment in reference to the "godly powers" of now Judge Stillwell, which was interpreted by Boyce as a reference that Stillwell might try to do something improper to help Smith out and handle the matter with secrecy, since the original error had been his. The bar and Respondent both agreed the statement was "inappropriate, flippant and [a] frustrated use of terminology," but did not find Butner intended anything improper. Smith's divorce wasn't even sought in Seminole County where Stillwell sits and the original 1980 petition and waiver were to have been filed in Hughes County. Butner stated that at no time did he represent Smith. At the same time, there was nothing showing he operated contrary to her interests.

Discussion

The Bar Association's asserted violation of Rule 4.2 was premised on a theory that Butner represented Stillwell to the adversity of Mrs. Smith. There was an ancillary argument as well in which the bar contended that Butner should not have spoken to Smith, knowing she was represented by Boyce in Stillwater. The trial panel correctly concluded there was no evidence to show Butner represented Stillwell in any capacity. Stillwell simply suggested to Smith that she see Butner for her own benefit and she did so. Butner "simply discussed the alternatives with Mrs. Smith and then with her attorney."

Butner discussed with Smith the possibility of getting her divorced finalized in 72 hours, as speed and no publicity were priorities for Mrs. Smith, now a minister's wife with two children. Neither party was able to find legal authority for or against the proposition that a 1980 petition could be filed sixteen years after being signed, possibly avoiding notice requirements to the first husband, Mr. Clayton. The evidence does not support the contention that Butner suggested anything dishonest or was more concerned with Judge Stillwell than with Smith. He was simply brainstorming methods by which Smith's divorce could be done as quickly and painlessly as possible.

With regard to Boyce, the panel specifically asked Butner if he knew Boyce had been retained when Smith came to his office. He said he was aware she had spoken with another attorney, but was not aware Boyce was her attorney until she said so at the end of the conversation. Even then, it was not clear if Boyce was retained or was simply going to be upon Smith's return to Stillwater. The panel chairman noted that the existence of an attorney-client relationship between Boyce and Smith was not material to Butner, the only question for Butner's concern was whether he knew or should have known the relationship existed. Given the extent of the information Butner had from Judge Stillwell and Smith, it is not apparent that Butner would have known Boyce was Smith's attorney; he only discovered the extent of Boyce's role in the course of his meeting with Smith. Also, it should be pointed out that Smith came to Butner, albeit at the suggestion of Stillwell, and Butner was under the reasonable belief that Smith was either shopping for an attorney or at least seeking a second opinion, neither of which would have required Butner to call Boyce in order to speak with Smith.

The bar association conceded that its alleged violations of 4.2 and 8.4(d) would stand or fall together. The 4.2 violation was the basis for the 8.4(d) violation. Having found no evidence to support the contention that Butner represented Stillwell's interests in opposition to Smith's or that Butner had improper contact with another attorney's client, no violation of 8.4(d) exists.

Respondent Exonerated.

Kentucky Bar Association v. Waller
929 S.W.2d 181 (Ky. 1996)

Attorney disciplinary proceeding was brought. The Supreme Court held that attorney's statement in court-filed papers that judge was a "lying incompetent ass-hole" violated rule prohibiting unfounded statements concerning qualifications and integrity of a judge and warranted six-month suspension from practice of law. Suspension ordered.

In June of 1994, respondent, Louis M. Waller, represented a client in a civil matter in the Logan Circuit Court. During the pendency of the action, but after having granted an injunction, the regular judge recused himself from hearing the case "because his impartiality might reasonably be questioned." A special judge, the Hon. William Harris, was then appointed. After the appointment of Judge Harris, Waller filed a motion to set aside the earlier temporary injunction. On June 21, 1994, Waller filed a memorandum styled as "Legal Authorities Supporting the Motion to Dismiss" which contained the following introductory language:

> Comes defendant, by counsel, and respectfully moves the Honorable
> Court, much better than that lying incompetent ass-hole it replaced ....

On June 24, 1994, Special Judge Harris ordered Waller to appear before the Logan Circuit Court and show cause why he should not be adjudged in contempt for filing such a scurrilous pleading. On June 29, 1994, Special Judge Harris rendered his findings of fact and conclusions of law, and found Waller to be in contempt of the Logan Circuit Court for his intemperate language and for his failure "to maintain the required respect due this court and the regular Judge thereof." For this contempt Waller was fined $499.00 and sentenced to thirty days in the county jail. The Court of Appeals affirmed the contempt judgment and we denied discretionary review on January 11, 1996.

A review of the record in this proceeding reveals that respondent's pleadings in the underlying civil action, in the contempt proceedings, and in the later disciplinary proceedings, are generally scandalous and bizarre. When given an opportunity to show cause why he should not be found in contempt, respondent filed a document styled "Memorandum In Defense of the Use of the Term 'As–Hole' (sic) to Draw the Attention of the Public to Corruption in Judicial Office" which, as indicated by its title, continued to assert corruption in the judicial system. He asserted that "[t]he undersigned would show the honorable reviewing tribunal that he does not know fear and if, while this case is pending in the courts, some interim punishment is deemed appropriate suggests, in all sincerity, flogging, caning or other physical torture." In an earlier pleading denominated "A Showing Of Cause," respondent asserted that the regular judge was a liar, a racist, that he was incompetent, and that he had a personal interest in proceedings before him. Respondent went further and offered:

> *Do with me what you will but it is and will be so done under like circumstances in the future. When this old honkey's sight fades, words once near seem far away, the pee runs down his leg in dribbles, his hands tremble and his wracked body aches, all that will remain is a wisp of a smile and a memory of a battle joined—first lost—then won.*

Apparently not yet satisfied, respondent continued filing similar bizarre pleadings throughout the disciplinary process. In his "Answer to First Amended Complaint," respondent repeated his allegations of corruption and included a "P.S.", as follows:

> *And so I place this message in a bottle and set it adrift on a sea of papers—hoping that someone of common sense will read it and ask about the kind of future we want for our children and whether or not the [corruption in] the judiciary should be exposed. My own methods have been unorthodox but techniques of controlling public opinion and property derived from military counter-intelligence are equally so. My prayer is that you measure reality not form ... [o]r is it too formitable (sic) a task and will you yourself have to forego a place at the trough? There is a better and happier way and—with due temerity I claim to have found it—it requires one to identify an ass hole when he sees one.*

Even in his brief to this Court, respondent takes the view that his statements were true, that the matter is not one that concerns the judiciary but rather "a private matter between the parties for which a private remedy exists," and that such comments are protected by the First Amendment to the United States Constitution. Such a claim is without merit. Respondent appears to believe that truth or some concept akin to truth, such as accuracy or correctness, is a defense to the charge against him. In this respect he has totally missed the point. There can never be a justification for a lawyer to use such scurrilous language with respect to a judge in pleadings or in open court. The reason is not that the judge is of such delicate sensibilities as to be unable to withstand the comment, but rather that such language promotes disrespect for the law and for the judicial system. Officers of the court are obligated to uphold the dignity of the Court of Justice and, at a minimum, this requires them to refrain from conduct of the type at issue here.

The Board of Governors recommended only that respondent be publicly reprimanded. While we have given due regard to the Board's recommendation and would agree if this were an isolated incident of intemperate language accompanied by a meaningful expression of regret, such is not the case. Respondent is utterly unrepentant and apparently intent on convincing this Court of the truth of his assertions. As such, we must impose a punishment of sufficient severity to forcefully inform respondent that he is wrong. Regardless of his personally-held views, if respondent desires to continue practicing law in the Commonwealth of Kentucky, he must conform his professional conduct to minimum acceptable standards. Consideration should be given to the desirability of professional counseling. It is therefore Ordered that Defendant Waller, be, and he is hereby, suspended from the practice of law in Kentucky for a period of six (6) months, and is further ordered to pay the costs of this proceeding.

****

Questions:

1. Lawyer blogs the following comments about a sitting judge, "the judge was either dishonest, or allowed others to be dishonest in the administration of the estate." The judge replied in a letter to the attorney where he stated, "One of the implications was that I was friends of the family, which I was not." "The implication was I somehow conspired with the executor to cheat some of the heirs out of the estate."

   The judge asked the attorney for an apology, stating "In 20 years on the bench, I have never had an attorney attack my integrity in writing in this manner." However, lawyer refused to apologize, and instead posted, "I stand by my statements regarding how you handled this estate". Do Lawyer's acts subject him to discipline for violating the model rules of professional conduct?[93]

2. Discuss whether the attorney in the following case should be sanctioned for violating ethical standards.

   In briefs filed with the Utah Supreme Court, the University of Utah S.J. Quinney College of Law professor wrote that "good judges never fabricate evidence," and that the appellate court opinion was "no innocent mistake."

   "So, if a court fabricates evidence, whether intentionally, negligently or through innocent mistake, it destroys the moral premise of the legal system," Dyer wrote. "A

---

[93] See Dave Stafford, Criticism of judge results in discipline case, The Indiana Lawyer.com available at http://www.theindianalawyer.com/criticism-of-judge-results-in-discipline-case/PARAMS/article/31510 last visited 7.4.14.

judge who fabricates evidence, even from a sincere motive to do justice in a particular case, has no moral standing whatsoever."[94]

****

REVIEW QUESTIONS

1. During settlement negotiations, Lawyer states that his client is unwilling to accept any amount less than $300,000. In fact, Client advised Lawyer that he would be happy with a $200,000 settlement. Is Lawyer subject to discipline for lying in his statement to opposing counsel?

2. Same facts as number 1 except Lawyer advises the Judge that the client would be unwilling to accept any amount less than $300,000. What result?

3. Lawyer represents Client who dies during settlement negotiations. Lawyer does not inform the opposing counsel or the court of the Client's death. Is Lawyer subject to discipline? Does Lawyer continue to represent Client after Client's death? See Virzi v Grand Trunk Warehouse & Cold Storage Co., 571 F. Supp. 507 (E.D. Mich.,1983.

4. Lawyer represents Defendant. Plaintiff is represented by counsel who has been attempting to negotiate settlement with Defendant's Lawyer. Plaintiff, seeing Defendant's Lawyer in the court building one day approaches her and says, "I want to settle this case as quickly as possible. What will it take to do that?" Defense counsel responds that his client will not be willing to pay a penny more than the $50,000 nuisance value of the suit. Plaintiff laughs and walks away. Later plaintiff tells his Lawyer what happened and Plaintiff's lawyer files a grievance against Defendant's Lawyer. Is Defendant's Lawyer subject to discipline? See Pleasant Management, LLC v. Carrasco, 870 A2d 443, 446 (RI, 2005)

5. Defendant is represented by Attorney. Responding to his Attorney's request for information, Defendant sends certain information to his Attorney inadvertently attaching the documents to a notice of hearing that had earlier been sent from his Attorney to him with a copy to opposing counsel. Defendant clicks the "reply all" button and opposing counsel receives a copy of the information, some of which would be very helpful to his client's position. Does Attorney have a duty under the model rules of professional conduct to notify defendant that he inadvertently sent a copy of the information to him? Does Attorney have a duty under the model rules of professional conduct to notify defendant's attorney that defendant inadvertently sent a copy of the information to him?

6. Plaintiff lawyers serve Defendant's Attorney with Interrogatories. Among other things the Plaintiff requests the names and contact information on any of the defendant's employees that may have information pertinent to the lawsuit filed. Defendant's Attorney knows about one employee who has very damaging information that if disclosed would ensure a Plaintiff victory. Attorney also knows that the defendant recently terminated employee's employment but contracted with employee as a highly paid consultant. Defendant also paid for the consultant to move to Ghana for an indefinite period but at least until the trial was concluded. Thereafter, in response to the interrogatories, Attorney's client provided a list of

---

[94] See Peters v. Pine Meadow Ranch Home Association, 2005 UT 295 (Utah Ct App., 2005) unpublished

employees with relevant, albeit insubstantial, information about the case. Defendant never disclosed the name or contact information for the recently hired "consultant." Has Attorney violated the model rules by permitting the Client to respond to the interrogatories in this manner?

7. Lawyer represented a client in the purchase of a take-out margarita business. The business' seller was not represented by counsel. The seller had sold other businesses on his own, without counsel and was a sophistocated negotiator. However, the Seller liked the way Lawyer handled the margarita transaction and asks the lawyer to represent him in his purchase of a downtown high rise property. This purchase is much more complicated than the small transactions the lawyer has previously handled during his five year legal career. May Lawyer represent Seller in the purchase of this property?

8. Plaintiff's Attorney (P) is copied on an e-mail from defendant that was meant for the various lawyers on the defense team. P realizes that the email includes the strategy of the defendant's case and that she was inadvertently included on the e-blast. What is Counsel required to do to comply with the model rules? What should Counsel do to comply with the model rules?

****

LAW FIRMS AND ASSOCIATIONS

IN THE NEWS:

In 2008, "[t]he Illinois Attorney Registration and Disciplinary Commission accused former high-ranking partner at Holland & Knight's Chicago office, Edward Ryan, 65, of billing fraud that lasted more than two years during his representation of Pinnacle Corp., a Midwestern home builder, in a copyright-infringement lawsuit." Ryan, who was served with the complaint earlier this month, denies the allegations, his attorney said Tuesday.

Considered one of the top ten ways that a lawyer fleeces his clients, bill padding has been referred to as "the "perfect crime" because it is nearly impossible for clients to detect if a lawyer charges for five hours reviewing documents when he really only spent three."

In Ryan's case, a junior lawyer at his firm blew the whistle on him.[95] "Much of the bill padding was for hours Ryan said he performed for the client but reassigned to other attorneys, the commission said."

Read more at Former partner with Holland & Knight charged with billing fraud: Edward Ryan inflated bills for Pinnacle Corp., says Illinois Attorney Registration and Disciplinary Commission, December 24, 2008 |By Ameet Sachdev, TRIBUNE REPORTER, http://articles.chicagotribune.com/2008-12-24/news/0812230601_1_billing-fraud-pinnacle-edward-ryan

---

[95] See Bohatch v. Butler & Binion, 977 S.W.2d 543 (1998) discussing a law partnership's right to expel a partner who reports another partner's overbilling

Ethical Considerations for Lawyers in Law Firms and Associations

Partners and supervisors

A partner and or supervising attorney in a law firm must rely on the staff to assist in carrying out the firm's legal services. The supervisor is generally liable for the wrongful and unethical acts of her staff. However, even in a small firm, it is impractical to expect the supervisor to be aware of everything that every employee does. Thus, it is important for the supervisor to ensure that there are procedural and practice standards that staff must follow in order to comply with the supervisor's obligations to the firm, the client and to the public.

At the minimum, the supervising attorney should take reasonable measures to ensure the staff is competent and trained to perform their duties in conformance with the rules of ethics.

Associates and other lawyer employees

An associate of a law firm is generally an employee who is also a lawyer and therefore is bound by obligations to the firm as well as its client. Some lawyers are contract workers with law firms and may be designated either an independent contractor or agent. Associates and other lawyer employees owe fiduciary duties of loyalty, care and obedience to their firm. The duty of loyalty requires the associate to place the interests of the firm above his own--a duty that could survive the termination of the relationship. In most jurisdictions, the associate may prepare to leave the firm without breaching the duty of loyalty so long as he acts candidly with respect to the firm and refrains from using improper methods of soliciting any of the firm's clients.

The associate warrants that he has the requisite skill to perform his professional duties on behalf of the firm. However, lawyers in the firm cannot turn a blind eye to evidence of the associate's incompetence. Depending on the extent of the associate's (or other lawyer's) disability the non-offending lawyer may be obligated to report the associate to the proper authorities.[96]

The associate is generally under an obligation to obey the reasonable instructions of the firm in performing his job. A challenge may arise when the associate believes that the instructions are in violation of the rules of ethics. Generally, if there is any reasonable basis for the instruction, then the associate may comply with immunity. However, the associate, himself an attorney, has an independent obligation to refrain from violating the rules of ethics. The shield from protection will not permit an associate from this obligation when the instruction constituted a clear violation of the rule.

Many times, the associate works on a case file but not directly with the clients so there may be no attorney client relationship between the associate and client. However, the associate who does work with the firm's client owes fiduciary duties to the client as well as the firm.[97]

---

[96] ABA Model Rule of Professional Conduct [Rule 8.3]
[97] Leonard Gross, *Ethical Problems of Law Firm Associates*, 26 Wm. & Mary L. Rev. 259 (1985)

Unauthorized practice of law (UPL)

The practice of law is generally restricted to members of the appropriate bar who are licensed and in good standing to practice law. The practice of law generally includes preparation of legal documents including pleadings, wills and contracts.[98]

Birbrower, Montalbano, Condon & Frank v.Superior Court
17 Cal.4th 119 , 70 Cal.Rptr.2d 304; 949 P.2d. 1 (1998)[99]

...

I. Background

The facts with respect to the unauthorized practice of law question are essentially undisputed. Birbrower is a professional law corporation incorporated in New York, with its principal place of business in New York. During 1992 and 1993, Birbrower attorneys, defendants Kevin F. Hobbs and Thomas A. Condon (Hobbs and Condon), performed substantial work in California relating to the law firm's representation of ESQ. Neither Hobbs nor Condon has ever been licensed to practice law in California. None of Birbrower's attorneys were licensed to practice law in California during Birbrower's ESQ representation.

ESQ is a California corporation with its principal place of business in Santa Clara County. In July 1992, the parties negotiated and executed the fee [17 Cal.4th 125] agreement in New York, providing that Birbrower would perform legal services for ESQ, including "All matters pertaining to the investigation of and prosecution of all claims and causes of action against Tandem Computers Incorporated [Tandem]." The "claims and causes of action" against Tandem, a Delaware corporation with its principal place of business in Santa Clara County, California, related to a software development and marketing contract between Tandem and ESQ dated March 16, 1990 (Tandem Agreement). The Tandem Agreement stated that "The internal laws of the State of California (irrespective of its choice of law principles) shall govern the validity of this Agreement, the construction of its terms, and the interpretation and enforcement of the rights and duties of the parties hereto." Birbrower asserts, and ESQ disputes, that ESQ knew Birbrower was not licensed to practice law in California.

---

[98] E.g. Texas courts have held numerous acts as constituting the unauthorized practice of law. See *Unauthorized Practice Committee v. Cortez*, 692 S.W.2d 47 (Tex. 1985): selecting and preparing immigration forms constitutes the practice of law. ; *Crain v. Unauthorized Practice of Law Committee*, 11 S.W.3d 328 (Tex.App. - Houston [1st Dist.] 1999, pet. den'd), cert denied, 532 U.S. 1067, 150 L. Ed. 2d 211, 121 S. Ct. 2218 (2001): preparing and filing mechanic's lien affidavits constitutes the practice of law. ; *Greene v. Unauthorized Practice of Law Committee*, 883 S.W.2d 293 (Tex.App. - Dallas 1994, no writ): preparing and sending demand letters on personal injury and property damage claims and negotiating and settling the claims with insurance companies constitutes the practice of law. ;*Fadia v. Unauthorized Practice of Law Committee*, 830 S.W.2d 162, 165 (Tex. App.-Dallas 1992, writ denied): selling will forms and manuals constitutes the practice of law.; *Brown v. Unauthorized Practice of Law Committee*, 742 S.W.2d 34 (Tex. App.--Dallas 1987, writ denied): contracting to represent persons with regard to personal injury and property damage claims constitutes the practice of law.

[99] But see Williamson, P. A., a Professional Association v. John D. Quinn Construction Corp., 537 F.Supp. 613 (United States District Court, S. D. New York, 1982)

While representing ESQ, Hobbs and Condon traveled to California on several occasions. In August 1992, they met in California with ESQ and its accountants. During these meetings, Hobbs and Condon discussed various matters related to ESQ's dispute with Tandem and strategy for resolving the dispute. They made recommendations and gave advice. During this California trip, Hobbs and Condon also met with Tandem representatives on four or five occasions during a two-day period. At the meetings, Hobbs and Condon spoke on ESQ's behalf. Hobbs demanded that Tandem pay ESQ $15 million. Condon told Tandem he believed that damages would exceed $15 million if the parties litigated the dispute.

Around March or April 1993, Hobbs, Condon, and another Birbrower attorney visited California to interview potential arbitrators and to meet again with ESQ and its accountants. Birbrower had previously filed a demand for arbitration against Tandem with the San Francisco offices of the American Arbitration Association (AAA). In August 1993, Hobbs returned to California to assist ESQ in settling the Tandem matter. While in California, Hobbs met with ESQ and its accountants to discuss a proposed settlement agreement Tandem authored. Hobbs also met with Tandem representatives to discuss possible changes in the proposed agreement. Hobbs gave ESQ legal advice during this trip, including his opinion that ESQ should not settle with Tandem on the terms proposed.

ESQ eventually settled the Tandem dispute, and the matter never went to arbitration. But before the settlement, ESQ and Birbrower modified the contingency fee agreement. The modification changed the fee arrangement from contingency to fixed fee, providing that ESQ would pay Birbrower [17 Cal.4th 126] over $1 million. The original contingency fee arrangement had called for Birbrower to receive "one-third (1/3) of all sums received for the benefit of the Clients ... whether obtained through settlement, motion practice, hearing, arbitration, or trial by way of judgment, award, settlement, or otherwise ...."

In January 1994, ESQ sued Birbrower for legal malpractice and related claims in Santa Clara County Superior Court. Birbrower removed the matter to federal court and filed a counterclaim, which included a claim for attorney fees for the work it performed in both California and New York. The matter was then remanded to the superior court. There ESQ moved for summary judgment and/or adjudication on the first through fourth causes of action of Birbrower's counterclaim, which asserted ESQ and its representatives breached the fee agreement. ESQ argued that by practicing law without a license in California and by failing to associate legal counsel while doing so, Birbrower violated section 6125, rendering the fee agreement unenforceable. Based on these undisputed facts, the Santa Clara Superior Court granted ESQ's motion for summary adjudication of the first through fourth causes of action in Birbrower's counterclaim. The court also granted summary adjudication in favor of ESQ's third and fourth causes of action in its second amended complaint, seeking declaratory relief as to the validity of the fee agreement and its modification. [1](See fn. 3)The court concluded that: (1) Birbrower was "not admitted to the practice of law in California"; (2) Birbrower "did not associate California counsel"; (3) Birbrower "provided legal services in this state"; and (4) "The law is clear that no one may recover compensation for services as an attorney in this state unless he or she was a member of the state bar at the time those services were performed."

Although the trial court's order stated that the fee agreements were unenforceable, at the hearing on the summary adjudication motion, the trial court also observed: "It seems to me that those are some of the issues that this Court has to struggle with, and then it becomes a question of if they aren't allowed to collect their attorney's fees here, I don't think that puts the attorneys in a position from being precluded from collecting all of their attorney's fees, only those fees probably that were generated by virtue of work that they performed in California and not that work that was performed in New York." [17 Cal.4th 127]

In granting limited summary adjudication, the trial court left open the following issues for resolution: ESQ's malpractice action against Birbrower, and the remaining causes of action in Birbrower's counterclaim, including Birbrower's fifth cause of action for quantum meruit (seeking the reasonable value of legal services provided).

Birbrower petitioned the Court of Appeal for a writ of mandate directing the trial court to vacate the summary adjudication order. The Court of Appeal denied Birbrower's petition and affirmed the trial court's order, holding that Birbrower violated section 6125. The Court of Appeal also concluded that Birbrower's violation barred the firm from recovering its legal fees under the written fee agreement, including fees generated in New York by the attorneys when they were physically present in New York, because the agreement included payment for California or "local" services for a California client in California. The Court of Appeal agreed with the trial court, however, in deciding that Birbrower could pursue its remaining claims against ESQ, including its equitable claim for recovery of its fees in quantum meruit.

We granted review to determine whether Birbrower's actions and services performed while representing ESQ in California constituted the unauthorized practice of law under section 6125 and, if so, whether a section 6125 violation rendered the fee agreement wholly unenforceable.

II. Discussion

A. The Unauthorized Practice of Law

The California Legislature enacted section 6125 in 1927 as part of the State Bar Act (the Act), a comprehensive scheme regulating the practice of law in the state. (J.W. v. Superior Court (1993) 17 Cal.App.4th 958, 965 [22 Cal.Rptr.2d 527] (J.W.).) Since the Act's passage, the general rule has been that, although persons may represent themselves and their own interests regardless of State Bar membership, no one but an active member of the State Bar may practice law for another person in California. (Ibid.) The prohibition against unauthorized law practice is within the state's police power and is designed to ensure that those performing legal services do so competently. (Id. at p. 969.)

A violation of section 6125 is a misdemeanor. (§ 6126.) Moreover, "No one may recover compensation for services as an attorney at law in this state unless [the person] was at the time the services were performed a member of The State Bar." (Hardy v. San Fernando Valley C. of C. (1950) 99 Cal.App.2d 572, 576 [222 P.2d 314] (Hardy).) [17 Cal.4th 128]

Although the Act did not define the term "practice law," case law explained it as "the doing and performing services in a court of justice in any matter depending therein throughout its various stages and in conformity with the adopted rules of procedure." (People v. Merchants Protective Corp. (1922) 189 Cal. 531, 535 [209 P. 363] (Merchants)) Merchants included in its definition legal advice and legal instrument and contract preparation, whether or not these subjects were rendered in the course of litigation. (Ibid.; see People v. Ring (1937) 26 Cal.App.2d. Supp. 768, 772-773 [70 P.2d 281] (Ring) [holding that single incident of practicing law in state without a license violates § 6125]; see also Mickel v. Murphy (1957) 147 Cal.App.2d 718, 721 [305 P.2d 993] [giving of legal advice on matter not pending before state court violates § 6125], disapproved on other grounds in Biakanja v. Irving (1958) 49 Cal.2d 647, 651 [320 P.2d 16, 65 A.L.R.2d 1358].) Ring later determined that the Legislature "accepted both the definition already judicially supplied for the term and the declaration of the Supreme Court [in Merchants] that it had a sufficiently definite meaning to need no further definition. The definition ... must be regarded as definitely establishing, for the jurisprudence of this state, the meaning of the term 'practice law.' " (Ring, supra, 26 Cal.App.2d at p. Supp. 772.)

In addition to not defining the term "practice law," the Act also did not define the meaning of "in California." In today's legal practice, questions often arise concerning whether the phrase refers to the nature of the legal services, or restricts the Act's application to those out-of-state attorneys who are physically present in the state.

Section 6125 has generated numerous opinions on the meaning of "practice law" but none on the meaning of "in California." In our view, the practice of law "in California" entails sufficient contact with the California client to render the nature of the legal service a clear legal representation. In addition to a quantitative analysis, we must consider the nature of the unlicensed lawyer's activities in the state. Mere fortuitous or attenuated contacts will not sustain a finding that the unlicensed lawyer practiced law "in California." The primary inquiry is whether the unlicensed lawyer engaged in sufficient activities in the state, or created a continuing relationship with the California client that included legal duties and obligations.

Our definition does not necessarily depend on or require the unlicensed lawyer's physical presence in the state. Physical presence here is one factor we may consider in deciding whether the unlicensed lawyer has violated section 6125, but it is by no means exclusive. For example, one may practice law in the state in violation of section 6125 although not physically present here by advising a California client on California law in connection with a [17 Cal.4th 129] California legal dispute by telephone, fax, computer, or other modern technological means. Conversely, although we decline to provide a comprehensive list of what activities constitute sufficient contact with the state, we do reject the notion that a person automatically practices law "in California" whenever that person practices California law anywhere, or "virtually" enters the state by telephone, fax, e-mail, or satellite. (See e.g., Baron v. City of Los Angeles (1970) 2 Cal.3d 535, 543 [86 Cal.Rptr. 673, 469 P.2d 353, 42 A.L.R.3d 1036] (Baron) ["practice law" does not encompass all professional activities].) Indeed, we disapprove Ring, supra, 26 Cal.App.2d Supp. 768, and its progeny to the extent the cases are inconsistent with our discussion. We must decide each case on its individual facts.

189

This interpretation acknowledges the tension that exists between interjurisdictional practice and the need to have a state-regulated bar. As stated in the American Bar Association Model Code of Professional Responsibility, Ethical Consideration EC 3-9, "Regulation of the practice of law is accomplished principally by the respective states. Authority to engage in the practice of law conferred in any jurisdiction is not per se a grant of the right to practice elsewhere, and it is improper for a lawyer to engage in practice where he is not permitted by law or by court order to do so. However, the demands of business and the mobility of our society pose distinct problems in the regulation of the practice of law by the states. In furtherance of the public interest, the legal profession should discourage regulation that unreasonably imposes territorial limitations upon the right of a lawyer to handle the legal affairs of his client or upon the opportunity of a client to obtain the services of a lawyer of his choice in all matters including the presentation of a contested matter in a tribunal before which the lawyer is not permanently admitted to practice." (Fns. omitted.) Baron implicitly agrees with this canon. (Baron, supra, 2 Cal.3d at p. 543.)…

Exceptions to section 6125 do exist, but are generally limited to allowing out-of-state attorneys to make brief appearances before a state court [17 Cal.4th 130] or tribunal. They are narrowly drawn and strictly interpreted. For example, an out-of-state attorney not licensed to practice in California may be permitted, by consent of a trial judge, to appear in California in a particular pending action. (See In re McCue (1930) 211 Cal. 57, 67 [293 P. 47]; 1 Witkin, Cal. Procedure (4th ed. 1996) Attorneys, § 402, p. 493.)

In addition, with the permission of the California court in which a particular cause is pending, out-of-state counsel may appear before a court as counsel pro hac vice. (Cal. Rules of Court, rule 983.) A court will approve a pro hac vice application only if the out-of-state attorney is a member in good standing of another state bar and is eligible to practice in any United States court or the highest court in another jurisdiction. (Cal. Rules of Court, rule 983(a).) The out-of-state attorney must also associate an active member of the California Bar as attorney of record and is subject to the Rules of Professional Conduct of the State Bar. (Cal. Rules of Court, rules 983(a), (d); see Rules Prof. Conduct, rule 1-100(D)(2) [includes lawyers from other jurisdictions authorized to practice in this state].)

The Act does not regulate practice before United States courts. Thus, an out-of-state attorney engaged to render services in bankruptcy proceedings was entitled to collect his fee. (Cowen v. Calabrese (1964) 230 Cal.App.2d 870, 872 [41 Cal.Rptr. 441, 11 A.L.R.3d 903] (Cowen); but see U.S. Dist. Ct. Local Rules, Northern Dist. Cal., rule 11-1(b); Eastern Dist. Cal., rule 83-180; Central Dist. Cal., rule 2.2.1; Southern Dist. Cal., rule 83.3 c.1.a. [today conditioning admission to their respective bars (with certain exceptions for some federal government employees) on active membership in good standing in California State Bar].)

Finally, California Rules of Court, rule 988, permits the State Bar to issue registration certificates to foreign legal consultants who may advise on the law of the foreign jurisdiction where they are admitted. These consultants may not, however, appear as attorneys before a California court or judicial officer or otherwise prepare pleadings and instruments in California or give advice on the law of California or any other state or jurisdiction except those where they are admitted.…

B. The Present Case

The undisputed facts here show that neither Baron's definition (Baron, supra, 2 Cal.3d at p. 543) nor our "sufficient contact" definition of "practice law in California" (ante, at pp. 128-129) would excuse Birbrower's extensive practice in this state. Nor would any of the limited statutory exceptions to section 6125 apply to Birbrower's California practice. As the Court of Appeal observed, Birbrower engaged in unauthorized law practice in California on more than a limited basis, and no firm attorney engaged in that practice was an active member of the California State Bar. As noted (ante, at p. 125), in 1992 and 1993, Birbrower attorneys traveled to California to discuss with ESQ and others various matters pertaining to the dispute between ESQ and Tandem. Hobbs and Condon discussed strategy for resolving the dispute and advised ESQ on this strategy. Furthermore, during California meetings with Tandem representatives in August 1992, Hobbs demanded Tandem pay $15 million, and Condon told Tandem he believed damages in the matter would exceed that amount if the parties proceeded to litigation. Also in California, Hobbs met with ESQ for the stated purpose of helping to reach a settlement agreement and to discuss the agreement that was eventually proposed. Birbrower attorneys also traveled to California to initiate arbitration proceedings before the matter was settled. As the Court of Appeal concluded, "... the Birbrower firm's in-state activities clearly constituted the [unauthorized] practice of law" in California. ...

Birbrower next argues that we do not further the statute's intent and purpose-to protect California citizens from incompetent attorneys-by enforcing it against out-of-state attorneys. Birbrower argues that because out-of-state attorneys have been licensed to practice in other jurisdictions, they have already demonstrated sufficient competence to protect California clients. But Birbrower's argument overlooks the obvious fact that other states' laws may differ substantially from California law. Competence in one jurisdiction does not necessarily guarantee competence in another. By applying section 6125 to out-of-state attorneys who engage in the extensive practice of law in California without becoming licensed in our state, we serve the statute's goal of assuring the competence of all attorneys practicing law in this state. (J.W., supra, 17 Cal.App.4th at p. 969.)

California is not alone in regulating who practices law in its jurisdiction. Many states have substantially similar statutes that serve to protect their citizens from unlicensed attorneys who engage in unauthorized legal practice. Like section 6125, these other state statutes protect local citizens "against the dangers of legal representation and advice given by persons not trained, examined and licensed for such work, whether they be laymen or lawyers from other jurisdictions." ...

We [also] decline Birbrower's invitation to craft an arbitration exception to section 6125's prohibition of the unlicensed practice of law in this state. Any [17 Cal.4th 134] exception for arbitration is best left to the Legislature, which has the authority to determine qualifications for admission to the State Bar and to decide what constitutes the practice of law. (Baron, supra, 2 Cal.3d at pp. 540-541; see also Eagle Indem. Co. v. Industrial Acc. Com. (1933) 217 Cal. 244, 247 [18 P.2d 341].) Even though the Legislature has spoken with respect to international arbitration and conciliation, it has not enacted a similar rule for private arbitration proceedings. Of course, private arbitration and other alternative dispute resolution practices are important aspects of our justice system. (See Moncharsh v. Heily & Blase (1992) 3 Cal.4th 1, 9 [10 Cal.Rptr.2d 183, 832 P.2d 899] [noting a strong public policy in favor of arbitration].) Section 6125, however, articulates a strong public policy favoring the practice of law in California by licensed State Bar members. In the face of the Legislature's silence, we will not create an arbitration exception under the facts presented. …

Finally, Birbrower urges us to adopt an exception to section 6125 based on the unique circumstances of this case. Birbrower notes that "Multistate relationships are a common part of today's society and are to be dealt with in commonsense fashion." (In re Estate of Waring (1966) 47 N.J. 367 [221 A.2d 193, 197].) In many situations, strict adherence to rules prohibiting the unauthorized practice of law by out-of-state attorneys would be "grossly impractical and inefficient." (Ibid.; see also Appell v. Reiner (1964) 43 N.J. 313 [204 A.2d 146, 148] [strict adherence to rule barring out-of-state lawyers from representing New Jersey residents on New Jersey matters may run against the public interest when case involves inseparable multistate transactions].)

Although, as discussed (ante, at pp. 129-130), we recognize the need to acknowledge and, in certain cases, to accommodate the multistate nature of law practice, the facts here show that Birbrower's extensive activities within California amounted to considerably more than any of our state's recognized exceptions to section 6125 would allow. Accordingly, we reject Birbrower's suggestion that we except the firm from section 6125's rule under the circumstances here.

C. Compensation for Legal Services

Because Birbrower violated section 6125 when it engaged in the unlawful practice of law in California, the Court of Appeal found its fee agreement with ESQ unenforceable in its entirety. Without crediting Birbrower for some services performed in New York, for which fees were generated under the fee agreement, the court reasoned that the agreement was void and unenforceable because it included payment for services rendered to a California client in the state by an unlicensed out-of-state lawyer. The court opined that "When New York counsel decided to accept [the] representation, it should have researched California law, including the law governing the practice of law in this state." The Court of Appeal let stand, however, the trial court's decision to allow Birbrower to pursue its fifth cause of action in quantum meruit. We agree with the Court of Appeal to the extent it barred Birbrower from recovering fees generated under the fee agreement for the unauthorized legal services it performed in California. We disagree with the same court to the extent it implicitly barred Birbrower [17 Cal.4th 136] from recovering fees generated under the fee agreement for the limited legal services the firm performed in New York.

… Because Birbrower practiced substantial law in this state in violation of section 6125, it cannot receive compensation under the fee agreement for any of the services it performed in California. Enforcing the fee agreement in its entirety would include payment for the unauthorized practice of law in California and would allow Birbrower to enforce an illegal contract. (See Hardy, supra, 99 Cal.App.2d at p. 576.) …

Therefore, we conclude the Court of Appeal erred in determining that the fee agreement between the parties was entirely unenforceable because Birbrower violated section 6125's prohibition against the unauthorized practice of law in California. Birbrower's statutory violation may require exclusion of the portion of the fee attributable to the substantial illegal services, but that violation does not necessarily entirely preclude its recovery under the fee agreement for the limited services it performed outside California. (Calvert, supra, 33 Cal.2d at pp. 104-105.)...

III. Disposition

We conclude that Birbrower violated section 6125 by practicing law in California. To the extent the fee agreement allows payment for those illegal local services, it is void, and Birbrower is not entitled to recover fees under the agreement for those services. The fee agreement is enforceable, however, to the extent it is possible to sever the portions of the consideration attributable to Birbrower's services illegally rendered in California from those attributable to Birbrower's New York services. Accordingly, we affirm the Court of Appeal judgment to the extent it concluded that Birbrower's representation of ESQ in California violated section 6125, and that Birbrower is not entitled to recover fees under the fee agreement for its local services. We reverse the judgment to the extent the court did not allow Birbrower to argue in favor of a severance of the illegal portion of the consideration (for the California fees) from the rest of the fee agreement, and remand for further proceedings consistent with this decision.

Garcia v. Commission For Lawyer Discipline
No. 03-05-00413CV (Tex. App.-Austin, 2007)

This disciplinary action was brought by the Commission for Lawyer Discipline against Raul Garcia, a Texas-licensed attorney, for violations of rules 5.04(a), 5.04(b), 5.05(b), and 7.01(a) of the Texas Disciplinary Rules of Professional Conduct. On cross-motions for summary judgment, the district court granted summary judgment for the Commission as to rules 5.04(a), 5.05(b), and 7.01(a), and for Garcia as to rule 5.04(b). Garcia appeals the district court's judgment partially granting the Commission summary judgment against him and partially denying his summary judgment motions. We affirm the district court's judgment.

Background

At relevant times, Garcia was employed by Cristo Vive, Christian Social Services, Inc. Cristo Vive is a nonprofit organization that, beginning in the late 1980s, provided services that have included assisting individuals with immigration-related legal matters, translation work, and social-service referrals. It is undisputed that some of these activities come within the statutory definition of the practice of law. It is also undisputed that Cristo Vive has charged fees for these legal services ranging from $250 to $450, depending on the nature of service provided, served between 3,400 and 5,400 clients annually during the 1999-2001 tax years, and collected fees ranging from approximately $230,000 to $619,000 annually during that period.

Cristo Vive was previously the target of a proceeding initiated by the Unauthorized Practice of Law Committee (UPLC). Cristo Vive ultimately entered into a consent decree with the UPLC under which Cristo Vive "and its agents, officers, directors, servants, employees, successors and assigns" were enjoined from engaging in a range of activities related to immigration legal services, [including]:

1. Contracting with individuals to represent them in preparing, filing, or assisting with the preparation or filing of any documents with the United States Immigration and Naturalization Service;

2. Advising individuals as to their legal rights, the advisability and time limits in the making of claims for temporary and permanent residence, as well as U.S. citizenship;

3. Advising individuals of their rights, duties, and privileges under the law;

4. Advising individuals that they do not require the advice or services of a duly licensed attorney;

5. Soliciting legal services on behalf of another for remuneration;

6. Holding itself out as an attorney authorized to practice law in the State of Texas;

7. Holding itself out as qualified to render professional legal services of any kind;

8. Advising individuals regarding (a) which specific documents or forms might be necessary for filing with a court or governmental agency to accomplish an individual's objective; (b) how to properly fill out such papers; (c) where to correctly fill out such papers; or (d) how to present additional information to a court, government agency or quasi-judicial body;

9. Employing the words "immigration services" or "immigration consultant" in relation to any business it conducts;

10. Advertising or representing in written or electronic media or in any documents ordinarily submitted to the United States Immigration and Naturalization Service that it renders or can render "immigration services," is an "immigration consultant," or any services relating to United States citizenship application, non-immigrant or immigrant status; or

11. Assisting any other individual in the unauthorized practice of law.

Expressly excluded from the prohibited activities were translating documents; taking identification pictures; taking and filing Immigration and Naturalization Service (INS) fingerprint forms; teaching and testing English as a second language, history, government, or other classes; notary services; and "providing community services to low income persons," such as referrals to social service agencies and charitable organizations regarding food, shelter, and benefits. Federal regulation permits non-profit organizations meeting certain criteria to obtain recognition or accreditation from the Board of Immigration Appeals permitting them to designate a representative to practice before the Board or INS. 8 C.F.R. § 292.2. Criteria for recognition include "ha[ving] at its disposal adequate knowledge, information and experience" and "mak[ing] only nominal charges ... for persons given assistance." *Id.* § 292.2(a). The Commission has acknowledged that "[i]f Cristo Vive and its non-lawyer employees were recognized/accredited," state unauthorized practice of law (UPL) limitations "would yield to this federal law." However, it is undisputed that Cristo Vive has never succeeded in obtaining the required status.

In the aftermath of the consent decree, Cristo Vive, through its board of directors, and Garcia executed an employment contract whereby Garcia agreed to serve as the entity's "In-House Staff Attorney ... to supervise, direct and control all legal services offered to the community by Cristo Vive." It is undisputed that Cristo Vive and Garcia crafted the contract language and the structure of their relationship with the intent of coming within the second exception of the consent decree; i.e., Cristo Vive's acts and conduct otherwise constituting UPL would be "perform[ed] ... under the direction, supervision and control of a member of the State Bar of Texas"-Garcia. Garcia accepted the position on June 26, 2001.

Thereafter, Garcia provided legal services to Cristo Vive's clients. Garcia worked full-time in this capacity for Cristo Vive and did not otherwise practice law other than occasional pro bono work through Volunteer Legal Services. It is undisputed that although Cristo Vive charges fees varying with the services provided to each client, Garcia received a salary of approximately $50,000 per year that was not tied to the type of services he provided or the number of clients he counseled.

The "process by which immigration clients are assisted by Cristo Vive" and Garcia's role in that process is as follows:

> *"Client comes to Cristo Vive and asks for assistance. If the assistance requires legal advice they are told that only an attorney can answer that question and that they cannot give legal advice. They are informed that there is an attorney in the office [who] can advise them. If they want to see the attorney the attorney performs an interview, offers a legal remedy if there is one available, and prescribes the appropriate applications. If they want to hire Cristo Vive to fill out the prescribed applications the attorney will direct, supervise and control the service."*

Garcia's duties as an attorney with Cristo Vive was as follows:

> *"to supervise, direct and control all services provided by the paralegals in connection with their petitions for status as lawful permanent residents or as citizens of the United States that [he] may have advised. In initial consultation, [to] ...determine what forms, if any, will achieve the result desired by the client, and advise them accordingly. If the client hired Cristo Vive to type out forms and prepare, [he would]... direct, supervise, and control the staff in typing out the form, and after they are typed out, review to make sure everything was answered correctly. [He]... then authorize[d] the client to mail the application [to] the [Bureau of Citizenship and Immigration Services] or [Department of State]."*

In June 2003, the Commission filed a disciplinary proceeding against Garcia alleging violations of the following provisions of the Texas Disciplinary Rules of Professional Conduct:

- 5.04(a) (fee-splitting with a non-lawyer);
- 5.04(b) (forming a partnership with a non-lawyer);

- 5.05(b) (assisting a person who is not a member of the state bar in committing UPL);
- 7.01(a) (practicing in private practice under a trade name).

The Commission subsequently sought partial summary judgment that Garcia had violated each of these rules. Garcia filed a response to the motion and separate cross-motions for traditional and "no evidence" summary judgment regarding each of the alleged rule violations. The district court granted the motions of both the Commission and Garcia in part and denied them in part. It rendered judgment that Garcia had violated rules 5.04(a), 5.05(b), and 7.01(a) but had not formed a partnership with a non-lawyer in violation of rule 5.05(b). The court further adjudged that the proper discipline for Garcia's violations was a public reprimand with an award of costs. This appeal ensued.

Analysis

Garcia appeals the district court's judgment that he violated rules 5.04(a), 5.05(b) and 7.01(a). The Commission does not appeal the district court's judgment for Garcia regarding rule 5.05(b).

Standard of review

We review the district court's summary judgment de novo. When reviewing a summary judgment, we take as true all evidence favorable to the non-movant, and we indulge every reasonable inference and resolve any doubts in the non-movant's favor. Summary judgment is proper when there are no disputed issues of material fact and the movant is entitled to judgment as a matter of law.

When, as here, both parties move for summary judgment on overlapping grounds and the district court grants one motion and denies the other, we ordinarily review the summary-judgment evidence presented by both sides, determine all questions presented, and render the judgment that the district court should have rendered.

Rule 5.05(b): Assisting UPL

Rule 5.05(b) provides that a lawyer shall not "assist a person who is not a member of the bar in the unauthorized practice of law." This prohibition against assisting UPL, as well as the underlying ban on UPL itself, is rooted in a "perceived need to protect individuals and the public from the mistakes of the untrained and the schemes of the unscrupulous, who are not subject to the judicially imposed disciplinary standards of competence, responsibility, and accountability."

The Commission's complaint that Garcia assisted in UPL is predicated on the UPL of Cristo Vive. Cristo Vive's alleged UPL, in turn, is predicated on the acts of Garcia in providing legal services in the name of Cristo Vive to its customers, which is imputed to Cristo Vive as Garcia's principal. It is undisputed that the services Garcia provided to third parties as an attorney for Cristo Vive included those constituting the practice of law. To date, Texas law remains that, at least where a corporation has no direct interest in legal work performed by a lawyer agent for the benefit of a third party, the corporation has practiced law through that lawyer.

Section 81.101(a) of the government code defines the "practice of law" as:

> *the preparation of a pleading or other document incident to an action or special proceeding or the management of the action or proceeding on behalf of a client before a judge in court as well as a service rendered out of court, including the giving of advice or the rendering of any service requiring the use of legal skill or knowledge, such as preparing a will, contract, or other instrument, the legal effect of which under the facts and conclusions involved must be carefully determined.*

However, this definition "is not exclusive and does not deprive the judicial branch of the power and authority under both [chapter 81 of the government code] and the adjudicated cases to determine whether other services and acts not enumerated may constitute the practice of law." The Texas Supreme Court has granted review in *American Home,* and it remains pending before the court.

To avoid the Commission's entitlement to summary judgment on this issue, Garcia relies principally on the affirmative defense that his actions for Cristo Vive were expressly permitted by that entity's consent decree with the UPLC. As noted previously, the consent decree enjoined Cristo Vive "and its agents, officers, directors, servants, employees, successors and assigns" from a range of activities related to immigration-related legal services, subject to [certain] provisions.

Garcia also suggests that "the Comments to the Rules of Professional Conduct expressly permit Garcia to undertake his employment with Cristo Vive." From context, it appears that Garcia is referring to comments 4, 5, and 6 to rule 5.04, which he suggests "contemplate situations in which a lawyer may be hired by an organization to provide legal services to another person," including employment with legal-aid offices. Rule 5.04 is concerned with maintaining the professional independence of lawyers. The three comments Garcia cites address the professional-independence concern where lawyers are hired to provide legal services to third persons. Contrary to what Garcia suggests, the comments do not imply that such arrangements are categorically permitted without regard to the limitations of other rules. *See Touchy v. Houston Legal Found.,* 432 S.W.2d 690, 694-95 (Tex.1968) (contrasting a non-profit corporation that is "directly representing clients as an attorney by signing pleadings in its name, or by appearing for such clients through its employees," which would constitute UPL, with "a legal aid society which acts merely as a conduit or intermediary to bring the attorney and client together," which would not).

Although Garcia admits that Cristo Vive has not been accredited under section 292.2, he contends that the entity complied with the consent decree by "perform[ing] any such acts [otherwise prohibited by the decree] under the direction, supervision and control of a member of the State Bar of Texas"-Garcia. In Garcia's view, compliance with the second exception alone is sufficient to bring Cristo Vive in compliance with the consent decree because the decree's two exceptions are stated in the alternative, not cumulatively. The Commission disputes Garcia's construction of the consent decree, maintaining that Cristo Vive was required to satisfy *both* exceptions to the consent decree's prohibitions and that its inability to obtain recognition under section 292.2 thus forecloses its reliance on either exception.

We need not reach the proper construction of the consent decree because we conclude that Garcia has not raised a fact issue as to each element of any cognizable defense to which it would be relevant.

Nor can Garcia raise a fact issue regarding equitable estoppel. *See City of White Settlement v. Super Wash Inc.,* 198 S.W.3d 770, 773 (Tex.2006) (noting that "equitable estoppel will not lie against the Government as against private litigants" because "legislative prerogative would be undermined if a government agent could-through mistake, neglect, or an intentional act-effectively repeal a law by ignoring, misrepresenting, or misinterpreting a duly enacted statute or regulation"). We, accordingly, conclude that the district court did not err in granting summary judgment that Garcia assisted Cristo Vive in the UPL, in violation of rule 5.04(b).

Rule 5.04(a): Fee splitting

Rule 5.04(a) provides, with exceptions not applicable here, that "a lawyer or law firm shall not share or promise to share legal fees with a non-lawyer." The rationale for this limitation is "to prevent solicitation by lay persons of clients for lawyers and to avoid encouraging or assisting nonlawyers in the practice of law."

It is undisputed that persons served by Cristo Vive pay the entity for legal services provided by or under the supervision of Garcia, that these revenues are commingled with other revenues, and that this common pool of revenues goes to pay Cristo Vive's expenses-including Garcia's approximately $50,000 annual salary and the $85,000 salary of Cristo Vive founder, Jorge Sanchez. Garcia's salary was not dependent on the amount of legal fees collected by Cristo Vive. We agree with the Commission that these undisputed facts establish a violation of rule 5.04(a). *See* Tex. Comm. on Prof'l Ethics, Op. 498, 58 Tex. B.J. 38 (1995) (holding that, when a lawyer is employed by a corporation not owned solely by licensed attorneys, "the arrangement would amount to an agreement by the lawyer to share legal fees with a non-lawyer (the corporation) in violation of Rule 5.04(a)" if the corporation were to receive payment for the lawyer's services).

Accordingly, we conclude that the district court did not err in granting summary judgment that Garcia violated rule 5.04(a) by sharing legal fees with a non-lawyer.

Rule 7.01(a): Practicing under a trade name

Rule 7.01(a) provides, in part, that "[a] lawyer in private practice shall not practice under a trade name." Rule 7.01 is broadly aimed at preventing lawyers from using the names of other lawyers or entities so as to mislead the public regarding their identity. In this regard, "Trade names are generally considered inherently misleading." *Id.*

The Commission presented undisputed summary-judgment evidence indicating that Garcia provided legal services to third parties under the name of Cristo Vive. This evidence included letters from Garcia to INS regarding, in his words, "clients" he "represent[ed]" in INS proceedings, on "Cristo Vive for Immigrants, C.S.S., Inc." letterhead indicating Cristo Vive's address, and signed "Raul Garcia, Attorney at Law." Similarly, Garcia's business cards were titled "Cristo Vive for Immigrant: Christian Social Services, Inc."; indicated the entity's address, phone number, and an email address "cristovive @ix.netcom.com"; and identified him as "Raul Garcia, Esq., Attorney at Law/Abogado." The evidence also indicated that Cristo Vive's signage at its offices, while indicating the presence of an "Attorney at Law," referred only to Cristo Vive and not Garcia.

Garcia asserts that rule 7.01(a) does not apply to him because he is not "in private practice," but is "an employee of a legal aid provider" or an in-house "corporate employee" of a non-profit. In support of this argument, Garcia points to the supreme court's attorney-occupancy-tax exemption form, which identifies an exempt category of "employee of a 501(c)(3) or 501(c)(6) non-profit corporation whose employees are prohibited from private practice," and the state bar's membership form, which distinguishes between a lawyer in "Private Law Practice" and "In-House/Corporate Counsel."

To construe rule 7.01(a), however, we seek the supreme court's intent as reflected in the text of the Disciplinary Rules of Professional Responsibility. The Commission points out that the term "private practice" as used in the rules distinguishes between governmental employment, in which a lawyer represents the public interest, and all other types of employment, in which the lawyer represents the interests of a private party. We agree with the Commission that, from context, "private practice" in rule 7.01(a) was intended to refer to lawyers representing private third-party clients. In light of our disposition of Garcia's other issues, we agree that the district court did not err in granting summary judgment that he violated rule 7.01(a) by using the trade name of Cristo Vive in his representation of private clients.

We affirm the judgment of the district court.

****

Questions:

1. What act(s) constituted the unauthorized practice of law? Why?

2. Discuss the result if Garcia had maintained a segregated account for fees paid to the attorney for legal services. If the funds maintained in the account were used by the non-profit only for the expenses connected with Garcia's legal services, would the corporation have been guilty of the unauthorized practice of law?

3. The ABA rules encourage lawyers to provide pro bono legal services to persons who could not otherwise afford representation. Why would the state bar, in Garcia, act in a way that would discourage the provision of such legal services?[100]

****

---

[100] See DC Rules of Prof'l Conduct R. 5.4 which permits "an individual nonlawyer who performs professional services which assist the organization in providing legal services to clients" to hold an ownership interest in a law firm; and District of Columbia Rule 5.4(a) permits the sharing of legal fees with such persons.

The People of the State of Colorado v. Casey
948 P.2d 1014 (Colo. 1997)

After attorney stipulated to violating rules of professional conduct by failing to inform tribunal that client facing trespassing charge was using another person's identity, hearing board and hearing panel recommended suspension of attorney for 45 days. Attorney excepted to the recommendation. The Supreme Court held that: (1) attorney was not "subordinate lawyer" who acted in accordance with supervisory lawyer's reasonable resolution of arguable question of professional duty, and (2) suspension for 45 days was appropriate sanction.

A hearing panel of the supreme court grievance committee approved the findings and the recommendation of a hearing board that the respondent in this lawyer discipline case be suspended for forty-five days from the practice of law and be ordered to take and pass the Multi-State Professional Responsibility Examination (MPRE). The respondent has excepted to the recommendation as too severe. We disagree, and we accept the recommendation of the hearing panel and hearing board.

The respondent was licensed to practice law in Colorado in 1989. The complainant and the respondent entered into an unconditional stipulation which the hearing board accepted. Based on the stipulation and evidence presented at the hearing, the board made the following findings by clear and convincing evidence.

In December 1994, S.R., a teenager, and her mother, met with the senior partner at the law firm where the respondent was an associate. In August 1994, S.R. attended a party held in the home of third parties. The police were called and they cited several persons at the party with trespassing and underage drinking. S.R. gave the police a driver's license in her possession that had been issued to her friend, S.J. A criminal summons charging trespass was issued to S.R. in the name of her friend, S.J. Since she was not aware of the summons in her name, S.J. failed to attend the first court hearing and a bench warrant was issued in her name. S.R., posing as S.J., later appeared to reset the matter. S.R. was arrested, jailed, and later released under the name of S.J.

After being assigned the case by the senior partner, the respondent wrote to the Colorado Springs City Attorney's Office, and advised the City Attorney, falsely, that he represented S.J., when he actually represented S.R. He requested and obtained discovery using S.J.'s name. He also notified the court clerk of his entry of appearance in the S.J. case. The senior partner "consulted and advised" the respondent, but the hearing board did not make findings as to when this occurred or as to the details of the conversation.

On February 14, 1995, the respondent appeared at a pretrial conference scheduled for S.J. His client, S.R., waited outside during the hearing. Although he spoke with an assistant city attorney about the case, the respondent did not reveal his client's true identity. The assistant city attorney agreed to dismiss the S.J. matter. The respondent presented the city's motion to dismiss the case and the court entered an order of dismissal on February 14, 1995.

Prior to the pretrial conference, S.J. called the respondent about the case. The respondent told her that he intended to get the trespassing charge dismissed, but that S.J. would then have to petition on her own to get the criminal record sealed. He also told S.J. the date and time of the pretrial hearing.

After the case was dismissed, the respondent met with his client and her mother, and S.J. and her stepfather. S.J. was upset that the respondent had spoken with the assistant city attorney outside of S.J.'s presence and she wanted to know if her name had been cleared. The respondent took S.J. and her stepfather outside, and explained that the trespassing charge had been dismissed and that his client would pay the court costs. The respondent admitted that S.J. would nevertheless have a criminal record and that she would have to petition the court to have her criminal record sealed. S.J.'s stepfather subsequently called his lawyer who reported the events to the district attorney.

The respondent stipulated that the foregoing conduct violated Colo. RPC 1.2(d) (counseling a client to engage, or assisting a client, in conduct that the lawyer knows is criminal or fraudulent); Colo. RPC 3.3(a)(1) (knowingly making a false statement of material fact or law to a tribunal); Colo. RPC 3.3(a)(2) (failing to disclose a material fact to a tribunal when disclosure is necessary to avoid assisting a criminal or fraudulent act by the client); Colo. RPC 8.4(c) (engaging in conduct involving dishonesty, fraud, deceit or misrepresentation); Colo. RPC 8.4(d) (engaging in conduct prejudicial to the administration of justice); and C.R.C.P. 241.6(3) (violating the highest standards of honesty, justice or morality).

The hearing panel approved the hearing board's recommendations that the respondent be suspended for forty-five days and be required to take and pass the MPRE. The respondent has excepted to the panel's action. He contends that a public censure rather than suspension is appropriate, primarily because his mental state at the time of the misconduct was at most "negligent," rather than "knowing" as found by the hearing board.

The respondent portrays his situation as involving a close question between the loyalty he owed his client, and his duty to the court. He apparently seeks to invoke the status of a "subordinate lawyer," …:

Rule 5.2. Responsibilities of a Subordinate Lawyer

(a) A lawyer is bound by the Rules of Professional Conduct notwithstanding that the lawyer acted at the direction of another person.

(b) *A subordinate lawyer does not violate the Rules of Professional Conduct if that lawyer acts in accordance with a supervisory lawyer's reasonable resolution of an arguable question of professional duty.* (Emphasis added.)

He asserts that before he succeeded in getting the trespass charge dismissed, he studied the applicable ethical rules. Colo. RPC 1.6 provides in part:

(a) A lawyer shall not reveal information relating to representation of a client unless the client consents after consultation, except for disclosures that are impliedly authorized in order to carry out the representation, and except as stated in paragraphs (b) and (c).

(b) A lawyer may reveal the intention of the lawyer's client to commit a crime and the information necessary to prevent the crime.

However, Colo. RPC 3.3, which the respondent admits to having violated, states:

Rule 3.3. Candor Toward the Tribunal

(a) A lawyer shall not knowingly:

(1) make a false statement of material fact or law to a tribunal;

(2) fail to disclose a material fact to a tribunal when disclosure is necessary to avoid assisting a criminal or fraudulent act by the client; ....

(b) *The duties stated in paragraph (a) continue to the conclusion of the proceeding, and apply even if compliance requires disclosure of information otherwise protected by Rule 1.6.* (Emphasis added).

Colo. RPC 3.3(a)(2) applies because of his initial appearance before the court in which he represented, falsely, that he was appearing on behalf of the named defendant, S.J. At the pretrial conference he presented the motion to dismiss to the court resulting in the case being dismissed. The respondent had the duty to disclose to the court that his client was impersonating S.J. in the criminal proceedings.

Further, Colo. RPC 3.3(b) clearly resolves the respondent's claimed dilemma in that it provides that the duty to be truthful to the court applies even if to do so requires disclosure of otherwise confidential information. It is not "arguable" that the respondent's duty to his client prevented him from fulfilling his duty to be truthful to the court. The protection afforded by Colo. RPC 5.2(b) for a subordinate who acts in accordance with a supervisory lawyer's direction is not available to the respondent. However, as discussed below a good-faith, but unsuccessful, attempt to bring an ethical problem to a superior's attention to receive guidance may be a mitigating factor.

We conclude that the hearing board's findings with respect to the respondent's mental state are supported by the record. The board stated:

Respondent's conduct and violations of the Rules of Professional Conduct was not done negligently, but instead reveals a course of knowing conduct over an appreciable period of time, resulting in false and material information being submitted to the court, which without any remedial action being taken by the Respondent, caused both potential injury to a party to the legal proceeding and an adverse effect on the legal proceeding.

The Terminology section of the Rules of Professional Conduct states, "'Knowingly,' 'known,' or 'knows' denotes actual knowledge of the fact in question. *A person's knowledge may be inferred from circumstances.*" (Emphasis added.) We agree with the board that the respondent engaged in "a course of knowing conduct over an appreciable period of time, resulting in false and material information being submitted to the court."

When they are approved by the hearing panel, the board's factual findings are binding on this court unless, after considering the record as a whole, the findings are unsupported by substantial evidence. When acting as a fact finder, the hearing board has the duty to assess the credibility of evidence before it, controverted and uncontroverted. In addition, by assisting his client in continuing her impersonation of S.J., the respondent's conduct resulted in at least potential harm to S.J.

Suspension is generally appropriate when a lawyer knows that false statements or documents are being submitted to the court or that material information is improperly being withheld, and takes no remedial action, and causes injury or potential injury to a party to the legal proceeding, or causes an adverse or potentially adverse effect on the legal proceeding. The hearing board found the following factors in mitigation: the absence of a prior disciplinary record; full and free disclosure to the board or a cooperative attitude in the disciplinary proceedings, inexperience in the practice of criminal law; and the expression of remorse. The respondent takes issue with the one aggravating factor that the hearing board found, that he has substantial experience in the general practice of law. We conclude that the record supports an additional factor in mitigation; the respondent tried to bring his claimed ethical dilemma to the senior partner for his advice. The record indicates that the senior partner failed to provide adequate guidance to the respondent.

While we have determined that Colo. RPC 5.2(b) does not entitle the respondent to immunity, an attempt to obtain guidance from a senior partner and a failure of a senior partner to suggest a reasonable and ethical course of conduct for the respondent could be a factor to be considered in mitigation. Here, the board's finding that the senior partner "consulted and advised" the respondent, without detail about the advice, if any, given is inadequate to allow us to conclude that the consultation is a mitigation factor. We conclude that the respondent's misconduct is serious enough to warrant a short suspension. The respondent's professed confusion regarding his professional responsibilities confirms that he should be required to take and pass the MPRE. Accordingly, we accept the board's and panel's recommendations. However, three members of the court would impose a more severe sanction.

It is hereby ordered that William M. Casey be suspended from the practice of law for forty-five days, effective thirty days after this opinion is released. The respondent is ordered to take and pass the Multi-State Professional Responsibility Examination within one year from the date of this opinion. The respondent is also ordered to pay the costs of this proceeding in the amount of $2,270.64.

****

Questions:

1. Why was the associate not permitted to rely on the advice of the senior partner to support immunity under the rules of professional conduct?

2. Suppose evidence had been introduced that showed that the senior partner advised Casey to 'proceed with the deception because it was his and the firm's duty to protect the client's interest even above their own.' If Casey had relied on the senior partner's advice, would he have been protected from discipline?

3. What if Casey had challenged the senior partner's advice because he believed the deception was unethical. In response, the senior partner told Casey that the choice was his if he wanted to continue working for the firm. Would Casey be able to successfully argue duress to avoid discipline under the rules of professional conduct?

4. What is the purpose of requiring Casey to take the Multi-State Professional Responsibility Exam? Does taking the MPRE fulfill that purpose? Why or why not?

****

In the Matter of John Clark Whatley, VI
279 Ga. 867 (Ga. 2005)

In attorney disciplinary proceedings, Investigative Panel found that attorney violated Rules of Professional Conduct and recommended disbarment. The Supreme Court held that: (1) attorney violated Rules of Professional Conduct governing attorney's responsibilities regarding nonlawyers, prohibiting lawyers to work in partnership with nonlawyer, prohibiting lawyer from assisting nonlawyers in engaging in practice of law, and requiring lawyer to keep safe client's property, and (2) disbarment was appropriate sanction for violation of Rules.

This disciplinary matter is before the Court pursuant to the Notice of Discipline filed by the State Bar alleging that John Clark Whatley VI violated Rules 1.15, 5.3, 5.4 and 5.5 of the Rules of Professional Conduct. The maximum sanction for a violation of Rules 1.15, 5.3 and 5.4 is disbarment.

According to the facts set forth in the Notice of Discipline, which was not timely rejected by the Respondent, a client hired Whatley's law firm in September 2000 to represent her in a Chapter 13 bankruptcy matter. Whatley, who had been admitted to the State Bar of Georgia in 1977, filed the Chapter 13 case in November 2000 at a time when the client owed a mortgage arrearage of more than $3,000. Although the client paid Whatley's firm $4,350 with the understanding that most of that money would go toward her mortgage arrearage, Whatley did not remit the amount the client paid for the mortgage arrearage. In January 2004, the bankruptcy court issued an order requiring the client to satisfy the arrearage and setting out a payment plan, but Whatley did not advise the client of the order. When the client defaulted on the payment plan, the mortgage company notified Whatley's client directly that it had obtained an order lifting the bankruptcy stay. The client then filed a grievance against Whatley and hired another attorney to file an emergency motion to re-impose the stay. After the client explained her situation to the bankruptcy court, it held a show cause hearing for Whatley to appear and account for the funds he had collected on the client's behalf. In the order entered after the show cause hearing, the bankruptcy court found that Whatley could not account for $1,600 of the funds and ordered him to refund that amount to the client and to pay attorney fees. The bankruptcy court also found, not only that Whatley had violated Bar Rule 1.15, but that reason existed to believe he had violated other Bar Rules as well.

Although Whatley acknowledged service of the State Bar's Notice of Investigation, he failed to respond within 30 days as required by Bar Rule 4-204.3(a) and therefore he was suspended pursuant to Bar Rule 4-204.3(d). Then, in April of 2005, Whatley submitted a letter in response to the Notice of Investigation, in which he contended that he had established the law firm of John C. Whatley & Associates P.C. in December 1997, together with and at the urging of a law school graduate who never passed the Bar exam, but who had worked for several law firms doing bankruptcy paperwork. According to Whatley this other man was responsible for setting up the firm, taking client calls, interviewing clients, opening and maintaining the bank accounts, controlling incoming mail, maintaining client files, and conducting the business of the firm. Under the agreement Whatley was only required to complete the bankruptcy filings and appear in court as needed. Initially, the man paid Whatley, who maintained a full time job elsewhere, a flat fee of $100 per bankruptcy case filed through the firm but later the two worked out a deal where he paid Whatley a flat fee of $1,500 per month. The law firm operated in this manner until 2004 when the man allegedly began telling Whatley that the firm was suffering from a lack of business. In May 2004, after leaving Whatley a voice mail message telling Whatley that he had decided to close the law firm, the man allegedly converted the firm's operating and other bank accounts for his own benefit. Whatley asserts that the man stole not only the client's funds, but also funds paid to the law firm for submission to the bankruptcy court in eight other matters. Whatley asserts that he has filed a lawsuit against the man and asserts that the blame for the client's grievance should rest on that man, rather than himself.

Based on the above, the Investigative Panel issued a Notice of Discipline charging Whatley with violations of Rules 1.15, 5.3, 5.4 and 5.5 of Bar Rule 4-102(d) in his handling of the client's matter. The Investigative Panel concluded that although Whatley has been subject to no prior disciplinary proceedings, disbarment would be the appropriate disciplinary sanction for him. The Panel noted in aggravation that, based on the allegations contained in his untimely response to the Notice of Investigation, Whatley appears to have engaged in a pattern of misconduct; that he has displayed a cavalier and arrogant attitude towards these proceedings; and that he does not appear to understand his obligations under the Bar Rules. Whatley acknowledged service of the Notice of Discipline but failed to timely file a Notice of Rejection. He therefore is in default; has no right to an evidentiary hearing; and is subject to such discipline and further proceedings as may be determined by this Court, see Bar Rule 4-208.1(b).

Under these circumstances, we agree with the findings of the Investigative Panel and find that disbarment is the appropriate discipline for Whatley's violations of Rules 1.15, 5.3, 5.4 and 5.5 of Bar Rule 4-102(d).

****

Questions:

1. Lawyer enters an agreement with Lawyer from a different law firm located in the United Kingdom. If the professional rules of conduct in the United Kingdom permit a lawyer to share legal fees with a non-lawyer, which the UK firm does. Would the American lawyer be in violation of the model rules prohibition against such fee sharing?[101]

2. During the Law firm's annual meeting with its non-lawyer staff, the senior partner states "We will pay you a bonus of $10,000 if the firm's revenue (or profit) for the year is at or above $1,000,000." Is such a promise in violation of the model rules of professional conduct?[102]

3. What if, in lieu of making the announcement, at the end of the year, the law firm considers its revenue, expenses and proft in determining whether to pay bonuses and, if so, how much. Would lawyer be in violation of the model rules of professional conduct?[103]

4. Local law firm contracts with temporary agency for assistance with document review, bate stamping and other legal services. Temporary agency hires law school graduates, some of whom are not licensed to practice law. The agency is hired by non-lawyers who collect the fees from the law firm and use such fees to pay its staff of non-lawyer professionals. Is law firm in violation of the model rules of professional conduct?

****

Mays v. Neal

327 Ark. 302 (Ark. 1997)

...Richard L. Mays brings this appeal from the appellee Supreme Court Professional Conduct Committee's reprimand sanction, having found Mays violated Rules 1.4(b) and 5.5(b) of the Model Rules of Professional Conduct. Rule 1.4(b) directs that a lawyer shall explain a matter to the extent reasonably necessary to permit the client to make informed decisions regarding the representation. Rule 5.5(b) prohibits a lawyer from assisting a person who is not a member of the bar in the performance of activity that constitutes the unauthorized practice of law.

---

[101] See James Podgers, ABA ethics opinion sparks renewed debate over nonlawyer ownership of law firms, ABA Journal, December 2013 Issue

[102] Texas Center for Legal Ethics, opinion 642, available at http://legalethicstexas.com/Ethics-Resources/Opinions/Opinion-642.aspx, last visited 7.5.14

[103] Id. Also see State Bar of Arizona Ethics Opinions, Opinion 98-08 available at http://www.azbar.org/Ethics/EthicsOpinions/ViewEthicsOpinion?id=493 holding that An attorney ethically may contract with a paralegal to have the paralegal assist with conducting initial interviews of and signing of documents by estate planning clients, as long as: 1) the attorney supervises and controls the paralegal's activities to assure that the paralegal does not engage in the unauthorized practice of law; 2) there is no fee sharing; 3) the initial interviews are only with existing clients; and 4) there is no solicitation of new business by the paralegal. [ER 1.6, 5.3, 5.4, 5.5, 7.3], last visited 7.5.14.

This dispute arose after Mays's law firm, Mays & Crutcher, P.A., undertook to represent Vanessa Conley, who on July 18, 1994, was involved in a motor vehicle accident in Little Rock. The other vehicle involved in the accident was a rental car, which was insured by Empire Insurance Company. At the scene of the accident, a man, later known to be Tim Mason, approached Conley, asking her who caused the accident. Conley said that Mason identified himself as an investigator, and suggested Conley needed legal representation. This interchange resulted in Conley signing a contract employing Mays as her attorney. Mason gave Conley a business card bearing the name of Catherine Stevens and instructed Conley that Stevens was the person Conley should call. Stevens later sent a copy of Conley's contract to Empire, along with her business card. The business card reflected the Mays & Crutcher Law Offices and showed Catherine Stevens as "Senior Claims Manager."

Conley said that, on July 19, 1994, Stevens called Conley's home and spoke with her husband, and Conley says she returned the call on July 20, 1994. Conley claims that, during her conversation with Stevens, Stevens referred her to the Price Chiropractic Clinic. Conley was subsequently treated by the Price Clinic from about July 25, 1994, to October 21, 1994. In November 1994, negotiations to settle Conley's claim took place between Stevens and Chuck Traylor, who was the claims adjuster with Empire Insurance Co. Some confusion and differences occurred between Stevens and Conley over the method and amount of payment Conley would approve before reaching any settlement. Conley also expressed that, although she had been released by the Price Clinic, she was still having pain and needed to see another doctor. Conley became dissatisfied with the manner in which her case was being handled, and on November 30, 1994, she went to Mays's office to retrieve her file. While Stevens retained possession of Conley's file because Mays was not present, it is clear the Mays–Conley relationship had been severed by December 6, 1994—the date Stevens had notified Empire Insurance by letter (with a copy to Conley) that Mays no longer represented Conley. The letter also reflected that Conley had rejected Empire's $9,000.00 offer to settle, but Mays had retained an attorney's lien on any proceeds to be paid Conley in the future. Conley later claimed she had been unaware of any $9,000.00 offer until she received a copy of the December 6 letter.

Stevens testified that she never called Conley on July 19, and that she never gave Conley only the Price Clinic's name, since it was Mays's practice to suggest several physicians' names and allow the client to choose.

Conley subsequently pursued her claim without the assistance of an attorney, and sought information from Empire Insurance by writing that Company on March 26, 1995. Empire's adjuster, Traylor, responded, indicating that he had not received the December 6 letter written by Mays, that he had already settled Conley's claim by having spoken with "Jim," who was with Mays's firm, and that Conley would have to obtain a letter reflecting Mays no longer represented her. In May of 1995, Conley forwarded to Traylor a copy of Mays's earlier December 6 letter, and informed Traylor that she had since contacted the Supreme Court Professional Conduct Committee and complained about Mays's representation. She further asked Traylor for a copy of the $9,000.00 check dated November 30, 1994, which purportedly had been sent to Mays in settlement of her claim. Upon receipt of Conley's May 1995 letter, Traylor sent Conley another letter, wherein he forwarded her a copy of the $9,000.00 check. The check had never been cashed. In August of 1995, Conley filed her formal complaint against Mays with the Professional

Conduct Committee, alleging eight violations of the Model Rules of Professional Conduct, two of which the Committee eventually found meritorious. Besides complaining to the Committee about her initial confusion concerning the manner in which Mays established his contractual relationship with Conley, she also complained he failed to communicate and keep her informed concerning the law firm's negotiations with Empire Insurance Company in her behalf.

Mays first controverts Conley's complaints by raising several procedural points. None has merit. Mays initially argues this court's Committee on the Unauthorized Practice of Law (CUPL) has prerequisite jurisdiction of this matter because its Rule III provides in part that " *all* inquiries and complaints relating to the unauthorized practice of law *shall* be directed to the Committee on the Unauthorized Practice of Law." He further argues that, because Rule 5.5(b) of the Model Rules of Professional Conduct prohibits a lawyer from assisting a person who is not a member of the bar in performing the unauthorized practice of law, Conley was required first to get CUPL to determine what is or is not " the unauthorized practice of law." We disagree. Nothing in either committee's rules reflect that CUPL's rules in any way preempted the Model Rules of Professional Conduct. As is obvious from reading them, the Model Rules deal only with the activities of licensed lawyers, whereas CUPL's rules are intended to prevent non-lawyers from practicing law.

We first address the Committee's decision that Mays violated Rule 1.4(b) by failing to communicate properly with his client, Conley. Rule 1.4(b) provides, "[A] lawyer shall explain a matter to the extent reasonably necessary to permit the client to make informed decisions regarding the representation." Adequacy of communication depends in part on the kind of advice or assistance involved. *See* Comment to Rule 1.4(b). The Comment further offers the example that, in negotiations where there is time to explain a proposal, the lawyer should review all important provisions with the client before proceeding to an agreement.

In the present case, such a review did not happen. In fact, from the beginning, there is proof that Mays's law firm failed to explain its contract with Conley or make clear early in the employment relationship the objectives of that legal representation. While Mays testified that he initially tries to make contact with his clients, he conceded that he never met with Conley or spoke to her by telephone. Mays further conceded that Conley's only contact with his firm was through his staff, and Stevens admitted that she had worked on Conley's case before Mays knew Conley was a client. In addition, Conley averred that her only contact with the firm was through Stevens even though, on several occasions, Conley had asked for an appointment with Mays. Each time Conley was told she should communicate with Stevens. In sum, although Mays and Stevens both related that Mays had instructed Stevens how Conley's case should be settled, the evidence is undisputed that Conley was afforded no opportunity to communicate directly with Mays and to ask him questions about her case. Obviously, the record supports the view that Mays had relied entirely upon his non-lawyer staff member to communicate with Conley even though Conley had posed questions concerning her legal representation, and was denied the opportunity to resolve those questions by meeting with him.

We next address Mays's argument that the evidence is insufficient to support the Committee's finding that he violated Rule 5.5(b) by assisting a person who is not a member of the bar to perform the unauthorized practice of the law. Again, it is helpful to our discussion to allude to the applicable comment to this model rule which in relevant part provides:

> Paragraph (b) [of Rule 5.5] does not prohibit a lawyer from employing the services of paraprofessionals and delegating functions to them, so long as the lawyer supervises the delegated work and retains responsibility for their work. Rule 5.3(b) further provides that a lawyer having direct supervisory authority over the non-lawyer shall make reasonable efforts to ensure that the person's conduct is compatible with the professional obligations of the lawyer. In this respect, a lawyer should give such assistants instruction and supervision concerning the ethical aspects of their employment.

The significance and meaning of Rules 5.3(b) and 5.5(b) is explained within the practice of law and why those matters are limited to performance by licensed lawyers:

> This [prohibition] is not only to ensure professional competence, but is in the public interest, to ensure that the public be not led to rely upon the counseling, in matters of law, by those who are not answerable to the courts in this state for the manner in which they meet their professional obligations by compliance with standards of professional conduct imposed upon those engaging in the practice of law.

While a lawyer may delegate certain tasks to his assistants, he or she, as supervising attorney, has the ultimate responsibility for compliance by the non-lawyer with the applicable provisions of the Model Rules. In reviewing the record, we conclude Mays failed in this respect both in his firm's initial contracting with Conley and when negotiating her claim.

We again review in more detail the events leading to the signing of Conley as a client. In fact, Conley's testimony reflects she was confused and dissatisfied with her legal representation beginning when she signed Mays's contract at the scene of her accident on July 18, 1994. She said that she did not know who Mason was or what she had signed. She thought the paper she signed was for Mason to investigate the accident and to authorize him to get information. Mays testified that he did not employ, nor did he know Tim Mason, even though Mason possessed Stevens's business card and the law firm's employment contract which Conley signed. Ray Keech, an investigator and process server hired by the Committee, testified that in his attempts to locate Mason he was given a phone number, which turned out to be that for Mays & Crutcher. When Keech called the number, the person answering indicated that Mason only came into the office about once a month.

Mays testified he later learned from his paraprofessional, Jimmy Morris, that Morris had given Mason a blank contract intended for another potential client, Bobby Jett, who lived in Pine Bluff. Morris had asked Mason to take the contract to Jett, who was interested in retaining the firm. Mason apparently gave that contract to Conley. Mays testified that he would have had grave concerns if he had known how his contract had been entered into with Conley. Even so, it is clear Mays would not have learned of the contract by signing it, because Mays's agreement did not require his signature and had no place for him or any other attorney to sign. Also, he could not have been apprised of the circumstances surrounding the procurement of the contract because, as Mays conceded, he never met with Conley. Instead, it was Stevens who first contacted Conley by letter dated July 19, 1994, confirming the law firm had commenced work in Conley's behalf. That correspondence bears Mays's stamped signature. From this and other evidence, we believe the Committee could reasonably conclude that Mays had failed to supervise his non-lawyer staff personnel in meeting his fundamental obligations owed any new client, namely, to explain the parties' responsibilities under the contract, and to permit the client to ask questions and to make informed decisions regarding the representation.

Jett testified that he had spoken with Morris about Mays's law firm because Jett was dissatisfied with his lawyer. He said he expected to receive a contract from Morris, but never received one.

We also note that there was substantial evidence that Mays had provided inadequate supervision over the manner in which his assistants negotiated Conley's claim. Mays testified that he monitored Conley's personal injury claim and evaluated it after receiving medical reports, bills, and wage-loss statements. He stated that he met with Stevens and Morris, and established a high and low range within which to settle. Mays said that Jimmy Morris had most of the contacts with Empire Insurance, and Stevens mostly dealt with Conley. Because Conley's injury was a "soft-tissue" injury and she had incurred medical expenses of $2,700.00 to $2,800.00, Mays said he set a settlement range between $6,500.00 and $10,500.00.

Contrary to Stevens's version, Conley testified that she had never told Stevens how much she wished to net and never authorized a settlement in any amount. Nonetheless, Mays stated that he had authorized settlement for $9,000.00 because he could make some money and satisfy Conley as well. Without obtaining Conley's approval, Morris called Traylor at Empire Insurance, and the Company sent Mays a check for $9,000.00. While Conley had advised Stevens she would not settle for the Company's offer, Conley was unaware the Company had sent a $9,000.00 check until months after she had terminated Mays's firm.

As confusion had resulted from Conley's signing of Mays's employment contract, confusion also arose during settlement negotiations of Conley's claim. It is obvious from the testimony that this confusion led to Mays extending a final offer to Empire Insurance without the offer having ever first been approved by Conley. A lawyer often delegates tasks to clerks, secretaries, and other lay persons. Such delegation is proper *if the lawyer maintains a direct relationship with his or her client,* supervises the delegated work, and has complete responsibility for the work product.

Mays's office procedures fostered confusion by permitting Stevens and Morris to act outside his close supervision. For example, these two paraprofessionals, when dealing with third parties, were authorized by Mays to refer to firm clients as their clients. In addition to being given broad authorization to use Mays's signature stamp and thereby act in Mays's stead, Mays also allowed Stevens to send correspondence to Empire Insurance referring to Conley as Stevens's client. Conley averred that she never understood how Stevens, rather than Mays, could advise her concerning the "equities" of her claim or had the authority to correspond with the insurance company. Also adding to Conley's confusion was that, while Conley knew of Stevens, she was wholly unaware of the role Morris played in the negotiations with Empire Insurance, and only learned of Morris's existence after the insurance company later told her it had settled Conley's claim with "Jim." Unlike with Stevens, Morris's name was never disclosed as an assistant on the law firm stationery.

In sum, we must conclude, as did the Committee, that Mays failed to properly delegate his legal work and responsibilities and failed to properly supervise work delegated to his assistants. If he had, he would have been in the position at the least to have tried to resolve the questions that continued to resurface during his legal representation of Conley. For these reasons, we affirm the Committee's decisions.

****

Questions:

1. New lawyer is on his way from court when he is approached by a man who tells him that he works for a local law firm that is looking for young aggressive lawyers to handle personal injury cases. He hands lawyer a card with the name of a law firm on it and a phone number. Lawyer, anxious to earn enough money to pay off his student loans and live well, calls the number. A man answers the call, who lawyer determines is the same non-lawyer who he met outside the courtroom. They talk and lawyer agrees to handle cases that the firm refers to him. Within days, five new personal injury files are delivered to lawyer. Lawyer dutifully meets with the clients, settles their cases and pays the doctors on the case. Lawyer never enters into a written representation agreement with the clients. This practice continues for about a year before lawyer is arrested for barratry and subject to discipline under the state bar rules. Is lawyer likely guilty of barratry? Subject to discipline? In each instance, Why? Why not?[104]

2. Barratry is commonly defined as the intent to gain employment by soliciting clients either in person, via telephone, or through written communication. Consider the difference between barratry and bar approved advertisement.[105]

****

---

[104] See e.g. State Bar of Texas, Solicitation and Barratry—Frequently Asked Questions, available at http://www.texasbar.com/Content/NavigationMenu/ForLawyers/GrievanceInfoandEthicsHelpline/BarratryFAQ.htm last visited 7.5.14 responding to question: *Under the Texas Disciplinary Rules of Professional Conduct, can I be disciplined if I pay someone not licensed to practice law to solicit clients for me or to refer clients to me? Response: With certain very limited exceptions, the answer is yes. See Rule 7.03(b). Also, see Rule 7.03(c) which prohibits payments to clients or anyone else in order to solicit employment. Additionally, accepting referrals from certain Lawyer Referral Services is also prohibited. See 7.03(e).*

[105] See Bob Bennett & Associates, Why Should Barratry be a Crime: Barratry Ethics and Keeping your Texas Law License, Harris County Democratic Lawyers' Association, June 9th 2013 CLE Event, available at http://www.google.com/url?sa=t&rct=j&q=&esrc=s&source=web&cd=7&ved=0CFMQFjAG&url=http%3A%2F%2Fmedia.avvosites.com%2Fupload%2F102%2F2013%2F04%2FWhy-Should-Barratry-be-a-Crime.pdf&ei=xCe4U76mIo-LqgaB-4CYBQ&usg=AFQjCNGmJ1mc4em9d79j5ROcPTe4XnMx4g&sig2=uJbtaYJONI3sd5NzENbQ-g&bvm=bv.70138588,d.b2k

REVIEW QUESTIONS

1.   You represent Plaintiff in her suit against Defendant. Defendant is represented by your arch nemesis since law school. The case is ripe for settlement but Nemesis pushes his client not to settle. However, Defendant, an honorable man, pushes back and insists Nemesis work with you to secure a fair and just settlement. Reluctantly, Nemesis agrees and accepts the terms of your proposed settlement adding one provision which Nemesis claims is non-negotiable. The provision requires you to agree that you will not represent any other Plaintiff in any matter against Defendant. As Plaintiff's attorney, you want what's best for your client and you do not envision an occasion that you would represent any other Plaintiff against this Defendant. Under these circumstances, is such an agreement permissible under the model rules?

2.   Lawyer discovers that her law firm is overbilling its clients. She reports her finding to another partner at the firm who reports her claim to the partners at their subsequent partners' meeting which was scheduled during a time that Lawyer could not be present. The partners attending the meeting voted unanimously to terminate Lawyer's employment with the law firm, effective immediately. Does Lawyer have a viable civil action against the law firm? Is the law firm and or any of its lawyers subject to discipline? See Bohatch v. Butler Binion 977 S.W.2d 543 (Tex. 1998)

3. Do the model rules of professional conduct permit lawyers to include their employees in a profit-sharing arrangement?

4.   Supervising Lawyer works well with supervised Associate who recently married his law school sweetheart. In fact, the two work so well together, that Supervisor saw no need for written office management policies or procedures. Associate rarely discussed office business with his spouse but one particular case bothered him and one night after the couple had celebrated their 721st day of marriage, Associate confided in spouse that the firm's client was hiding funds from his wife in anticipation of divorce proceedings. Associate did not know that his bride was Client's wife's lover and that the two of them planned to get divorces from their husbands, "hit the lottery with their divorce settlements" and then move to Delaware where they would wed. Client's wife informs Client that she knows that he has been hiding assets and she demands he produce them all by noon the next day "or else". Client was shocked that wife knew about the hidden assets and confronts Supervising Lawyer, telling her that he had told no one about what he was doing and demanding to know how wife discovered it. Associate admitted to Supervisor that he had told his bride but assured Supervisor that she would not have told anyone else. Is either or both Lawyers subject to discipline?

5.   Are profit-sharing employees permitted to participate in the management and control of the law practice?

6.   Lawyer is not admitted to practice law in the jurisdiction in which her mother resides. Mother is sued by a person claiming personal injury as the result of a car collision in that jurisdiction. Lawyer contacts the plaintiff's lawyer in an attempt to resolve the matter. Is Lawyer engaged in the unauthorized practice of law?

7.   Same facts as in number 6 except Lawyer does not 'appear' for mom, but instead advises mom, a person not licensed to practice law, what to do to handle the case. In fact Lawyer is silently on every telephone conversation that mom has with the plaintiff's lawyer. Is Lawyer assisting mom in the unauthorized practice of law?

8.   Corporation hires Lawyer as its general counsel. Lawyer is licensed in the states of Pennsylvania, New York and California. Lawyer is not licensed in the state of Texas, where the corporation assigns Lawyer and from where Lawyer advises Client. Does Lawyer's duties in Texas constitute an unauthorized practice of law?

9.   Attorney uses "the cloud" to maintain client files, providing access as he believes prudent. Attorney outsources to another company, the maintenance, retention and destruction of client files in accordance with the Attorneys File Maintenance and Retention Policies and Procedures. What measures, if any, should Attorney take to ensure that Clients' confidences are not in jeopardy.

10. Lawyer purchases the law practice from his Mentor. Their agreement is that Lawyer will make a cash down payment and pay the balance over five years. Lawyer pays diligently until Mentor dies in a plan crash. Mentor's heirs demand that Lawyer pay the remaining sums due on the debt to them. However, none of the heirs is an attorney and Lawyer's payments are all generated from earned attorney fees. Since Lawyer is prohibited from splitting attorney fees with non-lawyers, what if any, rights do the heirs have to the loan balance?

11. Lawyer just won a large verdict against defendant who has decided not to appeal and to pay the money. Lawyer could not have won the case but for the dedicated work of his two paralegals and secretary who worked night and day on the case. Desiring to show his appreciation, Lawyer, pays each of the employees a bonus as soon as the defendant's check cleared the bank. Has Lawyer violated the model rules of professional conduct?

12. Lawyer hires Law Graduate to manage the law office. Law graduate does a great job, brings in lots of business and handles all administrative duties. However, Graduate has never taken a bar examination. At the end of the year, Lawyer evaluates Graduate's performance and raises his salary and pays him a year-end bonus. Is Lawyer subject to discipline under the model rules of professional conduct?

13. Supervising Lawyer works well with supervised Associate who recently married his law school sweetheart. In fact, the two work so well together, that Supervisor saw no need for written office management policies or procedures. Associate rarely discussed office business with his spouse but one particular case bothered him and one night after the couple had celebrated their 721st day of marriage, Associate confided in spouse that the firm's client was hiding funds from his wife in anticipation of divorce proceedings. Associate did not know that his bride was Client's wife's lover and that the two of them planned to get divorces from their husbands, "hit the lottery with their divorce settlements" and then move to Delaware where they would wed. Client's wife informs Client that she knows that he has been hiding assets and she demands he produce them all by noon the next day "or else". Client was shocked that wife knew about the hidden assets and confronts Supervising Lawyer, telling her that he had told no one about what he was doing and demanding to know how wife discovered it. Associate admitted to Supervisor that he had told his bride but assured Supervisor that she would not have told anyone else. Is either or both Lawyers subject to discipline?

14. Supervising Attorney advises associate to file a motion for the purpose of delaying the proceedings. Associate believes the filing would violate the model rules and fails to file the motion. Supervisor is incensed, fires associate and informs Client that the motion was not filed. As a result of the failure, Client is damaged. Supervisor compensates Client but seeks

indemnification from Associate, who then files a claim against Supervisor with the state bar. What result and why?

15. Lawyer informed Secretary about the importance of confidentiality and advised her that her employment with the firm could be terminated if Secretary failed to adhere strictly to the rules. Lawyer knows that Secretary is a gossip and Lawyer is concerned that Secretary might improvidently release confidential information. What is Lawyer required to do to ensure clients' confidentiality? What should lawyer do to comply with the model rules?

16. Before Lawyer became a licensed attorney, she was a real estate broker. After becoming an attorney, Lawyer establishes a small business that offers legal representation, land title examinations, and contract negotiations and drafting. Lawyer has kept on four real estate agents to help in the business. Can Attorney maintain both a law practice and a real estate brokerage firm as a single business without violating the Model Rules of Professional Conduct?

17. Joseph has started a personal injury law firm in XYZ jurisdiction. He has decided to hire associates at entry-level positions, but wants to limit turnover. In furtherance of that goal, Joseph drafts an employment contract that provides: "1) any Attorney who leaves the firm within 3 years may only retain 50 percent of any vested retirement benefits, and 2) an attorney who leaves after 3 years may retain 80 percent of their vested retirement benefits, but cannot practice personal injury law in XYZ for at least 5 years after the date of separation. Do either of these terms of employment violate the rules of professional conduct?

****

PUBLIC SERVICE

Lawyers are expected provide legal services to those who would otherwise not have access to justice. According to the American Bar Association, the practice of law is a privilege that carries with it the obligation to make justice equally accessible to all.[106] Many states recognize the necessity of no or low cost legal services to the poor and to charitable organizations. [107] Pro Bono legal service is aspirational and not mandatory under the rules of ethics.

The State Bar of Texas v. Gomez
891 S.W.2d 243, 38 Tex. Sup. Ct. J. 140 *(1994)*

The sole question presented for our determination is whether the district court below has jurisdiction of this suit, which complains of the failure of the State Bar of Texas to compel member lawyers to provide free legal services to Texans who cannot pay for those services. We

---

[106] American Bar Association Standing Committee on Pro Bono and Public Service, available at http://www.americanbar.org/groups/legal_education/resources/pro_bono.html
[107] See e.g. TEX. DISCIPLINARY R. PROF'L CONDUCT, Preamble, *reprinted in* TEX. GOV'T CODE ANN., tit. 2, subtit. G app. A (Vernon 2005). Also See American Bar Association, State-By-State Pro Bono Service Rules, available at http://www.americanbar.org/groups/probono_public_service/policy/state_ethics_rules.html (last updated 01/30/2012)

conclude that the district court correctly dismissed the case for lack of jurisdiction. Thus, we reverse the judgment of the court of appeals and remand this case to the district court with instructions to dismiss.

After being refused free legal services, Maria Gomez, Alicia Naveja, and Leonardo Chaves, on behalf of themselves and others similarly situated (collectively, Gomez), filed suit in a Travis County district court against the State Bar of Texas and two of its officials at that time, James Parsons III, President, and Karen Johnson, Executive Director (collectively, State Bar). Gomez contends that the State Bar, by not effectively encouraging attorneys to volunteer free legal services, has illegally failed to meet the legal needs of indigent Texans.

Specifically, Gomez alleges violations of the following provisions of the Texas Constitution: (1) Article I, Section 13 (open courts); (2) Article I, Section 3 (equal protection); (3) Article I, Section 3a (equal rights); (4) Article I, Section 19 (due course of law); and (5) Article I, Section 29 (inviolate nature of the Bill of Rights). Gomez further asserts violations of the Texas antidiscrimination statute, the Texas Disciplinary Rules of Professional Conduct, and the Texas Lawyer's Creed.

The district court dismissed the case, concluding it lacked jurisdiction under Article V, Section 8, of the Texas Constitution. The court of appeals reversed, holding that the district court had jurisdiction to decide the merits of Gomez's claims, but because of this Court's exclusive authority to regulate the legal profession in Texas, it held that the district court could levy only a prohibitory, and not a mandatory injunction against the State Bar. 856 S.W.2d 804 (Tex.1993).

The court of appeals explained:

We conclude that a district court does not have authority to grant relief that would unreasonably usurp the supervisory control vested exclusively in the supreme court. By vesting the supreme court with supervisory control of the practice of law, the constitution and the State Bar Act grant the supreme court *discretion* to decide issues concerning the State Bar and the practice of law. Whether a district court has authority to grant a particular form of injunctive relief depends, we believe, on whether granting such relief would effectively exercise the kind of supervisory discretion that is vested exclusively in the supreme court. 856 S.W.2d at 815. We agree with the court of appeals' identification of the issue but not its conclusion. ...

The unique aspect of this jurisdictional inquiry, as the court of appeals recognized, arises out of this Court's power to regulate the practice of law in the State of Texas. This power is derived from both statutory and inherent powers. The primary statutory grant of power is found in the State Bar Act, which gives the Court administrative control over the State Bar and provides a statutory mechanism for promulgating regulations governing the practice of law. *See* Tex.Gov't Code § 81.011(c). The other source of this court's power to regulate the practice of law in this state, its inherent power, is not secured by any legislative grant or specific constitutional provision, but is necessarily implied to enable the Court to discharge its constitutionally imposed duties. *See Eichelberger v. Eichelberger,* 582 S.W.2d 395, 398–99 (Tex.1979) (noting that doctrine of inherent power is derived, in part, from the separation of powers dictated by Article II, Section 1 of the Texas Constitution). Those duties include our obligation, as the head of the judicial department, to regulate judicial affairs. Because the admission and practice of Texas attorneys is inextricably intertwined with the administration of justice, the Court must have the power to regulate these activities in order to fulfill its constitutional role. *See generally* Jim R. Carrigan, Inherent Powers of the Courts 2 (1973) (defining inherent powers as those "reasonably required to enable a court to perform efficiently its judicial functions, to protect its dignity, independence and integrity, and to make its lawful actions effective"). The Court's inherent powers, such as the power to regulate the practice of law, are not *jurisdictional* powers. *See Eichelberger,* 582 S.W.2d at 399. These powers are *administrative* powers, necessary to the preservation of the judiciary's independence and integrity.

Because the Court's power to regulate the practice of law is an administrative one, the exercise of that power does not in and of itself deprive lower courts of general subject matter jurisdiction over challenges to that governance. …

Gomez seeks to compel either the State Bar or this Court to implement a mandatory pro bono program for Texas lawyers. To the extent a remedy is sought against the State Bar, Gomez seeks relief from an entity that is powerless, acting alone, to implement that remedy. The State Bar's authority is limited to proposing regulations to this Court, which may accept or reject any recommendation, in whole or in part. *See* Tex.Gov't Code § 81.024(a). …

Moreover, to the extent the remedies are sought against the Supreme Court, they would clearly impinge on the Court's exclusive authority to regulate the practice of law. The Legislature itself implicitly acknowledged the Court's fundamental authority in this area when it enacted the State Bar Act as *an aid* to the Court in carrying out this function. *See* Tex.Gov't Code § 81.011(b). No subordinate court in Texas has the power to usurp our authority or responsibility in this area. …

This is not to say that all remedies bearing upon the regulation of the legal profession would be unacceptable infringements on the inherent powers of the Court. Had this Court actually promulgated rules establishing a pro bono program and had Gomez challenged the constitutionality of such rules, the district court would have jurisdiction to decide, in the first instance, whether such rules met constitutional standards. *See O'Quinn v. State Bar,* 763 S.W.2d 397 (Tex.1988) (upholding the trial court's decision on a constitutional challenge to the rules of disciplinary conduct promulgated by the Court). In due course, we would review any adverse determination in our adjudicative capacity. *See Cameron v. Greenhill,* 582 S.W.2d 775, 777 & n. 3 (Tex.1979) (holding that the Court could both promulgate a rule and determine its constitutionality). The important distinction between such a case and the one at hand is that in the former case, the district court would not be cast in the impermissible role of effectively promulgating policies and regulations governing Texas lawyers. Such a case would be justiciable because the district court would be capable of rendering a judgment that accords the parties complete relief, subject of course to appellate review.

But when, as here, the essence of a complaint is that this Court has failed to establish rules governing some aspect of lawyer conduct, a district court has no authority to assume this Court's authority to regulate the legal profession. …

Our decision that the district court lacks jurisdiction does not, however, leave the parties without a forum in which to seek redress of their grievances. This Court, in the exercise of its constitutional responsibilities, wants and needs input from interested persons concerning its supervisory responsibility over Texas lawyers. Ordinarily, interested parties would be free to informally petition this Court in its administrative capacity, to urge reconsideration of the proper constitutional mandates for this Court's regulation of attorney conduct. However, given the potentially far-reaching effects of this particular challenge to our scheme of regulation, we direct that this matter be placed on the Court's administrative agenda for further consideration. …

Accordingly, we reverse the judgment of the court of appeals and remand to the district court with instructions to dismiss for want of jurisdiction.

Brown v. Commission for Lawyer Discipline
980 S.W.2d 675 *(C.App.-San Antonio, 1998)*

Charles A. Brown appeals a judgment finding that he violated two rules of professional conduct, suspending him from the practice of law, and ordering him to pay attorney fees to the Commission for Lawyer Discipline. In five points of error, he argues that the evidence is factually and legally insufficient to sustain the findings that he violated the rules, that the rules are unconstitutionally vague, that the court held him responsible for violating a repealed rule, that the Commission is not entitled to the attorney fee award because it was represented by attorneys acting *pro bono,* and that the amount of attorney fees awarded was erroneous. We conclude that Brown's arguments are not well taken. Accordingly, we affirm the judgment, but reform it to delete the reference to the repealed rule.

Factual and Procedural Background

In November 1991, Brown agreed to represent Sucellen Humphrey (also known as Sucellen or Nicole Hayes) in a suit to recover damages arising from an automobile accident. Their written contract indicates that Brown would pursue a cause of action against the driver of the other vehicle and his insurer, State Farm. Brown testified that they also contemplated a product liability claim against General Motors, the manufacturer of Humphrey's car. During the course of the representation, Brown issued letters of protection to Humphrey's medical providers. The letters stated in relevant part:

Please forward all billings and medical reports directly to me, as I will pursue the recovery of all medical, hospital, etc. costs directly from State Farm Insurance Co., and assure that you are paid the amounts billed pursuant to this letter of protection.

Through these letters, Brown protected approximately $16,000 of Humphrey's medical expenses. He testified that he believed the letters obligated him to pay the medical providers. In September of 1992, State Farm settled the case with Humphrey for $50,000. State Farm deducted $3000 from this amount for insurance payments already made. Of the remaining $47,000, Brown gave himself $16,667 (representing his 1/3 contingency fee), gave Humphrey $6333, and deposited the remaining amount in a joint investment checking account in his and Humphrey's names.

Between December 1, 1992, and January 8, 1993, Brown wrote eight checks on the joint account. The first one, for $4500, was co-signed by Humphrey. This money was a loan from Humphrey to Brown so that Brown could buy office equipment. The money was eventually paid back with interest. The other seven checks were signed only by Brown. According to Brown, some of the money was used on behalf of Humphrey for items such as rental car expenses. But some of it was also used for Brown's personal or office expenses. Although he did not get Humphrey's permission before writing each check, he claimed that he and Humphrey had an informal agreement that he could take "advances" from the account and repay the money directly to the account or to the medical providers. Brown's testimony indicates that they agreed to put the money in the joint account, rather than paying the medical providers, so the money could be used to pursue litigation against General Motors.

In April of 1993, Humphrey filed a grievance against Brown, claiming he had taken money from the joint account without her consent and without repaying it. At that time, no more than $2500 of the $16,000 in medical bills had been paid and no money from the joint account had been expended toward the General Motors litigation. After the disciplinary petition was filed, Brown and Humphrey reached a settlement whereby Humphrey released Brown, and Brown paid Humphrey $3000 and assumed responsibility for paying certain medical providers to whom he had issued letters of protection. Humphrey did not testify at the disciplinary proceeding.

After a nonjury trial, the trial court determined that Brown violated Rules 1.14(c) and 8.04(a)(3) of the Texas Disciplinary Rules of Professional Conduct. Brown was suspended from the practice of law for nine months and ordered to pay the State Bar of Texas $7200 in attorney fees.

...
"Throughout the history of our profession, a lawyer has been required to treat the property of a client in accordance with the highest standards of accountability." Robert P. Schuwerk & John F. Sutton, Jr., *A Guide to the Texas Disciplinary Rules of Professional Conduct*, 27A Hous. L.Rev. 1, 199–200 (1990). The prohibition on commingling, set forth in Rule 1.14, is one of the principal aspects of those standards. *See id.* As one court has explained, the prohibition on commingling is both a prophylactic measure and a method for avoiding even the appearance of impropriety....

2. Violation of Rule 8.04(a)(3)

In his second point of error, Brown argues the evidence is legally and factually insufficient to support the court's finding that he violated Rule 8.04(a)(3), which provides that a lawyer shall not "engage in conduct involving dishonesty, fraud, deceit or misrepresentation." The letter of protection that Brown sent to Humphrey's medical providers stated, "Please forward all billings and medical reports directly to me, as I will pursue the recovery of all medical, hospital, etc. costs directly from *State Farm Insurance Co.,* and assure that you are paid the amounts billed pursuant to this letter of protection." The letters clearly indicated that Brown would pay the medical providers when he obtained a recovery from State Farm. Nevertheless, he deposited the State Farm recovery into the joint account, ostensibly to finance further litigation, and used part of the money for his own purposes. This evidence is legally and factually sufficient to establish dishonesty. ...

Attorney Fees

In his fifth point of error, Brown argues the trial court erred in awarding attorney fees to the Commission. The Rules of Disciplinary Procedure allow the Commission to receive an award for attorney fees. *See* Tex.R. Disciplinary P. 1.06(T)(b). A reviewing court will not overturn a trial court's allowance of attorney fees unless the award constitutes a clear abuse of discretion. *See Lancer Corp. v. Murillo,* 909 S.W.2d 122, 125–26 (Tex.App.—San Antonio 1995, no writ). The test for abuse of discretion is whether the trial court acted arbitrarily. *See id.* at 126.

1. Constitutionality

Brown asserts that the rule allowing an award of attorney fees to the Commission is unconstitutional because it does not also allow a prevailing defendant to recover attorney fees. This issue was not raised in the trial court; therefore, it is waived on appeal. *See Dreyer,* 871 S.W.2d at 698.

2. Recoverability of Pro Bono Fees

Brown also argues that the Commission is not entitled to an award of attorney fees because the lawyers representing the Commission in this case did so on a *pro bono* basis. The Commission acknowledges that the trial attorneys provided their services on a *pro bono* basis with the intention of donating the value of their services to the Bar. Brown asserts that an attorney fee award is only authorized if the Commission actually incurs or is contractually liable for attorney fees. The rule, however, is not written so narrowly. It states:

The term "Sanction" may include the following additional ancillary requirements: ....

b. Payment of Reasonable Attorneys' Fees and all direct expenses associated with the proceedings. Tex.R. Disciplinary P. 1.06(T)(b).

The term "Reasonable Attorneys' Fees" is defined as "a reasonable fee for a competent private attorney, under the circumstances." Tex.R. Disciplinary P. 1.06(R). Among the factors that may be considered in determining the reasonableness of the fee are the time, labor, and skill required; the novelty and difficulty of the issues; the customary fee in the locality; the amount involved and the results obtained; the time limitations imposed by the circumstances; and the experience, reputation, and ability of the lawyers performing the services. *See id.* Neither Rule 1.06(T)(b) nor Rule 1.06(R) expressly requires that fees be contracted-for or incurred; the rules merely require that an award of attorney fees be reasonable.

For reasons of public policy, the federal courts have allowed *pro bono* attorneys to recover attorney fees under the Equal Access to Justice Act. *[citations omitted]* The courts have reached this result even though the EAJA expressly authorizes a prevailing party to receive an award for attorney fees that have been "incurred." 28 U.S.C.A. § 2412(d)(1)(A) (West Supp.1998). For similar reasons of public policy, we are persuaded that the Commission is entitled to the attorney fee award in this case.

First, the rule authorizing the award of attorney fees describes the award as a "sanction." This is some indication that the primary purpose of the award is to deter and punish conduct that violates the disciplinary rules, rather than to reimburse the Commission for costs it has actually incurred. Second, allowing an attorney fee award in this situation encourages *pro bono* service to the Bar. The legal profession is charged with seeking improvement of the administration of justice and the quality of legal service rendered by the profession. *See* Tex. Disciplinary R. Prof. Conduct preamble ¶ 5 (1989). "A lawyer should aid the legal profession in pursuing these objectives and should help the bar regulate itself in the public interest." *Id.* By agreeing to represent the Commission *pro bono,* the lawyers sought to donate the value of their services, $7200, to the Commission. If we denied the attorney fee award in this case, the donation intended for the Commission would effectively go to the lawyer subjected to discipline instead. *Cf. Copeland v. Marshall,* 641 F.2d 880, 900 (D.C.Cir.1980) (en banc) (noting that there is "nothing 'inconsistent in prosecuting a case in the public interest, agreeing not to charge one's *own* client a fee, and thereafter seeking fees' from the losing *defendant* ") (quoting *Keyes v. School Dist. No. 1,* 439 F.Supp. 393, 406–07 (D.Colo.1977)). Such a result would hardly encourage future *pro bono* representation.

For these reasons, we conclude that the trial court did not abuse its discretion in awarding attorney fees to the Commission even though the lawyers representing it did so on a *pro bono* basis.

3. Failure to Segregate

Finally, Brown argues that the court abused its discretion by awarding $7200 as an attorney fee because the lawyers used part of their time pursuing another complaint against Brown which they eventually decided to drop.

Brown's attorney stipulated twice that the amount of fees requested was reasonable. In his opening statement, the attorney stated, "[W]e have no doubt that the amount involved is reasonable, so there's no reason for there to be testimony on that. We will stipulate to the reasonableness of that attorney's fee." Before the attorney fee testimony was taken, Brown's attorney stated, "I will stipulate that the attorney's fees are reasonable but it is my opinion that they cannot be recovered." ...

To establish the reasonableness of attorney fees, a party seeking attorney fees must show that the fees resulted from suing the party sought to be charged with the fees on a claim that allows recovery of the fees. *See Stewart Title Guar. Co. v. Sterling,* 822 S.W.2d 1, 10 (Tex.1991). A party seeking attorney fees has a duty to segregate nonrecoverable fees from recoverable fees. *See id.* at 11. A recognized exception to the segregation requirement exists when the attorney fees rendered are in connection with claims that are so interrelated that their prosecution or defense entails proof or denial of essentially the same facts. *See id.* ...

The lawyer's testimony indicates that $7200 was an approximation of the amount of reasonable fees. It did not include all work done on the case or the time spent at trial. The testimony is also far from certain regarding the amount of time spent on abandoned matters. But Brown failed to object to the Commission's unsegregated proof that $7200 was a reasonable fee. Instead, he stipulated twice that the amount was reasonable and stated that the matters were interrelated. Given this state of the record, the trial court would have been justified in concluding that the time spent on the abandoned matters did not constitute a substantial, severable portion of the $7200 requested and that $7200 was a reasonable approximation of the actual value of the representation. The court did not abuse its discretion.

Conclusion

For the reasons stated herein, the judgment of the trial court is affirmed as reformed.

****

QUESTIONS

1. Lawyer represents charitable organization for a fee of $10,000. Organization pays Lawyer $5,000 but cannot pay the balance. Lawyer accepts the reduced fee and counts the non-paid hours she works on the case as pro bono. Is Lawyer correct in charging the hours as pro bono service under the model rules of professional conduct?

2. Lawyer has passed the bar exam a year ago, but just started working earlier this month. In reporting pro bono hours for the prior year, Lawyer reports zero. Is Lawyer subject to discipline?

3. Lawyer refused to conduct pro bono legal services and in lieu thereof, donated $1,000 each year to the state's Legal Services Foundation. Is Lawyer in violation of the model rules of professional conduct?

4. Judge appoints Lawyer to represent Defendant pro bono in a complex matter that the Lawyer is competent to handle but desires not to. Can Lawyer refuse to represent the Defendant pro bono? See Powell v Alabama, 287 U.S. 45, 53 S.Ct.55, 77 L.Ed. 158 (1932) and see DeLisio v Alaska Superior Court, 740 P. 2d 437 (Alaska 1987)

****

SOLICITING LEGAL SERVICES

For many years, the legal profession prohibited lawyer advertising of legal services as reprehensible and offensive means of soliciting clients and business.[108] That changed in 1978 with the United States Supreme Court's decision in Bates v. State Bar of Arizona determining that lawyer advertising was constitutionally protected speech.[109] Since that decision, the various states have promulgated rules governing the extent and limitations on lawyer advertising within their jurisdictions. As a general rule, advertising that misleads or unduly pressures is prohibited. The bar seeks to ensure that the lawyer does not take unfair advantage of his ability to influence an unwary public.

---

[108] Canon 27, 1908 Canons of Professional Ethics
[109] 433 U.S. 447 (1978)

Barratry

The solicitation of professional employment rises to the level of a criminal offense when the person solicits employment for himself or another with the intent to obtain an economic benefit through the efforts of another on behalf of the attorney.[110] The attorney should also be mindful that accepting non recognized referrals could result in a charge of barratry. In addition to criminal laws, some states have civil barratry laws. These laws deal with, among other things, voidability of legal services contracts and providing for monetary penalties for the lawyer who commits barratry.[111] Civil and Criminal penalties are in addition to sanctions that the lawyer will be subject to under the applicable rules of ethics.

In re Charges of Unprofessional Conduct Against 95-30, an Attorney at Law of the State of Minnesota
550 N.W.2d 616 (Minn. 1996)

Director of Office of Lawyers Professional Responsibility issued private admonition based on misleading telephone directory advertisement. Lawyers Professional Responsibility Board Panel affirmed admonition. The [Minnesota] Supreme Court held that advertisement stating "we have an office near you" and "offices located in" were not materially misleading and did not warrant admonition. …

The appellant attorney was admitted to practice law in Minnesota in 1980 and currently practices in a two person criminal defense and personal injury firm. After receiving information regarding appellant's advertising practices, the Director of the Office of Lawyers Professional Responsibility (Director) conducted an investigation and concluded that the appellant's telephone directory advertisement and letterhead contained false or misleading communications about the appellant's practice, in violation of Minn.R.Prof.Conduct 7.1(a) and 7.5. On May 31, 1995, the Director issued a private admonition pursuant to Rule 8(d)(2), Rules on Lawyers Professional Responsibility (RLPR). The appellant demanded a Lawyers Professional Responsibility Board Panel hearing pursuant to Rule 8(d)(2)(iii), RLPR, and the panel affirmed the admonition, agreeing with the Director that the appellant's conduct violated Minn.R.Prof.Conduct 7.1(a) and 7.5 but was isolated and nonserious. We disagree with the panel and reverse the admonition.

The facts are essentially undisputed. The appellant placed an advertisement in the 1993 Minneapolis Yellow Pages containing the statement "we have an office near *you:* Anoka, Arden Hills, Brooklyn Center, Columbia Heights, …Eden Prairie, Minneapolis, St. Louis Park, St. Paul." His law firm letterhead also contained the representation that he had "OFFICES LOCATED AT: Anoka, Arden Hills, Brooklyn Center, Columbia Heights, … Eden Prairie, Minneapolis, St. Louis Park, St. Paul." Of the appellant's "offices," all but two of them are office buildings where the appellant had occasionally rented conference rooms on an hourly basis to meet with clients. Of the other two locations, one of them is also a conference room that the

---

[110] E.g. Texas Penal Code Barratry and Solicitation of Professional Employment §38.12
[111] E.g. Texas Government Code §§82.065; 82.0651.

appellant leases on a monthly basis. The last location is a fully staffed office and, according to the appellant's testimony, is the appellant's primary office.

The Hennepin County District Ethics Committee (DEC) investigator concluded, and the panel agreed that the appellant in fact had only two offices: the one that appellant called the primary office, and the conference room that appellant leases on a monthly basis. As for the other locations, according to the panel, the appellant only "used offices in those locations to confer with clients and others on an irregular basis as needed, renting them for the occasion on an hourly basis." Therefore, the panel concluded that appellant's statements in the advertisement and on the stationery were false and misleading communications. The appellant disputes this conclusion, arguing that each of the nine locations qualifies as an "office," defined as a place where a professional person conducts business. At the panel hearing the appellant testified that no client or prospective client had ever complained about the advertisement or letterhead and that some had expressed appreciation that the appellant made convenient locations available. Nevertheless, after the DEC investigation began and before the admonition was issued, the appellant changed the letterhead from "offices located at" to "appointments may be scheduled at."

Minn.R.Prof.Conduct 7.1(a) provides:

[a] lawyer shall not make a false or misleading communication about the lawyer or the lawyer's services. A communication is false or misleading if it:
(a) contains a material misrepresentation of fact or law, or omits a fact necessary to make the statement considered as a whole not materially misleading.

Rule 7.5 provides in relevant part, "[a] lawyer shall not use a firm name, letterhead or other professional designation that violates Rule 7.1."

The issue before us, then, is whether the appellant's use of the phrases "we have offices" and "offices located in," to refer to the conference room arrangements, was a *material* misrepresentation of fact or omitted any fact necessary to make the statement considered as a whole not *materially* misleading. Although we agree that the representations were vague, and we believe attorneys should be more forthcoming in their advertisements, we cannot say that the appellant's conduct warranted discipline. The Director presented no evidence disputing appellant's testimony that the statements were made to inform readers that they would not have to drive to a distant location to meet their attorney. Nor was there any evidence that whether the appellant met with clients in a fully staffed office or in a private conference room was material to the readers of the statements. We do not find clear and convincing evidence that the appellant's representations were *materially* misleading.

This court does not condone the use of unclear or less than wholly straightforward language in lawyer advertising. We expect attorneys to provide accurate and complete information that will assist people in making fully informed decisions about legal representation. Our conclusion that discipline was not appropriate under these facts does not indicate that we approve altogether of the appellant's conduct.

So long as lawyer advertising is not false, fraudulent, misleading or deceiving, it passes constitutional muster and the disciplinary code, but one hopes for more. * * * Simply because free speech allows us to make fools of ourselves is no reason we should avail ourselves of the opportunity. For then, sadly, it is the whole profession that suffers.

The appellant did change the language of the statements during the course of the DEC investigation to remove any possible ambiguity. This improvement by appellant is commendable because it showed a willingness to cooperate with the Director's Office and avoid further disputes. But more importantly, the substance of the alteration converted the language into a clearer representation of what the appellant offers his clients. We should be able to expect this level of clarity in all attorney advertising. Reversed.

Coyne, Justice (dissenting)

Although I agree that the Rules of Professional Responsibility do not define "office," it seems to me that the ordinary use and commonly accepted meaning of "office" suggests a permanency of presence. Surely, one would expect a lawyer's office to be staffed by a receptionist, a secretary, or a legal assistant to answer the telephone during business hours and to assist a walk-in client.

It may well be that neither the complainant nor any other person has sustained damage by reason of this lawyer's advertising, but the indication to the reader that this lawyer is the senior or managing partner of a thriving law firm that is so large that it maintains nine offices throughout the metropolitan area seems to me to be misleading and deceptive and, therefore, deserving of admonition. Therefore, I would affirm.

****

Questions:

Consider each of the following situations and determine whether the lawyer should be disciplined for misleading communication.

1. A back cover phone book advertisement that declared, "FOR OVER 40 YEARS, WE'VE BEEN PUTTING EXPERIENCE, KNOWLEDGE, AND SKILLS TO WORK FOR PEOPLE LIKE YOU." The firm had not been in existence for 40 years and none of the lawyers with the firm had 40 years of experience. However, the combined legal experience of the lawyers in the firm was more than "40 YEARS".[112]

2. A statement in a direct mail letter claiming that "[a]bsent a legitimate excuse, we require the officer to be present at the trial setting and to possess the proper documentation for your case."[113]

---

[112] See Alice Neece Mine, Misleading Communications: The Bad, The Ugly, and the ???, North Carolina State Bar Journal available at http://www.ncbar.gov/ethics/eth_articles_11,1.asp
[113] Id.

3. In a direct mail letter, the statement, "[w]e know the judges, the police, and the DAs and have good working relations with each of them."[114]

4. A postcard advertisement depicting two lawyers standing before a judge. One lawyer says, "Your Honor, we have photos, taped conversations, AND a signed contract." The judge responds, "Give it up, counselor. You can't win against ABC Law Firm."[115]

5. Lawyer advertises that she has offices throughout the United States and can "represent you regardless of the state you are in". In fact, lawyer maintains a virtual law office, is only licensed to practice law in one state and associates with lawyers in other states as necessary.

****

The State Bar of Texas v. Kilpatrick
874 SW 2d 656 (Tex. 1994)

In this disciplinary proceeding, the court of appeals reversed and remanded the trial court's order disbarring Donald Kilpatrick for soliciting employment in violation of State Bar disciplinary rules. We reverse the judgment of the court of appeals, and render judgment disbarring Kilpatrick.

Bill Camp, a Houston attorney, suffered brain damage during a routine medical procedure on June 13, 1989. A week later, on June 20, his wife was appointed as his temporary guardian. On September 1, 1989, she became his permanent guardian.

Kilpatrick visited Camp at the Texas Institute for Research and Rehabilitation on July 19, 1989. During this meeting, Kilpatrick obtained Camp's signature on a power of attorney, which purported to authorize Kilpatrick to represent Camp in a medical malpractice claim. Only Kilpatrick and Camp were present, and neither Camp, his family, nor any legal representative requested or authorized Kilpatrick's visit. Kilpatrick later testified he knew Camp only as a "brother in the bar," that they had not been close friends or socialized together, and that their only previous acquaintance had been as opposing counsel on some criminal cases. He said that he had heard of Camp's misfortune through a law firm that, in turn, had learned the news from the emergency room physician on duty at the time of Camp's injury. Kilpatrick learned of Camp's location by calling Camp's office.

On July 21, 1989, two days after Kilpatrick obtained Camp's signature, Hornbuckle & Montgomery, the firm that had contacted Kilpatrick, filed a malpractice lawsuit against the doctors who treated Camp. When Ms. Camp learned of Kilpatrick's actions, she told Kilpatrick that the power of attorney was invalid, that she was Camp's guardian, and that Bill Camp was in

---

[114] Id.
[115] Id.

no condition to retain a lawyer. Ms. Camp also hired a probate lawyer, Robert McIntyre, to assist her with the guardianship.

At Ms. Camp's behest, McIntyre went to Kilpatrick's office and demanded that Kilpatrick relinquish any claim to represent Camp under the power of attorney. Kilpatrick refused, and insisted on a referral fee. When McIntyre repeated his demand to Kilpatrick in a letter dated October 6, 1989, Kilpatrick demanded $277,000.00 in exchange for his release.

As guardian, Ms. Camp filed a Tex.R.Civ.P. 12 Motion for Attorney to Show Authority with the probate court concerning Kilpatrick's power of attorney. On November 17, 1989, the probate court determined that Camp was mentally incompetent on the date he signed the power of attorney, and that Kilpatrick had no authority to represent him. The probate court also directed Kilpatrick to reimburse Ms. Camp for the attorneys' fees she had incurred as a result of his actions. On December 8, 1989, the same day the court issued its order, Kilpatrick appeared at McIntyre's office with an unfiled Motion to Recuse the probate judge. Kilpatrick threatened to file the motion unless Ms. Camp paid him the requested referral fee.

In April 1991, the State Bar filed a disciplinary action against Kilpatrick, charging him with violations of five disciplinary rules. At trial, the jury found that Kilpatrick (1) initiated contact with a prospective client for the purpose of obtaining employment, (2) engaged in conduct involving dishonesty, deceit, or misrepresentation, and (3) with intent to obtain an economic benefit to himself, solicited employment for himself to prosecute or collect a claim. On March 13, the trial court rendered judgment on the verdict, disbarring Kilpatrick.

The court of appeals reversed the trial court's judgment and remanded for new trial on two grounds. 869 S.W.2d 361. First, the court of appeals held that the trial court had erroneously permitted the State Bar to amend its pleadings at trial to include an allegation of barratry. *Id.* at 364. Second, the court held that the trial court abused its discretion in ordering disbarment based on a single act of solicitation. *Id.* at 366. We disagree with the court of appeals on both counts.

The State Bar's expert witness, Fred Hagans, testified on the issue of barratry, first during cross-examination by Kilpatrick's attorney, and then on redirect examination. At the subsequent charge conference, the State Bar requested a trial amendment alleging barratry as defined in Tex. Penal Code Ann. § 38.12(a) (Vernon Supp.1993), *reprinted in* Tex. Penal Code Ann. § 38.12 note (Vernon Supp.1994) (Historical and Statutory Notes), *amended by* Tex.Penal Code Ann. § 38.12(a) (Vernon Supp.1994). Over Kilpatrick's objection, the trial court permitted the trial amendment, and included the issue in the charge.

If evidence is objected to at trial on the ground that it is not within the issues made by the pleadings, the court *may* allow the pleadings to be amended and *shall* do so freely when the presentation of the merits will be subserved thereby and the objecting party fails to satisfy the court that the amendment would prejudice that party in maintaining the action or defense on the merits. Tex.R.Civ.P. 66 (emphasis supplied). A court may not refuse a trial amendment unless (1) the opposing party presents evidence of surprise or prejudice, or (2) the amendment asserts a new cause of action or defense, and thus is prejudicial on its face. *Greenhalgh v. Service Lloyds Ins. Co.*, 787 S.W.2d 938, 939 (Tex.1990). The burden of showing surprise or prejudice rests on the party resisting the amendment. *Id.* If the trial amendment is not mandatory, then the decision to permit or deny the amendment rests within the sound discretion of the trial court. Tex.R.Civ.P. 66; *Greenhalgh*, 787 S.W.2d at 939. In such a case, the court's decision to allow or deny a trial amendment may be reversed only if it is a clear abuse of discretion. *Hardin v. Hardin*, 597 S.W.2d 347, 349–50 (Tex.1980).

The court of appeals held that the trial amendment alleging barratry was "prejudicial on its face" because it added a new cause of action. 869 S.W.2d at 365. In so doing the court of appeals effectively held that all nonmandatory trial amendments under Rule 66 must be rejected. To the contrary, we hold that the decision to grant or deny the trial amendment was discretionary, and under the circumstances the trial court did not abuse that discretion.

The central allegation in the State Bar's initial complaint was that Kilpatrick violated former Tex.Code Professional Responsibility DR 2–103(D)(1), which prohibited attorneys from initiating contact with prospective clients for the purpose of obtaining employment if the lawyer knew or reasonably should have known the person could not have exercised reasonable judgment in employing a lawyer. *See also*, Tex.Disciplinary R.Prof.Conduct 7.02 (1989), *reprinted in* Tex.Gov't Code Ann., tit. 2, subtit. G, app. A (Vernon Supp.1994) (State Bar Rules art. X § 9). Former DR 2–103(D)(1) shares common elements with the criminal offense of barratry, which " is the solicitation of employment to prosecute or defend a claim with intent to obtain a personal benefit. Tex. Penal Code Ann. § 38.12(a)(3) (Vernon Supp.1993), *amended by* Tex.Penal Code Ann. § 38.12(a) (Vernon Supp.1994)." The evidence presented at trial supported discipline under either theory. Thus, the trial court, in its discretion, could reasonably have concluded that the trial amendment did not impair Kilpatrick's ability to present his defense. We therefore hold that the trial amendment did not involve the kind of calculated surprise or unfair prejudice that would render it an abuse of discretion.

The court of appeals further based its reversal on the fact that Kilpatrick had not been convicted of barratry in criminal proceedings: "[T]here was no criminal prosecution, yet, the State Bar obtained a finding of criminal wrongdoing without the hardship of the higher burden of proof which is necessary for a conviction." 869 S.W.2d at 365. The court of appeals erred, however, in its assumption that an attorney may not be disciplined for barratry in civil proceedings without first being convicted in criminal proceedings. While barratry is a crime for which an attorney may be prosecuted, a criminal prosecution is not a prerequisite to disciplinary proceedings based on that offense. Tex.Gov't Code Ann. § 82.062 (Vernon 1988) ("Any attorney who is guilty of barratry ... may be [disciplined] ... regardless of whether the attorney is being prosecuted for, or has been convicted of the offense."). Thus, we hold that the trial amendment resulted in no unfair prejudice, and was clearly within the trial court's discretion.

The court of appeals also concluded that the trial court's judgment should be reversed because the sanction of disbarment was so disproportionate to Kilpatrick's misconduct that it constituted an abuse of discretion. 869 S.W.2d at 366. We disagree.

The court of appeals characterized Kilpatrick's misconduct as an "isolated act of solicitation." Comparing it to other reported disciplinary cases in which the attorney misconduct "was much more egregious but in which the appellate court approved lesser sanctions," the court concluded that the sanction of disbarment was "so heavy" as be an abuse of discretion. 869 S.W.2d at 366.

The trial court has broad discretion to determine whether an attorney guilty of professional misconduct should be reprimanded, suspended, or disbarred. *Id.; State v. O'Dowd,* 158 Tex. 348, 312 S.W.2d 217, 221 (Tex.1958). In determining the appropriate sanction for attorney misconduct, a trial court must consider the nature and degree of the professional misconduct, the seriousness of and circumstances surrounding the misconduct, the loss or damage to clients, the damage to the profession, the assurance that those who seek legal services in the future will be insulated from the type of misconduct found, the profit to the attorney, the avoidance of repetition, the deterrent effect on others, the maintenance of respect for the legal profession, the trial of the case, and other relevant evidence concerning the attorney's personal and professional background. Tex.R.Disciplinary P. 3.10 (1992).

The sanction of disbarment does not turn on whether an attorney has engaged in a single act, as opposed to repeated and systematic pattern, of misconduct. Under Disciplinary Rule 3.10, a multitude of factors must be considered. In light of the facts and circumstances presented, we cannot say that the trial court abused its discretion, and we disagree with the court of appeals that the sanction of disbarment is disproportionate to Kilpatrick's misconduct.

We therefore grant the application of the State Bar and, without hearing argument, a majority of the court reverses the judgment of the court of appeals, and renders judgment disbarring Donald Kilpatrick. TEX.R.APP.P. 170.

Rodgers v. Commission for Lawyer Discipline
151 S.W.3d 602 (Tex Ct.App.-Ft.Worth, 2004)

This is an appeal from a jury verdict finding that appellant Clifford B. Rodgers violated the State Bar of Texas rules of professional conduct regarding trade name usage, false or misleading advertising, required advertising disclosures, and filing of advertising with the State Bar. *See* Tex. Disciplinary R. Prof'l Conduct 7.01(a), (e), 7.02(a), 7.04(b), (j), 7.07(b), *reprinted in* Tex. Gov't Code Ann., tit. 2, subtit. G app. A (Vernon 1998) (Tex. State Bar R. art. X, § 9). After a jury found that Rodgers violated all of these rules, the trial court determined that Rodgers should receive a two-year, fully probated suspension of his law license.

In six issues on appeal, Rodgers contends that (1 & 2) the evidence is legally and factually insufficient to support the jury's findings that he violated the trade name and false or misleading advertising rules, (3) as a matter of law he did not violate the disclosure rule, (4) as a matter of law he did not violate the filing of advertising rule because the advertisement was either exempt from the filing requirement or because appellee the Commission for Lawyer Discipline (CLD) did not conclusively prove that it was not exempt, (5) the trial court abused its discretion in admitting the testimony of CLD's expert, and (6) the trial court abused its discretion in assessing Rodgers's punishment. Because we determine that the evidence is sufficient to prove that Rodgers violated the trade name and false or misleading advertising rules, that the jury's verdict regarding whether he violated the disclosure rule controls, that the advertisement was not exempt from the filing rule and CLD did not have the burden to prove it was, and that the trial court did not abuse its discretion in admitting the expert testimony of Lynette Fons or setting punishment, we affirm the trial court's judgment.

Background Facts

In 1994 Rodgers began running an advertisement in the Southwestern Bell Yellow Pages under the name "Accidental Injury Hotline." The advertisement was located in the "Attorney Referral & Information Serv" section of the book. The advertisement did not list Rodgers's or any other attorney's name, nor did it make any other disclosures required by the rules. *See* Tex. Disciplinary R. Prof'l Conduct 7.04. It did contain a telephone number and list of topics regarding what to do in case of accident or injury.

After pressing the code number next to one of the topic listings, the caller was directed to a prerecorded message advising the caller about that specific topic. At the end of each prerecorded message, the caller was prompted as follows: "To arrange a free, no obligation consultation about your case with an attorney, now press '0'." If the caller pressed 0, the call was forwarded to Rodgers's office, with the following recording:

Your call is being forwarded to the Fort Worth office of attorney Clifford Rodgers, the sponsor of the Accidental Injury Hotline, which is copyrighted 1994 by him. He is licensed to practice law by the Texas Supreme Court and is not certified by the Texas Board of Legal Specialization. This is an advertisement.

If the call took place after office hours, the caller was prompted to either press the " * " key for emergency matters or to leave a message.

Rodgers subsequently received a letter from the State Bar dated August 15, 1994, which indicated that the Bar had initiated a grievance committee complaint against Rodgers about the advertisement. The letter indicated that the advertisement was "alleged to be in violation of [former] Rule 7.04 Texas Disciplinary Rules of Professional Conduct, in that said rule forbids attorneys from practicing under a trade name or a name that is misleading as to the identity of the lawyer or lawyers practicing under that name." [*citation omitted*] Rodgers later received a letter indicating that an investigatory panel of the grievance committee found that he had not committed professional misconduct and that the matter had been dismissed. However, the letter also warned that "the complainant has the right to amend the complaint and refile with new information."

In 1995, new rules of professional disciplinary conduct regulating attorney advertising became effective. 892–893 S.W.2d (Tex. Cases) XXXIII (1995) (providing that rules would become effective 120 days after judgment in *Texans Against Censorship*); *see Texans Against Censorship, Inc. v. State Bar of Tex.,* 888 F.Supp. 1328 (E.D.Tex.1995) (judgment date March 31, 1995). The new rules imposed additional regulations on attorney advertising, including, among other things, prohibiting an attorney from advertising under a trade name and requiring all attorney advertising—with certain enumerated exceptions—to be filed with an advertising review committee of the State Bar. *See* Tex. Disciplinary R. Prof'l Conduct 7.01(e), 7.07.

Rodgers was aware of the new rules and continued to run his advertisements. He did not send copies to the review committee for approval.

In 1997, a few days before the deadline for approving copy for the upcoming publication of the Southwestern Bell Yellow Pages, Rodgers was contacted by a representative of Southwestern Bell, who told Rodgers that—based on its communications with the Bar—it could no longer run his advertisement under the "Attorney Information Referral Service" heading.

Rodgers filed suit against the State Bar and Southwestern Bell and obtained a temporary order restraining the Bar from talking to Southwestern Bell and telling it not to run Rodgers's advertisement and restraining Southwestern Bell from printing the directory without the advertisement in it. After a hearing, Rodgers and Southwestern Bell entered into a rule 11 agreement to run the advertisement with a disclaimer indicating that the advertisement was not a referral service, but an information service. *See* Tex.R. Civ. P. 11. The State Bar was not a party to the rule 11 agreement. Rodgers then nonsuited the litigation.

Rodgers subsequently ran the advertisement in the 1997 Southwestern Bell Yellow Pages, GTE Everything Pages, and Transwestern World Pages. CLD initiated the grievance process against Rodgers in 1998 and filed this suit in November 1999.

Whether the Law of the Case Doctrine Applies

…

The law of the case doctrine is defined as "that principle under which questions of law decided on appeal to a court of last resort will govern the case throughout its subsequent stages." *Briscoe v. Goodmark Corp.,* 102 S.W.3d 714, 716 (Tex.2003) (citing *Hudson v. Wakefield,* 711 S.W.2d 628, 630 (Tex.1986)). The doctrine prohibits relitigation of a question of law unless (1) the earlier holding is clearly erroneous or (2) the later stage of litigation presents different parties, different issues, or more fully developed facts. *Id.* at 716–17; *Hudson,* 711 S.W.2d at 630.

Here, the determination of whether more than a scintilla of evidence is shown in the record is being made at two different stages of litigation and may involve more fully developed facts at either stage. …It is possible that evidence considered at summary judgment may not have been introduced into the record at trial or vice versa. Thus, we do not believe the law of the case doctrine is applicable here. We will review the sufficiency of the evidence based on the evidence adduced at trial.

Legal and Factual Sufficiency of Evidence to Prove Violation of Trade Name and False or Misleading Advertising Rules

Violation of Trade Name Rule

Rule 7.01(a) provides that "[a] lawyer in private practice shall not practice under a trade name, a name that is misleading as to the identity of the lawyer or lawyers practicing under such name, or a firm name containing names other than those of one or more of the lawyers in the firm." Tex.R. Disciplinary Conduct 7.01(a). Rule 7.01(e) provides that "[a] lawyer shall not advertise in the public media or seek professional employment by written communication under a trade or fictitious name." *Id.* 7.01(e). Rodgers contends that the trade name rule prohibits only the use of deceptive trade names and that rule 7.01(a) defines trade name as "a name that is misleading as to ... identity."

We reject Rodgers's interpretation of rule 7.01(a). By its plain language, the rule prohibits a lawyer's use of three types of names: (1) a trade name; (2) a name that is misleading as to the lawyer's identity; or (3) a firm name with names other than those of the lawyers in the firm. *Id.* 7.01(a); *see* Tex. Gov't Code Ann. § 311.011(a) (Vernon 1998) (providing that "[w]ords and phrases shall be read in context and construed according to the rules of grammar and common usage"). We have previously defined a "trade name" as "a designation that is adopted and used by a person either to designate a good he markets, a service he renders, or a business he conducts." *C.R.,* 54 S.W.3d at 515. Moreover, comment 1 to rule 7.01 notes that "[t]rade names are inherently misleading." Tex.R. Disciplinary Conduct 7.01 cmt. 1. And, in ruling that rule 7.01 does not infringe on the First Amendment's protection of commercial speech, a federal district court has recognized the inherent risks of even a nondeceptive trade name used in attorney advertising because, by not identifying the name of the professional practicing under the trade name, the name frees the professional from dependence on his own personal reputation. *Texans Against Censorship, Inc.,* 888 F.Supp. at 1350 (analogizing to United States Supreme Court opinion regarding risks of use of nondeceptive trade name in optometrists' practices and holding rule limiting use of trade names constitutional). Thus, we conclude that to be prohibited under rule 7.01 a trade name does not have to be facially deceptive.

The evidence at trial showed that the advertisements Rodgers placed in the telephone books contained the name "Accidental Injury Hotline," but not Rodgers's name or any other attorney's name. Rodgers obtained a copyright on the name "Accidental Injury Hotline," registered a service mark for the hotline, and received more than fifty percent of his business from the hotline. Rodgers admitted to starting the hotline solely as an advertisement for his business because he thought "informational positioning," or providing helpful information to consumers to position the provider as knowledgeable, was the best way to obtain customers through advertising. The evidence also showed that the only place Rodgers used the name was in the advertisements; however, the fact that Rodgers used the name in only one facet of his business does not outweigh the evidence that with regard to the only medium in which he advertised his business, he used the name to designate a service he rendered or a business he conducted. We hold that the evidence is both legally and factually sufficient to prove Rodgers violated rule 7.01(a) and (e). We overrule Rodgers's second issue.

Violation of False or Misleading Advertising Rule

Rodgers further contends that the evidence is legally and factually insufficient to prove that he violated rule 7.02(a) by making a false or misleading communication. Rule 7.02 provides as follows:

(a) A lawyer shall not make a false or misleading communication about the qualifications or the services of any lawyer or firm. A communication is false or misleading if it:
(1) contains a material misrepresentation of fact or law, or omits a fact necessary to make the statement considered as a whole not materially misleading;

231

(2) is likely to create an unjustified expectation about results the lawyer can achieve, or states or implies that the lawyer can achieve results by means that violate these rules or other law;

(3) compares the lawyer's services with other lawyers' services, unless the comparison can be substantiated by reference to verifiable, objective data;

(4) states or implies that the lawyer is able to influence improperly or upon irrelevant grounds any tribunal, legislative body, or public official; or

(5) designates one or more specific areas of practice in an advertisement in the public media or in a written solicitation unless the advertising lawyer is competent to handle legal matters in each such area of practice. Tex.R. Disciplinary Conduct 7.02(a).

Rodgers claims that federal case law regarding the Lanham Act and trademark infringement cases required CLD to introduce evidence that at least one person was actually confused by Rodgers's advertisement. But Rodgers cites no authority applying this requirement outside the context of those cases, including the attorney disciplinary context. And the only case this court found addressing this issue in the professional disciplinary-advertising context concluded that the State of Maryland did not have to prove that a specific customer had been misled or deceived by the advertising. *See Barnett v. Md. State Bd. of Dental Exam'rs,* 293 Md. 361, 444 A.2d 1013, 1020 (1982).

Rule 7.02 itself does not require evidence of actual confusion. In the only other reported case from this State that we have found, *Musslewhite v. State Bar of Texas,* 786 S.W.2d 437 (Tex.App.-Houston [14th Dist.] 1990, writ denied), *cert. denied,* 501 U.S. 1251, 111 S.Ct. 2891, 115 L.Ed.2d 1056 (1991), the court held that an attorney's press release, letters, and advertisements were false and misleading on their face because they referred to a "team of internationally renowned U.S. lawyers" but did not identify those lawyers, and the information in them was not "susceptible to reasonable verification by the public." *Id.* at 441. The court did not require any showing that one or more persons had been actually confused or misled by the materials.

The purpose of the rules is to protect the public from deceptive advertising, which the Supreme Court has recognized as a substantial governmental interest. *Texans Against Censorship, Inc.,* 888 F.Supp. at 1348 (citing *Edenfield v. Fane,* 507 U.S. 761, 768, 113 S.Ct. 1792, 1799, 123 L.Ed.2d 543 (1993)). A federal court has recognized that one advantage to Texas's advertising filing requirements is that the state bar is not required to rely on consumers, who may not have enough information about the legal system in general, or a particular lawyer, to detect false or misleading advertising from lawyers. The state bar will not be forced to rely hereafter on consumers, to find deceptive advertising or misleading solicitation letters. Instead, the filing process will enable the state bar itself to winnow false or deceptive advertising from truthful advertising. *Id.* at 1364.

The evidence at trial showed that the advertisements did not identify Rodgers, the only attorney available through the hotline was Rodgers, and the caller did not learn the name of the attorney he would be referred to until he pressed "0." Thus, the only way a person could verify which attorney's office he would be speaking to was to actually connect to the attorney's office. This type of advertising creates the same types of problems as the use of a trade name, which is inherently misleading: a potential consumer has no name or other information to help her evaluate whether she wants to contact a particular attorney prior to being connected to that attorney's office. In fact, this advertisement is similar to a sample advertisement that the State Bar published as an example of a noncompliant advertisement in a 1995 Texas Bar Journal article that Rodgers included as one of this trial exhibits. That advertisement listed no attorney name or office information, just a telephone number and two trade names, "Child Support & Locating Clinic" and "Debt Relief Clinic." 58 Tex. B.J. 664 (1995).

We hold that the evidence is legally and factually sufficient to support the jury's finding that Rodgers made a false or misleading communication in violation of rule 7.02(a). We overrule Rodgers's first issue.

Whether Presence of Required Disclaimers in Second Part of Message Satisfies Rule 7.04

In his third issue, Rodgers claims that as a matter of law, he did not violate rule 7.04(b) and (j), which require that an advertisement in the public media contain certain disclaimers, because even though the disclaimers were not included in the print advertisement, they were included in the audio recording once a customer pressed the button indicating he wanted to speak to an attorney. He contends that the advertisement becomes a lawyer advertisement only when the caller presses the button indicating he or she wants to speak to a lawyer. Rodgers concedes, however, that if the disclosures are to be required in the print portion of the advertisement, then he violated rule 7.04(b) and (j). Tex. Disciplinary R. Prof'l Conduct 7.04(b), (j). Rodgers contends that we must determine whether the disclaimers were required in the print portion of the advertisement by applying the "anti-dissection" rule set forth in Lanham Act and trademark infringement cases. Again, Rodgers has not cited any cases indicating that these legal authorities have been applied in an attorney disciplinary case, nor do we believe they are appropriately applied to the attorney advertising context....

As we have previously discussed, an advertisement can be misleading by omission. In an advertisement such as Rodgers's, a caller wishing to speak to an attorney cannot verify any information regarding that attorney before pressing the button to speak to an attorney. CLD claims that "[o]ne of the fundamental purposes behind Rule 7.04 is to allow consumers to make an informed choice before seeking legal services, by ascertaining the names (and reputations), locations, and qualifications of potential attorneys." By not including his name or any of the required disclosures in the print portion of the advertisement, Rodgers violated this purpose. Thus, we hold that as a matter of law, the disclaimers were required to be in the printed portion of the advertisement. We overrule Rodgers's third issue.

Whether Rodgers's Advertisement Violated Rule 7.07(b)

The jury concluded that Rodgers violated rule 7.07(b) by failing to file the advertisement with the State Bar Advertising Review Committee (ARC) before its first dissemination. Rodgers disputes this finding on two grounds: (1) the rule does not apply to advertisements submitted before July 29, 1995 when the filing requirement first became effective and (2) it was CLD's burden to procure a finding that the public service announcement exception to the rule did not apply, and CLD did not. Rodgers argues that because CLD did not conclusively prove the nonexistence of the exemption, he could not have violated the rule.

Whether Pre–1995 Advertisements are "Grandfathered" Out of Rule 7.07(b) Filing Requirements?

Rule 7.07(b) provides that "a lawyer shall file with [ARC], either before or concurrently with the first dissemination of an advertisement in the public media, a copy of that advertisement." Tex. Disciplinary R. Prof'l Conduct 7.07(b). Rodgers contends that this rule does not apply to his 1997 advertisement because it was first disseminated in 1994, before the effective date of the rule. CLD contends that the phrase "first dissemination of an advertisement in the public media" means the first dissemination after the effective date of the rule. To determine which interpretation of the rule is correct, we must employ common rules of statutory construction. *See O'Quinn v. State Bar of Tex.*, 763 S.W.2d 397, 399 (Tex.1988) (holding that the rules of disciplinary conduct are to be treated like statutes). Our primary objective in construing a statute is to determine and give effect to the drafters' intent. *See Mitchell Energy Corp. v. Ashworth*, 943 S.W.2d 436, 438 (Tex.1997) (orig.proceeding); [citations omitted] The amendments to the advertising rules were promulgated in response to the perception that the prior rules did not adequately protect Texas citizens from false or deceptive lawyer advertising and solicitation. *See Texans Against Censorship, Inc.*, 888 F.Supp. at 1335, 1348. ...

Although an attorney may apply for preapproval of an advertisement, preapproval is not required. Tex.R. Disciplinary Conduct 7.07 cmt. 4. Rule 7.07 provides that filing may be made "concurrently with" the first dissemination of an advertisement. *Id.* 7.07(b). Along with a copy of the advertisement, the attorney must file "a statement of when and where the advertisement *has been,* is, or will be used." *Id.* 7.07(b)(3) (emphasis added). Furthermore, the rule contains an extensive list of advertisements that are exempt from the filing rules, but does not explicitly exempt advertisements that were first disseminated before rule 7.07 took effect. *See, e.g., Unigard Sec. Ins. Co. v. Schaefer,* 572 S.W.2d 303, 307 (Tex.1978) (holding that when statute contains specific exclusions or exceptions, no others usually apply). ...

We hold that the filing requirements of rule 7.07 apply to advertisements previously submitted before the effective date of rule 7.07 that are also being submitted for the first time after the effective date of the rule. ...

Here, CLD claimed that Rodgers violated rule 7.07(b) by failing to submit the advertisement to the ARC. Rodgers admits he did not submit the advertisement for review, but contends that he was not obligated to do so because it fits one of the exceptions to the rule. Thus, Rodgers asserts an independent reason why CLD should not recover on its claim that he violated rule 7.07(b) and had the burden of proof on that issue. Because Rodgers had the burden of proof, his challenge on appeal that CLD failed to conclusively prove the advertisement was not a public service announcement fails. We overrule Rodgers's fourth issue. ...

Did the Trial Court Abuse its Discretion in Setting Rodgers's Punishment?

Rodgers contends the trial court abused its discretion in sentencing him to a two-year, fully probated suspension because, "under the circumstances of this case, the sanction imposed smacks of punishment for [Rodgers] exercising [his] legal rights to determine how the [rules] should be applied to [his] advertising approach." According to Rodgers, the fact that he chose to litigate this issue rather than change his advertisement is justified in light of the prior State Bar ruling that his advertisement did not violate the trade name prohibition and the settlement he entered into with Southwestern Bell, and he should have received no more than a public reprimand.

Sanctions for professional misconduct may include disbarment, resignation in lieu of disbarment, indefinite disability suspension, suspension for a certain term, probation of suspension, interim suspension, public reprimand, and private reprimand. [citations omitted]

An appellate court should reverse the trial court's decision only if an abuse of discretion is shown. *Love,* 982 S.W.2d at 944. The court must consider the following factors in determining the appropriate sanction: (1) the nature and degree of the professional misconduct for which the respondent is being sanctioned; (2) the seriousness of and circumstances surrounding the professional misconduct; (3) the loss or damage to clients; (4) the damage to the profession; (5) the assurance that those who seek legal services in the future will be insulated from the type of professional misconduct found; (6) the profit to the attorney; (7) the avoidance of repetition; (8) the deterrent effect on others; (9) the maintenance of respect for the legal profession; (10) the conduct of the respondent during the course of the CLD action; (11) the trial of the case; and (12) other relevant evidence concerning the respondent's personal and professional background. Tex.R. Disciplinary P. 3.10; *Kilpatrick,* 874 S.W.2d at 659; *Curtis,* 20 S.W.3d at 235.

Although a prior State Bar grievance committee determined that Rodgers did not violate the version of the trade name rule in effect in 1994—which did not include the prohibition against advertising under a trade name—a grievance committee decision not to prosecute has no res judicata or collateral estoppel effect, which Rodgers concedes. In addition, the State Bar was not a party to the 1997 settlement with Southwestern Bell, and there is no evidence that it agreed the advertisement did not violate the advertising rules. ... Accordingly, we overrule Rodgers's sixth issue.

Conclusion

Having overruled Rodgers's issues on appeal, we affirm the trial court's judgment.

****

QUESTIONS

1. Tony Malone has a number of high end restaurants throughout the city. Attorney befriends Malone and asks him to refer any customers that he has to Attorney who practices business transactions law. Most of Malone's customers are entrepreneurs with various business interests. Attorney offers no quid pro quo but does pay a quarterly incentive to Malone. Is Attorney subject to discipline?

2. Four lawyers in a ten lawyer law firm decide to leave the firm to open their own law office. During the thirty days before their departure, they launch a solicitation campaign to gather as many Clients from the old law firm as possible. The solicitation states "Our offices are moving to 123 Main Street on January 1st. You may call us at 713-555-5555 after that date. We look forward to continuing to serve your legal needs". The letter was written on 'old' law firm's letterhead. Are the four lawyers subject to discipline for soliciting their own clients?

3. Lawyer has a facebook page with more than 5000 friends. If Lawyer posts that he provides legal services at reasonable rates, will the posting be considered prohibited solicitation or permitted advertisement?

4. Lawyer is among only fifteen lawyers that engage in a specialized area of practice in his state. State Bar offers no certification in the area so the 15 lawyers get together and establish their own certification which they call the Certifying Board for Specialization. Lawyer publishes in his advertisement that he is certified by the Certifying Board for Specialization. Is Lawyer in violation of the model rules of professional conduct?

5. Attorney advertises her law practice on a downtown billboard. The billboard shows a professional looking woman at a desk apparently hard at work. The billboard message states:

I handle 18-Wheeler Truck Accidents
Suma cum laude graduate
Fluent Spanish Spoken
Call me 713-333-3333

Attorney has never handled an 18-Wheeler Truck Accident case, but desires to. Attorney was a suma cum laude undergraduate but did not graduate suma cum laude from law school. There are three persons in Attorney's office who are fluent in Spanish; attorney is not one of them. Is Attorney subject to discipline?

6. A recent office building fire in Northeast Houston left four people dead and twenty badly injured. Lawyer is horrified when he hears the news reports. While at the hospital visiting a family friend, lawyer discovers that some of the victims of that fire are in the same hospital. Lawyer finds out where they are and contacts five of them to share his remorse and offer any legal assistance he could give. Is Lawyer subject to discipline?

7. If placed on the lawyer's letterhead, which of the following least likely violate(s) the model rules of professional conduct?

    A. ANY LAWYERS
       LEGAL SERVICES CORPORATION

    B. ANY LAWYER, PLLC
       Of Counsel: United States Congressperson Lynda Legislator

    C. ANY LAWYER & ASSOC.
       "WE PROVIDE LEGAL SERVICES"

    D. ANY LAWYERS, PC
       SPECIALISTS IN INDIGENT DEFENSE

****

Generally speaking, it is every lawyer's obligation to ensure that every member of the bar maintains the highest level of integrity and moral responsibility. Under the model rules, the lawyer is required to report any lawyer who fails to meet these standards to the degree that the lawyer is unable to provide competent representation to his clients.[116]

In the Matter of Jorge L. Rodriguez
753 N.E.2d 1289 (Ind. 2001)

Because the respondent failed on his Indiana Bar application to disclose attendance at two colleges, his academic dismissal from both, and a semester suspension from one, he will be suspended from the practice of law for 90 days.

This attorney disciplinary action comes before this Court now upon the respondent's and the Disciplinary Commission's *Statement of Circumstances and Conditional Agreement for Discipline.* In that agreement, the respondent admits to misconduct and agrees to be suspended for 90 days. The agreement is now before this Court for final approval. The respondent's admission to this state's bar in 1992 confers upon this Court disciplinary jurisdiction in this matter.

This is the second time this particular conditional agreement has been submitted to us for approval. Upon its first submission, we returned it to the parties for further information regarding the circumstances regarding the respondent's admitted 1980 suspension from the University of Miami. In response, the respondent tendered the requested information to augment the conditional agreement, along with a *Memorandum in Support of Nondisclosure,* in which the respondent argued that the acts underlying that suspension formed the basis for criminal charges as well as violations of school policy. Since the criminal records were later "released," then "expunged," the respondent argues that he should not be required to disclose the records to this Court. We disagree. The respondent opened his past for inspection through his purely voluntary act of seeking Indiana Bar admission. Accordingly, we deny his request for nondisclosure, and have arrived at our decision on the tendered conditional agreement with the benefit of the information describing the incident underlying his 1980 suspension from the University of Miami.

The parties agree that on April 19, 1991, the respondent submitted his *Application for Admission Upon Examination to Practice Law* to the Indiana State Board of Law Examiners. Paragraph 10 of the application asked the respondent to list colleges and universities he had attended. Although the respondent disclosed that he had attended the University of Florida for his undergraduate and masters' degrees, and Ohio Northern University for his law degree, he failed to disclose that he attended the University of Miami from 1979 to 1983 and the Nova University College of Law from 1986 to 1987.

---

[116] ABA Model Rules of Professional Conduct, Rule 8.3

Paragraph twelve of the application stated:

> The following is a complete report as to every incident in which I have
> ever been disciplined, expelled or suspended from any college, university
> or law school or other professional school or profession (to include
> academic suspension or probation) or have been removed from appointive
> or elected public office for cause:

> In response, the respondent stated, "None." In fact, the respondent was
> suspended from the University of Miami in 1980. He was academically
> dismissed from the University of Miami in 1983. He was academically
> dismissed from Nova University College of Law in 1987. In 1993, the
> respondent offered to the Board of Law Examiners to correct the
> omissions on his application.

Indiana Professional Conduct Rule 8.1 provides:

An applicant for admission to the bar, or a lawyer in connection with a bar admission
application or in connection with a disciplinary matter, shall not:

(a) knowingly make a false statement of material fact; or

(b) fail to disclose a fact necessary to correct a misapprehension known by the person to
have arisen in the matter, or knowingly fail to respond to a lawful demand for
information from an admissions or disciplinary authority, except that this Rule does not
require disclosure of information otherwise protected by Rule 1.6.

By failing to disclose his attendance at the University of Miami and Nova law school, his
suspension from the University of Miami, and his academic dismissals from the University of
Miami and Nova law school, the respondent violated Ind. Professional Conduct Rule 8.1.

This Court's discipline imposed for faulty disclosure on bar applications has varied,
depending on the circumstances and any mitigating or aggravating factors.

In a prior case, an attorney failed to disclose on both Indiana and Florida Bar admission
applications three lawsuits in which he was a named defendant, a speeding ticket, an arrest for
public intoxication, and various delinquent credit card accounts. Pursuant to a conditional
agreement, this Court accepted the agreed discipline of public reprimand, in large part because of
the parties' stipulation that the respondent's application omissions were the result of his "fail[ing]
to take sufficient care and time in completing [the applications] to reflect on the questions and
consider their import ..." rather than the product of a conscious objective to deceive admissions
authorities.

This Court disbarred an attorney in another case, upon finding that the attorney
deliberately falsified bar application responses on Pennsylvania and Maryland questionnaires.
His deceit was pervasive and included the forgery of certain documents to support his false

claims. That attorney, who failed to appear at hearing, had been previously disciplined by this Court for falsifying an application for federal employment. Due to the sheer gravity and breadth of his deceptions, this Court imposed disbarment.

The present case presents misconduct more akin to those cases in that it is mitigated by the respondent's acknowledgement of his wrongdoing and his subsequent efforts with the Board of Law Examiners to correct the errors. In light of that, along with the fact that the discipline is the product of an agreed resolution, we find that it should be approved, but wish to make clear that 90 days is the minimum discipline this Court would accept for the respondent's misconduct.

It is, therefore, ordered that the respondent, Jorge L. Rodriguez, be suspended from the practice of law in this state for ninety (90) days, beginning October 5, 2001, at the conclusion of which he shall be automatically reinstated.

Note: In 2014, in the California Supreme Court in an unanimous decision concluded that Respondent Glass had not sustained "his heavy burden of demonstrating rehabilitation and fitness for the practice of law."[117] The court wrote:

" Stephen Randall Glass made himself infamous as a dishonest journalist by fabricating material for more than 40 articles for The New Republic magazine and other publications. He also carefully fabricated supporting materials to delude The New Republic"s fact checkers. The articles appeared between June 1996 and May 1998, and included falsehoods that reflected negatively on individuals, political groups, and ethnic minorities. During the same period, starting in September 1997, he was also an evening law student at Georgetown University"s law school. Glass made every effort to avoid detection once suspicions were aroused, lobbied strenuously to keep his job at The New Republic, and, in the aftermath of his exposure, did not fully cooperate with the publications to identify his fabrications.

Glass applied to become a member of the New York bar in 2002, but withdrew his application after he was informally notified in 2004 that his moral character application would be rejected. In the New York bar application materials, he exaggerated his cooperation with the journals that had published his work and failed to supply a complete list of the fabricated articles that had injured others.

Glass passed the California bar examination in 2006 and filed an application for determination of moral character in 2007. It was not until the California State Bar moral character proceedings that Glass reviewed all of his articles, as well as the editorials The New Republic and other journals published to identify his fabrications, and ultimately identified fabrications that he previously had denied or failed to disclose. In the California proceedings, Glass was not forthright in acknowledging the defects in his New York bar application.[118]

---

[117] In re Stephen Randall Glass on admission, 58 Cal 4th 500, 316 P.3d 1199 (2014)
[118] Id.

The Glass facts paint a picture of a person with a pattern for lying and deception. Moreover, Glass has evidently profited from the lies in a 2003 book, purportedly a biographical novel titled, *The Fabulist* as well as a feature film titled *Shattered Glass*. Thus, while the specific acts of fabrication occurred between 1996 and 1998, his record since that time was considered insufficient to show rehabilitation requisite to being admitted to the bars in California or New York.

****

Iowa Supreme Court Board Of Professional Ethics And Conduct v. Lane
642 N.W.2d 296 (Iowa 2002)

In disciplinary proceeding, the Supreme Court, Streit, J., held that attorney's plagiarism of 18 pages of a brief from a treatise, and requesting attorney fees for 80 hours of work preparing the brief, warranted suspension of license for six months. License suspended.

An Iowa attorney passed someone else's writing as his own and claimed he spent almost two weeks writing that which he used. The Iowa Supreme Court Board of Professional Ethics and Conduct filed a complaint with our Grievance Commission against respondent, William J. Lane, alleging he violated several ethical rules and recommended we suspend Lane's license to practice law for three months. Our review is required by Court Rule 118.10. We agree with the Commission's findings of misconduct but suspend Lane's license for six months.

Background Facts and Proceedings

After the conclusion of a trial in federal court in which Daniel Sicard claimed a violation of the Americans with Disabilities Act, attorney Lane submitted a post-trial brief to the court. The legal portion of the brief was in great part plagiarized from a treatise written by Barbara Lindemann and Paul Grossman. Lane later applied to the court for attorney fees. Among other charges, Lane requested compensation for eighty hours of work spent to prepare the questioned brief. Charging $200 per hour, Lane asked for $16,000 to write the brief that was largely copied from an uncredited source. In total, Lane requested $104,127 in attorney fees plus $13,363.29 in costs for his representation of Sicard.

On May 5, 1998, there was a hearing on Lane's attorney fee application. The United States magistrate judge stated it did not appear to him that Lane wrote the legal portions of the brief. Lane responded, "I borrowed liberally from other sources. Yes, your Honor." The court noted, [b]ecause of the consistency of style and the sequence of footnotes, the court assumes that [the brief] is from a particular source. If the source is a published treatise, it can simply be identified by name, author, and publisher.

To address this suspicion, the judge ordered Lane to explain or identify the sources cited in his brief within ten days. At the end of the ten days, Lane did nothing to comply with the court's order. On June 4, 1998, a member of the judge's staff asked Lane if he intended to respond to the order. Only days later, a fire at Lane's home destroyed many of his files and records in the Sicard matter. In July 1998, Lane closed his office, but continued to practice out of his home.

Four months passed and Lane still did not respond to the judge's order. On September 30, 1998, the judge entered an order awarding Lane $20,000 in fees in the Sicard case. The judge stated "there [were] many serious problems with plaintiff's fees and cost claim." The court was particularly concerned because Lane did not support his contention he was entitled to receive compensation at the rate of $200 per hour for his services. Lane also requested $9000 as compensation for the time he spent preparing his bill. The judge stated Lane requested $16,000 for the lifted brief but failed to comply with the court's order to "disclose the sources from which counsel 'borrowed liberally.' " Lane also requested compensation for fifty-nine hours of legal research preceding the trial. The court concluded it is not reasonable to bill 59 hours of legal research in the two weeks prior to trial.... If counsel spent this amount for time performing research, it is further evidence that he does not possess the skill and experience of those who charge $200 per hour.

The court further explained its reduction of the attorney fees awarded by citing to Lane's charges of $5.00 per telephone call, $1.00 per page of facsimile transmissions, $191 for long distance transmission, and $.50 per photocopy. Finally, the court stated Lane did not cite authority for the ability to charge for estimated pretrial travel expenses. Lane did not appeal the $20,000 award of attorney fees.

On October 30, 1998, Lane filed a compliance with the judge's order to document his sources but the judge was not made aware of the compliance until March 1999. When the judge read Lane's compliance he did not notice any reference to the primary source of the legal portion of Lane's brief. Lane's compliance constituted four pages of single-spaced lists of authorities. Among them was the Grossman treatise. However, no particular attention was drawn to this source. Consequently, the judge undertook his own investigation and discovered Lane took the legal portion of his brief verbatim from the Grossman treatise.

Complaint

The Ethics Board alleges violations of DR 1-102(A)(1), (3), (4), (5), and (6). This rule provides in part, a lawyer shall not violate a disciplinary rule; engage in illegal conduct involving moral turpitude; engage in conduct involving dishonesty, fraud, deceit or misrepresentation; engage in conduct that is prejudicial to the administration of justice; and engage in any other conduct that adversely reflects on the fitness to practice law.

The Ethics Board also charges Lane with a violation of [rule] which states, "[a] lawyer shall not enter into an agreement for, charge, or collect an illegal or clearly excessive fee." The Commission found Lane violated rules by his handling of the Sicard case.

Ethical Violations

Lane plagiarized from a treatise and submitted his plagiarized work to the court as his own. This plagiarism constituted, among other things, a misrepresentation to the court. An attorney may not engage in conduct involving dishonesty, fraud, deceit, or misrepresentation. This issue is akin to the matter of ghost-writing attorneys who "author pleadings and necessarily guide the course of the litigation with unseen hand." In this situation, an attorney authors court documents for a pro se litigant who, in turn, submits the court document as his or her own writing. This practice is widely condemned as unethical and a "deliberate evasion of the responsibilities imposed on attorneys." Just as ghost writing constitutes a misrepresentation on the court, so does plagiarism of the type we have before us.

Plagiarism itself is unethical. "Plagiarism, the adoption of the work of others as one's own, does involve an element of deceit, which reflects on an individual's honesty." Use of "appropriated material ... cannot go undisciplined, especially because honesty is so fundamental to the functioning of the legal profession...." Undoubtedly, Lane's plagiarism reflects poorly on both his professional ethics and judgment.

On the first occasion plagiarism became an issue, Lane appeared to be forthcoming with the court and admitted "[he] borrowed liberally from other sources." It also appears Lane attempted to identify the source of his writing before the court but was unable to recall the exact title of the treatise. Lane later had the chance to identify his source to the court, but when he responded to the court's order, he failed to specifically draw the court's attention to the Grossman treatise. Instead, Lane buried the title within a list of over 200 other sources. Though a technical compliance with the court's order, Lane's continued lack of candor indicates he hoped, by concealing the treatise among 200 other titles, the judge would not recognize the extent of Lane's plagiarism.

We find the record shows Lane knowingly plagiarized and intended to deceive the court. Equally troubling is Lane's application for attorney fees. Lane copied the entire portion of his legal argument out of a book and then claimed it took him eighty hours to write the brief containing the copied material. He requested attorney fees for this work at the rate of $200 per hour. Other than Lane's assertions that perhaps he works less efficiently than other lawyers, there is little in the record to indicate Lane actually spent this amount of time writing the brief. Because he plagiarized the entire legal argument, the chances are remote that it took Lane eighty hours to write the argument. Rather, the facts show Lane stole all eighteen pages of his legal argument from a single source. Then to justify his request for attorney fees for the eighty hours it took to "write" the brief, Lane submitted a list of over 200 legal sources to the court. In doing so, Lane attempted to have the court believe he researched and relied on each of these sources in writing the brief. These circumstances only support the conclusion Lane endeavored to deceive the court.

The trial court properly considered several factors in reducing the award of attorney fees. These factors included: the time necessarily spent; the difficulty of handling and importance of the issues; the responsibility assumed and results obtained; the standing and experience of the attorney in the profession; and the customary charges for similar service.

In many cases a fee application may not necessarily be a precise measure of the time an attorney spent on a particular case. Ethics concerns are not unavoidably raised where the court reduces the attorney fee award merely reflecting considerations that do not bring into question the attorney's honesty or integrity in submitting the fee application. On the other hand, although ethics is not a matter of degree of misstatement-any knowing misstatement to the court being unethical-the nature and depth of Lane's misrepresentation speaks of knowing deception. The record before us amply supports the conclusion Lane's conduct rises to the level of intent to deceive. We conclude the record supports the Commission's findings that Lane charged a clearly excessive fee in the Sicard case.

Discipline

In determining the proper sanction, we consider the particular facts and circumstances of each case. Among the factors we give weight to are the need for deterrence, protection of the public, maintenance of the reputation of the Bar as a whole, and the violator's fitness to continue to practice law. We also consider any aggravating or mitigating circumstances.

One such aggravating circumstance is a lawyer's prior disciplinary history. Lane has once before faced attorney disciplinary proceedings. In 1997, the Commission sanctioned Lane for failing to respond to an inquiry. He was publicly reprimanded for conduct prejudicial to the administration of justice and conduct adversely reflecting on his fitness to practice law.

A mitigating factor to consider is Lane's recognition of some wrongdoing. Lane filed "Respondent's Statement" with this court. Although not evidence, we will treat this statement as a supplemental brief. Lane stated,

I can accept that my behavior was the result of bad judgment, ignorance, even stupidity or carelessness, or sloppiness, or any number of things, such as laziness, negligence, arrogance, indolence, pettiness, or just plain old incompetence....

Lane asserted he did not intend to deceive the court and cited his reputation for honesty. In support of this contention, several character witnesses testified on Lane's behalf at the hearing before the Commission. Despite Lane's statements to the court, he still does not appear to comprehend the wrongfulness of his actions. In requesting excessive and unreasonable attorney fees for a brief he did not write, Lane was not negligent, or even reckless. Rather, more seriously, he intended to deceive. Lane's purported acknowledgment of misconduct fails to recognize the full extent of his wrongdoing.

Mitigating factors alone do not overcome our responsibility to the public and to the legal profession. Though Lane offered evidence of difficult personal circumstances, this does not excuse his unethical conduct. ...[W}e conclude in cases of this type, fairness and justice require discipline be imposed to deter future misconduct, protect the public, and maintain the reputation of the bar as a whole. We conclude a six-month license suspension is warranted. We therefore suspend Lane's license to practice law in the State of Iowa, with no possibility of reinstatement for a period of six months from the date of the filing of this opinion.

* * * * * * * * * * * * * *

1. The court in Lane recognized Lane's "difficult personal circumstances" but stated that the circumstances would "not excuse his unethical conduct". Distinguish excusing unethical conduct from mitigating punishment despite unethical conduct.

2. What was Lane's responsibilities under the model rules of professional conduct in light of his personal circumstances?

****

In the Matter of Darrell Lester Diggs
344 S.C. 397 (S.C. 2001)

We suspend Darrell Lester Diggs ("Diggs") from the practice of law for 90 days for supplying incorrect information on his CLE compliance report.

Factual/Procedural Background

Diggs admits he submitted incorrect information to the Commission on Continuing Legal Education ("Commission") on his CLE compliance report, which he signed and had notarized. Specifically, on December 29, 1997, Diggs submitted a CLE compliance report claiming 7.5 hours of credit for CLEs that were to occur on January 10, 1998, and January 23, 1998. On January 2, 1998, the Commission advised Diggs he could not claim CLE credit for courses he planned to attend in the future, and he should reexecute the report once the CLE hours had been properly earned. Diggs reexecuted the report, which still claimed credit for the January 10, 1998, and January 23, 1998, seminars. The Commission selected Diggs' compliance report randomly for attendance verification. The sponsor of the January 10, 1998, seminar informed the Commission he had no record of Diggs' attendance.

Diggs admitted by letter that he did not attend the legal ethics seminar due to alleged extenuating circumstances, even though he registered and pre-paid for the seminar. According to Diggs, he planned to attend the Columbia CLE, but he did not realize the seminar was only two hours. He was under the mistaken belief the CLE was being held via satellite at Aiken Technical College and it would last most of the day. When he arrived at Aiken Technical College, he realized the seminar was scheduled live at the law school. Diggs drove to Columbia and when he arrived, the two hour ethics CLE was completed. According to Diggs, he believed at the time he traveled to the CLE that he would be able to claim the hours even though the seminar was over. At the time he filed his CLE compliance report, he did not think a late arrival to a CLE was a basis to nullify the hours.

Diggs refiled his application for CLE credit, omitting the January 10, 1998, seminar and adding a February 20, 1998, seminar. He also re-signed the report and had it notarized.

On September 11, 1998, the Commission served Diggs with a Notice of Filing of Formal Charges, which alleged Diggs violated Rule 7 of the Rules of Lawyer Disciplinary Enforcement,

Rule 413, SCACR, and the Rules of Professional Conduct, Rule 407, SCACR. Diggs filed an Answer on October 14, 1998, admitting he committed misconduct with respect to his CLE requirements, but denying those allegations made out a case of attorney misconduct.

Diggs argues that certain rules are inapplicable to his disciplinary matter because they concern the representation of clients, and no clients were involved. He acknowledges his original CLE compliance report contained incorrect information. Specifically, that he attended a January 10, 1998, seminar when he never had the opportunity to sign the attendance roll at the seminar. According to Diggs, "I point out that having made an effort to attend (arriving shortly after its conclusion), having preregistered for and paid for the seminar, I reasonably believed that I could claim credit." According to his Reply, Diggs does not think claiming credit for a CLE he did not attend was wrong, he thinks his only mistake was not signing the roll. Diggs states: "In retrospect, I am not so sure that I had, at that time, instant consideration of my failure to sign the roll on January 10 th. Also in retrospect, I may have compared my situation with lawyers, who largely without impunity [sic], travel to a seminar, arrive before it actually begins, sign the attendance roll, and leave without actually participating." Diggs claims he would consent to a private reprimand in this matter if the Commission found it desirable to use his case "to send a message to attorneys that honesty-in-fact is the gravaman of compliance in the annual reports ..."

On November 18, 1998, a hearing was held before a subpanel of the Commission. The subpanel recommended a public reprimand, but did not direct Diggs to pay for the costs incurred by the Commission in this matter. Both Disciplinary Counsel and Diggs filed exceptions. On September 29, 2000, the full panel adopted the subpanel report and recommended a public reprimand. The following factors were considered as mitigation by the full panel: (1) Diggs has been practicing law for eighteen years with no apparent prior record of difficulties from a grievance perspective; (2) he candidly admitted wrong doing in this matter; and (3) he cooperated in all aspects of the investigation. The full panel concluded as a matter of law Diggs violated: (1) Rule 408, SCACR, which requires mandatory attendance at CLEs; (2) Rule 407, SCACR, which prohibits engaging in conduct tending to pollute the administration of justice or to bring the courts or legal profession into disrepute or conduct demonstrating an unfitness to practice law; (3) Rule 3.3 of Rule 407, which provides that a lawyer shall not knowingly make a false statement of material fact or law to a tribunal; and (4) Rule 8.4(a) of Rule 407, which prohibits an attorney from engaging in conduct involving dishonesty, fraud, deceit, or misrepresentation.

The authority to discipline attorneys and the manner in which the discipline is given rests entirely with this Court. In an attorney disciplinary proceeding, this Court is not bound by the findings made by the panel of the Commission on Lawyer Conduct or by the Commission itself. However, these findings are entitled to great weight. Therefore, this Court may make its own findings of fact and conclusions of law in an attorney disciplinary proceeding. Furthermore, an attorney disciplinary violation must be proven by clear and convincing evidence. Disciplinary Counsel argues the full panel should have recommended a sanction harsher than a public reprimand, given the level of Diggs' misconduct proven by the clear and convincing evidence standard. We agree.

Diggs has violated several Rules of Professional Conduct. First, Diggs knowingly made a false statement of material fact or law to a tribunal in violation of the Rules of Professional Conduct. Second, Diggs has engaged in conduct involving dishonesty, fraud, deceit, and misrepresentation in violation of Rule 8.4(d) of the Rules of Professional Conduct. The sanction recommended by the subpanel and full panel was insufficient, given the nature of the misconduct. The authority to determine the appropriate sanction for attorney misconduct rests solely with this Court. A sentence harsher than a public reprimand is warranted for submitting a false sworn document to a tribunal. Therefore, Diggs is suspended from the practice of law for 90 days.

Truthful representations on CLE compliance reports are essential to the successful operation of the South Carolina CLE program. Our CLE program operates on an honor system. The Commission does not check the accuracy of every attorney's CLE compliance report. The Commission audits the accuracy of approximately 2% of the CLE compliance reports. In order for the CLE program to be successful, and provide the public with competent, educated attorneys, South Carolina attorneys must complete the required number of CLE hours. Diggs argues it is a common practice for attorneys to receive full CLE credit for seminars when they leave early. Diggs also claims attorneys receive CLE credit when they just pay the CLE registration fee, show up to sign the roll, and leave. We emphasize that any attorney who provides false information on a notarized CLE compliance report commits a false swearing to a tribunal, which constitutes perjury.

The Court does not consider the fact Diggs eventually complied with the CLE requirements as mitigation because such compliance is required for an attorney to continue practicing law. Furthermore, if Diggs continued to practice law during the time when he was not in compliance with the CLE requirements, he practiced without being properly approved by the Commission, and engaged in the unauthorized practice of law. We, therefore, suspend Diggs from the practice of law for 90 days.

Based on the foregoing, we hereby: (1) suspend Diggs from the practice of law for 90 days commencing on the date of filing of this decision; and (2) find Diggs responsible for $193.50, the cost incurred by the Commission in this matter.

****

Questions:

1. Lawyer registered for a continuing legal education program that began at 9:00 a.m. on Thursday ending at 5p.m. and reconvening the following Friday at 9:00 a.m. and ending at 4:00 p.m. the following Friday. Both days included a lunch period of one hour during which time there was a sponsored lecture. Lawyer attended all sessions and was at the program both days. When completing his application for credit, lawyer certified that he was entitled to 15 hours; 8 hours on Thursday and 7 hours on Friday. Has Lawyer violated the model rules of professional conduct?

2. What if Lawyer failed to attend the sponsored lunch lectures on either Thursday or Friday, merely taking an one hour lunch break alone each day. Would Lawyer be entitled

to 15 hours credit without violating the model rules of professional conduct?

3. What if Lawyer attended the session all day Thursday. Planning to return the following Friday, lawyer completed the application for 15 hours. However, upon returning to his office on Thursday evening, he read a message from the court ordering him to appear to an emergency show cause hearing at 8:00 a.m. Friday. Has Lawyer violated the model rules of professional conduct?

****

The People of the State of Colorado v. Parsley
109 P.3d 1060 (Colo. 2005)

Upon conclusion of a sanctions hearing, the Presiding Disciplinary Judge disbarred Respondent Jeffrey A. Parsley (Registration No. 8069) from the practice of law, effective April 10, 2005. Respondent was also ordered to pay the costs incurred in conjunction with this proceeding. It was established through the entry of default that Respondent knowingly made material false statements in applying for a loan. Thereby, he engaged in a scheme to fraudulently obtain $180,000. This conduct constitutes a felony under federal and state law. Accordingly, Respondent violated Colo. RPC 8.4(b) (commission of a criminal act that reflects adversely on the lawyer's honesty, trustworthiness or fitness as a lawyer in other respects), 8.4(c) (conduct involving dishonesty, fraud, deceit or misrepresentation), and C.R.C.P. 251.5(b) (conduct that violates the criminal laws of this state or ... the United States). Disbarment is the presumptive sanction for the commission of a serious crime involving dishonesty. The Judge found a number of aggravating factors, including prior discipline, a dishonest and selfish motive, substantial experience in the practice of law, and indifference to making restitution. Respondent did not appear or present any evidence in mitigation.

As established by default, Respondent knowingly made material false statements in applying for a loan, and thereby fraudulently received $180,000. Respondent's conduct constitutes a felony under federal and state law. Disbarment is the presumed sanction for a lawyer who commits a serious crime involving dishonesty. As Respondent did not answer the Complaint or participate in the Sanctions Hearing, there is no evidence of mitigation. Under these circumstances, what is the appropriate sanction? Upon review of the case file, the ABA *Standards for Imposing Lawyer Sanctions* (1991 & Supp.1992), and the relevant Colorado Supreme Court case law, the Court finds that disbarment is the appropriate sanction.

The Complaint contains all factual details. In summary, Respondent applied for and received a $180,000 loan from Equity Mortgage based upon fraud and misrepresentation. On July 20, 2001, Respondent executed the loan paperwork, including a Deed of Trust. In doing so, he secured the loan with real property in Boulder County ("the Boulder property" or "the property"). Before and during the loan closing, Respondent represented that he held fee simple title to the property. For example, he prepared a Title Commitment to prove ownership. Respondent, however, did not own the property, and did not have the authority to offer it as security for the loan. Rather, his parents held title to the property, and they had already encumbered it with a "reverse mortgage" in the face amount of $232,875. Respondent did not inform Equity Mortgage of the existing mortgage, and allowed Equity Mortgage to believe it had obtained a first position mortgage. In addition to the Deed of Trust, Respondent executed a number of other fraudulent documents, which he certified to be true and upon which the lender relied in approving the loan. Thus, Respondent received the loan proceeds ($180,000) based upon fraud and misrepresentation.

Respondent knew at the closing that Equity Mortgage planned to sell Respondent's mortgage to Flagstar Bank, which is insured by the Federal Deposit Insurance Corporation ("FDIC"). Equity Mortgage did so. When Respondent defaulted on the loan, the note holder hired a lawyer to collect the money owed. Upon completion of a title search, the lawyer discovered that the Boulder property did not belong to Respondent. As a result, the lawyer also discovered that the Title Commitment falsely stated that Respondent was vested in fee simple title to the Boulder property.

These facts constitute professional misconduct on the following grounds: Colo. RPC 8.4(b) (commission of a criminal act that reflects adversely on the lawyer's honesty, trustworthiness, or fitness as a lawyer in other respects); Colo. RPC 8.4(c) (conduct involving dishonesty, fraud, deceit or misrepresentation); and C.R.C.P. 251.5(b) (conduct which violates the criminal laws of this state or ... the United States). While Respondent has not been convicted in a state or federal court for his misconduct, such is not required before addressing these matters in disciplinary proceedings. C.R.C.P. 251.5; *People v. Morley,* 725 P.2d 510, 514 (Colo.1986) (conviction of criminal offense is not a condition precedent to attorney disciplinary proceedings involving the offense).

The ABA *Standards for Imposing Lawyer Sanctions* (1991 & Supp.1992) ("ABA *Standards"*) and Colorado Supreme Court case law are the authorities for selecting and imposing sanctions for lawyer misconduct. The appropriate sanction depends upon the facts and circumstances of each case.

Under ABA *Standard* 5.11 "[d]isbarment is generally appropriate when a lawyer engages in serious criminal conduct a necessary element of which includes ... false swearing, misrepresentation, fraud, extortion, misappropriation, or theft...." Colorado Supreme Court decisions are in accord with ABA *Standard* 5.11. We have previously held that conduct constituting a felony and evidencing dishonesty may result in disbarment. This is especially true when the conduct is intentional, involves a dishonest motive, and is coupled with previous discipline.

As set forth in the Complaint and established by default, Respondent committed both federal and state crimes with respect to the loan. In knowingly making false statements to an FDIC-insured institution for the purpose of influencing action on the loan, Respondent violated 18 U.S.C. § 1014. This crime is punishable by a fine of up to $1,000,000 and/or a term of imprisonment up to 30 years. In knowingly obtaining the bank's money by deception, Respondent violated C.R.S. § 18–4–401 (theft), a Class 3 Felony. For disciplinary purposes, the term "serious crime" is defined to include any felony. C.R.C.P. 251.20(e)(1). Therefore, the Court finds that Respondent's conduct constituted serious federal and state crimes. Respondent's conduct also evidenced dishonesty, because his actions involved a conscious effort to deceive.

Accordingly, disbarment is the presumptive sanction for Respondent's misconduct. However, disbarment is not mandated. Before determining the appropriate sanction, ABA *Standard* 3.0 directs the Court to examine the following factors:

(1) the duty violated;
(2) the mental state of the lawyer;
(3) the injury or potential injury caused; and
(4) the aggravating and mitigating evidence.

Duties Violated

Respondent had a duty to deal honestly and openly with the lender and underwriters on the loan. Instead, Respondent used his imprimatur as a lawyer in good standing to persuade the underwriter that he was a worthy credit risk and that he indeed owned the Boulder property. Attorneys are officers of the court and pledge to uphold the law. Consequently, they must adhere to high moral and ethical standards.

Mental State

While no testimony was offered in this regard, the Complaint establishes that prior to Respondent's loan application, he was going through a divorce "resulting in emotional and financial distress and hardship." The Court previously found in its Report re: Petition for Immediate Suspension (entered on June 22, 2004) that Respondent had lost over $200,000 in bad investments and admittedly need more funds to meet his obligations. While these facts provide an explanation for Respondent's actions, they also tend to show that he knowingly deceived the lender to assure loan approval.

Injury Caused

Respondent unquestionably obtained a loan based upon false pretenses. Although Respondent serviced the loan for a little over one year, he then defaulted. Upon Respondent's default, the lender was left with little recourse in recovering its funds, as it could not foreclose on the Boulder property. This fact alone demonstrates serious injury to the lender. Respondent also caused injury to the legal profession, by using his status as a lawyer to obtain the loan on false pretenses and thereby undermining confidence in the profession.

Aggravating and Mitigating Evidence

Matters In Aggravation

Prior Discipline

Respondent has previously been disciplined for attorney misconduct. In 1992, the Supreme Court issued a letter of admonition for neglect of a legal matter with respect to a single client. In 2000, the Supreme Court suspended Respondent for 90 days for neglect of a legal matter, failure to provide competent representation, and conduct prejudicial to the administration of justice with respect to a single client.

Dishonest or Selfish Motive

Respondent engaged in a conscious effort to deceive in order to personally benefit from loan proceeds in the amount of $180,000. Respondent applied for and obtained the loan by misrepresenting first that he owned the Boulder property in fee simple and second that the lender would receive a first position mortgage. This conduct was dishonest. Further, Respondent received the proceeds of this loan to meet personal obligations. Thus, Respondent chose to carry out a scheme of misrepresentation for his own monetary benefit.

Substantial Experience in the Practice of Law

Respondent has been practicing law for nearly 30 years and therefore should be well aware of his professional responsibilities as an attorney. Experience in the law, however, is not required to understand every citizen's obligation to refrain from illegal conduct.

Indifference to Making Restitution

Respondent has not made restitution. Nevertheless, there is no evidence in the record to show that his failure to do so is the result of indifference rather than a lack of ability. Therefore, the PDJ finds no aggravation for this factor.

Matters In Mitigation

Respondent failed to appear for the Sanctions Hearing. As a result, there are no mitigating factors supported by the record.

Conclusion

Upon consideration of the duties breached, Respondent's mental state, the injuries caused, the aggravating factors present, and the absence of mitigating factors, the Court concludes that the gravity of Respondent's conduct substantially outweighs any justification for deviation from the presumptive sanction of disbarment.

While the conduct in this case involves a single loan, this was not a simple act of deception. Rather, Respondent engaged in a fairly sophisticated scheme to defraud a lender and thereby obtain a large amount of money (approximately $180,000). It has been established by default that Respondent caused a number of fraudulent documents to be drafted, including a title commitment. Respondent executed his scheme over an extended period of time and involved innocent parties, including his own parents. In addition, Respondent was the only person to benefit from the deception, as he received all the funds disbursed. A number of parties and the financial system as a whole were directly affected by Respondent's actions. Respondent's dire financial position cannot excuse his scheme to defraud or ameliorate the sanction for such conduct.

Although Respondent's actions did not directly concern the practice of law, they harmed a number of parties, as well as the legal profession and respect for the law in general. The rules governing lawyer discipline support disbarment for serious criminal conduct involving false swearing, misrepresentation, fraud, or theft. While Respondent has not been convicted of any offense beyond a reasonable doubt, proof of commission of such a crime by clear and convincing evidence, as established by default, is sufficient for disciplinary purposes. Respondent's breach of integrity is simply unacceptable for a member of the legal profession. The Court therefore finds that disbarment is the appropriate sanction.

IN THE NEWS:

"A disbarred South Florida attorney who is serving a hefty prison term for masterminding the state's biggest swindle says some lawyers at his former Fort Lauderdale law firm, but not others, had knowledge of his wrongdoing. ... Scott Rothstein says he himself lied to investors about nonexistent structured settlements in sex-abuse litigation against billionaire Jeffrey Epstein, in order to persuade them to "invest" in fictitious settlements resulting in an ...estimated $1.2 billion fraud for which Rothstein is now serving a 50-year sentence."

For more see: Imprisoned Ex-Attorney Scott Rothstein: Other Lawyers Had Some Knowledge of State's Biggest Swindle Posted Jun 27, 2012 11:25 AM CDT By Martha Neil at
http://www.abajournal.com/news/article/imprisoned_ex-attorney_scott_rothstein_other_lawyers_had_some_knowledge_of_/

****

REVIEW QUESTIONS

1. Clyde, Attorney's client, asked Attorney to write a letter recommending Client's daughter for admission to the bar. Clyde has been Attorney's client for more than ten years. However, Attorney has never met daughter and knows nothing about her qualifications to be admitted to the bar. Client tells Attorney that a letter of recommendation would mean the world to him, suggesting that a refusal to write such a letter could have a detrimental effect on their business relationship. Client assures you that his daughter, "while she has faced some major obstacles in her life, including drug addiction, is the salt of the earth".   What would Attorney be required to do under the model rules?

2. Attorney is licensed to practice law in the jurisdiction but has never practiced law. Attorney has instead worked as an investment broker.   After more than a decade as a broker, Attorney was accused of participating in an investment fraud scheme that bilked hundreds of investors out of millions of dollars. Some of the investors filed a class action lawsuit against Attorney, alleging in part, that Attorney had masterminded the scheme and had benefited financially from the fraud.   The plaintiffs won their class action lawsuit and Attorney was ordered to repay the plaintiffs based on their individual losses. Is Attorney subject to discipline?

3. Two law graduates were arrested when they were roommates in undergraduate school. Adjudication of both their cases was deferred pending successful completion of conditions of

their probation. Both graduates successfully completed the conditions and their cases were dismissed. Law Graduate One applies for admission to the state bar but neglects to inform the bar of the arrest, even though the application for admission asked if he had ever been arrested and convicted of a crime. Graduate Two did not apply for admissions to the state's bar, however, he had similarly failed to reveal the arrest on his application to law school. Are the two graduates, or either of them subject to discipline under the model rules of professional conduct?

4. During election season, well-known liberal attorney was asked his opinion about the candidate for county prosecutor. Attorney responded that the candidate was an ass, who, if elected would set the county judicial system back fifty years. Is attorney subject to discipline.

5. Alice Attorney was dating Lov R Mann, a lawyer who Alice had met while in law school. The two dated for more than three years, when on Valentine's Day, Alice expecting an engagement ring, got notice that Mann was marrying someone else. Alice reported Mann's conduct to the state bar. In response to the charge, Mann replied that he had wanted to marry Alice but that he wanted children and Alice refused to have children. In fact, he added in his response, she had become pregnant on at least one occasion but had chosen to have an abortion. Was Alice required to file the information with the state bar officials? Did Mann's response subject him to discipline?

6. Can a lawyer be disciplined solely for the failure to report the improper conduct of another lawyer?[119]

7. Is a Lawyer required to report his own ethical indiscretions to the proper state authority under model rule 8?

8. Lawyer's wife was diagnosed with cancer and given a few short months to live. Doctors inform Lawyer of a test being conducted in Sweden that might help wife live for a period up to five years. The cost to enroll in the test is exorbitant but Lawyer agrees to pay the money. Unfortunately, wife's medical treatment to date has exhausted the couple's savings so Lawyer takes the needed funds from a Client trust fund with the intent to return the money as soon as practicable. During a routine audit of the firm's accounts, the theft is uncovered and reported to the firm's executive committee. The committee investigates the charge against Lawyer who admits to the theft and explains the extraordinary circumstances that lead him to commit such an act. The executive committee places Lawyer on a six months leave of absence with pay, refuses to accept his resignation and votes to lend Lawyer enough money to repay the Client fund. Are the Lawyers on the executive committee subject to discipline?[120]

9. While a freshman in undergraduate school, Law Graduate was arrested and charged with possession of a controlled substance. Adjudication of his case was deferred pending successful completion of 200 hours of community service. Once Graduate completed the service, the possession charge was dismissed. Four years after the possession case was dismissed, and while a student in law school, Graduate reported on his application for admission to the bar that he had never been charged with a crime. The question on the application read, "Have you ever been arrested or convicted of a crime"? Does Graduate's response violate model rules of professional conduct?

---

[119] *See In re Himmel, 125 Ill 2d 531, 127 Ill. Dec. 708, 533 N.E.2d 790 (1988)*
[120] *See Board of Overseers of the Bar v Warren, 34 A. 3d 1103 (Me. 2011).*

10. Last week State Bar distributed judicial evaluation forms to attorneys for their assessment of judges' performance in office. Lawyer received a form for Judge Thibodeaux, a judge that Lawyer regular practices before. Lawyer has not been fond of the judge since they were in law school together. Lawyer's completed the evaluation form, scoring Judge Thibodeaux as one of the least qualified judges on the bench. In doing so, has Lawyer violated the Model Rules?

11. A first-year associate joined a law firm where she is supervised by one of the founding and most senior partners. The partner is over 80 years old and is very knowledgeable and highly respected among the bench and bar. He teaches the first year associate some brilliant trial tactics. However, sometimes the partner speaks in a language that he made up, walks through the office in his underwear, and appears moody. The firm's other partners ignore these antics and call them "insignificant displays of aging". Since they respect him so much for his contribution to the firm over the years, they refuse to take action. Should the associate report the elderly attorney's behavior to disciplinary authorities?

12. Attorney Sue lnnron observed another associate in her firm shredding what she believes were incriminating client documents. The other attorney is unaware Sue observed her. The client in question is one of the firm's biggest and the firm often goes to great lengths to please this client to retain the business. What <u>must</u> Sue do to comply with the model rules? What <u>should</u> Sue do to comply with the model rules?

JUDICIAL CONDUCT

PROFESSIONAL CONDUCT FOR SOME JUDGES AND JUDICIAL CANDIDATES

Judges have an important role in the system of justice.[121] Symbolically, it is the judge who is viewed as the guardian of basic principles of justice. Sworn to be impartial and unbiased, the judge's principal role is to ensure that justice is done. The public perception of the judge directly correlates with their respect for the judicial system.[122] The ABA Judicial Code and those of the various states provide guidance for how the judge, and in some cases, the judicial candidate must behave to comply with minimal standards of conduct.[123]

The codes cover a myriad of areas that the judge must be mindful of including (1) exercising legal discretion, (2) exercising administrative responsibilities so that court personnel nor facilities are misused, (3) maintaining the proper court decorum, (4) avoiding impropriety and the appearance of impropriety, (5) avoiding ex parte communications except where permitted by law or agreement, (6) conduct off-the-bench including speaking engagements and organization memberships, (7) proper maintainance of business activities, (8) participation in civic and charitable activities, and (9) independence from undue and improper influences[124]

Judges have a duty to uphold the independence and impartiality of the judiciary and the judicial system,[125] avoid impropriety and the appearance of impropriety at all times.[126]

Judges should perform their responsibilities competently, diligently, civilly and without partiality.[127] The burden of meeting these standards lies with the judge. In many cases, judges are elected by the general electorate who may not have enough information to determine the competence of the judicial candidate.[128] Therefore, the burden of accountability may lie with the judge, the candidate and the bar.

The judge's primary responsibility is to her duties as judge and she must conduct her extrajudicial duties to avoid conflicts with her judicial responsibilities.[129] The judge is expected to ensure that her personal and business activities conform to the highest of ethical standards.

---

[121] See Cynthia Gray and Frances Kahn Zemans, Instructing Judges: Ethical Experience and Educational Technique, 58 Law and Contemporary Problems 305 (1996)

[122] Shira J. Goodman, The *Danger Inherent In The Public Perception That Justice Is For Sale*, 60 Drake L. Rev. 807 (2012) *Also See* American Bar Association, *Perceptions of the U.S. Justice System*, http://www.americanbar.org/content/dam/aba/migrated/marketresearch/PublicDocuments/perceptions_of_justice_system_1999_1st_half.authcheckdam.pdf

[123] ABA Model Code of Judicial Conduct, Preamble and Scope. Also See Preface

[124] Supra, note 58 at 307 identifying the Keck Judicial Conduct and Ethics Curriculum, slightly modified in this text

[125] ABA Model Code of Judicial Conduct Canon 1

[126] Id.

[127] See generally, Alex Kozinski, The Real Issues of Judicial Ethics, 32 Hofstra Law Rev 1095 (2004) where author discusses many challenges a judge faces, particularly in those cases where the judge believes that following the law will cause an unjust result

[128] ABA Model Code of Judicial Conduct, Canon 2

[129] ABA Model Code of Judicial Conduct, Canon 3

In recent years, certain advocacy groups have called on the United States Supreme Court justices to be bound by the ABA Model Code of Judicial Conduct. The court has rejected the demand, claiming instead, that they follow an internal code of conduct. For some, that internal code has been deficient in preventing the justices from acting unethically and leaves no process for discipline.

IN THE NEWS:

Should United States Supreme Court Justices be governed by a Code of Judicial Ethics?

A group of democratic congressmen think so and introduced a bill in 2013 which will hold the Supreme Court Justices to the same Ethical Code of Conduct as United States Judges. The bill is in response to potential partisan conflicts of interest that may have arisen by actions from the Supreme Court Justices or their spouses, notably Justice Thomas and Justice Scalia. Currently, the justices of the United States Supreme Court are not bound by any formal judicial code of ethics.

For the full story see: Supreme Court Ethics Act Proposed In Response To Controversial Behavior By Justices Scalia, Thomas, The Huffington Post | By Nick Wing Posted: 08/01/2013 1:45 pm EDT | Updated: 08/01/2013 7:06 pm EDT
http://www.huffingtonpost.com/2013/08/01/supreme-court-ethics-act_n_3689351.html

6.16.14 Update: On 9.13.2013 the bill was referred to the Subcommittee on Courts, Intellectual Property and the Internet. Govtrack.us gives the bill a 6% chance of being enacted.
https://www.govtrack.us/congress/bills/113/hr2902

****

Questions:

1. Should United States Supreme Court justices be subject to the Judicial Code of Conduct?

2. Canon 2 of the Code of Conduct mandates that "A judge should not allow family, social, political, financial, or other relationships to influence judicial conduct or judgment. A judge should neither lend the prestige of the judicial office to advance the private interests of the judge or others nor convey or permit others to convey the impression that they are in a special position to influence the judge." Justice Antonin Scalia (75, an appointee of Ronald Reagan) and Justice Clarence Thomas (63, an appointee of George H.W. Bush) have attended exclusive events at private resorts orchestrated by the billionaire oil barons Charles and David Koch, which the brothers use to advance their partisan political agenda. The invitation to the Koch Brothers event stated in part:

> "Twice a year our network meets to review strategies for combating the multitude
> of public policies that threaten to destroy America as we know it. ...

In Palm Springs, we will assemble an exceptional group of leaders.along with a strong line-up of speakers. Together, we will develop strategies to counter the most severe threats facing our free society and outline a vision of how we can foster a renewal of American free enterprise and prosperity."

3. Do United States Supreme Court justices violate their ethical mandates when they attend these kinds of events? Why or why not?[130]

****

In the News:

It may be difficult to imagine that judges would abuse their office by ruining the lives of teenaged students who come before them on often minor offenses. In Harris County and throughout Texas school-aged children are subject to tickets for violating some rule of conduct at school. The tickets subject the students to court adjudications that could stay on their record well into adulthood.

But that's nothing compared to what happened to Hillary Transue, 14, charged with creating a fake, humorous Myspace page about her school's vice principal; Justin Bodnar, 12, who was charged with cursing at another student's mother and Ed Kenzakoski, 17, who evidently did nothing at all.

For these students, victimized by corrupt judge Mark A. Ciavarella in Pennsylvania, were all pronounced guilty, shackled and sentenced to months of detention in a cockroach-infested jail. Some of these children spent their entire high-school ensnared by the juvenile justice system.

Judge Ciavarella, who sentenced around 3,000 children in a similar manner, was later sentenced himself to 28 years in prison for financial crimes related to his acceptance of $2.2 million as a finder's fee for the construction of a for-profit facility in which to house these so-called delinquents.

Read more at: *Corrupt 'Kids for Cash' judge ruined more than 2,000 lives* By Larry Getlen, http://nypost.com/2014/02/23/film-details-teens-struggles-in-state-detention-in-payoff-scandal/ February 23, 2014 | 1:41am

---

****

---

[130] Consider Emily Bazelon, Sounding Off, Legal Affairs, November/December 2002 where the writer states that "Thurgood Marshall denounced Supreme Court decisions restricting prisoners' rights. Warren Burger advocated for prison reform, appearing on *Nightline* and taking an influential group of Americans to visit Scandinavian prisons. Harry Blackmun discussed the opinion he wrote in favor of abortion rights in *Roe v. Wade*. Lewis Powell expressed regrets about having cast the swing vote in *Bowers v. Hardwick*, the decision that upheld the prosecution of a gay man under Georgia's sodomy law. Sandra Day O'Connor, a swing vote in many death-penalty cases, made news when she said that innocent people were likely being executed and questioned whether poor defendants were getting decent representation from court-appointed lawyers."

Questions:

1. Lawyer pleads guilty to bribing a state district court judge, by paying over $5,000 in cash and services, including washing the judge's car. Lawyer testifies that in exchange for value, judge granted favorable rulings on the Lawyer's cases that came before him. However, the only cases included changing a defendant's sentence from three years in prison to four years probation, leniency at sentencing and less restrictive conditions of release, all things within the discretion of the district court judge. What would the judge have to argue to avoid discipline by the state bar?[131]

2. Judge participated in a plot along with lawyers from his prior law firm to benefit their criminal defense client. The judge was paid $3,500 to accept and help elicit a false confession from a man on a gun charge. The law firm client, who was guilty of the offense had a lengthy criminal record and would have faced a stiff prison sentence if convicted. Under the conspiracy, the confessor would likely have received probation. Discuss the various actions of judicial misconduct and your recommended sanction, if any.[132]

****

IN THE NEWS

It is no secret that law schools and their alumni benefit from the school's reputation. Among the things that schools do to enhance their reputation are to bring celebrated scholars and speakers to campus, and often to hire judges to teach classes as adjunct faculty. Some challenge this practice as unethical, especially in those cases where the school that the judge works for is the subject of litigation and or when that litigation is pending before the judge's court.

A recent article in the National Law Journal discusses the issue. It states that "Law schools paid federal appeals judges thousands of dollars for lecturing or teaching full-time semesters that may go beyond what federal laws allow. Under federal law, active judges were barred from earning more than $26,955 off the bench during 2012…The law schools say that they are receiving a benefit from donors, reputation among students and prospective students and law school ranking voters. The law schools say that the students benefit from building of relationships, clerkships, expertise and understanding of what is expected from them in practice.

To find out more about the ethical dilemma that this scenario presents and the subject in general see: Law Schools Paid Judges Nearly $2M to Teach, Lecture in 2012 by Zoe Tillman, The National Law Journal, June 9, 2014 at http://www.nationallawjournal.com/id=1202656334413/Law-Schools-Paid-Judges-Nearly-%242M-to-Teach%2C-Lecture-in-2012#ixzz349m0tF6g

---

[131] See Guillermo Contreras, San Antonio lawyer bribed Bexar judge, my San Antonio, March 18, 2014 available at http://www.mysanantonio.com/news/local/article/San-Antonio-lawyer-bribed-Bexar-judge-5323573.php
[132] See James Queally, Former Essex County Prosecutor Clifford Minor disbarred by NJ Supreme Court, The Star Ledger, March 31, 2014

****

Questions:

1. While still hearing a case, Judge reports to news media that Defendant, a large corporation, had "proved, time and time again, to be inaccurate, misleading, evasive, and transparently false. ... the company has an institutional disdain for both the truth and for rules of law that lesser entities must respect. It is also a company whose senior management is not averse to offering specious testimony to support spurious defenses to claims of its wrongdoing." Is judge subject to discipline for violating the judicial code?[133]

2. In Narrowing the Nation's Power, Judge John T. Noonan, Jr. writes "It is the duty of lawyers to work for the reform of the law. It is their duty because lawyers best know its imperfections. Lawyers do not cease to have this duty when they become judges."[134] The book is critical of recent decisions of the United States Supreme Court as well as its anticipated rulings. Is Judge Noonan in violation of the Judicial Code's mandate that a judge avoid even the appearance of impropriety or of appearing biased?[135]

3. May a Judicial Official teach a course at a state university regarding the legislative process and, if so, are there any restrictions other than not discussing current or pending cases? If teaching is permitted, may the Judicial Official be compensated for teaching the class.[136]

4. If judges teach at a university are they compromised in their judgment? Must they recuse themselves from any case where the university is involved? If they fail to recuse themselves could they be subject to discipline?

****

The special temperament of Judges

Extreme cases of judicial misconduct negatively impact the public's perception of the justice system. In many cases the question is whether the accused party has violated the spirit, if not the letter, of the law. It seems reasonable to expect that one honored to serve as a judge would not mince words but would carry herself personally and professionally within the spirit of ethical rules. In *People v. Black* the California appeals court's opinion captured the essence of the ethical values of judicial codes.[137]

---

[133] See United States v Microsoft Corporation, 253 F.3d 34, 107 (2001)

[134] John T. Noonan, Jr., Narrowing the Nation's Power: The Supreme Court sides with the states (2002)

[135] Bazelon, supra note 129; and see Matthew Fogelson, narrowing the Nation's Power: The Supreme Court Sides with the States, by John T. Noonan, Jr., book report, 3 U Md L J of Race, Religiion, Gender and Class 167 (2003).

[136] See Connecticut Committee on Judicial Ethics, 2009-24 (july 27, 2009)

[137] (150 Cal. App. 2d 494, 500-01 (1957). In the book, Noonan is critical of the United States Supreme Court and writes "No defensible theory of the Constitution justifies the justices preferring their hunch to the work of the

"A judge should be temperate, attentive, patient, impartial. A judge should be courteous to counsel, especially to those who are young and inexperienced, and also to all others appearing or concerned in the administration of justice in the court."

"A judge may properly intervene during the trial of a case where this appears reasonably necessary in order to expedite proceedings, for clarification of any point, or to prevent injustice. ... Litigants, witnesses, and attorneys alike are entitled to have a court function as a court of justice in fact as well as in theory."

"In exercising the firmness necessary to the dignity and efficient conduct of court proceedings, a judge's attitude should not reflect undue impatience or severity toward either counsel, litigant, or witnesses."

"Justice should not be molded by the individual idiosyncrasies of those who administer it. A judge should adopt the usual and expected method of doing justice, and not seek to be extreme or peculiar in his [or her] judgments, or spectacular or sensational in the conduct of the court."

In Re Hecht
213 S.W.3d 547 (2006)

Special Court of Review Appointed by the Supreme Court.

This case focuses on whether the Texas Code of Judicial Conduct, the judicial "rules of the road," so to speak, prohibit a Texas state judge from speaking out favorably in behalf of a close friend nominated to the United States Supreme Court. This case hinges on the meaning of words in this Code and what words were spoken by the judge. This case involves a composite of two different political systems for the selection of judges. In Texas, we have an elective process, whereas in the federal system, we have a nomination-confirmation process.

We recognize at the outset a considerable hurdle must be overcome: the Texas Code is decidedly deficient in a pivotal area important in this case, that is, providing definitive meanings to words in the political arena, words such as "authorized," "endorsing," and "private interests." We are all familiar with certain axioms in particular disciplines, some of which capsulize the core of the undertaking. For example, in real estate, the appropriate axiom is "location, location, location." In music, "practice." In law, "definitions." The relevant provisions of the Texas Code, Canons 5(2) and 2B, quite candidly, lack definitive meaning.

The political processes offer a unique twist. The state judge is up for re-election and is in a political campaign. The state judge speaks of his friend, the nominee, whose nomination is

---

legislators. Judicial restraint is abandoned when they do." Himself a conservative, Noonan argues that recent supreme court decisions abandon the rights of individuals in favor of states rights.

pending before the Senate Judicial Committee of the United States Congress. In this federal process, the public expects a thorough examination of the background, qualifications, and experience of the nominee in public, and most assuredly, at the Senate committee hearings. The Senate committee fully intended to call the state judge as a witness during the confirmation hearings, and the state judge fully intended to testify to the same statements before the committee which are at issue here. No one claims such statements would have violated the Texas Code of Judicial Conduct. Had the confirmation proceeded as scheduled and the state judge testified, it is highly doubtful we would be considering any of these matters, anonymous complaint or not.

We also recognize the commission's approach and this Court's approach are substantially different. The commission, according to the evidence, assumed the Code prohibited endorsing and supporting, terms it used interchangeably, and proceeded to devote substantially all of its efforts to determining the penalty to be imposed. This Court performs a de novo review. We consider the evidence presented before us (which differs markedly in some respects from evidence presented to the commission), we review Canons 5(2) and 2B, with our starting point being the determination of the meaning of pivotal terms, such as "authorized," "endorsing," and "private interests" (rather than assuming certain of these terms can be used interchangeably), and we decide whether the judge's public statements violated Canons 5(2) and 2B.

II.

The Preamble to the Texas Code of Judicial Conduct provides:

Our legal system is based on the principle that an independent, fair and competent judiciary will interpret and apply the laws that govern us. The role of the judiciary is central to American concepts of justice and the rule of law. Intrinsic to all sections of this Code of Judicial Conduct are the precepts that judges, individually and collectively, must respect and honor the judicial office as a public trust and strive to enhance and maintain confidence in our legal system. The judge is an arbiter of facts and law for the resolution of disputes and a highly visible symbol of government under the rule of law. . . . The Code [of Judicial Conduct] is intended . . . to state basic standards which should govern the conduct of all judges and to provide guidance to assist judges in establishing and maintaining high standards of judicial and personal conduct.

Tex.Code Jud. Conduct, Preamble, reprinted in Tex. Gov't Code Ann., tit. 2, subtit. G app. B (Vernon 2005). The Preamble reminds us of the high ideals and noble principles this Court is called upon to apply. This case presents substantial issues of first impression. First, we must determine whether public statements of a judge supporting a nominee to the United States Supreme Court violate the Texas Code of Judicial Conduct, specifically Canons 2B and 5(2). If so, we must determine whether the Texas Code abridges the Petitioner's freedom of speech guaranteed by the First Amendment to the United States Constitution. However, because we conclude Petitioner did not violate the Canons, we do not address the constitutional question.

III.

The events leading to the public admonition revolve around President George W. Bush's nomination of Harriet Miers to the United States Supreme Court in October 2005 and statements of the Honorable Nathan Hecht, Texas Supreme Court Justice, (hereafter "Petitioner") to the news media concerning her nomination.

On October 14, the commission voted to initiate an investigation of Petitioner based on the October 12 complaint and, on its own motion, an article published on October 6 in The New York Times. On October 17, 2005, the State Commission on Judicial Conduct received a confidential complaint about Petitioner based on the October 10 article in the Texas Lawyer newspaper. The commission informed Petitioner of the investigation and requested that he answer a questionnaire about the news articles and his actions preceding and during Miers' nomination. Petitioner cooperated with the commission and provided detailed responses to the questions. Petitioner voluntarily appeared at a hearing before eight[6] members of the commission. The commission voted and issued its Public Admonition, containing its findings of fact and conclusions of law. The commission determined Petitioner violated Canons 2B and 5(2) of the Texas Code of Judicial Conduct. See Tex.Code Jud. Conduct, Canon 2B ("A judge shall not lend the prestige of judicial office to advance the private interests of the judge or others. . . ."), & Canon 5(2) ("A judge shall not authorize the public use of his or her name endorsing another candidate for any public office. . . . ").

Petitioner requested de novo review of the public admonition rendered by the commission. Texas Supreme Court Chief Justice Wallace Jefferson appointed, by random selection, this panel to the Special Court of Review to review the commission's decision. See Tex. Gov't Code Ann. § 33.034(c) (Vernon 2004). This Court subsequently conducted an evidentiary hearing. See id. § 33.034(e) (review "is by trial de novo as that term is used in the appeal of cases from justice to county court"). Following the presentation of evidence and arguments, the commission sought a public admonition, and Petitioner requested dismissal of the sanction imposed on him.

IV.

The parties entered into a written "Parties' Stipulations of Fact" (hereafter "Stipulation"). At the hearing before this Special Court of Review, the commission called one witness, Petitioner; the remainder of its presentation centered around documentary evidence, including news stories, public admonishments relative to other judges bearing generally on the two Canons at issue, several volumes of committee hearings involving the current Task Force on the Code of Judicial Conduct and its recommendations, several videos, and the Stipulation. The commission presented no expert testimony related to whether Petitioner violated the Code or whether the Code was constitutional under Republican Party v. White, 536 U.S. 765, 122 S.Ct. 2528, 153 L.Ed.2d 694 (2002).

Petitioner's testimony will be detailed below. In addition, Petitioner presented, without objection by the commission, the expert testimony of former Chief Justice Tom Phillips through his affidavit; the testimony of Judge Jim Parsons and Judge Monica Gonzalez; the expert testimony of Professor Geoffrey Hazard and Blake Tartt by stipulation; Senator Arlen Specter's oral deposition; official transcripts from numerous Senate confirmation hearings of past United States Supreme Court Justices; and copies of the Codes of Judicial Conduct from many states.

The evidence shows Petitioner and Miers became close friends beginning in 1976 when they practiced in the same law firm, Locke Purnell. Petitioner left the firm in 1981 to become a district court judge. He subsequently served on the appellate bench, first on the Fifth District Court of Appeals at Dallas, and then the Texas Supreme Court, his current position. It is undisputed that Petitioner's record is unblemished. The Stipulation recites that Petitioner "has never been sanctioned by the State Commission on Judicial Conduct."

Miers became head partner of Locke Purnell, and eventually became White House Counsel to President Bush. She also served as president of the State Bar of Texas and as a member of the Dallas City Council. Petitioner and Miers have remained close friends through the succeeding thirty-five years, including regularly attending the same church and going to dinners and social occasions together.

Besides being a long-time, close friend of Miers, Petitioner was also a friend of White House Deputy Chief of Staff, Karl Rove. On October 1, 2005, two days before Miers' nomination, Rove and Petitioner had a telephone conversation, and Rove told him Miers might be nominated to fill retiring Justice Sandra Day O'Connor's place on the Supreme Court. Rove asked Petitioner if he would agree to speak with Dr. James Dobson (the founder of Focus on the Family, a conservative religious organization that emphasizes family values) about Miers' faith. Petitioner agreed to speak to Dr. Dobson, and he told Rove he was willing to speak to the media about Miers as he considered himself one of the most knowledgeable people, if not the most knowledgeable person, about Miers' personal and professional beliefs and accomplishments.

Out of an abundance of caution, Petitioner consulted first with former Texas Supreme Court Chief Justice Tom Phillips, considered a legal scholar and knowledgeable and experienced with respect to the Code of Judicial Conduct. Petitioner also consulted with former Texas Supreme Court Justice Priscilla Owen, a friend with similar experience involving the Code of Judicial Conduct. Both assured Petitioner that the statements in question did not violate the Code.

Between Miers' nomination on October 3 and the announcement of her withdrawal on October 27, Petitioner responded to more than 120 requests for media interviews. Petitioner appeared on television news programs, and he was quoted or referenced in many newspaper and internet news articles. Petitioner's comments included discussions of his personal relationship with Miers, her professional background and accomplishments, her conservative political philosophy, her attendance and participation at an evangelical Christian church, and her pro-life and anti-abortion views. He expressed his opinion in a variety of ways that she would be a "great" Justice of the Supreme Court. Some news articles also reported that Petitioner said President Bush had known Miers for many years and that conservatives had no need to be concerned that she was an unknown entity. Petitioner was continuously identified as a close personal friend of Miers and as a Justice of the Texas Supreme Court.

Much of the commission's evidence consisted of media reports between October 3 and 27. The Texas Lawyer published an article on October 10, 2005 about Petitioner's and other present and former Texas Supreme Court Justices' participation in supporting the Miers nomination. Although Petitioner was never interviewed, The New York Times published an article on October 6, 2005. These were the only news articles presented at the commission's hearing.

Evidence of additional articles and interviews were presented before this Court. Rather than selecting "representative statements" from these sources, which are often redundant, and quoting them verbatim, we choose a more succinct method, excerpting from the commission's brief the primary statements it asserts violate Canons 2B and 5(2):

For the most part, Petitioner provided reporters and interviewers with factual information about Miers' background and experience, including information about her views on religion and abortion and his own personal relationship with her. However, beyond the factual information, Petitioner repeatedly expressed his opinion that the Miers' appointment was "great," "solid," "strong," and that after the American people had been given a chance to review her record, they were "going to herald this nomination as a good one." When asked about the opposition to Miers' nomination during an interview reported by the Washington Post, Petitioner replied that he believed that Miers' detractors were "going to be happy as clams" after they learned more about her. When asked by another interviewer about the need to prove the President's "case" in favor of the Miers' nomination, Petitioner agreed that a "case has to be made," but went on to claim that a "case has been made in Texas for the last 30-plus years. We think of her as a hero down here already." Petitioner went on to predict that during the confirmation process, Senators would be "convinced that this is the right person for the job." Tellingly, in one interview with an ABC news reporter, Petitioner expressly opined that Miers would be a "great justice." On a more personal note, Petitioner acknowledged publicly that he had a close personal relationship with Miers, and frequently spoke of his "admiration" for Miers, describing her in various interviews as being "remarkable," "charming," "gracious," "solid," "strong," "sterling," and "stellar."

Former Chief Justice Phillips, whose extensive curriculum vitae was admitted, furnished an affidavit in support of Petitioner's position.

Judge Jim Parsons testified he was a district judge in Palestine and a long time Democrat. He did not believe Canon 5(2)'s restrictions on endorsements applied outside partisan electoral politics, and he viewed the public statements about Miers' nomination as "an administration of justice issue," particularly at the level involving a nominee to the United States Supreme Court, not a matter of partisan politics.

Senator Arlen Specter, the Chairman of the Senate Judiciary Committee of the United States Congress, testified by deposition that the committee would have considered Miers' nomination to the United States Supreme Court had it not been withdrawn. If the Miers nomination had gone forward, his chief counsel would have recommended asking Petitioner to testify before the committee and the Senator would have honored this recommendation. Senator Specter testified that frequently, judges appear and testify voluntarily in hearings involving nominees to the United States Supreme Court. The Senator saw no difference between speaking at the committee hearing and speaking informally to the press. He also stated that had Miers' nomination gone forward, his interest in Petitioner's testimony would have been based on Petitioner's personal and deep knowledge of Miers' background, not his position as a Texas Supreme Court Justice.

The parties stipulated that Geoffrey C. Hazard, Jr., Professor of Law at the University of Pennsylvania Law School, would testify Petitioner's speech did not violate Canon 2B or 5(2) of the Texas Code of Judicial Conduct, and that [Petitioner] had a First Amendment right to engage in the speech which is subject of the censure by the State Commission on Judicial Conduct. He would further say that judges talk to the media and public about nominees to the federal bench, and he is not aware of any judge who has been sanctioned by a state or federal committee or by a court for making comments to the press or public about a nominee to the federal bench.

The commission further stipulated that Blake Tartt would testify:

[H]e is a former member of the Commission on Judicial Conduct, and a former president of the State Bar of Texas, and he has served on numerous ABA committees, which have vetted nominees for the federal bench, and in performing those tasks has frequently sought the comments of judges about the nominees. Many of these judges have made favorable comments in support of the nominees. . . .

V.

The Texas Constitution and Government Code do not set forth expressly the commission's burden of proof. The parties assert and we agree that the commission has the burden of proof and that the standard is by a preponderance of the evidence, as is applicable "to the trial of civil actions generally." Tex. Gov't Code Ann. § 33.034(f) (Vernon 2004); In re Davis, 82 S.W.3d 140, 142 (Tex. Spec.Ct.Rev.2002); In re Bell, 894 S.W.2d 119, 123 (Tex.Spec.Ct.Rev.1995); In re Jimenez, 841 S.W.2d 572, 579 (Tex. Spec.Ct.Rev.1992). Thus, the commission must prove each element of a charge by a preponderance of the evidence.

VI.

The commission's first charge alleges that Petitioner violated Canon 5(2) when he "authorized the public use of his name and title to endorse his close friend, Harriet Miers, a candidate for public office." The question presented is whether the commission proved by a preponderance of the evidence that Petitioner authorized the public use of his name endorsing another candidate, Miers, for public office. We hold the commission did not.

Until 1974, there was no Code of Judicial Conduct in Texas. In 1974, the Texas Supreme Court enacted the initial Code of Judicial Conduct, which contained an "endorsement" prohibition:

A judge or candidate for election to judicial office should not: . . . (b) make political speeches for a political organization or candidate or publicly endorse a candidate for public office.

Tex.Code Jud. Conduct, Canon 7A(1)(b), 37 Tex. B.J. 853 (1974).

In 1976, the Texas Supreme Court removed the endorsement prohibition from the Code. In 1980, the Committee on Judicial Ethics issued an opinion in answer to the question: "May a judge endorse a specific candidate or candidates?" The opinion stated the Code did not "specifically prohibit a judge from supporting a candidate or candidates." After reviewing the provisions of Canon 2, the opinion concluded:

The Committee is of the opinion that endorsing a candidate or candidates is within the discretion of a judge provided the nature and type of endorsement does not contravene Canon 1, Canon 2A and Canon 2B of the Code of Judicial Conduct. Comm. on Jud. Ethics, State Bar of Tex., Op. 53A (1980).

In 1990, the Texas Supreme Court amended Canon 7(3) as follows:

A judge or judicial candidate shall not authorize the public use of his or her name endorsing another candidate for any public office, except that a candidate may indicate support for a political party.

Tex.Code Jud. Conduct, Canon 7(3), 53 Tex. B.J. 240-41 (1990) (emphasis added). Today, this provision (hereafter, "authorization" provision) is found in Canon 5(2) and provides in pertinent part: "A judge or judicial candidate shall not authorize the public use of his or her name endorsing another candidate for any public office, except that either may indicate support for a political party." Tex.Code Jud. Conduct, Canon 5(2). Petitioner, who was on the Texas Supreme Court in 1990, testified that the "authorization" provision was generated at the request of the judges. In response to questions by the commission, Petitioner provided significant insights about the circumstances leading to the creation of the "authorization" provision:

The problem, the reason that 5(2) was proposed in the first place, the judges were concerned that county officials were muscling them into endorsements that they didn't want to make. And they said, look, you've got to endorse me for, let's say a district judge, you have to endorse me for County Commissioner. The district judge didn't want to do it, but he didn't have any way of saying no. If he said no, then he was afraid of what was going to happen to him in the budgeting process. So he wanted cover for that. So that's why the judges came to us back in '88 and said, we're tired of getting hammered on here, and we want an excuse that we can hold up and say, we don't have to do this any more. In essence, Petitioner explained that the purpose of inserting the "authorization" language into Canon 5(2) was to provide "cover" for judges to refuse to authorize endorsements of partisan elected candidates.

…We recognize it is integral to the commission's position that the "authorization" provision of Canon 5(2) be read and interpreted to prohibit a judge from "endorsing" or "supporting" another candidate. The commission's first charge contains no factual allegations Petitioner "authorized" the public use of his name endorsing Miers' nomination to the United States Supreme Court. The commission's evidence focused exclusively on establishing Petitioner had supported Miers' nomination. The commission urged this Court to hold that as Petitioner was a sitting Justice on the Texas Supreme Court and made public statements to the news media supporting Miers' nomination, Petitioner was guilty of endorsing another candidate, in violation of the "authorization" provision of Canon 5(2).

The commission primarily relies upon its own Public Statement PS-2000-2.[23] This Public Statement firmly espoused a broad view of the term "authorize." See Public Statement, No. PS-2000-2 (Comm'n Jud. Conduct Mar. 24, 2000). The commission essentially declared "personally publishing an endorsement of another candidate for public office" was synonymous with "giving permission to or `authorizing' the candidate or a third party to use the judge's name in such a public endorsement." Id. The commission took the position that no distinction was to be made "between acting on one's own behalf and empowering another to act on one's behalf as [Canon

5(2)] necessarily encompasses the broadest definition of the term `authorize.'" Id. The commission cited no legal precedent.

...The issue before us is the construction of the "authorization" provision of Canon 5(2), including examining the meaning of "authorize." In our analysis of this issue, this Court recognizes the wisdom and value of the cautionary mandate incorporated within Canon 8A:

The Sections are rules of reason, which should be applied consistent with constitutional requirements, statutes, other court rules and decisional law and in the context of all relevant circumstances.

Tex.Code Of Jud. Conduct, Canon 8A (emphasis added). This provision also encourages "reasonable and reasoned application of the text." Id. Accordingly, we endeavor to construe Canon 5(2) as written, in accordance with the rules of reason.

We also recognize our judicial system is based upon the cornerstones of integrity, impartiality, fairness, and independence. In discharging judicial responsibilities, the judge must be governed by the Rule of Law, conduct a fair and impartial hearing, and dispense justice as well as equity under the law, according to the particular facts and circumstances presented in each individual case.

We therefore undertake to construe and apply the language in dispute in Canon 5(2) consistent with "rules of reason" to the facts presented. Our analysis should focus upon key language and its relationship to the entire Code.

...If the supreme court had intended by its 1990 amendments to reinstate the 1974 "endorsement" prohibition, it would have done so, but it did not. Instead, it used substantially different language by adding the "authorization" provision. We conclude the Texas Supreme Court intended for the 1990 amendment inserting the "authorization" provision into the Canon governing political activity to effect a substantial change, not simply a technical refinement, from the "endorsement" prohibition. See Gold v. City of Coll. Station, 40 S.W.3d 637, 649 (Tex.App.-Houston [1st Dist.] 2001, pet. granted, judgm't vacated w.r.m. by agr.) ("Moreover, the fact that the legislature enacts an amendment indicates that it thereby intended to change the original act by creating a new right or withdrawing an old one."). Such a significant modification in terminology (deleting "endorse" and inserting "authorize") and the concomitant shift in meaning certainly signals that the Texas Supreme Court intended to confine the restriction to a prohibition of a judge's authorization of the public use of his or her name endorsing a candidate.

In determining what constitutes a judge's authorizing the public use of his or her name endorsing a candidate for any public office, we examine a recent incident involving such conduct. A judge's act of giving a candidate express permission to include the judge's name on a publicly distributed list of persons endorsing the candidate would violate Canon 5(2). See Public Admonition of Justice of the Peace Torres, No. 00-0689-JP (Comm'n Jud. Conduct Aug. 16, 2000). Any other fact scenario must be analogous to this situation to constitute a violation of Canon 5(2). That is, the facts must show the judge gave permission for others to publicly use the judge's name in endorsements of the candidate.

...The Texas Supreme Court defines "authorized" as follows: "The primary meaning of `authorize' is to empower, or give a right to act." Caller Times Publ'g Co. v. Chandler, 134 Tex. 1, 7, 130 S.W.2d 853, 856 (1939); see Cox, Inc. v. Humble Oil & Ref. Co., 16 S.W.2d 285, 286 (Tex. Comm'n App.1929, judgm't adopted) (same). ...

When the commission called Petitioner as its only witness, the commission never asked Petitioner if he "authorize[d] the public use of his . . . name endorsing" Miers' nomination. In addition, the commission failed to question Petitioner about this matter at the hearing before the commission. The commission's questions to Petitioner recognized he had no control or authority over what the media broadcast or printed. In the media interviews, Petitioner could anticipate the use of his name as the person being interviewed, if the media chose to identify him. However, having reviewed Petitioner's statements, we do not find any evidence that he authorized the media to use his name publicly endorsing Miers. Any argument that Petitioner impliedly authorized the public use of his name endorsing Miers would be futile and unavailing. We therefore conclude the commission failed to prove by a preponderance of the evidence that Petitioner authorized the public use of his name endorsing Miers.

VII.

While we have rejected the commission's argument that Canon 5(2) prohibits "endorsing," we conclude that, even under its construction, the commission failed to prove by a preponderance of evidence that Petitioner's public statements endorsed Miers.

...The commission's brief essentially contends Petitioner's public statements provided more than "factual information about Miers' background and experience." Specifically, the commission stated: "[Petitioner's] praise of Miers' 'sterling' character and his opinion that she would make `a great justice,' and his repeated public statements that her nomination was 'good' and 'solid,' certainly sound like approval and support of the President's nomination." In a footnote, the commission refers us Merriam-Webster OnLine Dictionary's definition of "endorse": "[T]o approve openly, especially: to express support or approval of publicly and definitely [as in] endors[ing] a mayoral candidate." The commission's ultimate argument is that "endorsement" is equivalent to "support," and it is undisputed that Petitioner supported Miers.

...QUESTION: May a Texas judge privately introduce candidates for judicial office to his friends and recommend that such friends vote for such candidates? ANSWER: It is the opinion of the Committee on Judicial Ethics that a Texas judge would not violate the Code of Judicial Conduct by privately introducing candidates for judicial office to his friends and recommending that such friends vote for such candidates. Comm. on Jud. Ethics, State Bar of Tex., Op. 2 (1975). In its opinion No. 13, the committee stated,

QUESTION: May a district judge introduce a candidate for the state Legislature to his personal friends and recommend that such friends vote for such candidate? ANSWER: The Committee on Judicial Ethics is of the opinion that the question should be answered in the affirmative. In Opinion Number 2 this Committee held that a Texas judge would not violate the Code of Judicial Conduct by privately introducing candidates for judicial office to his friends and recommending that such friends vote for such candidates. The Committee now reaffirms that opinion and extends its scope so that henceforth it will be applicable to all candidates for public office. Comm. on Jud. Ethics, State Bar of Tex., Op. 13 (1976).

These ethics opinions are noteworthy for several reasons. These opinions do not conclude that "endorsing," as a matter of principle, is evil, corrupt, ill-advised, undignified, or inherently injudicious. Both opinions hold "endorsing" is acceptable conduct within certain boundaries. These holdings are consistent with, if not as expansive as, the new draft rules of the American Bar Association's joint commission and a significant number of state Codes throughout the country that expressly permit judges to endorse other candidates in certain circumstances or which have no express prohibitions.

In addition, these ethics opinions contradict the assertion that the "authorization" provision of Canon 5(2) constitutes a blanket prohibition, banning a judge from endorsing another candidate. These opinions only limit "endorsing" in scope. In effect, these opinions approve the practice of "endorsing" by allowing a judge to introduce a candidate to personal friends and recommend to friends that they vote for the candidate.

The text of Canon 5(2), the lack of any definition of the term "endorse," and the problematic ethical opinions provide marginal guidance. A survey of the respective Codes of a majority of states shows that they prohibit either "endorsing" or "endorsing and opposing," but for the most part these state Codes fail to define "endorse."

…We interpret "endorsing" under the circumstances of this case to mean more than support, that is, more than spoken praise.

…Our conclusion is reinforced by examining Petitioner's public statements in the context of several relevant provisions of the Canons. The Preamble and Canon 2 stress the need for a competent judiciary and maintaining public confidence. Petitioner made a number of remarks which asserted Miers' character, experience, and career reflected the type of competence necessary on the bench. His remarks were designed to instill public confidence in the Miers nomination.

Canons 3B(10), 4B(1), and 5(2) encourage participation by judges in the legal system, the administration of justice, and the political process. Petitioner's public statements concerning Miers' nomination detailed her personal life, her positions on various sensitive issues, her professional career, her character, and her work ethic. It is undisputed that Canon 5(2) permits a judge to speak out "on political matters." Petitioner's statements were within the boundaries of these Canons. The commission's interpretation and application of the authorization provision minimizes Canon 5(2)'s provision empowering a judge to speak on political matters.

Canon 5(1)(ii) prohibits misrepresentations. Petitioner took the position that he "was uniquely situated to get the truth out about Harriet [Miers]." He described the times as truly "chaotic" and that "the publicity coming out about Harriet Miers [was] negative," "false," and "untrue." He perceived that "more information" needed to be developed about her background. His public statements were "truthful" on matters "of enormous concern to the American public." Petitioner was also "worried" that if he did not speak up, it could be perceived that he knew something that would hurt her nomination, which was false.

Canon 5(2) should permit a judge to respond to any untruthful or inaccurate statements, thereby affording a judge able and willing to do so an effective and timely avenue of recourse to correct misrepresentations in a public forum. Otherwise, this provision provides minimal utility at such a critical juncture. A construction of this provision that bars a judge from publicly responding to misrepresentations absent express permission to do so leaves a judge vulnerable to potentially inaccurate and untruthful attacks without any effective remedy and deprives the public of correct and accurate background information on judicial candidates and nominees. A reasonable construction of this provision affords an immediate and practical method to counter public attacks and criticisms and protects the public's right to truthful and important information, particularly as to a nominee to the United States Supreme Court. In addition, the purposes of the Code are promoted and enhanced, not hindered and frustrated. This provision should not censor or silence a judge.

The American Bar Association Model Code of Judicial Conduct and other state Codes make ample provision enabling a judicial candidate to respond to misrepresentations. The ABA Model Code of Judicial Conduct includes a comment addressing "false information" stating, "Where false information concerning a judicial candidate is made public, a judge or another judicial candidate having knowledge of the facts is not prohibited by Section 5A(1) from making the facts public." ABA Model Code Jud. Conduct, Canon 5A(1), Commentary (2004). This comment or a variation of this comment has been included in the Codes of Judicial Conduct of several states including Alaska, Florida, Idaho, Indiana, Kansas, Kentucky, Mississippi, Nebraska, Nevada, North Dakota, South Carolina, South Dakota, and Tennessee. We conclude Petitioner's public statements are consistent with a judge's right, if not his responsibility, to respond to misrepresentations.

…We conclude the commission has failed to prove by a preponderance of the evidence that Petitioner endorsed Miers. We conclude under the particular circumstances presented that Petitioner complied with the spirit and letter of the Texas Code of Judicial Conduct. Accordingly, we conclude Petitioner is not guilty of violating Canon 5(2).

VIII.

The commission's second charge alleges: "[Petitioner] lent the prestige of his judicial office to advance the private interests of his close friend, Harriet Miers in violation of Canon 2B of the Texas Code of Judicial Conduct." We conclude Canon 2B is inapplicable to the conduct at issue.

Canon 2 is entitled: "Avoiding Impropriety and the Appearance of Impropriety in All of the Judge's Activities." Tex.Code Jud. Conduct, Canon 2. Canon 2B of the Code provides, in relevant part: "A judge shall not lend the prestige of judicial office to advance the private interests of the judge or others. . . ." Tex.Code Jud. Conduct, 2B. The second charge was limited to the private interests of "others," namely, Miers.

We first address whether Canon 2B applies to the conduct at issue in this case. In so doing, our inquiry focuses again on a definition, this time, of the term "private interests." The Code of Judicial Conduct does not contain a definition of "private interests."

In re Jimenez, 841 S.W.2d 572 (Tex. Spec.Ct.Rev.1992), provides some guidance. In that case, the commission, after finding the judge had a private interest in retaliating against a policeman, privately admonished the judge for violating Canon 2B for making statements accusing a policeman of perjuring himself and selectively prosecuting Hispanic males for DWI. The judge's communications followed a telephone conversation in which the policeman criticized the judge's dismissal of a suit against an Hispanic male for DWI as a "[expletive deleted] . . . decision." Id. at 573-74. The Special Court of Review determined that the judge's actions, including one of the letters and later "media interviews" stemming from the letters and the judge's testimony in a lawsuit as to the truthfulness of the policeman, were to advance the public interest. Id. at 579. The court reasoned that all these communications dealt with the policeman's "alleged crimes," not with his "private insulting remarks," and were, therefore, motivated by public interest. Id. at 580. The court considered a "matter of public interest" to be "one that affected his [i.e., the policeman's] performance of duty." Id. at 580. In considering a second letter in which the judge did not mention possible crimes and public misconduct but instead referred to the judge taking "particular offense" to the comment, the court concluded the letter was not written to retaliate. Id. at 581. Instead, the court concluded that, even if the judge had a "personal motive of retaliation," it was not convinced by a preponderance of the evidence that his personal motive "exceeded the public motive of disciplining a police officer reasonably suspected of major crimes and minor bad manners." Id.

Thus, the focus of the Jimenez court was on the public interest of the policeman's performance of his duties as a police officer, not the judge's private interest in retaliating against an ill-mannered individual. See id. at 580. The Jimenez court also recognized a balancing between private and public motivation. See id. at 581. Finally, the Jimenez court stressed the commission never alleged any of the judge's statements were false in any respect.

…The commission asserts that a benefit of office, life tenure, as well as power and prestige, constitute "private interests" under Canon 2B. We disagree. Although the position of Supreme Court Justice comes with life tenure and as well as a guaranteed salary, see U.S. CONST. art. III, § 1, those factors are not necessarily private interests. Rather, they are the perquisites of the public office. Lifetime tenure and guaranteed salary safeguard the judiciary from interference from the other branches of government and promote judicial independence; thus, they are public, rather than private, interests. …

The evidence before us, including numerous transcriptions of congressional hearings, clearly demonstrates candidates seeking federal judicial positions are driven by the desire and passion to engage in public service and promote the rule of law in a meaningful capacity. Furthermore, all of the expert witness testimony, most of which was stipulated to by the commission, opined that Petitioner's conduct did not advance the private interests of Miers. Under the facts presented, we are convinced this level of dedication and commitment is best described as one of public, not private, interest. …

Petitioner testified about the purpose of Canon 2B:

[T]he purpose for 2B is to keep judges from calling the district attorney, trying to get him to go easy on their kid, or the neighbor's kid, or trying to get the county commissioners to give a contract to somebody that's more friendly or less friendly, or those kinds of things. It's not the idea that by speaking in favor of someone who is trying to get confirmed, and has already been nominated to the U.S. Supreme Court, that that somehow advances a private interest, no one would have ever thought that. If you made a list this canon is old, so if you made a list a long time ago and said, check off the ten things this is supposed to stop, and one of them was keeping people from promoting nominees to the U.S. Supreme Court, nobody would check that off. . . .

Canon 2B prohibits a judge from using the prestige of judicial office to pursue "private interests" such as using the position of judge to extort a financial benefit, to retaliate against another, or to obtain preferential treatment for the judge or another person. Such conduct is generally perpetrated in secret or in a clandestine manner. The conduct at issue, however, is the public dissemination of information about Miers in a political context. The record does not even intimate that Petitioner engaged in any surreptitious conduct.

We hold Canon 2B was not intended to apply and does not apply to the conduct at issue in the political environment described. Under these circumstances, we can hardly conclude that Petitioner's public statements would have constituted an advancement of Miers' "private interests." Accordingly, we find Petitioner not guilty of the charge of violating Canon 2B by lending the prestige of his judicial office to advance Miers' private interests.

IX.

… Although we have not resolved the meaning of "endorsing," we conclude there are alternative, reasonable definitions of "endorsing" and that, even if we accepted the commission's interpretation of Canon 5(2) as prohibiting "endorsing," a strict construction of "endorsing" means a narrower construction than just broad support, and, therefore, does not encompass Petitioner's public statements. The commission failed to prove Petitioner's public statements "endorsed" Miers. Thus, we cannot conclude Petitioner violated Canon 5(2) by "endorsing."

We also conclude Petitioner's public statements are, under the particular facts presented, permitted by the Canons because they qualify as legitimate responses to misrepresentations (Canon 5(1)(ii)), expressions of views on political matters (Canon 5(2)), statements that promote public confidence in the competence of the judiciary, and statements which involve the law, the legal system, and the administration of justice (Preamble, Canons 2 & 4).

Finally, we conclude Canon 2B does not apply to the political conduct at issue, and, therefore, no violation can be found.

Accordingly, we conclude the commission has failed to meet its burden of proving Petitioner violated the Canons, we dismiss the commission's public admonition, and we find him not guilty of the charges.

In The News:

The AfterMath

In 2008, the Texas Ethics Commission fined then Justice Hecht $29,000 for accepting a large in-kind donation (in the form of a discount on legal fees) and then failing to report it as a political contribution.

History: In 2006, "the Texas Commission on Judicial Conduct (CJC) reprimanded then Texas Supreme Court Justice Nathan Hecht, finding that he had misused his judicial position by becoming a public champion for long-time friend Harriet Miers, the former Lottery Commission official who President George W. Bush nominated to the U.S. Supreme Court in 2005. Hecht hired the law firm of Jackson Walker to appeal the CJC finding, and ultimately had it dismissed.

When his law firm billed him about a half-million in legal fees – Justice Hecht and the firm negotiated a fee, whereby the firm agreed to knock off part of the fee as pro bono work, since the case was really about the free speech rights of Texas judges. Hecht paid the bill with campaign funds. Nonpartisan *Texas Watch* filed an official complaint with the commission.

Acknowledging that it isn't illegal to use campaign cash for legal expenses, the commission concluded that the discount Hecht received was not just a reduction in fees, but in fact a campaign donation -- and one that far exceeded the $5,000 cap on donations from individual lawyers and their firms. In part, … Hecht was done in by the language he chose to use in an email to supporters, wherein he explained that Jackson Walker not only reduced his bill, but also "agreed to designate a large part of the fees as an in-kind contribution to my campaign."

For more read: Jordan Smith, Ethics Commission Fines Hecht: Texas Supreme will have to pay $29,000 fine for accepting a donation larger than the law allows, and for failing to report it, Fri. Dec. 5, 2008 available at http://www.austinchronicle.com/daily/news/2008-12-05/711190/

Oh, Hecht!

Following the decision that the fees represented a Texas Ethics violation, Texas Supreme Court Justice Nathan Hecht decided to appeal, arguing that the commission's ruling conflicts with the Rules of Professional Conduct for lawyers, which includes the admonition that lawyers "must charge reasonable fees." That's all Jackson Walker was doing when it lowered Hecht's bill, he argues. "The commission itself mandates that politicians and judges be charged for goods and services like any other customer," Hecht's petition reads. "Nevertheless, the commission's decision creates a different legal fee structure for judges alone. Under this new structure, adjustments to legal bills to establish a reasonable fee turn into improper campaign contributions."

For more read: Jordan Smith, *State Supreme Court Justice says he was denied justice from Ethics Commission. Fancy that. ,* Fri., Feb. 6, 2009, available at http://www.austinchronicle.com/news/2009-02-06/736737/

In Re: Judge Frank A. Marullo, Jr.
No. 96-O-2222 (1997) Supreme Court of Louisiana
On Recommendation for Discipline from the Judiciary
Commission of Louisiana

Facts and Procedural History

On February 13, 1996, Respondent wrote a letter on his official stationery to the Honorable Edith Brown Clement, Judge of the United States District Court for the Eastern District of Louisiana. This letter concerned the sentencing of Anthony Carollo, a man who had pled guilty in Judge Clement's court to a conspiracy involving illegal video poker operation. Respondent has known Carollo for more than twenty-five years, and testified that he consistently patronized Carollo's restaurant since his days in law school. Based on this acquaintance, Respondent stated in his letter to Judge Clement that Carollo is a generous, loving man who is a good father. Respondent also stated:

> [an]y considerations that can be given to this kind and gentle man will be
> greatly appreciated. I know sentencing is a very difficult thing to do, but
> Mr. Carollo is not a young man and he is in failing health, and I am sure
> he wouldn't pose any risks at all to society.

The letter was solicited by Carollo's attorney, Arthur Lemann. Respondent wrote the letter and gave it to Lemann for delivery to Judge Clement. According to Respondent, he wrote the letter in an attempt to avoid being subpoenaed to appear in open court and believed only Judge Clement would be privy to the information contained in the letter. However, a copy of the letter was published in the *Times-Picayune.* Prior to Carollo's sentencing, but after Respondent wrote the letter, Respondent was subpoenaed by Lemann to appear at Carollo's sentencing hearing; however, the letter was used in lieu of Respondent's testimony.

On April 2, 1996, the Judiciary Commission filed a Formal Charge against Respondent alleging that he violated Canon 2B of the Code of Judicial Conduct, and engaged in willful misconduct related to his official duty and persistent and public conduct prejudicial to the administration of justice that brings the judicial office into disrepute. On July 13, 1996, the Judiciary Commission conducted a hearing on this matter. The Judiciary Commission concluded that Respondent violated Canon 2B of the Code of Judicial Conduct and that his action constituted public conduct prejudicial to the administration of justice that brings the judicial office into disrepute. However, the Judiciary Commission concluded that Respondent's writing of the one letter was not persistent conduct. As a result of this finding, the Judiciary Commission recommended that this court publicly censure Respondent pursuant to La. Const. art. V., § 25(C), and order Respondent to reimburse the Commission the costs incurred in the investigation and prosecution of the case, in the amount of $580.00, pursuant to La. S.Ct. R. 23, § 22.

At the time Respondent wrote the letter, Canon 2B provided:

> A judge should not allow family, social, or other relationships to influence judicial conductor judgment. A judge should not lend the prestige of judicial office to advance the private interest of others; nor should a judge convey or permit others to convey the impression that they are in a special position to influence the judge. A judge should not testify voluntarily as a character witness.

Law and Discussion

This court has original jurisdiction in judicial disciplinary proceedings. La. Const. art. V., § 25(C). Therefore, this court has the power to make original determinations of fact based upon the evidence in the record and is not bound by the findings and recommendations of the Judiciary Commission. The grounds for disciplinary action against a judge are set forth in La. Const. art. V., § 25(C), which provides:

> On recommendation of the judiciary commission, the supreme court may censure, suspend with or without salary, remove from office, or retire involuntarily a judge for willful misconduct relating to his official duty, willful and persistent failure to perform his duty, persistent and public conduct prejudicial to the administration of justice that brings the judicial office into disrepute, conduct while in office which would constitute a felony, or conviction of a felony. On recommendation of the judiciary commission, the supreme court may disqualify a judge from exercising any judicial function, without loss of salary, during pendency of proceedings in the supreme court. On recommendation of the judiciary commission, the supreme court may retire involuntarily a judge for disability that seriously interferes with the performance of his duties and that is or is likely to become permanent. The supreme court shall make rules implementing this Section and providing for confidentiality and privilege of commission proceedings.

Under its supervisory authority over all lower courts, this court adopted the Code of Judicial

Conduct, effective January 1, 1976. This Code of Judicial Conduct is binding on all judges, and violations of the Canons contained therein may serve as the basis for the disciplinary action provided for by La. Const. art. V., § *25(C)*. *In re Decuir*, 95-0056 (La. *5/22/95), 654* So.2d 687, 692; *In re Wilkes,* 403 So. 2d *35,* 40 (La. 1981); *In re Babineaux*, 346 So. 2d 676, 680-81 (La.), *cert. denied sub nom. Berry v. Judiciary Commission of Louisiana*, 434 U.S. 940, 98 S.Ct. 431 (1977). A violation of the Code of Judicial Conduct must be proven by clear and convincing evidence. *In re Huckaby*, 95-0041 (La. *5/22/95), 656* So.2d 292, 296.

Violation of Canon 2B

The basis for the complaint against Respondent is that he used the efficacy of judicial office for another's gain by writing the letter in dispute on official court stationery which identified him as a Judge of the Criminal District Court for the Parish of Orleans, State of Louisiana. At the time Respondent wrote the letter, Canon 2B of the Code of Judicial Conduct did not contain a specific provision which prohibited writing this type of letter on official court stationery. In fact, Canon 2B was amended to clarify the confusion concerning the propriety of judges writing these types of letters. Respondent's conduct clearly violates the current version of Canon 2B of the Code of Judicial Conduct. However, the only issue presented by this case is whether Respondent violated Canon 2B as it existed *before* the recent amendment.

At the time Respondent wrote the letter, the propriety of judges writing letters of recommendation or letters regarding convicted felons was less than clear. There were three advisory opinions prepared by the Supreme Court Committee on Judicial Ethics and one Louisiana Supreme Court case dealing with this exact issue. In Opinion No. 64, dated in December 1984, a majority of the Supreme Court Committee on Judicial Ethics stated that while a judge in his private capacity *may* write a letter to the Louisiana Board of Pardons recommending an individual be granted commutation of sentence, he *may not* ethically use his official stationery. In Opinion No. 76, dated September *25,* 1989, the Supreme Court Committee on Judicial Ethics concluded that a judge *may* write a letter of recommendation on his personal stationery. Finally, in Opinion No. 102, dated May 7, 1992, the Supreme Court Committee on Judicial Ethics stated that it is ethically *impermissible* for a judge to write a letter of recommendation on official stationery. While these opinions are not the law, and were not universally circulated to the judiciary, they do serve as advisory opinions which help members of the judiciary determine the types of conduct which may be ethically impermissible under the Code of Judicial Conduct. Based on these standards, at the time of Respondent's action, a letter could be written on a convicted felon's behalf--if it was written on personal stationary.

In addition to these advisory opinions, this court in 1995 publicly censured a judge, in part, for conduct similar to that engaged in by Respondent. *In re Decuir*, 95-0056 (La *5/22/95), 654* So.2d 687. *The Decuir* case involved the imposition of public censure upon a judge for the following offenses, only one of which bears similarity to the instant case: (1) allowing a former law partner to share the court of appeal's secretary, telephone system, post office box, office supplies, and law library; (2) failing to properly supervise and report campaign contributions on his Campaign Finance Report; (3) allowing his law clerk to work as an independent contractor for a law firm and research a case in which the clerk's firm was involved; and *(4)* writing a letter on temporary personal judiciary stationary that identified him as a court of appeal judge to a federal district judge concerning the sentencing of a friend, who was a criminal defendant, in a criminal case. For these violations, this court, speaking through Justice Victory, determined "the violations are serious enough to merit the most lenient type of discipline by the Court," and ordered censure of Judge Decuir in a public opinion. *Id.* at p.10, *654* So. 2d at 693.

Respondent maintains he was not aware he was violating Canon 2B of the Code of Judicial Conduct when he wrote the letter to Judge Clement. While it is true that Canon 213, prior to its recent amendment, was unclear as to what was and was not ethically permissible,' the existence of three advisory opinions composed by the Supreme Court Committee on Judicial Ethics and the *Decuir* decision conveyed the fact that it was ethically impermissible under Canon 2B to write the letter on official stationery. In addition, we note the Florida State Supreme Court faced this same issue in *In re Fogan, 646* So. 2d 191 (Fla 1994). In *Fogan,* the sole charge levied against Judge Fogan concerned the writing of a character reference letter, on his official stationery, for a friend who was awaiting sentencing in federal court. The Florida Supreme Court held that while there may be general confusion over the writing of character reference letters, the numerous advisory opinions on the issue should have alerted Judge Fogan that it was ethically impermissible under Canon 2B to write a character reference letter to a judge presiding over his friends sentencing hearing. *Fogan, 646* So.2d at 194.

Based upon the foregoing, we find by clear and convincing evidence that Respondent did violate Canon 2B of the Code of Judicial Conduct by writing the character reference letter on his official stationery. Having found an ethical violation, we must assess whether the conduct rises to the level of sanctionable misconduct under our law.

Sanctions

Initially, we recognize the primary purpose of the Code of Judicial Conduct is to protect the public rather than to discipline a judge. Leslie W. Abramson, *canon 2 of the Code of Judicial Conduct,* 79 Marq. L. Rev., *950,* 951 (1996). As ministers of justice entrusted with the duty to preserve the integrity of the bench for the benefit of the public, the judges of this State should conduct themselves in a manner above reproach and suspicion. *Huckaby,* 95-0041 plo, 656 So.2d at 298. While the public cannot expect their judges to be completely without fault, in order to protect and earn the public trust, judges must be accountable for all their actions. Harold T. Kelly, Jr., *Hart Failure: The Supreme Judicial Court's Interpretation of Nonjudicial Demeanor,* 44 Me. L. Rev., *175,* 177 (1992). However, all violations of the Canons of the Code of Judicial Conduct do not always rise to the level of sanctionable misconduct. *In re Hart, 577* A. 2d *351* (Me. 1990). Indeed, La Const. art. V., § 25(C) provides this court with the power to determine whether formal discipline is warranted for a violation of a Canon of the Code of Judicial Conduct. In this case, Respondent is charged with a violation of one Canon of the Code of Judicial Conduct. Unquestionably, under the current version of Canon 213, Respondent's actions clearly would violate the letter of the Code. However, we find that at the time Respondent wrote the letter at issue, it did not violate the Code of Judicial Conduct to actually write the letter. Rather, Respondent's violation stemmed from writing the letter on official stationery instead of personal stationery. While we certainly do not condone the conduct herein complained of, we recognize that sanctionable misconduct 's more than that conduct which comes about by reason of error of judgment or lack of diligence." *State ex rel. Gremillion v. O'Hara,* 252 La. 540, 211 So.2d 641 (1968). Considering the confounded state of ethics law in this area at the time of Respondent's action, which apparently led to a detailed revision of Canon 2B, together with the facts and circumstances of this case, we find the prospect of censure on the instant violation when compared with the *Decuir* case, in which the respondent stipulated to no less than four ethical offenses, would be a disproportionate sanction.

In addition, over a twenty-two year judicial career, Respondent has never been the subject of official disciplinary proceedings before now. We also find it significant that Respondent did not write the letter for personal gain; rather, the record reflects he acted in good faith to provide information he believed his acquaintance was entitled to under law. While good faith is not an affirmative defense to a Canon violation, it is a mitigating factor which militates in favor of a lesser sanction. *In re Chaisson, 549* So.2d *259,* 267 (La. 1989).

La. Const. art. V., § 25(C) provides four punishment alternatives for disciplining a judge. This court may: (1) censure; (2) suspend the judge with or without salary; (3) remove the judge from office; or (4) retire the judge involuntarily. The punishment imposed depends upon the seriousness of the violation and the presence of mitigating factors. Censure is the most lenient form of discipline which may be imposed by this court. Decuir, p. 10, 654 So.2d at 693. As mentioned previously, in *Decuir,* this court censured Judge Decuir for three other violations in addition to his writing of a letter of recommendation on his temporary judicial stationery. In this case, Respondent is only charged with an isolated and technical violation of the Code of Judicial Conduct, a blemish on an otherwise clean professional slate.

We do not find that official judicial discipline is warranted in this case considering the totality of the circumstances surrounding the writing of this letter, the fact Canon 2B of the Code of Judicial Conduct was unclear as it existed at the time the letter was written, and the fact this was an isolated transgression.

Decree

The recommendation of the Judiciary Commission of Louisiana is hereby rejected; no official discipline imposed.

****

Questions:

1. Law professor also serves as municipal court judge. Professor's student asks if she will prepare a letter of recommendation to a law firm that student desires to work with. The firm is the premier traffic tickets firm in the city. Student has been in two of professor's class and did well in both. If Law Professor writes a letter of reference for the student, will she be in violation of the judicial code?

2. Would your answer to question 1 above be different if Professor wrote the letter on official municipal court stationery? Why? Why not?

3. Would Judge Marullo have been subject to discipline if the letter he wrote was for the benefit of a close family member?

4. The Marullo court found that the pre-Canon 2B clarification left open the question of whether a judge violated the judicial code if (s)he wrote a letter of recommendation on

official stationery. However, the court cited three advisory opinions which addressed the issue. What factors persuaded the court that Judge Marullo had not violated the earlier version of Judicial Code Canon 2B?

****

In Re: Honorable Elizabeth E. Coker
Before the State Commission on Judicial Conduct
CJC Nos. 13-0376-DI, 13-0448-DI, 13-0471-DI, 13-0712-DI, 13-0815-DI, 13-0101-DI

VOLUNTARY AGREEMENT TO RESIGN FROM
JUDICIAL OFFICE IN LIEU OF DISCIPLINARY ACTION

This Agreement is being entered into by the undersigned parties pursuant to Section 33.032(h) of the Texas Government Code.

WHEREAS at all times relevant hereto, the Honorable Elizabeth E. Coker was Judge of the 258th Judicial District Court in Livingston, Polk County, Texas; and

WHEREAS in late December 2012 and early January 2013, complaints and media stories were brought to the Commission's attention alleging that Judge Coker had engaged in improper ex parte text communications with Polk County Assistant District Attorney Kaycee Jones while Judge Coker presided over the criminal jury trial of *State v David M. Reeves in* August 2012; and

WHEREAS based on the above-referenced complaints, the Commission commenced an investigation into allegations that Judge Coker used Assistant District Attorney Jones to privately communicate information about the *Reeves case* to the assistant district attorney prosecuting the case; to suggest questions for the prosecutor to ask during the trial; to ensure that a witness was able to refresh his memory and rehabilitate his testimony by reviewing his videotaped interview with law enforcement before he took the stand for the second time the following day; and to discuss legal issues pertinent to the case, in an unsuccessful effort to assist the State obtain a guilty verdict in the case;

WHEREAS in addition to the allegations arising out of the *Reeves* trial, the Commission investigated claims that Judge Coker allegedly engaged in other improper ex *parte* communications and meetings with Jones, other members of the Polk County District Attorney's Office, the San Jacinto County District Attorney, and certain defense attorneys regarding various cases pending in her court; Judge Coker allegedly exhibited a bias in favor of certain attorneys and a prejudice against others in both her judicial rulings and her court appointments and Judge Coker allegedly met with jurors in an inappropriate manner, outside the presence of counsel, while the jurors were deliberating in one or more criminal trials;

WHEREAS following a full investigation into the complaints, the Commission conducted informal hearings in the matter and obtained the sworn oral testimony of several witnesses and Judge Coker; and

WHEREAS the Commission also expressed concerns that Judge Coker discussed the Commission's investigation and Judge Coker's written, responses to the investigation with a material witness prior to that witness testimony before the Commission in an apparent attempt to influence that witness, and that the judge may not have been candid and truthful in her testimony before the Commission when questioned about her contact with the witness; and

WHEREAS no Findings of Fact or Conclusions of Law have been made by the

278

Commission in connection with the above-referenced matters; and

WHEREAS the parties agree that the allegations of judicial misconduct, if found to be true, could result in disciplinary action against Judge Coker; and

WHEREAS the parties to this Agreement wish to resolve this matter without the time and expense of further disciplinary proceedings.

IT IS THEREFORE AGREED that Judge Coker, upon the signing of this Agreement, agrees that she will officially and formally resign her judicial office effective December, 6, 2013. On October 21, 2013 Judge Coker shall send a formal letter of resignation to the Governor notifying him of the effective resignation date, and will take a voluntary leave of absence from all of her ditties and responsibilities as Judge of the 258th Judicial District Court starting October 21, 2013 through December 6, 2013. Judge Coker is entering into this Agreement to resolve the above-referenced complaints in lieu of disciplinary action by the Commission, pursuant to Section 33.032(h) of the Texas Government Code. The Commission agrees that it shall pursue no further disciplinary proceedings against Judge Coker in connection with the above-referenced matters.

IT IS FURTHER AGREED that, upon the effective date of Judge Coker's resignation, Judge Coker shall thereafter he disqualified in the future from: sitting or serving as a judge in the State of Texas; standing for election or appointment to judicial office in the State of Texas; or performing or exercising any judicial duties or functions of a judicial officer in the State of Texas, including the performance of wedding ceremonies.

IT IS FURTHER AGREED that any violation of this Agreement by Judge Coker would constitute willful or persistent conduct that is clearly inconsistent with the proper performance of her duties or casts public discredit upon the judiciary or administration of justice in violation of Art. *5, §1-a(6)*A of the Texas Constitution, and Section 33.001(b) of the Texas Government Code, and would result in the commencement of formal proceedings against Judge Coker by the Commission, and the release of an Agreed Statement of Facts in support of the Commission's charges against Judge Coker.

IT IS FURTHER AGREED that the Commission may enforce this Agreement through any legal process necessary, including injunctive relief that Travis County, Texas, shall be the proper venue for any dispute between the parties or proceeding relating to this Agreement; and that Judge Coker, individually, shall bear the expense, cost, and any reasonable and necessary attorneys' fees in the event any dispute arising tinder this Agreement is decided against her by any court or tribunal.

IT **IS FURTHER AGREED** that Judge Coker, by her execution of this voluntary agreement, does not admit guilt, fault or liability regarding the matters contained in the complaints and allegations referenced above.

AGREED TO AND ACCEPTED upon its execution by the parties,

EL1ZABETH E. COKER   TOM CUNNINGHAM, CHAIR
                                 STATE COMMISSION ON JUDICIAL
                                 CONDUCT

Date: Date:

AGREED AS TO FORM:

****

Questions:

1. Judge Firstyear was new to the bench. Prior to her election to the bench, she had been a personal injury attorney for 30 years. One of the first cases on her docket was a whistleblower action. Judge Firstyear heard the preliminary motions and realized that she was completely incompetent in that area. Her clerk suggested that she contact a local law school dean who was an expert in the field. The dean drafted a written memorandum containing a summary of the law and references to secondary sources that contained issues expected in the upcoming trial. Judge Firstyear informed counsel for both parties of her communication with the dean, provided them the citations to the sources, and told them they could submit any written comments they might have. Has Judge Firstyear acted properly?

2. Judge is a single woman who was elected last year. Five years before her election, while practicing law, she was involved in a nasty divorce from her then husband. By the time the divorce case was over, Judge was very upset with her husband's attorney, Harry Hardnose and the way he treated her throughout the divorce proceeding. Judge was recently assigned a criminal theft case where Hardnose is defense counsel. The trial began, and neither Judge nor Hardnose said anything about the prior divorce trial. Is Judge subject to discipline for not disqualifying herself in the criminal theft trial?

3. Highly regarded state district court judge is offered a position at a local law school. The judge would be required to teach one course that will be taught from 5:00 p.m. - 6:00 p.m. Monday through Friday. The school is within walking distance from the judge's court room. The judge will be paid commensurate with her experience as any other adjunct professor. Is it proper for the jdge to accept the offer of employment with the law school?

4. Judge's son has decided to get married and desires to purchase a home. Son has recently graduated and begun a new job that would easily allow him to make monthly mortgage payments. However, son has not established credit in his own name nor has he saved enough money for a down payment. Judge agrees to give son $50,000 as a wedding gift so that he can make the down payment. Judge also agrees to guarantee the repayment of the loan that is made through Mega Mortgage Company (MMC). MMC agrees to make the loan at below interest rate because judge recently ruled in their favor on a case significant to MMC. If son accepts the terms of the mortgage, will judge be in violation of the Code of Judicial Conduct?

5. Judge had been a district court judge for 20 years when he announced his engagement to be married. Lawyer has regularly appeared in Judge's court over the past two decades and has, on occasion, played golf with the judge. Lawyer considered himself to be a friend of Judge, so he decided to give Judge a wedding gift of a two week honeymoon to his chalet in Tuscany valued at $15,000. He also paid for the Judge and his bride to fly to Tuscany in his private jet. Is it proper for Judge to accept these gifts?

280

6. Bernie Barpasser was the president of the Student Bar Association of All-4.0 Law School. Upon graduation, he went to work for the county prosecutor's office. While there, he was involved in a number of high profile cases. This gave him a platform and public support that allowed him to run for an open judicial district court position. During his judicial campaign for the judicial court seat, Bernie participated with other candidates for office whereby the candidates endorsed one another for the positions they were seeking. This they called a candidate ticket and all encouraged voters to vote the straight ticket. The group, including Bernie also made public appearances and participated in coordinated advertisement campaigns. Their ads indicated that Bernie was a Democrat. Bernie also agreed that the County Democratic Party could include his name on their list of "recommended candidates". What actions, if any, will subject Bernie to discipline?

7. Not long after graduating from Law School, Angelica was elected to a state judicial seat. Law School was very proud of the accomplishments of its alumni. Accordingly, the law school alumni director asked Angelica to lead its Capital Campaign to obtain alumni contributions. An automated voice system called each alumnus and Angelica's pre-recorded message was played which requested large donations to the law school. If no contribution was received from the first call, then a second call would be made two weeks later where Judge Angelica would firmly remind the alumnus of all the school had done for them and of their responsibility to contribute. Was Judge Angelica's participation in the contribution campaign proper?

8. Tracy was an attorney who served on the town council of Blimpville prior to running for Criminal Court Judge. She was elected, but after eight years, Judge Tracy became increasingly tired of hearing criminal cases. When the Mayor stepped down amid a career-ending scandal, the city council scheduled a special election and Judge Tracy was urged by supporters to run for Mayor. She decided, however, that she needed to feel out how much campaign support she could count on from local political leaders. She decided to meet with them to discuss the likelihood and extent of their support. Is Judge Tracy's conduct proper?

****

INDEX OF CASES

Ethics Advisory Opinions

INDEX

INDEX TO ABA RULES